Columbanus and the Peoples
of Post-Roman Europe

OXFORD STUDIES IN LATE ANTIQUITY

Series Editor
Ralph Mathisen

Late Antiquity has unified what in the past were disparate disciplinary, chronological, and geographical areas of study. Welcoming a wide array of methodological approaches, this book series provides a venue for the finest new scholarship on the period, ranging from the later Roman Empire to the Byzantine, Sasanid, early Islamic, and early Carolingian worlds.

The Arabic Hermes
From Pagan Sage to Prophet of Science
Kevin van Bladel

Two Romes
Rome and Constantinople in Late Antiquity
Edited by Lucy Grig and Gavin Kelly

Disciplining Christians
Correction and Community in Augustine's Letters
Jennifer V. Ebbeler

History and Identity in the Late Antique Near East
Edited by Philip Wood

Explaining the Cosmos
Creation and Cultural Interaction in Late-Antique Gaza
Michael W. Champion

Universal Salvation in Late Antiquity
Porphyry of Tyre and the Pagan-Christian Debate in Late Antiquity
Michael Bland Simmons

The Poetics of Late Latin Literature
Edited by Jaś Elsner and Jesús Hernández Lobato

Rome's Holy Mountain
The Capitoline Hill in Late Antiquity
Jason Moralee

Columbanus and the Peoples of Post-Roman Europe
Edited by Alexander O'Hara

Columbanus and the Peoples of Post-Roman Europe

Edited by
Alexander O'Hara

OXFORD
UNIVERSITY PRESS

OXFORD
UNIVERSITY PRESS

Oxford University Press is a department of the University of Oxford. It furthers
the University's objective of excellence in research, scholarship, and education
by publishing worldwide. Oxford is a registered trade mark of Oxford University
Press in the UK and certain other countries.

Published in the United States of America by Oxford University Press
198 Madison Avenue, New York, NY 10016, United States of America.

CIP data is on file at the Library of Congress
ISBN 978-0-19-085796-7

1 3 5 7 9 8 6 4 2
Printed by Sheridan Books, Inc., United States of America

To Patrick J. Geary

Contents

List of Maps   ix
Foreword by Walter Pohl   xi
Preface   xv
List of Contributors   xvii
List of Abbreviations   xix
Maps   xxi

Part I   Columbanus in Context

1. Introduction: Columbanus and Europe   3
   Alexander O'Hara

2. Columbanus and the Language of Concord   19
   Damian Bracken

Part II   The Insular Background

3. The Political Background to Columbanus's Irish Career   53
   Dáibhí Ó Cróinín

4. Movers and Shakers? How Women Shaped the Career of Columbanus   69
   Elva Johnston

5. Columbanus's Ulster Education   91
   Alex Woolf

Part III   The Frankish World

6. Columbanus in Brittany   103
   Ian Wood

7. Columbanus and Shunning: The Irish *peregrinus* between Gildas,
   Gaul, and Gregory   113
   Clare Stancliffe

8. Orthodoxy and Authority: Jonas, Eustasius, and the Agrestius Affair   143
   Andreas Fischer

9. Columbanus and the Mission to the Bavarians and the Slavs in
   the Seventh Century   165
   Herwig Wolfram

Part IV   On the Fringe: Columbanus and Gallus in Alamannia

10. Between the Devil and the Deep Lake Constance: Jonas of Bobbio, *interpretatio
    Christiana*, and the Pagan Religion of the Alamanni   177
    Bernhard Maier

11. Drinking with Woden: A Re-examination of Jonas's *Vita Columbani* I.27   189
    Francesco Borri

12. Between Metz and Überlingen: Columbanus and Gallus in Alamannia   205
    Yaniv Fox

13. *Quicumque sunt rebelles, foras exeant!* Columbanus's Rebellious
    Disciple Gallus   225
    Philipp Dörler

Part V   Lombard Italy and Columbanus's Legacy

14. Columbanus, Bobbio, and the Lombards   243
    Stefano Gasparri

15. Disputing Columbanus's Heritage: The *Regula cuiusdam patris*
    (with a Translation of the Rule)   259
    Albrecht Diem

Index   307

Maps

1. Ireland at the time of Columbanus   xxi
2. Columbanus's itinerary from Bangor to Bobbio   xxii
3. Alamannia and Bavaria in the seventh century   xxiii
4. The Columbanian monastic network, showing principal monasteries and towns   xxiv

Foreword

WALTER POHL

This volume grew out of a conference held in Vienna in November 2013 on Columbanus and the peoples of post-Roman Europe. Columbanus never got as far as Vienna (unlike other places where the anniversary of his death was celebrated in 2015). As we know, it was an angel who kept him from going there.[1] Had he traveled east along the Danube, he would have crossed from Bavaria into Avar territory at the Enns River, near Lauriacum, attested in the late eighth century as *limes certus*, the secure frontier of the Avar khaganate. Near Vienna he would have passed into Avar territory proper, the settlement area of the Avar and Slavic subjects of the khagan. Perhaps he considered traveling to the Slavs in the eastern Alps, to the Marca Vinedorum, as Fredegar later called it, which had been a Christian country until very recently. But these were boundaries that he never crossed, and Avars and Slavs were *gentes* that he never met.

I will not say much more about Columbanus here, but rather about the *gentes*, the peoples that are also the focus of this volume. Perhaps this is not the most obvious topic to be treated in the context of Columbanian studies. G. S. M. Walker, the editor of the works of Columbanus for the *Scriptores Latini Hiberniae*, was so little interested in the peoples in the text that his elaborate indices contain almost nothing about them. The *Index verborum et locutionum* does not include *gens/gentes, populus, barbarus, patria,* or *gentilis,* but only the more exquisite word *ethnici* and the composite *gentiles barbari.* The index of names only includes Lombards, omitting Hebrews/Jews/Israel, Gaul/Gauls, Britons, Italians (also called Ausonians by Columbanus), Greeks, and the very interesting mentions of Europe—and worst of all, it does not include the Irish

---

1. *VC* I.27.

and all the different names by which Columbanus calls them: Scoti, Hiberni, and Iberi. The entries for Italy and Ireland only refer to his Introduction and not to the texts.

This brief list of omitted names of peoples and of their countries demonstrates that the letters of Columbanus can be contextualized in a world of *gentes*, although he mentions most of them only in passing. The letter to Pope Boniface uses the image of Christ in a chariot drawn by Saints Peter and Paul, who "riding over the sea of *gentes* troubled many waters, and increased his chariot with thousands of innumerable peoples *(populi)*."[2] The semantic distinction between pagan *gentes* and Christian *populi* is often used in the period, though it had never been applied exclusively, and of course many *gentes* had meanwhile become more or less Christian. Columbanus's use of names also shows that he often resorts to classical usage. No mention of the Franks, but only of Gauls and Gaul, and only one of the Lombards, in the pointed phrase that underlines the paradoxical character of the letter written to Pope Boniface IV in matters of faith: "*rex gentilis peregrinum scribere Longobardus Scotum hebetem rogat*," a gentile Lombard king asks a dull Irish pilgrim to write.[3] Rome, at whose foundation almost all *gentes* once rejoiced,[4] was now only relevant because of the Cathedra Sancti Petri and as a *caput ecclesiarum*, and it risked squandering even this glory.

Several chapters in this volume deal with all aspects of Columbanus's relations with the peoples and kingdoms of his time, and they can build on substantial research. At the same time, the letters of Columbanus, and of course from a somewhat different angle, Jonas of Bobbio's *Life of Columbanus*, are important textual witnesses to how these peoples and their political role in general were perceived, and to an extent also shaped by writing. In the late sixth and the first half of the seventh centuries in the West these perceptions were transformed, and the ethnic self-identification of the *regna* was consolidated. Of course Franks, Goths, or Lombards had been present for a while, and barbarian rule over former Roman provinces had become self-evident for many authors. A late-sixth-century letter by Pope Pelagius II stating that Lombard domination over Italy would pass *sicut fumus* ("like smoke") is a rare expression of hopes that barbarian rule might disappear.[5] But this adaptation to barbarian rule did not mean that the concept of a kingdom defined by the ethnic affiliation

---

2. *Ep. 5.11, 48: per mare gentium equitans turbavit aquas multas et innumerabilium populorum millibus multiplicavit quadrigas.*

3. *Ep. 5.14.*

4. *Ep. 5.11: urbis quondam conditae nomen nimio favore omnium prope gentium.*

5. *Epistulae Aevi Merowingici Collectae* no. 9 : 449. Cf. Pohl 1997: 101f.

of its ruling elite had necessarily taken root. Gregory of Tours subtly avoids highlighting the Frankishness of the Merovingian kingdoms, and equally, the Romanness of its ecclesiastical elites: his overarching concept of the polity he lived in was the sacred topography and ecclesiastical structure of Gaul. Helmut Reimitz has shown that this was only one of the contemporary approaches possible, and that Gregory clearly reacts against other options.[6] Venantius Fortunatus, for example, repeatedly lauded the Christian synthesis of Roman and barbarian virtues in the elite of the kingdom. We have no direct statement of a more Frankish view from the same period.

But that would change in the seventh century, most notably with the Chronicle of Fredegar. Here the Frankish origin story from Troy that Gregory had excluded was extensively narrated, and the name of the Franks was even added to passages that Fredegar had taken from Gregory. In Fredegar's wide perspective, the Franks were surrounded by other *gentes* and their polities. Similar views of the political landscape are expressed in other seventh-century works, such as the *Origo gentis Langobardorum* and Isidore of Seville's *History of the Goths*. These two works of historiography are remarkably different from each other and in their treatment of the identity of the respective peoples; both of them, however, buttress the ethnic legitimation of each kingdom and its historical basis. In the seventh century we also find increasing evidence of the use of the ethnic title in the *regna: rex Francorum, rex gentis Langobardorum*, and so forth.

The *gentes* that had grabbed power in the fifth and sixth centuries had not trumpeted the ethnic character of their rule from the start, although the Romans had always distinguished them by their ethnonyms. Explicit ethnic identifications only gradually pervaded texts written in the Latin language of state; but after AD 600 they certainly became more frequent. Still, other texts continued to shape contemporary political identities differently.[7]

It is in this context that the writings of Columbanus, and his *Life* written by Jonas, can profitably be studied. Hagiography, letters about Church policy, or sermons are of course not focused on affairs of state or of peoples as historiographical texts, but they can also contain traces of shifting concepts of community and identity. Such casual glances at the political landscape are important precisely inasmuch as they are casual and may not always be central to their author's agenda. On the other hand, some of the earliest surviving manuscripts of Gregory of Tours's *Histories* (more specifically, the six-book

6. Reimitz 2015.
7. Pohl 2013.

version) were produced in Columbanian monasteries. Their horizon remained wide. Columbanus had met many *gentes*: Irish, Britons, Franks, Alamanni, Lombards, and others. He had come, as he said, from the ends of the earth, from the *transmundialis limes*,[8] and he possibly crossed more boundaries than many of his contemporaries. Still, he wanted the peoples all accommodated within a single Roman, Western, "European" Church, which was as pure in belief as that of his native Ireland. The chapters in this volume explore these encounters and the complex perspective from which Columbanus and his successors perceived them.

BIBLIOGRAPHY

Epistulae Aevi Merowingici Collectae. (1892), ed. W. Gundlach. MGH, *Epistulae* III. Berlin.
Pohl, W.. (1997) "The Empire and the Lombards: Treaties and Negotiations in the Sixth Century." In W. Pohl (ed.), *Kingdoms of the Empire: The Integration of Barbarians in Late Antiquity*. Leiden, Brill, 75–133.
Pohl, W. (2013) "Christian and Barbarian Identities in the Early Medieval West: Introduction." In W. Pohl and G. Heydemann (eds.), *Post-Roman Transitions: Christian and Barbarian Identities in the Early Medieval West*. Turnhout, Brepols, 1–46.
Reimitz, H. (2015) *History, Frankish Identity and the Framing of Western Ethnicity, 550–850*. Cambridge, Cambridge University Press.

8. *Ep.* 5.11; cf. 5.5.3; 5.8.

Preface

This volume developed from a conference held in Vienna on November 22–23, 2013, to mark the start of a three-year research project at the Austrian Academy of Sciences funded by the Austrian Science Fund, titled "The Columbanian Network: Social Networks, Elite Identities, and Christian Communities in Europe, 550–750" (FWF P25175), which ran from 2013 to 2016. The conference was titled "Meeting the *Gentes*—Crossing Boundaries: Columbanus and the Peoples of Post-Roman Europe" and was the first in a series of international conferences leading up to the fourteenth centenary of Columbanus's death in 2015. I wish to thank Abbot Johannes Jung OSB and Professor Georg Braulik OSB for hosting the conference in the Schottenstift; H. E. Ambassador James Brennan for his opening remarks and for the reception at the Irish embassy; Professor Walter Pohl and my colleagues at the Institut für Mittelalterforschung, especially Maximilian Diesenberger; the speakers at the conference—Walter Pohl, Damian Bracken, Clare Stancliffe, Ian Wood, Herwig Wolfram, Andreas Fischer, Bernhard Maier, Francesco Borri, Barbara Theune-Großkopf, Yaniv Fox, Roberta Conversi and Eleonora Destefanis, Gisella Cantino-Wataghin, Conor Newman, Sébastien Bully and Emmet Marron, Dominique Barbet-Massin, Ann Buckley, and Jean-Michel Picard; and most especially all those who contributed to the final volume. I am grateful to the Austrian Science Fund (FWF) for funding the project and to the Society of Authors' Foundation in London for the award of an Authors' Foundation grant. I am also very grateful to series editor Ralph Mathisen, Stefan Vranka, and the editorial team at Oxford University Press for their patience and interest in this volume; and to Jaroslav Synek of the Czech Academy of Sciences for drawing the maps. The volume is dedicated to Professor Patrick J. Geary, who I first met as a PhD student living in Oslo in 2006 and who encouraged my interest in this field. In the summer of 2016 I had the privilege of editing the final volume at the Institute for Advanced Study in Princeton, and my sincere thanks go to Professor Geary and the Faculty of the IAS for making me so welcome there. It was the perfect *locus amoenus* in which to finish this work.

A. O'H

Contributors

Francesco Borri, Austrian Academy of Sciences

Damian Bracken, University College Cork

Albrecht Diem, Syracuse University

Philipp Dörler, University of Vienna

Andreas Fischer, Austrian Academy of Sciences

Yaniv Fox, Bar-Ilan University

Stefano Gasparri, Università Ca'Foscari Venezia

Elva Johnston, University College Dublin

Bernhard Maier, University of Tübingen

Dáibhí Ó Cróinín, National University of Ireland, Galway

Alexander O'Hara, Austrian Academy of Sciences, University of St Andrews

Walter Pohl, Austrian Academy of Sciences

Clare Stancliffe, University of Durham

Herwig Wolfram, University of Vienna

Ian Wood, University of Leeds

Alex Woolf, University of St. Andrews

Abbreviations

AU Annals of Ulster, ed. S. Mac Airt and G. Mac Niocaill. *The Annals of Ulster to A.D. 1131*, Pt. 1, *Text and Translation*. Dublin, Dublin Institute for Advanced Studies, 1983.

CSEL *Corpus Sciptorum Ecclesiasticorum Latinorum*, Brepols.

CCSL *Corpus Christianorum Series Latina*, Brepols.

CDL *Codice diplomatico longobardo*, III, ed. C. Brühl. Rome, Istituto storico italiano per il medioevo, 1973.

CDSCB *Codice Diplomatico del monastero di San Colombano di Bobbio fino all'anno MCCVIII*, I, ed. C. Cipolla. Rome, Istituto storico italiano per il medioevo, 1918.

DEB Gildas, *De excidio et conquestu Brittaniae*, ed. M. Winterbottom. *Gildas: The Ruin of Britain and Other Documents*. Chichester, Phillimore, 1978.

DLH Gregory of Tours, *Decem Libri Historiarum*, ed. B. Krusch and W. Levison. MGH, *Scriptores rerum Merovingicarum* 1,1. Hanover, 1951. *Gregory of Tours: The History of the Franks*, trans. L. Thorpe. London, Penguin, 1974.

Ep. or *Epp.* Columbanus's *Epistula(e)*. In *Sancti Columbani Opera*, ed. G. S. M. Walker. *Scriptores Latini Hiberniae* II. Dublin, Dublin Institute for Advanced Study, 1957 (reprinted 1970).

Fredegar Chronicle of Fredegar = *Chronicae*, ed. B. Krusch. MGH, *Scriptores rerum Merovingicarum* 2. Hanover, 1888. *The Fourth Book of the Chronicle of Fredegar, with Its Continuations*, ed. and trans. J. M. Wallace-Hadrill. London, Nelson, 1960.

HE Bede, *Historia ecclesiastica gentis Anglorum*, ed. C. Plummer. *Venerabilis Baedae Opera Historica*. Oxford, Oxford University Press, 1896; *Bede's Ecclesiastical History of the English People*,

	ed. and trans. B. Colgrave and R. A. B. Mynors. Oxford, Oxford University Press, 1969; rev. edition, 1992.
MGH	Monumenta Germaniae Historica
PG	*Patrologia Graeca* = J.-P. Migne (ed.), *Patrologiae cursus completus, Series Graeca*. Paris, Imprimerie Catholique, 1857–1866.
PL	*Patrologia Latina* = J.-P. Migne (ed.), *Patrologiae cursus completus, Series Latina*. Paris, Imprimerie Catholique, 1844–1855.
Reg.Ep.	*S. Gregorii magni opera. Registrum epistularum: Libri 1–7, 8–14*, ed. Dag Norberg. Corpus Christianorum Series Latina 140–140 A. 2 vols. Turnhout, Brepols, 1982; translated into English and annotated by J. R. C. Martyn as *The Letters of Gregory the Great*. 3 vols. Toronto, Pontifical Institute of Mediaeval Studies, 2004.
VC	Jonas of Bobbio, *Vita Columbani abbatis et disciplorumque eius*. In B. Krusch (ed.), *Ionae Vitae sanctorum Columbani, Vedastis, Iohannis*. MGH, *Scriptores Rerum Germanicarum in usum scholarum separatim editi*. Hanover and Leipzig, 1905, 144–294. *Jonas of Bobbio: Life of Columbanus, Life of John of Réomé, and Life of Vedast*, trans. A. O'Hara and I. Wood. Translated Texts for Historians 64. Liverpool, Liverpool University Press, 2017.

Maps

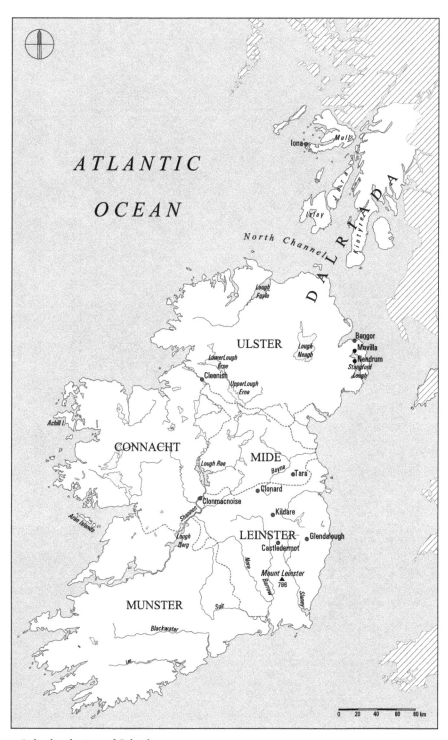

1. Ireland at the time of Columbanus

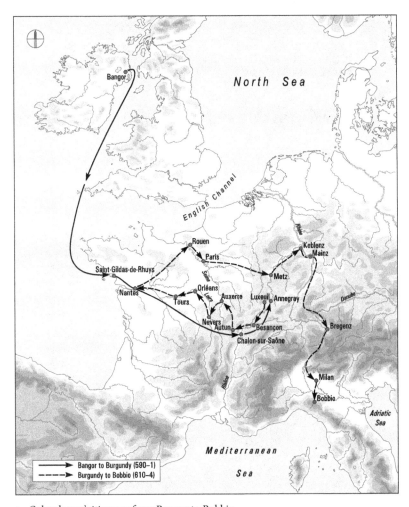

North Sea

Bangor

English Channel

Rouen
Paris
Saint-Gildas-de-Rhuys
Nantes
Orléans
Tours
Auxerre
Nevers
Autun
Chalon-sur-Saône
Besançon

Metz
Koblenz
Mainz
Luxeuil Annegray
Danube
Bregenz

Milan
Bobbio

Adriatic
Sea

Mediterranean
Sea

Rhine
Saône
Loire
Rhône

Bangor to Burgundy (590–1)
Burgundy to Bobbio (610–4)

2. Columbanus's itinerary from Bangor to Bobbio

3. Alamannia and Bavaria in the seventh century

4. The Columbanian monastic network, showing principal monasteries and towns

PART I

Columbanus in Context

Introduction

Columbanus and Europe

ALEXANDER O'HARA

Five years after the end of the Second World War, a group of statesmen and scholars met in the sleepy market town of Luxeuil-les-Bains in the Franche-Comté region of eastern France. They were there to commemorate the fourteenth centenary of the birth of the Irish abbot and monastic founder Columbanus, who was born in Leinster in the south of Ireland around the middle of the sixth century and founded the famous monastery of Luxeuil soon after his arrival in this region of France in 591. An academic congress had been organized alongside other festive commemorations to celebrate his legacy. What was unusual about this congress was its political profile: it had been orchestrated by the French Foreign Minister, Robert Schuman. A bevy of leading European statesmen and diplomats that included Taoiseach John A. Costello and Seán MacBride (the Irish prime minister and the Minister for Foreign Affairs, respectively), as well as the Papal Nuncio Angelo Roncalli, the future Pope John XXIII, converged on Luxeuil in response to Schuman's invitation.[1] Schuman was a devout Catholic deeply influenced by the Catholic social teaching of Pope Leo XIII and Jacques Maritain.[2] Only two months before the Luxeuil conference, on May 9, 1950, Schuman had made the historic declaration in Paris that would mark the foundation of the European Community: the Schuman Doctrine. The previous summer in Strasbourg he had declared:

> We are carrying out a great experiment, the fulfillment of the same recurrent dream that for ten centuries has revisited the peoples of Europe: creating between them an organization putting an end to war and guaranteeing an eternal peace. . . . Our century, that has witnessed the catastrophes resulting in the unending clash of nationalities and nationalisms, must attempt and succeed in reconciling nations in a supranational association. This would safeguard the diversities and aspirations of each nation while

---

1. On the conference and the historical context, see Picard 2015.
2. On the influences that shaped Schuman, see Fimister 2008; and Krijtenburg 2012, 2015. For his political writings, see Schuman 2010.

4 Columbanus in Context

coordinating them in the same manner as the regions are coordinated within the unity of the nation.[3]

He followed Maritain's belief that a united European federation of states would ultimately lead to the establishment of a new Christendom. Behind the arcane academic discussions that were taking place at Luxeuil, Schuman had a pragmatic reason for bringing together leading European statesmen: he wanted to sound out the idea of a European coal and steel community based on the premise that by pooling coal and steel production (the most important materials for the arms industry) and by merging economic interests, war in Europe could be prevented. In his vision for a united Europe, Schuman drew inspiration from the unlikely figure of Columbanus, whom he praised as "the patron saint of all those who seek to construct a united Europe."[4] While it would not be until April 1951 that the European Coal and Steel Community (ECSC), the forerunner of the modern European Union, was launched, the conference in Luxeuil gave a new lease of life to a long-dead saint, more recently lauded as a "Father of Europe" by Pope Benedict XVI.[5]

Almost sixty-five years later, when Schuman's grand vision for a united Europe appeared increasingly unstable and threatened, a number of pan-European conferences were organized to mark the fourteenth centenary, in 2015, of Columbanus's death. All of them were decidedly more academic and less political or high profile than the Luxeuil conference of 1950, as European leaders were busy dealing with a new immigration crisis. This book grew out of the first of these international conferences, which I organized in Vienna in November 2013, called "Meeting the *Gentes*-Crossing Boundaries: Columbanus and the Peoples of Post-Roman Europe" and held in the Prälatensaal of the Benedictine abbey of the Schottenstift, itself founded by a group of Irish monks in 1155 under the aegis of the Babenberg duke of Austria. The conference also marked the start of a three-year research project at the Austrian Academy of Sciences funded by the Austrian Science Fund, titled "The Columbanian Network: Social Networks, Elite Identities, and Christian Communities in Europe".[6] A number of publications have stemmed from this project, of which this volume is the

---

3. From Schuman's speech at Strasbourg on May 16, 1949, announcing the coming supranational European Community (www.schuman.info/Strasbourg549.htm).

4. From a speech given by Schuman at the Luxeuil conference on July 23, 1950 (on the background see: http://www.amisaintcolomban.org/wordpress/wp-content/uploads/Secret_de_Luxeuil-1950.pdf).

5. Pope Benedict XVI, General Audience of June 11, 2008, at the Vatican, https://w2.vatican.va/content/benedict-xvi/en/audiences/2008/documents/hf_ben-xvi_aud_20080611.html.

6. The conference booklet and overview of the project are available at https://www.academia.edu/6309221/Meeting_the_Gentes_Crossing_Boundaries_Columbanus_and_the_Peoples_of_Post-Roman_Europe.

culmination.[7] In 2015 three further international conferences were organized by a separate team of European scholars in Bangor, Luxeuil, and Bobbio, and other volumes are in preparation based on these conferences. As the Luxeuil conference of 1950, held on the advent of European unification and to commemorate the fourteenth centenary of Columbanus's birth, gave a new impulse to the scholarship of this figure in the postwar period, so too the fourteenth centenary of his death in 2015 provided an opportunity for a new generation of scholars to engage afresh with this material. As is to be expected in a volume focusing on the life and legacy of a single figure, there are many overlaps and common themes among the contributions. But the different perspectives from which they are discussed provide a differentiated and nuanced discussion not only of Columbanus but also of the multiple and various efforts of contemporary and successive generations at the end of the sixth and beginning of the seventh centuries to find order and orientation in a rapidly changing world.

SCOPE AND APPROACH OF THE VOLUME

Columbanus left Ireland in 590 to pursue an ideal of ascetic exile, a commitment to live the rest of his life in religious exile.[8] This ideal of alienation informed every aspect of his exile on the Continent, the organization of his communities, and his relations with the Frankish and Lombard elites.[9] Columbanus attempted to shape his communities as separated, sacred spaces with clear boundaries and rules of access. As an abbot and monastic founder, his radical monasticism appealed to the Frankish elite, who increasingly sought to invest in religious institutions. But there was a distinction between what Columbanus sought to create—an ideal Christian ascetic community independent of secular and ecclesiastical power structures—and what the Frankish elites wanted: monastic foundations plugged into the social and political sphere. Conflict and tension ensued from these divergent aims, but in time the Frankish elite accepted the boundaries established by Columbanus, while conflict within his communities eventually led them to conform to Frankish ecclesiastical norms. The resolution of this conflict during the first decades of the seventh century led to a revolution in monastic foundation, as more than a hundred monasteries were founded

7. O'Hara 2012, 2013, 2015a, 2015b, 2015c, forthcoming; O'Hara and Wood 2017; O'Hara and Taylor 2013.

8. On Columbanus's spiritual writings and theology, see de Vogüé 2004, Mackey 1996, and Gionta 2017. Flood 2004 provides a useful, broader theoretical framework for approaching this type of subject.

9. On Columbanus's identification as an exile and on the construction of identity more generally in the age of Columbanus, see O'Hara 2013, Geary, forthcoming b, and Johnston 2016.

within a century of Columbanus's death that transformed the ritual economy of Merovingian Gaul and subsequently that of the early Middle Ages.[10]

The world of Late Antiquity that Columbanus entered when he left Ireland toward the end of the sixth century was a world of *gentes*. The pluralistic political landscape of the *gentes* had replaced a world of empire. The post-Roman kingdoms of Europe through which Columbanus traveled and established his monastic foundations were comprised of many different communities of peoples. As an outsider and an immigrant, how did Columbanus and his communities interact with these peoples? How did he and the diverse members of his communities negotiate their differences, and what emerged from these encounters? How societies interact with outsiders can reveal the inner workings and social norms of those cultures, as the recent migrant crisis in the European Union has shown.[11]

During his two-thousand-mile odyssey through France, Germany, Austria, Switzerland, and Italy, Columbanus crossed many boundaries (both literally and figuratively) that brought him into contact with the religious and secular elites and local communities of post-Roman Europe. He and his contemporaries operated in a gift-giving society that was rooted in reciprocal relations. As an outsider, Columbanus relied on the most powerful people in society for patronage and protection, even if he consciously sought to position his monasteries on the frontiers of the political orbit. He always went directly to the cities and the courts of kings to seek their support, but he established his monasteries on the rural peripheries of their kingdoms. In return for the gift of land and patronage, the kings expected a spiritual counter-gift of intercessory prayer and blessing from Columbanus and his communities. Initially Columbanus appears to have been a kind of spiritual adviser to the young Merovingian king of Burgundy, Theuderic II, and their relations were amicable. He appears to have been shocked at the moral turpitude of some members of the Gallic episcopate, who were essentially state bureaucrats, as Clare Stancliffe discusses in chapter 7 of this volume. Columbanus refused to deal with them or acknowledge their authority, and he fell afoul of them because he followed a different method for calculating the date of Easter, the most important feast in the Christian liturgical calendar. He also refused the laity access to the inner confines of his monasteries, which were strictly demarcated for members of his communities.[12] While he had the protection of the king, Columbanus was safe from the machinations of the bishops. However, his influence over the young king threatened the position

10. Atsma 1976; Prinz 1965, 1981; Fox 2014.
11. On boundaries and community-building, see Cohen 1985, 1994.
12. *VC* I.19; on Insular concepts of sacred space, see Jenkins 2010 and MacDonald 2001.

of the latter's grandmother, the dowager queen Brunhild, who was the power behind the throne.[13] Columbanus became more embedded in court politics when he chastised the king for his sexual conduct and urged him to take a wife. Columbanus's refusal to bless the king's illegitimate children by concubines and his later refusal of commensality with the king led to a deterioration in relations and ultimately to his banishment in 610 along with the Insular members of his communities, those monks who had followed him from Ireland and Britain.[14] His rigid adherence to the precepts of the gospel and his unwillingness to compromise with the cultural and ecclesiastical norms of Gaul led to a breakdown in reciprocal relations. Columbanus was unwilling to give the counter-gift of his prayers and blessing fully if this meant compromising his own ethical, religious, and cultural values. However, out of this conflicting cultural encounter emerged new forms of community-building and engagement in the decades following Columbanus's death. The monastic model that Columbanus advocated as a founder—rural monasteries that were "pure spaces" of intercessory prayer independent of bishops and secular authorities—became a new form of cultural contact that transformed the interrelationship between monastic groups and secular authorities. During the course of the seventh century the foundation of monasteries by the Frankish elite became a new way for them to assert their investment in the welfare of the kingdom while winning spiritual, social, and political prestige for themselves and their families. The new monasteries that were founded throughout the kingdom and their close links to the court fostered new types of community and ways of exercising power that would continue to have a long reach into the Middle Ages.

In planning this volume and in my initial contact with contributors, I sought to approach this topic from two angles: reciprocity (people's informal economic systems of exchange) and cultural hybridity (new forms that emerge from cultural contact). Contributors were invited to approach these avenues of inquiry within the context of all of the geographical spheres in which Columbanus and his monastic communities operated (the Insular world, Merovingian Gaul, Alamannia, and Lombard Italy) and the varieties of communities he came in contact with, whether they were royal, ecclesiastical, aristocratic, or grassroots.

In cultural anthropology and sociology, reciprocity is a way of defining people's informal exchanges of goods and labor; that is, people's informal economic systems. Columbanus's troubled relations with the Frankish elite can perhaps best be understood in terms of reciprocity. Holy men had to provide

13. On the career of Brunhild, see Nelson 1978 and Dumézil 2008.
14. *VC* I.18–9.

spiritual benefits, which in turn could have social and political ramifications. Power and dominance derive not only from possession of material resources, but also from possession of cultural and social resources.[15] Columbanus's role as a catalyst needs to be understood not from the perspective of his supposed role in transforming a decadent Merovingian Church, but as an outsider who provided an alternative framework for the new Frankish elites that were emerging at this time. As an outsider, Columbanus needed the patronage of the Frankish elite but was unwilling to assimilate to their customs, while the Frankish elite were initially unwilling to give Columbanus and his communities the independence he desired. It was only later, when the Frankish elite had accepted the boundaries set by Columbanus and his successors had modified their norms and practices, that the movement gained momentum.

Columbanus's ascetic exile was the first sustained contact in the historical record between a group of Irish men from a non-Romanized society and groups from different ethnic and cultural backgrounds whom they encountered on the Continent. As such, this contact provides an interesting case study for looking at the development of cultural hybridity that came about through this exchange.[16] What were the effects of this contact between these different groups? Peter Burke (2009) has delineated three stages in the formation of cultural hybridity: cultural encounter, appropriation, and fusion.[17] The responses to exchange can vary from acceptance, to rejection, to segregation, to adaptation. Burke has identified the city and the frontier as two specific locales that are particularly favorable for cultural exchange. These are places at the "intersections between cultures, in which the process of mixing ends in the creation of something new and distinctive."[18] Columbanus's monasteries, located in border areas, can be understood as vibrant cultural contact zones where men from different ethnic and cultural backgrounds formed communities together, not always harmoniously. Indeed, conflict is an important lens through which to study this phenomenon. Through the conflict and rejection that Columbanus experienced both within his own communities and from the Gallic episcopate, and later through the conflict that erupted in his own communities after his death, we can trace the stages by which these communities negotiated and worked out their own identities. From these liminal monastic communities we can also trace how, like cultural routers, their norms and *habitus* were transported to the city, to the royal court

---

15. Bourdieu 1985, 1992.
16. On cultural hybridity, see Yazdiha 2010; Bergolte and Schneidmüller 2010; Burke 2009; Kapchan and Turner Strong 1999; and Bhabha 1994.
17. Burke 2009.
18. Burke 2009: 76.

in Paris, where monastic culture came to play an increasingly important role in influencing the court culture of Chlothar II and his successors.[19] What emerges from these processes of encounter, conflict, negotiation, and adaptation are new forms of cultural order, which we see gradually crystallizing in Merovingian Gaul from the mid-seventh century onwards. Something new emerged from this encounter, and we can see how religion increasingly comes to shape the vocabulary of identity politics in the early Middle Ages.[20] Columbanus's *peregrinatio* and the establishment of his communities can in one sense be understood as a utopian project, as the activation of what had been for Augustine a key way of imagining the new chosen people in contrast to Roman models of identification.[21] Coming from a non-Roman society on the fringes of the Roman world, Columbanus's Christian universalist perspective allowed him to approach the world he encountered from the perspective of a plurality of *gentes* who, despite political and ethnic boundaries, could and should be united by their common Christian faith.[22]

But the essays in this volume are not only about Columbanus and his perspective. Many contributions also deal with perspectives on Columbanus by members of the societies with which Columbanus came to live and work and in which his legacy continued to play an important role. In doing so they reconstruct the circuits of communication in which positions, identities, notions of Christianity and orthodoxy, and different views of the world were discussed in the post-Roman West. Taken together, the chapters in this book reconstruct the formation of the horizons of a distinct post-Roman European world. As Peter Brown has observed, it is precisely in the seventh century that we can trace the emergence of a Western Christendom in the former provinces of the Western Roman Empire, which is much more recognizable to modern Christianity than it was to the more ancient Christianity of the time of Augustine.[23]

OVERVIEW AND INTRODUCTION TO CONTRIBUTORS

Columbanus lived during a period of profound transformation following the breakup of the Roman Empire in the West and the consolidation of the post-Roman successor kingdoms in the sixth and seventh centuries. He had the

---

19. On these new emotional communities tied to the Frankish court, see Rosenwein 2006 and Hen 2007.

20. On the role of religion in the shaping of identity politics in the early Middle Ages, see the methodological profile in Pohl 2013.

21. See Corradini 2013 on the concept of *peregrinatio* in Augustine's thought.

22. See Heydemann 2013 in the context of Cassiodorus's *Expositio psalmorum*.

23. Brown 2003: 217–9.

perspective of an outsider coming from the edges of this world, and he was conscious of the divisions and disunity that characterized the societies through which he traveled. Concord and unity are recurring themes throughout his writings, and in chapter 2 Damian Bracken deftly traces Columbanus's language of concord, following the literary vein back to the classical and patristic authorities who shaped the political ideology of the Roman Empire and later the Christian Commonwealth. He shows how the adoption and transformation of the language and imagery of concord by Christian thinkers was central to early Christian identity formation and how it influenced Columbanus's understanding of the Church as the home of all the *gentes*. Bracken shows Columbanus to have been a man fully engaged with and aware of the traditions he encountered on the Continent, someone who could employ the imagery and the deftness of language to engage the attention of those in power.

From Columbanus's attempt to shape concord and instill unity within the Christian Commonwealth we turn to the topsy-turvy political melting pot of his Ireland. If Columbanus could behave and write as an equal of the Frankish kings and ecclesiastical leaders of Europe, he may have done so because he thought of himself as their social equal. In chapter 3 Dáibhí Ó Cróinín introduces us to the Ireland of the sixth century, where new dynasties were on the make and carving out their territories. This was a violently competitive social and political arena, and Ó Cróinín intriguingly proposes that Columbanus may have been a member of the royal Leinster dynasty of the Uí Bairrche. He suggests that Columbanus's entry into monastic life in Bangor may have been politically expedient, as his family was gradually sidelined and ousted from power in the later sixth century. The Uí Bairrche dynasty had links to Bangor, where one of its kings retired in the sixth century, and the monastery in turn also had land holdings in Uí Bairrche territory in Leinster. Like his elder near contemporary, Columba of Iona, who was also a member of a royal dynasty and who left Ireland in 563 after a political debacle, Columbanus's decision to undertake ascetic exile (*peregrinatio*) may have been in part politically motivated and expedient. Columbanus's Irish background, particularly his dealings with women, is explored by Elva Johnston in her thought-provoking contribution, chapter 4, which deals with gender, status, social practices, and the contrast in power between queens on the Continent and women in Ireland, while Alex Woolf in chapter 5 looks more closely at Columbanus's links to the British Church and the networks linked to Bangor, in particular to Bishop Uinnianus, which proved to be defining influences on Columbanus's monastic formation in Ulster.

After leaving Bangor for the Continent in around 590, Columbanus landed in not-so-unfamiliar territory on the west coast of Brittany, which was part of the Insular world. As Ian Wood argues in chapter 6, Columbanus's veneration for the British ecclesiastical author Gildas may have led him to settle briefly near the reputed burial place of Gildas on the Morbihan peninsula of Brittany; a Frankish incursion into the area may have forced him and his monks to move to the Vosges region of Burgundy, where a settlement of British monks was already in existence at Salicis. Columbanus chose to found his first monastic foundation at Annegray, not far from this community of British monks. The leader of the Frankish incursion, King Guntram, may have been Columbanus's initial patron, as he was a known benefactor of the Church and religious life. As Ian Wood shows, Columbanus's work in Gaul followed on from the work of British ascetics in the region, and Jonas of Bobbio mentions a number of British monks who were also members of Columbanus's communities. Clare Stancliffe then turns in chapter 7 to Columbanus's dealings with the Gallic bishops, discussing how he looked to the writings of Gregory the Great and Gildas for support in his escalating conflict with the bishops and how this was grounded in fundamentally differing views on authority and the nature of Christian leadership, issues that also appear in Damian Bracken's contribution.

Religious deviance and heresy were topical issues during Columbanus's lifetime and continued to influence the communities after his death, as Andreas Fischer explores in chapter 8 in the context of the Agrestius affair of the 620s, when a renegade Luxeuil monk accused Columbanus and his monastic practices of being heretical. Fischer sheds light on the tensions between the missions among the *gentes* spearheaded by Columbanus's successor at Luxeuil, Eustasius, and the role of allegations of heresy in the internal conflicts of Columbanus's communities in the 620s, seen against the backdrop of broader concerns about orthodoxy in the seventh century. Abbot Eustasius was involved in a mission to the Bavarians and the extension of Frankish royal and ecclesiastical influence in Bavaria in the period after Columbanus's death, as Herwig Wolfram explores in chapter 9 in the context of the archaeological discovery of a seventh-century monastery on the island of Herrenchiemsee in Bavaria, which may have been a mission station established from Luxeuil. Columbanus briefly considered going farther east from Bregenz to preach to the heathen Slavs, but according to Jonas of Bobbio, he was reputedly persuaded by an angel to discard the notion and cross the Alps into Italy instead. Wolfram sets the political context for this decision and notes that it took another Irish émigré, Bishop Virgil of Salzburg (d. 784), to undertake the first successful mission to the Slavs in the eighth century, when the Carantanians became the first Christianized Slavonic people.

Although Columbanus only spent two years in Alamannia around the shores of Lake Constance at Bregenz (now in western Austria), a number of

contributions are specifically concentrated on this period because it is generally the least understood and studied within the context of Coumbanus's career
on the Continent. The Christianization of Alamannia was already under way
before Columbanus arrived in the region after he had won the support of King
Theudebert II of Austrasia (the eastern Merovingian kingdom with its centre at
Metz), the half-brother of Theuderic II, who had expelled Columbanus and his
Insular monks from Burgundy in 610. But it was a region where the old gods
were slow to die out. According to Jonas of Bobbio, Columbanus encountered
a feasting ritual organized by both baptized Christians and pagans, who had
dedicated a huge vat of beer to the Germanic god Woden.[24] Jonas's account is
the earliest reference to Woden in the historical record, and both Bernhard
Maier (chapter 10) and Francesco Borri (chapter 11) tease out the broader
contexts of this account, reading it as indicative of changing barbarian identity
politics of the seventh century. Columbanus's stay in Bregenz was short lived,
and it appears that he and his followers angered the local people with forceful
proselytization. In chapter 12 Yaniv Fox discusses the political background to
Columbanus's time in Alamannia; Columbanus's relationship to the local duke;
and the later achievements of his Irish disciple Gallus, who remained behind as
a hermit in the Steinach (now in Switzerland) after Columbanus and the rest
of his monks left for Italy in 612. Philipp Dörler also focuses in chapter 13 on
Columbanus's rebellious disciple Gallus, who refused to travel across the Alps
due to illness and who fell out with his abbot as a consequence. But Gallus's influence in the area proved much longer lasting and significant than that of his
master, as the great Carolingian monastery of St Gallen grew up on the site of
Gallus's hermitage. Recent excavations in the town of St Gallen have shed new
light on this UNESCO World Heritage site, which preserves the greatest monastic library from medieval Europe.[25] Dörler tries to situate Gallus and his hermitage within the context of the wider Columbanian network and why Gallus's
influence proved to be of more significance among the local elites in the area.

   Columbanus was more successful in Lombard Italy, where he won patronage
at the Lombard court in Milan. King Agilulf granted him the site of Bobbio in the
Ligurian Apennines in 613 while Columbanus acted as a cultural broker between
the Lombard court and the papacy in Rome, attempting to resolve the complex
theological dispute known as the Three Chapters Controversy (see chapters 8
and 14). His views on this schism would have won him support from Agilulf's
Bavarian queen, Theodelinda, who shared Columbanus's position. Stefano

24. *VC* I.27.
25. See the contributions in Schmuki, Schnoor et al. 2015.

Gasparri discusses in chapter 14 the close links that Columbanus fostered with the Lombard monarchy and how Bobbio became the first royal monastery in Italy. Columbanus's European journey finally came to an end at Bobbio, where he died on November 23, 615, probably aged in his midsixties,[26] after a meandering odyssey of some two thousand miles since he left the shores of Belfast Lough in northern Ireland. He was buried in the new monastery he had helped build with his monks during the last year of his life.[27] Columbanus remained a controversial figure even after his death, as monastic rebellions soon erupted in both Bobbio and Luxeuil under his abbatial successors.[28] His legacy was a disputed one, as Albrecht Diem concludes in chapter 15, the final contribution to this volume, which provides a translation of the enigmatic *Regula cuiusdam patris*, a monastic rule from this period written for one of the Columbanian communities, or perhaps for the rebel breakaway monks from Luxeuil or Bobbio. Diem interprets this within the context of factional disputes concerning Columbanus's legacy and tries from a close and detailed study of this Rule to disentangle some of the issues that may have preoccupied the communities in the years following Columbanus's death.

Columbanus was venerated as a saint throughout the Middle Ages (though he was never officially canonized, and his cult was not widespread),[29] thanks in large part to the successful *Life* written by Jonas of Bobbio some two decades after his death, which survives in more than 180 manuscripts dating from the ninth to the sixteenth centuries.[30] It was only during the Catholic Revival of the nineteenth century that French Catholic writers began to see Columbanus as a significant catalyst in European history and as a father of Europe, the image that captivated Robert Schuman in his dream for a united Europe and one that he sought to build on from 1950.[31] As an immigrant and outsider from the margins of Europe, Columbanus was one of the first to express an idea of Europe unfettered by ethnic and political divisions that was deeply grounded in the message of the gospel and the idea of a Christian commonwealth that transcended boundaries. In his writings and travels that marked out the boundaries of the Europe of his day, which can be seen as a gradual movement from the periphery into the center of his world, Columbanus was one of the

26. Given a year of birth in around 550; see Bullough 1997: 3.

27. *VC* I.30.

28. *VC* II.1; II.9–10. On the Bobbio revolt see Dunn 2008; on the Luxeuil revolt see Dumézil 2007.

29. On Columbanus remembered, forgotten, and transformed in the Middle Ages, see Geary, forthcoming a. I am grateful to Professor Geary for sharing this work prior to publication.

30. On the manuscript tradition, see discussion in O'Hara and Wood 2017.

31. On the context of Columbanus and the Catholic Revival of the nineteenth century, see Wood 2015: 175–8, 2013: 137–53 (in general), 143–7 (on Columbanus).

first to express a sense of a pan-European collectivity, albeit within the context of the Church.[32] On two occasions in his letters he uses the phrase "the whole of Europe" (*totius Europae*) when addressing the pope.[33] Although the self-assured world of the Roman Empire had disintegrated in the West, and Columbanus already saw Europe as "wilting"—as a decaying flower, an image he may have sought to associate with Ovid's depiction of Europa and her flowers in the *Metamorphoses*—he shared Gregory the Great's view of unity in diversity.[34] As one historian has commented on this passage: "The rhetorical contrast between a wilting Europe and its spiritual head, bathed in light and clothed in imperial epithet, reveals a new cultural landscape, however rugged and as yet fitful."[35] By contrast, Pope Gregory the Great still saw himself and Rome in an imperial context of the Eastern Roman Empire; he was a loyal servant of the emperor in Constantinople, and Rome was the westernmost frontier of the Byzantine Empire.[36] Columbanus voices a different view, one in which the pope is the head of a European body of churches. Grounded in biblical authority and Pauline theology, Columbanus could express the radical notion that "we are all joint members of one body, whether Gauls, or Britons, or Irish, or whatever people we come from."[37] The Christian barbarian kingdoms that formed the post-Roman successor states, although constituting many different ethnic groups, could be united within a common Christian framework and political theology. In this sense, Columbanus anticipated by some two hundred years the political theology of the Carolingian Empire and the Holy Roman Empire, with its symbiotic relationship with the papacy. Though he was persecuted and driven out for holding to his own cultural traditions and beliefs, Columbanus's message of unity transcended boundaries during the Europe of his day and inspired Robert Schuman some sixty-five years ago at the beginning of another European venture. May the contributions in this volume reflect the new directions and angles of approach from which Columbanus and this dynamic period of Late Antiquity and the early Middle Ages can be studied, while also posing broader questions about the role of exile and outsiders in reciprocal relations and cultural change.

32. For the development of the idea of Europe and context, see Oschema 2013, 119–24, 123 (on Columbanus).

33. Columbanus, *Epp.* 1.1, 5.1.

34. Columbanus, *Ep.* 1.1 to Gregory the Great: *totius Europae flaccentis augustissimo quasi cuidam Flori.* Cf. Ov., *Metamorphoseon* 2.858–68 on Europa's wreath of flowers.

35. Leyser 1992: 31.

36. Markus 1981: 33. "The vision of a Western Christian society subject to the *principatus* of the Roman Church and unrestricted by its subjection to the ecclesiastical establishment of the Byzantine Empire was not Gregory's vision."

37. Columbanus, *Ep.* 2.9: *unius enim sumus corporis commembra, sive Galli, sive Britanni, sive Iberi, sive quaeque gentes.* Based on Gal. 3:27–9; 1 Cor. 12:12–4; and Col. 3:8–11.

BIBLIOGRAPHY

Atsma, H. (1976) "Les monastères urbains du Nord de la Gaule." *Revue d'Histoire de l'Église de France* 62: 163–87.

Bergolte, M., and B. Schneidmüller (eds.) (2010) *Hybride Kulturen im mittelalterlichen Europa: Vorträge und Workshops einer internationalen Frühlingsschule* [Hybrid cultures in medieval Europe: Papers and workshops of an international spring school]. Berlin, de Gruyter.

Bhabha, H. K. (1994) *The Location of Culture.* London and New York, Routledge.

Bourdieu, P. (1985) "Social Space and the Genesis of Groups." *Theory and Society* 14: 723–44.

Bourdieu, P. (1992) "Social Space and the Genesis of 'Classes.'" In *Language and Symbolic Power.* Cambridge, UK, Polity, 227–51.

Brown, P. (2003) *The Rise of Western Christendom: Triumph and Diversity, A.D. 200–1000.* 2nd edition. Oxford, Blackwell.

Bullough, D. (1997) "The Career of Columbanus." In M. Lapidge (ed.), *Columbanus: Studies on the Latin Writings.* Woodbridge, UK, Boydell Press, 1–28.

Burke, P. (2009) *Cultural Hybridity.* Cambridge, UK, Polity.

Cohen, A. P. (1985) *The Symbolic Construction of Community.* London and New York, Routledge.

Cohen, A. P. (1994) "Culture, Identity, and the Concept of Boundary." *Revista de antropolgía social* 3: 49–61.

Corradini, R. (2013) "Die Ankunft der Zukunft: Babylon, Jerusalem und Rom als Modelle von Aneignung und Entfremdung bei Augustinus." In W. Pohl and G. Heydemann (eds.), *Strategies of Identification: Ethnicity and Religion in Early Medieval Europe.* Turnhout, Brepols, 65–142.

de Vogüé, A. (2004) "L'idéal monastique de saint Colomban." *Studia Monastica* 46: 253–68.

Dumézil, B. (2007) "L'Affaire Agrestius de Luxeuil: hérésie et regionalisme dans la Burgondie du VIIe siècle." *Médiévales* 52: 135–52.

Dumézil, B. (2008) *La Reine Brunehaut.* Paris, Fayard.

Dunn, M. (2008) "Columbanus, Charisma and the Revolt of the Monks of Bobbio." *Peritia* 20: 1–27.

Fimister, A P. (2008) *Robert Schuman: Neo-Scholastic Humanism and the Reunification of Europe.* Brussels, Peter Lang.

Flood, G. (2004) *The Ascetic Self: Subjectivity, Memory, and Tradition.* Cambridge, Cambridge University Press.

Fox, Y. (2014) *Power and Religion in Merovingian Gaul: Columbanian Monasticism and the Frankish Elites.* Cambridge, Cambridge University Press.

Geary, P. (forthcoming a) "Columbanus Remembered, Forgotten, and Transformed in the Long Middle Ages." In the Proceedings of the Bobbio conference of 2015, forthcoming in Press, Universitaires de Rennes.

Geary, P. (forthcoming b) "Construction of Identity in the Age of Columbanus." In the Proceedings of the Bangor conference of 2015, forthcoming in Press, Universitaires de Rennes.

Gionta, P. (2017) "The Spirituality of Saint Colomban (615–2015): An Outline." *The American Benedictine Review* 68: 88–97.

Hen, Y. (2007) *Roman Barbarians: The Royal Court and Culture in the Early Medieval West.* New York, Palgrave.

Heydemann, G. (2013) "Biblical Israel and the Christian *gentes*: Social Metaphors and the Language of Identity in Cassiodorus's *Expositio psalmorum*." In W. Pohl and

G. Heydemann (eds.), *Strategies of Identification: Ethnicity and Religion in Early Medieval Europe*. Turnhout, Brepols, 143–208.

Kapchan, D. A., and P. T. Strong. (1999) "Theorizing the Hybrid." *Journal of American Folklore* 112: 239–53.

Krijtenburg, M. (2012) *Schuman's Europe: His Frame of Reference*. Leiden, Leiden University Press.

Krijtenburg, M. (2015) "Robert Schuman's Commitment to European Unification: The Inspiring Role of His Roman Catholic Faith." *Philosophia Reformata* 80: 140–57.

Jenkins, D. (2010) *"Holy, Holier, Holiest": The Sacred Topography of the Early Medieval Irish Church*. Turnhout, Brepols.

Johnston, E. (2016) "Exiles from the Edge? The Irish Contexts of *Peregrinatio*." In R. Flechner and S. Meeder (eds.), *The Irish in Early Medieval Europe: Identity, Culture and Religion*. London, Palgrave Macmillan, 38–52 .

Leyser, K. (1992) "Concepts of Europe in the Early and High Middle Ages." *Past and Present* 137: 25–47.

MacDonald, A. (2001) "Aspects of the Monastic Landscape in Adomnán's *Life of Columba*." In J. Carey, M. Herbert, et al. (eds.), *Studies in Irish Hagiography: Saints and Scholars*. Dublin, Four Courts Press, 15–30.

Mackey, J. P. (1996) "The Theology of Columbanus." In P. N. Chatháin and M. Richter (eds.), *Irland und Europa im früheren Mittelalter: Bildung und Literatur*. Stuttgart, Klett-Cotta, 228–39.

Markus, R. A. (1981) "Gregory the Great's Europe." *Transactions of the Royal Historical Society*, 5th Series, 31: 21–36.

Nelson, J. (1978). "Queens as Jezebels: Brunhild and Balthild in Merovingian History." In D. Baker (ed.), *Medieval Women: Essays Dedicated and Presented to Rosalind M. T. Hill*. Studies in Church History, Subsidia 1. Oxford, Blackwell, 31–77.

O'Hara, A. (2012) "Columbanus and Jonas: New Textual Witnesses." *Peritia* 22–23: 188–90.

O'Hara, A. (2013) "*Patria, peregrinatio*, and *paenitentia*: Identities of Alienation in the Seventh Century." In W. Pohl and G. Heydemann (eds.), *Post-Roman Transitions: Christian and Barbarian Identities in the Early Medieval West*. Turnhout, Brepols, 89–124.

O'Hara, A. (2015a) *Saint Columbanus: Selected Writings*. Dublin, Veritas.

O'Hara, A. (2015b) "The Babenbergs and the Cult of St. Coloman: Saint Formation and Political Cohesion in Eleventh-Century Austria." *Journal of Medieval Latin* 25: 131–72 (with an edition and translation of the Passio et Miracula S. Cholomanni).

O'Hara, A. (2015c) "Columbanus *ad locum*: The Establishment of the Monastic Foundations." *Peritia* 26: 143–70.

O'Hara, A. (forthcoming) "The Politics of Piety: Ritual Communities and Social Cohesion in Merovingian Gaul." In W. Pohl and A. Fischer (eds.), *Social Cohesion and Its Limits*. Vienna, Austrian Academy of Sciences Press,.

O'Hara, A., and F.Taylor. (2013) "Aristocratic and Monastic Conflict in Tenth-Century Italy: The Case of Bobbio and the *Miracula Sancti Columbani*." *Viator* 44: 43–62.

O'Hara, A., and I. Wood (eds. and trans.). (2017) *Jonas of Bobbio: Life of Columbanus and His Disciples, Life of John, Life of Vedast*. Translated Texts for Historians. Liverpool, University of Liverpool Press.

Oschema, K.. (2013) *Bilder von Europa im Mittelalter*. Ostfildern, Jan Thorbecke Verlag.

Picard, J.-M. (2015) "Colomban, Luxeuil et la naissance de l'Union Européenne." *Gazette des Amis de Saint Colomban*, Amis de Saint Colomban, Luxeuil, 33–37.

Pohl, W. (2013) "Introduction-Strategies of Identification: A Methodological Profile." In W. Pohl and G. Heydemann (eds.), *Strategies of Identification: Ethnicity and Religion in Early Medieval Europe*. Turnhout, Brepols, 1–64.

Prinz, F. (1965) *Frühes Mönchtum im Frankenreich: Kultur und Gesellschaft in Gallien, den Rheinlanden und Bayern am Beispiel der monastischen Entwicklung (4. bis 8. Jahrhundert)*. Munich,, Oldenbourg.

Prinz, F. (1981) "Columbanus, the Frankish nobility and the territories east of the Rhine." In H. B. Clarke and M. Brennan (eds.), *Columbanus and Merovingian Monasticism*. BAR International Series no. 114. Oxford, British Archaeological Reports, 73–87.

Rosenwein, B. (2006) *Emotional Communities in the Early Middle Ages*. Ithaca, NY, Cornell University Press.

Schmuki, K., F. Schnoor, et al. (eds.). (2015) *Gallus und seine Zeit: Leben, Wirken, Nachleben*. St. Gallen, Kloster Verlag.

Schuman, R. (2010) *For Europe: Political Writings*. Geneva, Les Éditions Nagel.

Wood, I. (2013) *The Modern Origins of the Early Middle Ages*. Oxford, Oxford University Press.

Wood, I. (2015) "The Irish in England and on the Continent in the Seventh Century: Part I." *Peritia* 26: 171–98.

Yazdiha, H. (2010) "Conceptualizing Hybridity: Deconstructing Boundaries through the Hybrid." *Formations* 1: 31–8.

Columbanus and the Language of Concord

DAMIAN BRACKEN

The voice of Columbanus is one of the most distinctive of the early Middle Ages. It comes down to us in his series of moral exhortations (*instructiones*), monastic and penitential rules, and letters, which together are the earliest works of literature by a known Irish writer.[1] Columbanus's surviving letters cover a mere decade or so of an eventful life, but they give the clearest impression of his forceful character and an insight into the ideals and concerns of a Christian of the early seventh century who wrote with a strong awareness of his origins on the extreme periphery of the Christian world. The strident tone of the letters has perhaps deflected attention from the subtlety of Columbanus's arguments. He was a master of the literary conventions that he believed protected him from accusations of overstepping the mark in his direct expression of his concerns, forthright demand for principled leadership, and call for those responsible for causing and prolonging the divisions among Christians to be held accountable. However distinctive his voice, Columbanus was motivated to write by the perennial concerns that preoccupied Christians throughout the history of the Church. His letters focus on the divisions caused by theological conflicts and disputes about orthodox practice. In his call for harmony, both among his followers and in the wider Church that was riven by dissent, he recalls the controversialists to unity using the appropriate rhetoric and established literary conventions that demonstrate theological sophistication and affirm his pastoral competence.

Columbanus's theology was practical, but he wrote for a theologically literate readership. He used biblical passages, images, and exegetical traditions that had been invested with significance through constant iteration in theological debates about the role and duties of the ecclesiastical leader. Columbanus had bishops clearly in his sights, for they were the source of most of his difficulties. What he wrote shows that he had little experience of working within an episcopally controlled Church, and also that he had little intention of compromising his own ideals to conform to that system. His letter (*Ep.* 2, c. AD 603) to the Gallic bishops is, pointedly, a disquisition on the proper exercise of spiritual authority

---

1. The edition and translation of Columbanus's works followed here (with occasional modifications) are Walker 1957 and Gundlach 1892.

and a guide to the type of people best suited to fulfill the requirements. The short *Epistula 3* (Columbanus calls it a *cartula; Ep.* 3.2) to the pope ends with an extraordinary declaration of independence from episcopal authority; although he was working in the jurisdiction of the Gallic bishops, his mode of life and historical precedent led Columbanus to claim that he and his followers were still "in our homeland" (*Constat enim nos in nostra esse patria; Ep.* 3.2). He evokes in the most forthright way the monastic nature of his community's life; they are "settled in the deserts" (*in desertis sedentes*) following the rules of their elders (*nostrorum regulis . . . seniorum*). He explicitly rejects the rules of the Gauls (*regulas Gallorum*) and is ready to defend his position to the Gallic clergy, for whom he had little regard. In this letter he repeatedly applies the pronoun *iste* to them with a pejorative force ("those Gauls"; "those Gallic friends of yours").² Much more significantly, he is also willing to defend himself and his monks against the "apostolic fathers" (*apostolicos patres*), that is, the bishops of Rome.

Columbanus found historical precedent for papal toleration of diverse practices, including those the papacy had sought to stamp out, in an event that occurred in the reign of Pope Anicetus. Eusebius of Caesarea related the details in his *Ecclesiastical History*, a work Columbanus refers to explicitly in his letter to Pope Gregory (*Ep.* 1.3) and in his letter to the Gallic clergy (*Ep.* 2.7).³ When Bishop Polycarp (d. AD 155) came to Rome from the East, he continued to follow eastern practice in the celebration of Easter, which set him against the Roman insistence that Easter must be celebrated only on Sunday. Despite their differences, Anicetus acknowledged his communion in the faith with Polycarp and his church by consenting to his administration of the Eucharist in Rome. For Columbanus, therefore, the earliest tradition of the Church was to tolerate diversity. He ends letter 3 by asking to be allowed to live "among those Gauls (*inter istos*) in the peace of the unity of the Church" and supports his appeal with a subtle, but highly effective, allusion to the example of Polycarp and Anicetus, who coexisted "without scandal to the faith; on the contrary, with complete charity" (*Ep.* 3.2). In the letter Columbanus adheres to the straightforward principle that unity in the faith should override considerations of uniformity of practice, but his language belies the simplicity of the idea because it shows how Columbanus drew on the ancient language of concord in its Christian guise and transformed meaning. Much of what he says on the subject of the toleration of

2. The phrase *[i]storum liber Gallorum* is translated by Walker as "the book of your Frankish friends," whereas Smit is satisfied with the prosaic "the book of those Franks"; *dum nullas istorum suscipimus regulas Gallorum; inter istos* [sc *Gallos*] *possimus vivere*; Walker 1957: 24–5; Smit 1971: 7. On the classical use of *iste*, see de Jong 1998: esp. 33ff.

3. Columbanus was familiar with an abridged version of the text in the translation of Rufinus; see Wright 1997.

diversity is found in his treatment of the Easter controversy. He adduces historical precedent in support of his argument, but his most effective defense is theological, and he draws on ideas about the nature of the Church as a community joined in a common belief, united in the bonds of *caritas* ("love," "charity"). The historical records transmit the arguments of the victors in the Easter debate and allow us to appreciate the sophistication of their theological arguments, which led the defenders of the "Roman" Easter to triumph over those who favored the traditional, or "Celtic," Easter. The records, not surprisingly, are almost silent on the reasons put forward by those who advocated adherence to the traditional practices. Columbanus writes scathingly of the Victorian Easter cycle; the Irish experts (*nostris magistris et Hibernicis antiquis philosophis*), he says, laughed at it. Considerations of the reliability of the various methods for calculating Easter Sunday were central to the debate but not decisive because that debate was never about mere mathematics. It is likely that something of the lost voice of the defenders of the traditional Easter can be recovered from Columbanus's ecclesiology and his arguments in favor of the toleration of diversity, arguments that go to the center of early medieval ideals about the nature of the Church.

Columbanus was not the only seventh-century Irish or Insular writer to consider the authority of the bishop of Rome, but he uniquely observed at close hand the effects of delinquent papal leadership on his journeys through Merovingian Gaul and northern Italy, and he alone wrote to condemn that failure of leadership and division in the body of the Church. For him, the theological principle that failure to live up to the standards of the founder would lead to pastoral disaster was a theoretical principle that had been realized in the deeply divided Church in which he operated. He was the most informed of all seventh-century Irish writers who considered papal primacy, but unlike his compatriots, for whom the papacy was a distant notion, Columbanus had lived with the reality of papal leadership and the effects of its failure.

The Language of Concord

The ideals of doctrinal unity and the universality of the faith were central to early Christian identity formation and expression, and studies have concentrated on their biblical origins and theological elaboration. However, the principles and rhetoric of late antique *concordia* found in the political propaganda and political philosophies of the Roman Empire also influenced the development of the Christian understanding of orthodoxy at its formative stage. The Romans, in turn, derived their understanding of *concordia* from the Greek idea of *homonoia* (ὁμόνοια, "harmony"). The desire for concord was used to concentrate the loyalties of a culturally and socially diverse empire and to provide a framework that reconciled a degree of local autonomy with the reality of an empire that claimed the loyalty of all its citizens.[4] *Concordia* was an important element in the philosophic system of Stoic cosmopolitanism that went on to play a significant role in Roman imperial political rhetoric. It asserted that their shared rational nature united all beings, human and divine.[5] The order of the cosmos, even though composed of such diverse elements and creatures, was a reflection of the rationality of the gods who controlled it. The order of the well-regulated city and the stable relationship among its diverse social orders, in turn, was a reflection of the wisdom and rationality of the civilized inhabitants who controlled it. Such ideas had political consequences.

During Augustus's reign (27 BC–14 AD), Stoic metaphysics was used to link *concordia* (the harmonious existence that is possible only within the empire and, especially, in its well-ordered cities) with pax (the cosmic harmony and peace of the universe).[6] The Pax Romana, and more particularly, the Pax Augusta, were part of the divine order whose destiny was to unite all peoples in a global commonwealth of shared values, holding together the different and mutually antagonistic peoples of the *oikouméné* in the bonds of peace and harmony. The peace and harmony of the empire reflected the peace and order of the cosmos, and the imperial Pax Romana was therefore an earthly reflection of the cosmic Pax deorum. The sophisticated ideals of Roman imperial cosmopolitanism were thus used to accommodate the local autonomy of the city-state within the empire, powerfully demonstrating the ecumenical nature of imperial civilization, and legitimizing the empire's universal ambitions.

These philosophical and political theories claimed to derive their authority from the diversity of the natural world. That diversity and the complexity of creation sustained life and provided for the many and varied needs of humanity. Furthermore, diversity was viewed as a positive attribute that, paradoxically, promoted unity and fellowship among the nations. These ideas directly influenced the thinking of early Christians on the nature of the Church as a composite body made up of disparate peoples, united not by imperial dominion but by bonds of caritas. In the fourth century the rhetor Libanius taught that the divinely ordained diversity of creation determined that the fruits of nature are never produced all together in one region, but rather the different parts of the earth should specialize in their own particular crops. Of necessity, therefore, the nations had to engage in trade to meet their needs, and natural diversity was a

---

4. For a recent study of *concordia* in its early stages of development in Roman political rhetoric, see Akar 2013. For a survey of the imperial politics of concord, see Lobur 2008.

5. Cicero, *Leg.* 1.7.23; see Lee 2006: 62.

6. Brent 2006a: 309.

source of unity and peaceful interaction rather than division. Libanius, a pagan monotheist, wrote that in establishing the earth:

[God] included everything in this creation—seeds and cattle and in short all that human nature was going to need. However he did not assign everything to every part, but divided the gifts throughout the countries, bringing mankind into partnership through mutual need; and so he reveals commerce, so that he may make common to all the enjoyment of what is produced among the few.[7]

These classical ideals that promoted unity and peace were naturally amenable to Christian thinkers and were adopted into Christian theology at an early date.[8] By the beginning of the medieval era, these views were pervasive and influenced Gregory the Great's thought on issues as fundamental as the nature of the Christian commonwealth and the obligation of members of the Church to exercise charity toward one another.

In his letter to Pope Gregory (*Ep.* 1), Columbanus asks for a copy of his *Homilies on Ezekiel*, "which, as I have heard, you have compiled with wonderful skill (*miro . . . ingenio*) upon Ezekiel" (*Ep.* 1.9). Whether Gregory obliged, or Columbanus had to look elsewhere for the homilies, he would have encountered in Christian guise the ideas that Libanius had expressed about the importance of natural diversity, leading to trade, peaceful interaction, and the solidarity of the peoples. Gregory wrote:,

Almighty God so acts in the hearts of men as He does in the regions of the earth. For He could grant all fruits to any region but if one region did not need the fruits of another it would not have communion with the other. Thus it happens that He gives to this abundance of wine but to another of oil; He makes this region to abound with the multitude of cattle but that one with a wealth of pulses so that when that one offers what the other lacks, and the other renders what that one did not bring, countries at the same time separate from each other are joined together (*coniunctae sint*) by the communion of grace. As therefore the regions of the earth, so are the minds of the Saints which when they transfer to each other what they received, like the regions disburse their fruits to regions, so that all are joined in a single charity (*in una . . . caritate iungantur*).[9]

---

7. Libanius, *Or.* 59.169; Dogeon 1996: 204. See also Irwin 1996: 15–8 for further patristic and early Christian reflections of Libanius's principles.

8. Recent studies include Thorsteinsson 2010. See, however, the review by Volp 2012.

9. *CCSL* 142, 162; trans. Gray 1990: 124–25. On this passage, see Meyvaert 1963: 154. On the knowledge of Gregory's works in early Ireland, see Kerlouégan 1986.

Gregory's ideas, and the very language and images that he uses to express them, clearly have their origins in classical cosmopolitanism. However, this is not simply an uncritical appropriation by a Christian thinker of classical philosophy and imperial political rhetoric. Gregory transforms the meaning of Stoic cosmopolitanism by applying it in a theological and spiritual context to argue that Christian ecumenicity can exist only when charity prevails and diversity is tolerated. Interpreting Gregory and his contemporaries in their late antique context shows their indebtedness to classical philosophy, but also how the theologians fundamentally reshaped the philosophers' ideas. Columbanus, one of Gregory's contemporaries, took his inspiration on the theme of unity in diversity from the theology of figures like Gregory. Yet the classical sources reveal the extraordinary staying power of these ideas from Antiquity to the Middle Ages and their formative impact on the emerging identity of the Christian world. As this was the world within which Columbanus sought to make himself understood, the classical sources, as well as the Christian sources that directly influenced him, help us to interpret his subtle allusions to the language of concord as it applied to his own identity as a Christian from beyond the frontiers of the old empire.

Gregory returns to the subject of the importance of diversity in another work with which Columbanus was also familiar. He wrote to Gregory that he had read "your book containing the pastoral rule" (*Ep.* 1.9). In a letter written in 594, Gregory had himself instructed Venantius, bishop of Luni, not to keep the copy of the *Pastoral Rule* that accompanied his letter, but to hand it over "to the noble priest Columba" (*domno Columbo presbytero*).[10] It is far from certain that the reference in the letter is to Columbanus, but it is very likely that Columbanus was familiar with Gregory's work. There Columbanus found the core of Gregory's ecclesiology and his understanding of the Church as a body composed of different members "joined together in the union of charity" (*in collectione . . . caritatis uniti*).[11] That varied community (Gregory lists preachers and listeners, rulers and subjects, the married and unmarried, penitents, and virgins) "who were before of different sentiments" but are now "so agreed in that most peaceful concord of unanimity (*in illa pacatissima unanimitatis concordia conuenerunt*), that . . . it was said, as Scripture witnesses, 'That there was in them one heart and one soul' (Acts 4.32). The Lord . . . collects together faithful people in the Church according to the difference of their customs and languages."[12]

---

10. Gregory the Great, *Ep.* 5.17 to Venantius, bishop of Luni, November 594, MGH, *Epp.* 1, 299; trans. Martyn 2004: 2, 335.

11. On Gregory's ecclesiology, see ch. 6 of Leyser 2007: esp. 156ff.

12. Gregory the Great, *Mor.* 30.6.33; CCSL 143B, 1506; trans. *Morals on the Book of Job*, 3, pt. 2, 378.

Unity prevails not through uniformity and the elimination of difference, but when the different members are joined "through the bond of charity that knits the whole body together." In fact, for Gregory the presence of diversity was essential for progression in spiritual perfection. Difference does not compromise unity, but leads to cooperation in the forging of ties, just as in classical political theory the mixed constitution is the basis of harmony and, as Saint Paul admonishes the Corinthians, the diversity of the community was devised by God to the same ends, so that "the members may be mutually careful one for another" (1 Cor. 12:25).[13] No one possesses all the gifts; some excel in wisdom, some in the practice of good works, some in the rigors of asceticism. Gregory argued that such a healthy diversity encouraged others to learn from the example of those who are adept in these virtues, while the failure of the adepts to perfect other virtues prevents them from falling into the sin of pride.[14]

Columbanus appealed to this theology and its positive view of diversity. He used the language of ecclesiastical concord in defense of his community and way of life. The differences between his followers and the Gallic Church were brought into sharp focus during the Easter controversy, a traumatic episode that compromised the unity of the Church. The rancorous dispute, ostensibly about the correct method for setting the date of Easter Sunday, became so fractious because it involved questions of the nature of ecclesiastical authority and of those competent to exercise it. It brought those who adhered to the "traditional" Easter practices, sometimes called the "Celtic" Easter, into conflict with the promoters of what they claimed was the "universal" practice of the Church (sometimes, confusingly and illogically, called the "Roman" Easter). Significantly, the split reflected different conceptions of the nature of spiritual authority. Columbanus and his monks adhered to what could be termed a charismatic ideal, in which those who exercised authority did so because of their spiritual qualities, and whose holiness maintained and transmitted the standards of the saintly patrons they succeeded. Another view of the nature of authority could be termed "prelatic"; power rested with the senior cleric because of the level he had reached in the hierarchy of the Church. Authority was inherent in the office and would not be compromised by any shortcomings of the officeholder. This view, which saw authority devolving from the institution, contrasted with the principles of Columbanus, who throughout his writings saw the moral fitness of the officeholder as qualifying him to exercise authority. It would be a mistake to see in Columbanus's position a resistance to institutional authority; he and his fellow

---

13. Mitchell 1991: 160.
14. Gregory the Great, *Hom. in Ezech*, I.10.32; *PL* 76, 899–900; trans Gray 1990: 122–3.

Irish writers of the seventh century had a worldview that was resolutely hierarchical. It does indicate, however, that there was competition in the early Irish Church between those championing a monastic and charismatic ideal of authority and promoters of the episcopal model. In advocating for toleration of his vision of the structures of authority, Columbanus could cite historical precedent and the theological tradition of concord, which saw diversity as an essential condition of existence, and although his ideas had the support of a venerable antiquity, they proved weaker in the long run against the arguments of those promoting the "Roman" Easter and a model of authority in which bishops called the shots.

COLUMBANUS AND THE LANGUAGE OF CONCORD

Long before it influenced Christianity, the language of concord had acquired stability, with a set rhetoric and range of topoi to the extent that the "concord speech" became a recognizable genre. The speech was intended to remind the inhabitants of the city of the benefits of urban life and urged them to strive to maintain the peace and order of their community as a reflection of the perfect harmony of the cosmos. The Epistle to the Corinthians, attributed to Clement of Rome (d. 99), evokes the regular progress of day to night, the evolving seasons, and the revolutions of the heavenly bodies as evidence of the controlling hand of a benign and omnipotent deity. God's direction extends everywhere, from the greatest to the least of creatures for even the "smallest of the animals meet in peaceful harmony" (1 Clem. 20.10).[15] In the original Greek, the last phrase is a word pair, "peace and harmony," and it appears in the second- or third-century Latin translation of the letter as *pace et concordia*. The twin virtues of peace and harmony were so closely associated in this rhetoric that the words were interchangeable.[16] This pairing of "peace and concord" (εἰρήνη καί ὁμόνοια or ὁμό νοια καί εἰρήνη) is found five times in the course of the letter.[17] The pairing is significant, for 1 Clement is, in effect, an extended appeal for "peace and concord." The letter advises that because the Creator ordained all creatures to act "in peace and concord" (*cum pace et concordia*; 1 Clem. 20.11), the Corinthians must cease from dissension and division, as directed by the counsels found in "this letter for peace and concord" (*de pace et concordia in epistola hac*; 1 Clem. 63.2).

15. Kleist 1961: 22. 1 Clem. 20 is also translated in Van Unnik 1950: 181–2. Against Van Unnik, see Ullmann 1972.

16. "The word pair appears to constitute a single concept in *1 Clement*, and it is therefore appropriate to view the terms ὁμόνοια and εἰρήνη as a *hendiadys*." Bakke 2001: 82. "[L]e terme *pax* se changeait lui-même parfois, dans les texts, en *pax ciuilis* ou en *concordia*," Jal 1961: 210.

17. As noted by Pétré 1948: 315; Bakke 2001: 1, 75.

The repetition of this formula is not casual. The word pairing of "peace and concord" was the most succinct and direct appeal to the tradition of concord in the classical tradition and in early Christianity. It was a shorthand way to alert the reader that the writer was drawing on the ramified "deliberative rhetoric"[18] of the concord tradition that was forcefully directed to combating factionalism and defending the established order.

The rhetoric of concord was used particularly in sources that promoted unity and urged obedience to authority. When used more deliberatively, it recalled the fractious to order and demanded respect for the discipline of the Church. The fundamental values of peace and concord were so integral to the nature of the Church that actions threatening them were actions against Christ. In his treatise "On the Unity of the Catholic Church," Cyprian of Carthage wrote, "Whoever breaks the peace and concord of Christ acts against Christ."[19] Augustine counseled that "[i]ndeed we have been called to concord, we are ordered to have peace among ourselves."[20] In *Epistula* 5, his longest and most complex composition, Columbanus writes to Pope Boniface that his motive in expressing himself so directly (he worries that his words "have caused offence to godly ears") is "the greatness of my concern for your concord and peace" (*magnitudo sollicitudinis meae pro concordia et pace vestra; Ep.* 5.11). As will be shown, Columbanus's use of the word pairing of "peace and concord" is also not casual, as it occurs in the context of images and key biblical texts of Christian concord. He uses the language of concord and evokes the standard images of ecclesiastical unity throughout his letters.

In the letter to the Gallic clergy, Columbanus compares the Church leaders to the sailors of a ship: "yet let it be first your part like those mariners (*illorum nautarum*) to seek to save the shipwrecked by the bowels of godliness, and to draw the ship to land" (*Ep.* 2.7). In the letter to Pope Boniface he adopts the voice of a "fearful sailor" (*timidus nauta*) and warns the masters, helmsmen, and lookouts to "Wake up" (*Vigilate!; Ep.* 5.3). In classical and patristic literature, the ship can represent the journey through life.[21] In the early Christian sources, when that vessel draws safely into port it signifies the Church leading the faithful through the storms of this world to the rewards of the next. The ship

---

18. On the "deliberative" rhetoric of the "concord speech," see ch. 1 of Mitchell 1991: 10; Breytenbach 2003: 259ff.

19. *Qui pacem Christi et concordiam rumpit, adversus Christum facit: PL* 4, 503; Pétré 1948: 317, n. 2. On the subject of heresy and disunity in Cyprian, see Mattei 2013.

20. *Ad concordiam quidem vocati sumus, jubemur pacem habere inter nos*: Augustine, *Tract. in Ioh.* 34, 10; *PL* 35, 1656; Pétré 1948: 318, n. 1. Augustine examines the role of peace, based on concord, in *Civ. Dei* 19, esp. chs. 13 and 17.

21. See Bonner 1941.

of the Church completes its journey through choppy waters when its captain (*gubernator*), representing the ecclesiastical leader, fulfills his duty of watchfulness, and this is clearly the tradition on which Columbanus drew in *Epistula* 2.7. Cyprian of Carthage's influential "On the Unity of the Catholic Church" may have been known to Columbanus, whose ecclesiology certainly reflects the ideals of Cyprian. Cyprian illustrates the intractability of those who compromise the unity of the Church: just as the stream cannot survive without the link to its source, or the ray of light without the sun, groups that sunder their link to the mother Church cannot be orthodox. The unity of the orthodox is a reflection of the "oneness" (*unitatem; De unit. ecc.* 6) of the Trinity, and the single, true Church is signified by the one ark of Noah, whose passengers survive the Flood, while all outside it are lost. Cyprian associates the ship image with ecclesiastical concord and the doctrinal imperative to maintain unity, for he writes, using the familiar couplet, that whoever threatens unity "breaks the peace and concord" (*pacem . . . et concordiam rumpit*) of Christ. His warning that outside the ark, as outside the Church, there is no salvation[22] finds a parallel in Augustine: "For if there are dangers in the ship, without the ship ruin is certain."[23] A seventh-century commentary on the Catholic epistles, perhaps the work of an Irish exegete, sees the Church in the reference to Noah's ark in 1 Peter 3.20. Those outside the ark of the Church appreciate its shelter in tough times: "Those, however, who are outside the Church, when they see challenging misfortunes, seek the straitness of the Church."[24]

Columbanus provides a more expansive treatment of the theme in his letter to Pope Boniface demanding action in the midst of doctrinal divisions from the "masters and helmsmen of the spiritual ship and mystic sentinels" (*magistris ac spiritalis navis gubernatoribus ac mysticis proretis; Ep.* 5.3). He presents the conventional interpretation of the storm and threatening seas that the ship faces: they are divisions, challenges to orthodoxy, worldly temptations, and the wiles of the devil that the Church must combat on its journey through time. The storm "threatens the wreck of the mystic ship" (*mysticae navis naufragium intentat*) and, indeed, "water has already entered the ship of the Church, and the ship is in danger" (*aqua iam intravit in ecclesiae navem, et navis periclitatur*). By the first century, the ship was a popular image in the language of concord. The cooperation among the crew represented the unity that was essential for

22. *Si potuit evadere quisquam qui extra arcam Noe fuit, et qui extra ecclesiam foris fuerit evadit:PL* 4: 503.

23. *Nam si in navi pericula sunt, sine navi certus interitus: PL* 38: 475.

24. *Qui autem foris aecclaesia sunt, quando plagas inuitatas uident, angustias aecclesiarum desiderant: CCSL* 108B, 91.

the survival of the community. In a Christian context, the role of the captain in achieving that focus of intention and unity of purpose was analogous to the duty of the bishop to maintain order in his Church and guarantee its doctrinal integrity through decisive leadership and effective teaching. Discipline was essential for the ship's survival, and the harmonious crew united in their respect for their vigilant captain led the ship metaphor to be cited in the ecclesiastical literature of concord. The image of the ship with its crew united under the direction of a captain who knows his job was suited to Columbanus's purposes in calling on the bishop of Rome to exercise his duty of vigilance and principled leadership in the aftermath of the Three Chapters controversy, which had sundered the unity of the Church.

In the letter to Boniface, Columbanus lists the crew whose cooperation and discipline are essential if the ship is to sail safely. They are the masters (*magistri*), helmsmen (*gubernatores*), and lookouts or anchormen (*proretae*) "of the mystic ship." The naming of the crew according to rank in this manner is a feature of the ship topos and demonstrates the discipline of a well-run vessel; it serves as a model for order within the Church, where precedence within the hierarchy is respected and unity is maintained. Most especially for Columbanus's purpose, it shows that the safety of the vessel depends on its personnel performing their duties well, particularly those at the top of the chain of command. In the Ps-Clementine letter to James, Saint Peter compares the Church to a great ship (*magnae navi*) and warns all on board to remain of one mind "so that you keep hold of concord" (*ut concordiam teneatis*). The letter describes God as the shipmaster (*dominus*); Christ is the captain (*gubernator*), the bishop is the lookout (*proreta*), the deacons are the ship stewards (*dispensatores*), the catechists are the midshipmen (*naustologi*),[25] and the marine soldiers (*epibates*) are the multitude of laypeople.[26] These last are expected to stay restful and silent (*cum quiete et silentio*); otherwise their disorderliness could capsize the boat.[27] The fifth-century *De uita contemplatiua* by Pomerius is the oldest pastoral instruction to survive in the West. Pomerius, too, compares the Church to a great ship (*navis magna*)[28] sailing on the sea of the world, buffeted by the stormy waves whipped up by evil spirits. He emphasizes the responsibility of senior ecclesiastics to lead well, for the ship will reach port safely when it is guided by the watchfulness (*vigilantia*) of its pilot (*gubernatoris*). Among the Insular sources to take up the theme, a

---

25. Casson 1971: 397; s.v. "naustologos."
26. *PG* 2: 49; *PL* 56: 737; trans. Cox 1868, 220. The *epibatae* are later (col. 738) defined as *laici* in the letter.
27. *PL* 56: 738.
28. *PL* 59: 432; trans. Suelzer 1947: 38.

seventh-century commentary on the Catholic Epistles by the so-called Scottus Anonymus sees the Church as a ship (Jm 3.4) sailing on the sea of the world and steered (*gubernatur*) by the tongue (cf. Jm 3.6) of the teacher.[29] The *Catechesis Cracoviensis*, an eighth- or ninth-century collection of moral exhortations, says that the ship signifies the Church, and the seas represent this world. The lookouts (*probisores*) are the teachers who spy out and warn of dangers and are the first to see port, that is, the day of judgment. The *Catechesis* spells out the lesson ecclesiastical leaders should draw from the topos: true churches are led by captains (*gubernatores*), that is, ecclesiastical leaders (*principes*), with monks "who serve in unfeigned love (cf. 2 Cor. 6:6) . . . those churches which gather [such clerics] do not doubt that they can escape the dangers of the sea of this world."[30] Columbanus himself is associated with the metaphor in the *Life of Gallus* transmitted in the long-winded letter of Ermenrich of Ellwangen to Abbot Grimald of St. Gallen.[31] The *Life* implies that Ireland is like a ship tossed on the dangerous waters of the world. Columbanus and his follower, Gallus, are its captains and sailors. As evangelizers, they share company with another Insular saint, Boniface, who "manfully led all his followers to the harbour of everlasting rest."[32] The piece lists, in descending order, the personnel of the ship and relates them to the ecclesiastical grades, spelling out the duties of the leaders:

> [The ship's] captain (*gubernator*) is God himself, the man Jesus Christ. Indeed, the apostles and their successors are its sailors (*nautae*); moreover we, all entering the Church with faith, are its marine soldiers (*epibates*). Saint Columbanus and Saint Gallus, with their companions, having set out from that corner of the earth, were the captains and sailors (*gubernatores*

---

29. *CCSL* 108B, 16. The comment is on *naves* of Jm 3.4: *Id est, aeclesia in mare mundi huius gubernatur a lingua doctoris ad portum vitae.*

30. [Q]ui seruiunt . . . in dilectione non ficta sine murmuratione. Sine detractione. Sine blasphemia liveri et separati ab omnibus negotiis secularibus. Et cupiditatibus huius saeculi . . . Ille ecclesie, qui eos colligunt. Non dubitant possunt euadere pericula maris huius seculi; Kürbis et al. 2010: 178; and David 1937: 78.

The term *princeps* to denote an ecclesiastical leader has special significance in a Hiberno-Latin context; see Picard 2000.

31. The letter has been described as a paean to *amicitia*, an ideal that bears a close relationship to *concordia*; see Casaretto 1999.

32. Cuius gubernator est deus . . . nautae, uero, eius apostoli et successores eorum; epibates autem nos omnes in ecclesiam cum fide intrantes, cuius fidei seu ecclesiae gubernatores sue nautae fuere sanctus columbanus et sanctus gallus cum sociis suis de illo angulo terrarum egressi. Sicuti et [sup. sanctus] bonifacius martyr christi cum suis hinc emersus lumen nostrae patriae attulit et ad portum quietis aeternae omnes obsequentes uiriliter produxit: St. Gallen, Stiftsbibliothek, MS 265, fol. 86. See Bracken 2012: 84–5, and 337–40, 340, n. 47.

sue nautae) of that faith and of that Church, just as also Saint Boniface, the martyr of Christ, having come forth from there with his followers and brought the light to our homeland, and manfully led all his followers to the harbour of everlasting rest.

Columbanus, therefore, draws on an ancient and ramified tradition in support of his demand for effective leadership. As the shipmaster or supreme pastor of the Church, it is Pope Boniface's duty to lead and give direction. Like the captain, he must be vigilant, as Pomerius warned, and the words *vigilantia* and *vigilare* occur some fourteen times in Columbanus's letter to Boniface. The ship image, as an established topos in the rhetoric of concord, provided Columbanus with the pretext to draw attention to Boniface's primary function, as the supreme shipmaster, to "Be watchful" (*Vigilate*) for the faith and to take action when it is threatened. Should Boniface demonstrate his orthodox credentials and restore concord, Columbanus writes of the comprehensive nature of that restored unity, for the Lombard king, Agilulf, will abjure his Arian beliefs and turn to Rome, and his Catholic queen, Theodelinda, will accept the authority of the Church of Rome, which the north Italians had rejected as a consequence of the Three Chapters debacle (*Ep.* 5.14).

As bishop of Rome, Boniface was expected to act as the bridge builder, joining different factions, just as the traditional founders of the Roman Church, Peter, the apostle of the Jews, and Paul, the apostle of the Gentiles (Gal. 2.8), had united the peoples in the bonds of concord. The unity between the founders of Christian Rome (Columbanus calls them "Christ's twin apostles," *Christi geminos apostolos; Ep.* 5.11) had made Rome the focus for the unity of the Christian world and established their successors' role as the promoters of concord within the Church. Columbanus refers to Peter and Paul, the *principes apostolorum*, throughout the letter to Boniface. They are the "two most fiery steeds" who draw the chariot of Christ across the skies into the West, and they are the means by which Christian Rome continued the imperial Roman rhetoric of the "concord of brothers" (*concordia fratrum*) in the guise of the "concord of the apostles" (*concordia apostolorum*).[33] The importance of unity and universality as the defining attributes of orthodoxy played a major part in the Easter controversy debate and explains the dogged resolve of Columbanus in arguing his case in his letters to the Gallic clerics on the subject of Easter, and to Pope Boniface on the issue of the rupture in communion caused by the Three Chapters controversy.

---

33. Major studies include Pietri 1961; Huskinson 1982; Kessler 1987; Lønstrup Dal Santo 2015; O'Connor 1969; Maccarrone 1976: 183–90; and Curran 2000: 152. On the importance attached to fraternal relations in ancient Rome, see Bannon 1997.

The doctrinal imperative to maintain unity led to the impassioned defense of orthodoxy in the works of the Christian imperial official, Prudentius (d. c. 413), and explains the categorical nature of his statement: "Only concord knows God (*sola Deum novit concordia*); it alone worships the beneficent Father aright in peace."[34] Prudentius shows the importance attached to *concordia* in a late imperial, Christian context, and how firmly entrenched the rhetoric of concord had become in debates about the nature of the Church, where it remained influential for centuries. Although the failure of the empire in the fifth century forced a reconsideration of these ideas, the writings of Pope Gregory show that *concordia* continued to be central in Christian theology. *Quia autem nil sine concordia Deo placeat*[35] ("Because, however, nothing is pleasing to God without concord"), he wrote in his *Homilies on Ezekiel*. Through his references to Peter and Paul, Columbanus emphasizes the ideal of concord and the duty of the bishop of Rome, the successor of the "men equally great captains" and "most brave warriors" (*viros similiter et magnos . . . duces ac fortissimos . . . bellatores; Ep.* 5.17) to maintain that concord. In his portrayal of the apostles in the letter, acting in unison, drawing the carriage of Christ across the sky, Columbanus references yet another symbol of harmony: the chariot, with its horses harnessed to each other, their concerted efforts directed by the charioteer.[36] This particularly dense section of a complex letter is intended to impress on Boniface the duties of his office and the high expectations his followers have, for he must live up to the standards of the founders of his see. While the images and language of unity recur throughout this section of *Epistula* 5, Columbanus follows his treatment of the expectations of papal leadership with a subtle, but highly effective, warning to Boniface that the bishop of Rome has not met those standards or fulfilled his duty to promote the concord of the Church. As a consequence, the divided Church is in perilous straits without a competent leader. While he draws on the traditional portrayal of Peter and Paul as blood brothers joined not by biological ties, but by the blood they both shed in witnessing to the faith, Columbanus subtly references another example of fraternal bonds, but in this instance the

---

34. *Symm.* 2.593–4. On this subject and its treatment by Prudentius see Evenepoel 2010: 69; Torti 1970: 338; Cacitti 1972: 425; Allard 1884: 385; Argenio 1965; and Fontaine 1981. On the empire as preparation for Christianity in Prudentius, see Capizzi 2006: 148; Bartnik 1968: 757; Argenio 1965; and Fontaine 1981.

35. Gregory the Great, *Hom. in Ezech.* 1.8.9; *PL* 76: 858; see Catry 1978: 325.

36. Virgil, *Aen.* 3.543, in which the taming of wild horses under a yoke is seen by Anchises to foretell an era of peace. In *Symm.* 2.583–92, Prudentius lauds Rome for putting a civilizing rein on the world, whose peoples "bear gentle bonds in harmony" (*concordi*). The chariot is intended by Eusebius to represent the sun (as in Columbanus), but also the unifying and civilizing mission of Constantine, *In Praise of Constantine* 3.4, Drake 1976: 87. For the positive, civilizing associations of the yoke in Roman literature, see Nisbet and Hubbard 1970: 373–4.

twins he refers to represent discord, not unity. Columbanus writes of Rebecca, the mother of the twins Jacob and Esau (Gen. 25), whom he associates with "the Church, our common mother." Columbanus here draws on the tradition of *ecclesia mater* from anti-heretical polemic, where it was used to emphasize unity and the single and indivisible source of the faith: there can be only one Church, for it is impossible to have more than one mother.[37] Columbanus argues that it should be possible for subordinates (*iunioribus*) to exhort the pope: "for the unity of the Church, our common mother, who is indeed torn asunder like Rebekah in her maternal womb, and grieves for the strife and civil warfare (*rixa ac intestino bello*) of her sons, and in sorrow bewails the discord (*divisionem*) of her dearest" (*Ep.* 5.12).

Homonoia ("harmony," the Greek equivalent of *concordia*) is the perfect state of relations among the members of society, in which everyone acts in concert, being mindful of the interests and security of each other. The perfect charity of the primitive Church is described in the Acts of the Apostles, where the members of the Jerusalem community lived together as "one heart and one soul" (Acts 4:32). For early Christian writers, the word itself (*concordia* from *cum+ cor*) reflected the ideal of a community in peace where all are animated as if by a single heart. Augustine interpreted the peace left by Christ to his followers (John 14:27) as such a joining of hearts: "For as one is said to be a consort (*consors*) who joins together his part (*sors*), so that man must be called concordant (*concors*) who joins hearts (*corda*) together. Therefore, let us, beloved, to whom Christ leaves peace . . . join with one another our hearts that we may be concordant . . . and let us hold one heart uplifted."[38] Isidore gives a similar interpretation of the word in the *Etymologies*.[39] The opposite of this state of perfect harmony is when the citizens cease to care for one another and society disintegrates into internecine violence. In these conditions, according to the principles of concord, *stasis* (στάσις) replaces harmony, and the unity of society is sundered by civil war. As concord was the best state for society, making it resilient and able to fight off an attack, civil strife was dangerous because internal dissent left the community weak and vulnerable. This was the central tenet of

37. Delahaye 1964; Plumpe 1943,1939.

38. *Quomodo enim consors dicitur qui sortem iungit, ita ille concors dicendus est qui corda iungit. Nos ergo, charissimi, quibus Christus pacem relinquit, et pacem suam nobis dat, non sicut mundus, sed sicut ille per quem factus est mundus, ut concordes simus; jungamus invicem corda, et cor unum sursum habeamus*: Augustine, *Enarr. in Io.* 77.5; *PL* 35: 1835; for translations, see Gibb 1888: 340; and Rettig 1994: 105.

39. "Concordant (*concors*) is so called from 'joining of the heart' (*coniunctio cordis*), for as one who shares one's lot (*sors*) is called a 'partner' (*consors*), so one who is joined in heart (*cor*) is called *concors*"; Isidore of Seville, *Etym.* 10.B.37; trans. Barney et al. 2006: 215. The passages in Augustine and Isidore are identified by Pétré 1948: 318.

concord rhetoric, which sought to promote internal cohesion and to warn of the disastrous consequences of discord. The abhorrence of civil war as the antithesis of the classical ideals of peace and harmony, and as the greatest threat to the empire founded on such principles, left its mark on Christianity. The influence of these ideas on Christian writers can be seen in the works of Ambrose of Milan. Ambrose and others interpreted Psalm 45:9–10 ("Come and behold ye the works of the Lord . . . making wars to cease even to the end of the earth") in the context of the Pax Romana:

> Indeed, before the Roman Empire had time to spread, not only did the kings of every city war against each other, but the Romans themselves frequently burst into civil war (*bellis . . . civilibus*). . . . It thus happened that weary of civil strife the Roman Empire was handed over to Julius Augustus, when intestine warfare (*praelia intestina*) ceased. The result was that the apostles could be sent throughout the world at the command of the Lord Jesus: "Go and teach all nations" (Mt. 28.19). . . . At the same time, as [the apostles] spread over the earth, the power of the Roman Empire followed in the wake of the Church, whilst discordant minds and hostile nations settled down in peace.[40]

Columbanus's views of the Roman Empire cannot be explored here. What can be said is that he did not subscribe to this historiography of the empire, but clearly he was influenced by the philosophy of concord in his treatment of Rebecca, the mother of the twins Jacob and Esau. In contrast to the concord displayed by the "twin apostles" Peter and Paul, the twin sons of Rebecca lived in strife and mutual enmity. According to some traditions, the adherence to unity that, despite their differences, Peter and Paul displayed in their joint missions was maintained throughout their lives to the end, culminating in their joint martyrdom in the same place, Rome, on the same day. Through the triumph of that martyrdom, they established Rome as the primatial see for the whole world.[41] In contrast to the example of concord shown by Peter and Paul in their deaths, the twins Jacob and Esau, who represent discord, began their rivalry at birth and even before; they fought in utero. Columbanus warns Pope Boniface that the state of the Church reflects the hardships of Rebecca, "torn apart in her

---

40. Ambrose, *Explanations of the Twelve Psalms of David*, Ps 45, § 21; *PL* 14, 1142–3; Dvornik 1966: 681. See Mommsen 1951: 363 for similar early Christian interpretations.

41. In the words of Gelasius I: *Addita est etiam societas beatissimi Pauli apostoli vasis electionis . . . uno eodemque die gloriosa morte cum Petro in urbe Roma sub Caesare Nerone agonizans, coronatus est: et pariter supradictam sanctam Romanam ecclesiam Christo Domino consecrarunt, aliisque omnibus urbibus in universo mundo sua praesentia atque venerando triumpho praetulerunt:* Thiel 1867: 455. Similar sentiments are expressed by Eusebius, *Ecclesiastical History* ii 27.7; see Twomey 1982: 64–66.

maternal womb" (*intra viscera . . . discerpitur materna*) by her warring twins, rather than the harmony and concord of Peter and Paul, "Christ's twin apostles." In juxtaposing the twins Peter and Paul with Jacob and Easu, Columbanus reminds the pope that in contrast to the ideal of Church unity that Peter and Paul represent, the reality is that the barque of Peter is in a precarious position following the vacillating and indecisive leadership of Pope Vigilius at the start of the Three Chapters controversy. Those divisions in the Church will continue unless Boniface lives up to the demands of his office and returns the Church to unity through principled leadership. Columbanus's remedy is to "agree (*concordate*) and meet together (*conuenite in unum*) and refuse to argue over ancient quarrels." In the midst of this assertion of his right to speak out in defense of unity, Columbanus laments that all "ought to have been one choir" (*Ep.* 5.13) and so references yet another image of concord. In the ancient world, the choir reflected the varied yet harmonious elements of nature and symbolized the unity that prevailed when diverse elements worked together for the general good. The image was adopted and elaborated by early Christian writers to express the character of the Church as a diverse community united in faith. Late antique literature shows that the image had been invested with a theological significance, and his readers would have recognized that, in his subtle allusion to the choir, Columbanus was appealing to a ramified and authoritative tradition that justified the toleration of diversity as the basis of unity. In his explanation of the origins and significance of the word *concordia*, Columbanus's contemporary, Isidore of Seville, explained, "Others say the word "choir" is from the "concord" (*concordia*) that exists in charity, because without charity it is impossible to sing responses harmoniously."[42] In the rhetoric of concord, the choir could represent the harmony of the city or, on a grander scale, the peaceful empire, which takes its keynote from its leader, the emperor.[43]

When praising the Rome of the empire, its mixed political constitution, and its universal dominance, the second-century Greek orator Aristides chose the image of the choir, a symbol par excellence of concord in the ancient world. The signal achievement of the empire was to bring different, often mutually hostile, races together in the bonds of peace, "So the whole inhabited world speaks in greater harmony than a chorus . . . forged together by this chorus-leader prince."[44] An early Christian appropriation of the image is found in the letter of Ignatius to the Ephesians, in which the community is told that "in your

---

42. Isidore of Seville, *Etym.* VI.xxix.5: *Alii chorum dixerunt a concordia, qua in cariate consistit; quia, si caritatem non habeat, respondere convenienter non potest.* Lindsay 1957; trans. Barney et al 2006: 147.

43. The image and its significance are discussed in Oliver 1953: 876–930.

44. Behr 1981: 79.

concord (*homonoia*) and in the symphony of your love Jesus Christ is sung. You must join this chorus, every one of you, so that being harmonious in concord (*homonoia*) and taking your note from God you may sing in unity with one voice through Jesus Christ to the Father . . . being members of his Son."[45] Here, two traditional motifs representing harmony are combined: the Hellenistic political ideal of ὁμόνοια is expressed through the image of the choir, and the Pauline "body metaphor" represents the faithful as members of the body of Christ.[46] Early Christian sources applied the choir as an image of harmony in an explicitly episcopal context, in which the choir singing in harmony is the Church obedient to the direction of a bishop. By Augustine's time, the choir could represent more generally a harmonious Christian community.[47] Columbanus may have intended his references to musical harmony to be interpreted as a call for unity in an unfocused way, but the reference occurs in the context of his defense of his right to speak out and his call on Pope Boniface not to act capriciously or autocratically. Historically, the power of the choir image rested on the belief that the singers contributed to the work of the whole choir because humans naturally desire harmony. Harmony is the result of contentment; it cannot be enforced by a despot. As Isidore wrote, it results from the love each member directs to the other, for "without charity it is impossible to sing responses harmoniously." Order comes about because those who contribute to it make a rational choice to do so and the choirmaster acts to support that choice for harmony, nothing more.[48] There is an aspect of the image that, one can say with more certainty, suited Columbanus's purposes. The choir represented the cooperation of the constituent parts of the corporation working together, but like the singers in the choir, each retains its distinctive voice and register. This image was appropriated by Christian writers to express their understanding of the Church as united in diversity. Augustine drew the conventional lesson from the organ as an instrument that emits different notes, but those notes "sound together in most harmonious diversity (*diversitate concordissima*). For even then the saints of God will have their differences, accordant, not discordant (*consonantes, non dissonantes*), that is, agreeing, not disagreeing, just as sweetest harmony arises from sounds differing indeed, but not opposed to one another."[49] As a choir sings more than one note, so each community in the Church should retain its traditions while remaining united in the faith. In his letter to the Gallic bishops Columbanus

45. Brent 2007: 84, 2006a: 239, 306, 1998: 35; Lotz 2007: 55.

46. The order and harmony of the cosmos itself is compared to a "great circular choir moving evenly in rhythm," by Eusebius, *Praep. Ev.* 14.26; Gifford 1903: 839.

47. Augustine, *Enarr. in Ps.*, 150.6.

48. Brent 1998: 34, 63–4.

49. Augustine, *Enarr. in Ps.* 150.7; *PL* 37: 1964; trans. Cox 1887: 683.

writes that those involved in the factious debate about Easter should be as "single harmonious (*consonantia*) members of one body" (*Ep.* 2.8). In the letter to Pope Boniface, he offers similar counsel and writes that all "ought to have been one choir, and this motive is joined by the greatness for my concern for your concord and peace; 'for if one member suffers, all the members suffer with it' (1 Cor. 12:26)" (*Ep.* 5.11). In both examples, after he depicts the unity of the Church as musical harmony, Columbanus references the human body as another example of unity in diversity. Of all the topoi that appeared in the rhetoric of concord, the "body metaphor" was the most frequently cited both in political rhetoric and, through the influence of Saint Paul, in the rhetoric of orthodoxy and ecclesiastical unity.[50] Paul's First Epistle to the Corinthians and the Epistle to the Ephesians bear the heavy imprint of this political rhetoric in presenting the Church as the body of Christ, or the Church as a body with Christ as its head. In 1 Corinthians 12 Christians are advised that in their different roles they must work together in harmony, like the various limbs of the human body, motivated not by self-interest, but with a view to the good of the entire body. Charity (1 Cor. 13) is therefore to replace sectional interests within the body of the Church, whose head is Christ (Col. 1:18), he who left his followers the greatest example of charity by sacrificing himself for them. The analysis of examples of Columbanus's use of these Pauline ideas reveals something of his conception of the Church, whose members, united in the bonds of charity under sure leadership, adhere to their own traditions, where each is "allowed to remain in the condition in which he was called" (1 Cor. 7, 20; quoted by Columbanus in *Epp.* 2.7, 3.2). An exploration of Columbanus's arguments in favor of the toleration of diversity with reference to the "body metaphor" allows something of the voice of those on the wrong side of the Easter debate to be recovered.

THE BODY METAPHOR IN THE LETTERS OF COLUMBANUS

Columbanus drew on biblical sources for the "body metaphor" in his appeal for respect for diversity as the basis of peace. In his *Epistula* 2 he calls for unity between his monastic followers and the Gallic clergy, wishing that both parties would act like "single harmonious members of one body" (*Ep.* 2.8). He ends the letter with the same image, this time not to reconcile politicking ecclesiastics, but to draw attention to a Christian identity that transcends racial cleavages, "for we are all joint members of one body, whether Gauls or Britons or Irish or whatever *gens* we may be" (*Ep.* 2.9). The image of the body recurs in his letter to

---

50. Paul presents the Church as Christ's body in Rom. 12:4–5; 1 Cor. 12:12–31; Eph. 1:22–3, 2:16, 3:6, 4:4, 12, 16, 5:23; Col. 1:18, 24, 2:19, 3:15.

Pope Boniface. He quotes 1 Corinthians 12:26 in the same context as the rhetoric of concord: the word pairing of "peace and concord" and the image of the choir (*Ep.* 5.11). Later, he writes that those responsible for the schism within the Italian church are trying "to divide the body of Christ and separate his members" (*Ep.* 5.12). In so doing, Columbanus engaged with a dominant theme in contemporary theological thought that originated in the political propaganda of the empire and made his letters into a deliberative discourse that attempted to convince his readers to follow his plan for restoring unity to a divided Church.

In the *City of God*, Augustine repeated verbatim Cicero's comparison of social concord (*in civitate concordiam*) to musical harmony, revealing the influence of classical ideals of civic harmony on the mainstream of Christian thought. Cicero argued that just as harmony is made by the regulation of voices that are most unalike (*dissimillimarum vocum*), so the state may produce concord (*concordiam*) by regulating elements that are most unalike (*consensu dissimillimorum*).[51] The peaceful society, like the harmonious choir, achieves concord only through the toleration of the natural diversity of the body politic. The choir as a symbol stood for variety that is no threat to stability and for unity that is no threat to freedom. Augustine's teacher, Ambrose of Milan, quoted Cicero on this subject. His literary model for *De officiis* was Cicero's work by the same name, and he borrowed Cicero's words that expressed the ideas of unity and concord through the image of the body. In *De officiis*, Cicero argues that to defraud or injure a fellow citizen to gain a personal profit is unjust because it is motivated by greed rather than by concern for the welfare of all, and it is unnatural because it goes against the instinct to care for oneself and for one's fellow. To illustrate his point, he gives the example of a bodily member wishing to injure another member of the same body. Such a scenario is implausible because it goes against nature, and the result would be the weakening or even death of the whole body. Ambrose borrowed Cicero's ideas in his own *De officiis*, recasting philosophical principles as Christian theology:

> [L]et us suppose that you could give the eye the power to take away intelligence from the head, or hearing from the ears, or thinking from the mind, or the sense of smell from the nose, or taste from the mouth, and to assume these capacities itself. This would destroy the whole order of nature, would it not? The apostle puts it so well: "If the whole body were an eye, where would our hearing be? If the whole body had the gift of hearing, where would our sense of smell be?" (1 Cor 12:17). So we are all one body and different members, but all are necessary to the body, for one

---

51. Cicero, *De re publica* 2.42; Augustine, *De civitate Dei* 2.21.

member cannot say of another: "I do not need you." Far from it.[52]

Ambrose shows the congruence of the political philosophy of Cicero with Christianity by citing Saint Paul, who was himself influenced by the political rhetoric of the empire and who appropriated the body metaphor in his letters, interpreting it in a Christological sense and as an image of the Church, especially in 1 Corinthians 12.[53] In classical literature, the metaphor of the human body was the most common topos that allowed ancient writers to explore the need for cooperation and unity among the members for the progress and very survival of society. The body image was used to reconcile the plebs to the dominance of the patricians and to convince them to be happy with their lot. In a Christian setting, the image also appeared as a way of illustrating the disastrous consequences of the breakdown in social order. Augustine's student, the historian and theologian Paulus Orosius, described the revolt of the plebs of 494 BC in his *History* as an internal wickedness (*intestina pernicie*) "when a body severed from its head wished to destroy that from which it drew its life."[54]

Columbanus's letters to the Gallic bishops and to Pope Boniface, in which he refers to the Church as the body of Christ and to Christ as the head, are attempts to heal division in the Church or divisions between Columbanus's followers and the Gallic clergy. Although Columbanus's theology is not speculative, he is creative in how he interprets key passages relating to the body of the Church/ Christ from the Pauline epistles to defend his position. His main concern is to recover unity, but unity comes not when everyone agrees to submit to the will of a single authority; unity, for Columbanus, is *consensus*, the ideal of agreement (*unanimitas*) among all the members. His use of the body metaphor is, therefore, to promote unity, but also to defend his view of what unity should be. Columbanus was heir to the elaborate Stoic tradition of representing united humanity as a body as transmitted, and developed, by biblical and patristic writers. Cicero acknowledged his debt to Stoic philosophy when he set out his ideas on *concordia*. The Stoics argued that reason (*ratio*) unified the inhabitants of organized communities, creating fellowship among all communities [55] and uniting them with the gods, the source of reason.[56] Furthermore, each person has a

52. Davidson 2001: 362–5.

53. Studies include Mitchell 1991; Howard Marshall 2004. For a compendium and discussion of the sources, see Larchet 2012; Best 1955. On ecclesiastical unity and Saint Paul, see Hanson 1946. On Paul and political concord, see Harrison 2013; Ilsley Hicks, 1963; McVay 2000; Minear 2004: ch. 6; Tilley 2007; van Rensburg 1992.

54. Paulus Orosius, *Seven Books of History against the Pagans* 2.5.5; PL 31, 755; trans. Fear 2010: 81–2.

55. On the Stoic concept of reason and the perfecting of reason, see Vogt 2008: 4–16. See the section on *oikeiōsis* in Fraisse 1974: 338–47; Baldry 1965: 178–99.

56. Obbink 1999: 189.

natural affinity for his fellow, beginning with the family, extending to friends and neighbors, then to the wider community, and eventually embracing all human-kind.[57] That perfect community could be the cosmic city of the gods and humans, or it could be the empire.[58] For Christians, the basis of unity was not political or ideological, but spiritual, and terms of biological affinity were given a spiritual significance to express unity in faith. According to Hélène Pétré, Cicero may not have used the words *frater*, "brother," and *fraternitas*, "brotherhood," to convey a sense of shared identity, but by the end of the second century among Christian Latin writers these words were being used expressly to denote Christians who, as a people, were strongly linked through spiritual bonds. A lexical innova-tion that arose from this spiritual identity were the words *compati* (*cum+ pati*), meaning "to suffer with," and *compassio*. A member has compassion on, or shares in the suffering of, a fellow member of the body.[59] These ideas were pre-sent in Irish Christianity from the beginning. Saint Patrick called his converts in Ireland his brothers and sons (*fratribus et filiis*),[60] and the British chieftain Coroticus and his band, who enslaved or killed them, were therefore kin slayers; Patrick calls them father killers and brother killers (*patricida, fratricida*).[61] As the Irish captives were his fellow Christians, Patrick paraphrases the supreme Pauline formulation of shared suffering based on shared membership in the body of Christ: "If one member suffers, all suffer together (*compatiuntur*)" (cf. 1 Cor. 12:26).[62] Patrick's contemporary, the extreme Paulinus of Nola,[63] wrote informing Severus, who was also not in full health, that they were joined by "a most gracious sign of concord" (*gratissimum signum concordiae*) and that the ailing Vigilantius also shared in this "union of suffering" (*conjunctio passionis*) because Paul had taught that all shared in the suffering of a single member of the body. 1 Corinthians 12:26 expresses the cohesion of the body, but also the duty of its members to care for one another. In the letter to Boniface in which he runs a series of symbols of concord together, Columbanus writes that he acts from concern for Boniface's "concord and peace; for if one member suffers, all the members suffer with it" (*Ep.* 5.11). It is their common membership in the body of Christ, and the responsibility of care that it entails, that gives Columbanus

---

57. Cicero, *De fin.* 5.65.
58. Richter 2011: 84.
59. Pétré 1948: 107–38 on *frater/fraternitas*, 341–5 on *compati*. Lee 2006: 148–9 explores the idea of co-suffering in its classical context.
60. Conneely 1993: 34.
61. Conneely 1993: 51.
62. The Patrician formulation is: *Si dolet unum membrum condoleant omnia membra.*
63. Paulinus, *Ep.* 5.9–10.

his authority to speak out and admonish the head of the body, the bishop of Rome.[64]

The well-being of an individual member of the body should concern all members; if one is impaired, the entire body is weakened. This interdependence was explored by Paul's contemporary, the Stoic Seneca. If we honor our country, he argued, we must honor its parts, that is, our fellow citizens. Seneca points out the irrationality of wishing harm to our compatriots: "What if the hands should desire to harm the feet, or the eyes the hands?"[65] Each of these members has its particular duty, which it alone can fulfill, and any impairment affects the whole body. In *De officiis*, Ambrose argued that the form of the body should teach humans to respect difference and to expect unity:

> Can any one of your members claim the functions of any other? Can, say, the eye claim the function of the mouth, or the mouth the function of the eye; or can the hand take over the work of the feet, or the foot the work of the hands?[66]

An early Irish reflection of such principles is found in a tract on the responsibilities of the twelve grades of society, illustrated by negative examples. The first of the grades in the seventh-century *De duodecim abusiuis saeculi* is the *Sapiens sine operibus*, "The wise man without [good] deeds." The wise teacher is expected to guide with his words and through the example of his behavior. However, "if the teacher errs, by which teacher will he be corrected again?" To illustrate the intractability of the dilemma, the treatise warns, "If in as much as the eye fails in the duty of seeing, how is that service to be demanded of the hand, or from the foot or from the rest of the body?" [67] The same parts of the body listed in 1 Corinthians 12:15–16[68] are named in the Irish source; furthermore, to illustrate the importance of cooperation, these are members and limbs that occur in pairs in the body.[69] Ambrose argues that there is an obligation to help those in difficulty, because "[t]his is undoubtedly the law of nature, which binds us all to humanity: we must show respect for one another as we are all part of one body." This applies in particular to the Church, "for it rises into one body, joined

---

64. Columbanus addresses the bishops of Rome as "head" of the Church in his letters. His intentions are explored in Bracken 2002: 182–8.

65. Seneca, *De ira* 2.31.7; Basore 1928: 234–7.

66. Ambrose, *De officiis* 3.3.18–9; Davidson 2002: 1, 362–5.

67. *Si namque oculus a videndi officio desiverit, quis a manu aut pede vel reliquo corpore illud ministerium exigit?*: Hellmann 1909: 33.

68. "For the body also is not one member, but many. If the foot should say, because I am not the hand, I am not of the body; is it therefore not of the body? And if the ear should say, because I am not the eye, I am not of the body; is it therefore not of the body?"

69. See Mitchell 1991: 157 n. 570 for more classical examples.

and bound together in the unity of faith and love." However, these examples also illustrate how the individual members have their own particular tasks and responsibilities, which they alone can fulfill. Difference is therefore an essential feature of the members of the body, for it allows the body to function. Unity is not uniformity, but rather the toleration of diversity so that all the members can perform the individual tasks for which they were created, to the benefit of the whole body.

The body as a representation of ecclesiastical unity is the subject on which Columbanus begins his *Epistula* 2, and the topic allows him to end the letter with a flourish. The letter opens on the theme of the maturing of the people of God to form a single body through their shared faith. The section includes a biblical quotation that is not noted in the modern editions of Columbanus's letters by Gundlach and Walker.[70] Columbanus writes that the divines gathering in council to discuss the question of Easter are engaging in the task of debating "the truth of faith and good works" (*Ep.* 2.2: *de fidei et bonorum operum veritate*), and that they will undertake this endeavor "through senses exercised to the discerning of good and evil" (*per exercitatos sensus ad discretionem boni ac mali*). The quotation here is from the Epistle to the Hebrews, 5:14: "But strong meat is for the perfect; for them who by custom have their senses exercised to the discerning of good and evil" (*eorum qui pro consuetudine exercitatos habent sensus ad discretionem boni ac mali*). The author of Hebrews takes up a Pauline theme here. Paul compares those who have knowledge, but incomplete understanding, of the faith to babes who are fed with milk before they become fully grown and conform to the perfect body of Christ. The author of Hebrews continues: "Wherefore, leaving the word of the beginning of Christ, let us go on to things more perfect" (6:1). This topic bookends *Epistula* 2 when Columbanus returns to the subject of the growth and maturity of the body of the Church in conformity to the perfect body of Christ at the end of the letter. His words, evoking the body metaphor to show the ideal of an ethnically diverse but doctrinally united Church, have been commented on many times: "for we are all joint members of one body, whether Gauls or Britons or Irish or whatever *gens* " (*Ep.* 2.9). Columbanus then writes:

> Thus let all our peoples (*omnes gentes*) rejoice in the comprehension of faith and the apprehension of the Son of God, and let us all hasten to approach to perfect manhood, to the measure of the completed growth of the fulness of Jesus Christ.

70. Gundlach 1892: 160; Walker 1957: 12.

The biblical quotation is from Ephesians 4:13, "Until we all meet into the unity of faith and of the knowledge of the Son of God, unto a perfect man, unto the measure of the age of the fulness of Christ." The perfection referred to at the end of the letter refers to the mature body of the Church when it develops to conform to the perfect body of Christ. Paul writes that the Corinthians have to be fed on milk, not meat (1 Cor. 3:2), because they are immature and carnal. This immaturity and their carnal nature mean that they have as yet an incomplete understanding of Christ, and they are therefore prone to strife and factiousness (1 Cor. 3:3). They define themselves as followers of Paul, Apollo (1 Cor. 3:4), and, perhaps, of Cephas, or Christ. Had the ethnic groups within the Church grown to maturity, the British, Gauls, and Irish would no longer constitute separate parties, but would recognize the importance of unity and agree to be joined as a united body of believers. The allusions to the body in Columbanus's *Epistula* 2 are a compelling presentation of the Christian ideal of unity and a direct appeal to the disputants in the Easter controversy to work toward that ideal. There is also no doubt, however, in Columbanus's mind about which side (his monks, or the Gallic bishops) is further along the path toward perfection.

The representation of the Church as a body allowed Columbanus to explore the nature of ecclesiastical unity. For him, the Church was composed of individual communities, each with its traditions and history but united in the faith. The analogy of the body, with its limbs performing their own functions but united in their care for the whole of the body, suited his purposes in demanding that the Easter traditions of the Irish Church should be respected. He also used the body metaphor to insist that those in authority, like the head of the body, should fulfill their function and lead. However, Columbanus's interest in the metaphor goes deeper than a plea for the toleration of diversity within the Church. The body represented unity, but it also represented stability. Each member of the body is formed for a specific purpose, and the well-being of the body is assured when its members fulfill their individual functions. In a social context, peace and stability are assured when the orders meet their obligations. Problems arise when there is a failure to respect social division and when a group assumes a position or role within the social hierarchy other than the one it has been assigned or the one it has historically fulfilled. Sedition is therefore represented as a disease in the body politic.[71] As Christian writers appropriated, and transformed, the classical language of concord to convey their ideal ecclesiastical order, so too they went to the same sources to present heresy as a disease in the body of the Church. Augustine engaged directly with Cicero's

71. Lotz 2007: 132–3.

ideas on the nature of the state in the *City of God* XIX. A *populus* is a gathering of rational beings, united in fellowship (*concordi communione*) in the object of their love. However, the descent into civil war disrupted "that concord (*concordiam*) which is, so to speak, the health (*salus*) of the people."[72] The integrity of the body, therefore, depends on the willingness of its members to fulfill their assigned roles, as any innovation impairs its equilibrium. Ambrose and the author of *De duodecim abusivis saeculi* wrote of the impossibility of parts of the body fulfilling the duties of another, and Columbanus wrote to Pope Boniface warning him of the fatal inversion of the body of the Church should he fail to govern: Boniface's subordinates will become the head, while he will be transformed into the tail.[73] Columbanus quotes 1 Corinthians 7:20 ("Let every man abide in the same calling in which he was called") in his request to Pope Gregory that he be allowed to continue to adhere to the Easter practices of his homeland, so that "each should remain in the condition in which he was called" (*Ep.* 2.7). He repeats the quotation from 1 Corinthians when arguing for the importance of respecting the particular character of each Christian community in his letter to the pope defending the practices of the Irish Church. Following his allusion to the agreement reached between Pope Anicetus and Polycarp to tolerate their differing Easter practices, Columbanus writes that they remained united in charity, "each preserving what he had received and abiding in the condition in which he had been called" (*in quo vocatus est permanens; Ep.* 3.2).

De duodecim abusivis saeculi appeals to one of the major New Testament symbols of the unity of the Church, and that unity is linked explicitly to the body of Christ, within which there is absolute stability and no possibility of change. Christ's tunic is described in John's Gospel as being woven in a single piece "from the top throughout"; even the soldiers at the crucifixion refused to divide it, casting lots for ownership instead (John 19:23–24). For Cyprian, writing in *On the Unity of the Catholic Church*, and for Augustine, the tunic becomes an emblem of the indivisibility of the true Church. It represents the "bond of concord (*vinculum concordiae*) that is held together in a way that cannot be split."[74] *De XII* lists "the people without discipline" (*Plebs sine disciplina*) as the eleventh level of depravity in society and predicts dreadful retribution for their waywardness. They are outside the unity of the Church, which the tract compares to Christ's tunic: "Just as the whole body is covered by the tunic except the head, so too all the Church is protected and adorned by discipline, except for Christ, who

---

72. Augustine, *De civitate Dei* 19.24; *PL* 41: 655; Greene 1960: 232–3. For discussion, see Dvornik 1966: 2, 841; Duquesnay Adams 1971: 19.

73. *Ep.* 5.10; "tail" is Walker's polite translation of *caudam*.

74. *PL* 4: 504; Brent 2006b: 158.

is the head of the Church and is not subject to discipline. This tunic was woven from the top throughout (John 19:23), because the same discipline is renewed and bestowed on the Church by the Lord from heaven. . . . The tunic of the body of Christ is, therefore, the discipline of the Church; whoever is beyond discipline is separated from the body of Christ."[75] The tract portrays unity as an essential attribute of the body, and that unity, the tunic of Christ, is incapable of change because it cannot be torn. Those without discipline will have to stand before God's law, but they can expect no quarter because that law cannot be changed capriciously, and the commands of Christ cannot be broken. To show the impossibility of change, the chapter in *De XII* closes the argument by quoting 1 Corinthians 7:20: "Let every man abide in the same calling in which he was called."[76] Columbanus himself appealed to the established interpretation of Christ's tunic in his letter to Pope Boniface: "To divide the body of Christ and separate his members and part the vesture (*tunicam scindere*) which means unity" is Satan's plan, he writes, but Christ's plan is for unity because "he has made both one" (*Ep.* 5.12; cf. Eph. 2:14). The demands of the Gallic bishops that he conform to their Easter practices required Columbanus to abandon and change the traditions of the Church in which he was called (1 Cor. 7, 20). The delinquent leadership of the popes was dangerous for the body of the Church. In failing to act the part of the head through principled leadership, their negligence left open the possibility that junior members of the body would act as the head. The implication of Columbanus's line of reasoning is that to expect the members of the body to change is unnatural, and to expect churches to change their traditions is an affront to unity.

BIBLIOGRAPHY

Akar, P. (2013) *Concordia: Un idéal de la classe dirigeante romaine à la fin de la République.* Paris, Publications de la Sorbonne.

Allard, P. (1884) "Prudence historien." *Revue des Questions Historiques* 35: 345–85.

Argenio, R. (1965) "Roma nel concetto degli scrittori pagani e cristiani." *Studi Romani* 13: 14–20.

Augustine (1887) *Enarrationes in Psalmos = Enarrations on the Book of Psalms*, trans. A. Cleveland Cox. A Select Library of the Nicene and Post-Nicene Fathers of the Christian Church 8. New York, Christian Literature Co; repr. Grand Rapids, MI, 1996.

---

75. Hellmann 1909: 57–58: *Sicut enim tunica totum corpus praeter caput tegitur, ita disciplina omnia ecclesia praeter Christum, qui est caput ecclesiae et sub disciplina non est, protegitur et ornatur. Ipsa vero tunica texta desuper fuerat per totum, quia eadem ecclesiae disciplina a Domino in caelo tribuitur et integratur. . . . Tunica ergo corporis Christi disciplina ecclesiae est; qui autem extra disciplinam est alienus est a corpore Christi.*

76. Hellmann 1909: 58: *non solvamus quicquam de mandatis Christi, sed unusquisque in quo vocatus est in eo permaneat apud Deum.*

Augustine (1888) *Tractatus in Iohannis Evangelium* = *Tractates on the Gospel of John*, trans. J. Gibb. A Select Library of the Nicene and Post-Nicene Fathers of the Christian Church 7. New York, Christian Literature Co.; repr. Grand Rapids, MI, 1974; *St. Augustine: Tractates on the Gospel of John*, 55–111, trans. J. W. Rettig. Fathers of the Church 90. Washington, DC, Catholic University of America Press, 1994.

Bakke, O. M. (2001) *"Concord and Peace": A Rhetorical Analysis of the First Letter of Clement with an Emphasis on the Language of Unity and Sedition.* 2 vols. Wissenschaftliche zum Neuen Testament 141, vol. 1. Tübingen, Mohr Siebeck.

Baldry, H. C. (1965) *The Unity of Mankind in Greek Thought.* Cambridge, Cambridge University Press.

Bannon, Cynthia L. (1997). *The Brothers of Romulus: Fraternal Pietas in Roman Law, Literature, and Society.* Princeton, NJ, Princeton University Press.

Bartnik, C. (1968) "L'interpétation théologique de la crise de l'empire romain par Léon le Grand." *Revue d'Histoire Ecclésiastique* 63: 745–84.

Basore, J. W. (trans.) (1928) *Seneca: Moral Essays*, vol. 1, *De ira.* Loeb Classical Library 214. Cambridge, MA, Harvard University Press.

Behr, C. A. (ed.) (1981) *P. Aelius Aristides: The Complete Works*, vol. 2, *Orations XVII–LII.* Leiden, Brill.

Best, E. (1955) *One Body in Christ: A Study in the Relationship of the Church to Christ in the Epistles of the Apostle Paul.* London, SPCK.

Bonner, C. (1941) "Desired Haven." *Harvard Theological Review* 34: 49–67.

Bracken, D. (2002) "Authority and Duty: Columbanus and the Primacy of Rome." *Peritia* 16: 168–213.

Bracken, D. (2012) "'Whence the Splendour of Such Light Came to Us': The Account of Ireland in Ermenrich's Life of St Gall." In E. Mullins and D. Scully (eds.), *"Listen, o Isles, unto Me": Studies in Medieval Word and Image in Honour of Jennifer O'Reilly.* Cork, Cork University Press, 73–86, 337–40.

Brent, A. (1998) "Ignatius of Antioch and the Imperial Cult." *Vigiliae Christianae* 52: 30–58.

Brent, A. (2006a) *Ignatius of Antioch and the Second Sophistic: A Study of an Early Christian Transformation of Pagan Culture.* Studien und Texte zu Antike und Christentum 36. Tübingen, Mohr Siebeck.

Brent, A. (trans.) (2006b). *St. Cyprian of Carthage: On the Church, Select Treatises.* Popular Patristics Series 33. Crestwood NY, St. Vladimir's Seminary Press.

Brent, A. (2007). *Ignatius of Antioch: A Martyr Bishop and the Origin of Episcopacy.* London, Continuum.

Breytenbach, C. (2003) "Civic Concord and Cosmic Harmony: Sources of Metaphoric Mapping in *1 Clement* 20:3." In J. T. Fitzgerald et al. (eds.), *Early Christianity and Classical Culture: Comparative Studies in Honor of Abraham J. Malherbe.* Supplements to Novum Testamentum 110. Leiden, Brill, 259–73.

Cacitti, R. (1972) "*Subita Christo servit Roma Deo*: Osservazioni sulla teologia politica di Prudenzio." *Aevum* 46: 402–35.

Capizzi, C. (2006) "La *pax romana* e Giustiniano." In P. Catalano and P. Siniscalco (eds.), *Concezioni della pace.* Da Roma alla Terza Roma, Studi 6. Rome: Herder, 139–60.

Casaretto, F. M. (1999) "L'*amicitia*, chiave ermeneutica dell'*Epistola ad Grimaldum abbatem* di Ermenrico de Ellwangen." *Revue Bénédictine* 109: 117–47.

Casson, L. (1971) *Ships and Seamanship in the Ancient World.* Princeton, NJ, Princeton University Press.

Catry, P. (1978) "L'amour du prochain chez Saint Grégoire le Grand." *Studia Monastica* 20: 287–344.

CCSL = *Corpus Christianorum Series Latina*, Brepols, Turnhout.

Conneely, D. (1993) *St. Patrick's Letters: A Study of Their Theological Dimension*. Maynooth, An Sagart.

Curran, J. R. (2000) *Pagan City and Christian Capital: Rome in the Fourth Century*. Oxford Classical Monographs. Oxford, Clarendon Press.

David, P. (1937) "Un recueil de conférences monastiques irlandaises du viiie siècle: Notes sur le manuscript 43 de la bibliothèque du chapitre de Cracovie." *Revue Bénédictine* 49: 62–89.

Davidson, I. J. (ed. and trans.) (2002) *Ambrose: De officiis*, vol. 1. Oxford, Oxford University Press.

De Jong, J. (1998) "Deictic and (Pseudo)anaphoric Functions of the Pronoun *iste*." In R. Risselada (ed.), *Latin in Use: Amsterdam Studies in the Pragmatics of Latin*. Amsterdam Studies in Classical Philology 8. Amsterdam, J. C. Gieben, 19–37.

Delahaye, K. (1964) *Ecclesia mater chez les Pères des trois premiers siècles: Pour un renouvellement de la pastorale d'aujourd'hui*. Unam Sanctam 46. Paris, Éditions du Cerf.

Dogeon, M. H. (trans.) (1996) [revised by M. Vermes and S. Lieu]. "Libanius, *Oratio* LIX (Royal Discourse upon Constatius and Constans)." In S. N. C. Lieu and D. Montserrat (eds.), *From Constantine to Julian: Pagan and Byzantine Views: A Source History*. London, Routledge, 164–209.

Drake, H. A. (1976). *In Praise of Constantine: A Historical Study and New Translation of Eusebius' Tricennial Orations*. University of California Publications, Classical Studies 15. Berkeley, University of California Press.

Duquesnay Adams, J. (1971) *The "Populus" of Augustine and Jerome: A Study in the Patristic Sense of Community*. New Haven, CT, Yale University Press.

Dvornik, F. (1966) *Early Christian and Byzantine Political Philosophy: Origins and Background*, vol. 2. Dumbarton Oaks Studies 9. Washington, DC, Dumbarton Oaks Center for Byzantine Studies.

Evenepoel, W. (2010) "The Theme of *Concordia/pax* in the Words of the Poet Prudentius." *Sacris Erudiri* 49: 67–80.

Fontaine, J. (1981) "La dernière éopée de la Rome chrétienne: Le *Contre Symmaque* de Prudence." *Vita Latina* 81: 3–14.

Fraisse, J.-C. (1974) *"Philia": La nation d'amitié dans la philosophie antique; essai sur un problème perdu retrouvé*. Bibliothèque d'Histoire de la Philosophie. Paris, Vrin.

Gifford, E. H. (trans.) (1903) *Eusebii Pamphili evangelicae praeparationis libri xv*, vol. 2. Oxford, E Typrographeo Academico.

Gray, T. (1990). *The Homilies of St. Gregory the Great on the Book of the Prophet Ezekiel*. Etna, CA. Center for Traditionalist Orthodox Studies.

Greene, W. C. (trans.) (1960) *Augustine: City of God against the Pagans*, vol 6, *Books XVIII.36–XX*. Loeb Classical Library 416. Cambridge MA, Harvard University Press.

Gregory the Great (1971) *Homilies on Ezekiel* = *Sancti Gregorii Magni: Homiliae in Hiezechihelem prophetam*, ed. M. Adriaen. Corpus Christianorum Series Latina 142. Turhnout, Brepols.

Gregory the Great (1982) *Letters* = *S. Gregorii magni opera. Registrum epistularum: Libri 1–7, 8–14*, ed. D. Norberg. Corpus Christianorum Series Latina 140–40A. 2 vols. Turnhout, Brepols; English trans. J. R. C. Martyn, *The Letters of Gregory the Great*. 3 vols. Toronto, Pontifical Institute of Mediaeval Studies, 2004.

Gregory the Great (1979–1985) *Morals on the Book of Job* = *S. Gregorii. Moralia in Iob*, ed. M. Adriaen. 3 vols. Corpus Christianorum Series Latina 142–3B. Turnhout, Brepols; trans. *Morals on the Book of Job*. A Library of Fathers of the Holy Catholic Church. 3 vols. Oxford, 1850.

Gundlach, W. (ed.) (1892) Columbae sive Columbani abbatis Luxoviensis et Bobbiensis epistolae. In *Epistolae Merowingici et Karolini Aevi i*, MGH, Epp. III. Berlin, 154–90.

Hanson, S. (1946) *The Unity of the Church in the New Testament: Colossians and Ephesians*. Acta Seminarii Neotestamentici Upsaliensis 14. Uppsala, Almquist & Wiksells.

Harrison, J. R. (2013) "Augustan Rome and the Body of Christ: A Comparison of the Social Vision of the *Res gestae* and Paul's Letter to the Romans." *Harvard Theological Review* 106: 1–36.

Hellmann, S. (ed.) (1909) *Pseudo-Cyprianus: De xii abusiuis saeculi*. Texte und Untersuchungen zur Geschichte der altchristlichen Literatur 34. Leipzig, J. C. Hinrichs'sche Buchhandlung.

Howard Marshall, I. (2004) "'For the Husband Is Head of the Wife': Paul's Use of Head and Body Language." In P. J. Williams et al. (eds.), *The New Testament in Its First Century Setting: Essays on Context and Background in Honour of B. W. Winter on His 65th Birthday*. Grand Rapids MI, Wm. B. Eerdmans, 165–89.

Huskinson, J. (1982) *Concordia apostolorum: Christian Propaganda at Rome in the Fourth and Fifth Centuries*. BAR International Series 148. Oxford, Oxford University Press.

Ilsley Hicks, R. (1963) "The Body Political and the Body Ecclesiastical." *Journal of Bible and Religion* 31: 29–35.

Irwin, D. A. (1996) *Against the Tide: An Intellectual History of Free Trade*. Princeton, NJ, Princeton University Press.

Isidore of Seville (1957) *Etymologies = Isidori Hispalensis episcopi Etymologiarum sive originum libri XX*, ed. W. M. Lindsay. 2 vols. Oxford, Clarendon Press; *The Etymologies of Isidore of Seville*, trans. S. A. Barney et al. Cambridge, Cambridge University Press, 2006.

Jal, P. (1961) "*Pax civilis—Concordia*." *Revue des Études Latines* 39: 210–31.

Kerlouégan, F. (1986) "Grégoire le Grand et les pays celtiques." In J. Fontaine, R. Gillet, and S. Pellistrandi (eds.), *Grégoire de Grand*. Paris, Éditions du Centre National de la Recherche Scientifique, 589–96.

Kessler, H. L. (1987) "The Meeting of Peter and Paul in Rome: An Emblematic Narrative of Spiritual Brotherhood." *Dumbarton Oaks Papers* 41: 265–75; repr. Kessler, *Old St. Peter's and Church Decoration in Medieval Italy*, Spoleto, 2002, 109–25.

Kleist, J. A. (1961) *The Epistles of St Clement of Rome and St Ignatius of Antioch*. Ancient Christian Writers 1. London, Newman Press.

Kürbis, B., J. Wolny, D. Zydorek and M. Sobieraj (2010). *Kazania na różne dni postne i inne teksty z kodeksu krakowskiego 140 (43)*. Monumenta Sacra Polonorum 4. Krakow, Polska Akademia Umiejętności.

Larchet, J.-C. (2012) *L'Église corps du Christ*, vol. I, *Les relations entre les Églises*; vol. ii, *Nature et structure*. Paris, Éditions du CERF.

Lee, M. V. (2006) *Paul, the Stoics, and the Body of Christ*. Society for New Testament Studies Monograph Series 137. Cambridge, Cambridge University Press.

Leyser, C. (2007) *Authority and Asceticism from Augustine to Gregory the Great*. Oxford Historical Monographs. Oxford, Clarendon Press.

Lobur, J. A. (2008) *"Consensus", "Concordia", and the Formation of Roman Imperial Ideology*. Studies in Classics. New York, Routledge.

Lønstrup Dal Santo, G. (2015) "*Concordia apostolorum—concordia augustorum*: Building a Corporate Image for the Theodosian Dynasty." In R. Dijkstra et al. (eds.), *East and West in the Roman Empire of the Fourth Century: An End to Unity*. Leiden, Brill, 99–120.

Lotz, J.-P. (2007) *Ignatius and Concord: The Background and Use of the Language of Concord in the Letters of Ignatius of Antioch*. Patristic Studies 8. New York, Peter Lang.

Maccarrone, M. (1976) "Devozione a S. Pietro: Missione ed evangelizzazione nell'alto medioevo." In *Evangelizzazione e culture: Atti del congresso internazionale scientifico di missiologia, Roma, 5-12 ottobre 1975*, 3 vols. Rome, Pontificia Università Urbaniana, 2:180-205.

Mattei, P. (2013) "Schisme, hérésie, et autres détails dans saint Cyprien (à propos d'une édition récente du *De zelo et liuore*)." *Latomus* 72: 761-9.

McVay, J. K. (2000) "The Human Body as Social and Political Metaphor in Stoic Literature and Early Christian Writers." *Bulletin of the American Society of Papyrologists* 37: 135-47.

Meyvaert, P. (1963) "Diversity within Unity, a Gregorian Theme." *Heythrop Journal* 4: 141-62; repr. as section 6 of Meyvaert, *Benedict, Gregory, Bede and Others*. London, Variorum, 1977.

Minear, P. S. (2004). *Images of the Church in the New Testament*. Louisville, KY, Westminster Press.

Mitchell, M. M. (1991) *Paul and the Rhetoric of Reconciliation: An Exegetical Investigation of the Language and Composition of 1 Corinthians*. Louisville, KY, John Knox Press.

Mommsen, T. E. (1951) "St Augustine and the Christian Idea of Progress: The Background of the *City of God*." *Journal of the History of Ideas* 12: 346-74.

Nisbet, R. G. M., and M. Hubbard (1970) *A Commentary on Horace: Odes*, book 1. Oxford, Clarendon Press.

O'Connor, D. W. (1969). *Peter in Rome: The Literary, Liturgical and Archaeological Evidence*. New York, Columbia University Press.

Obbink, D. (1999) "The Stoic Sage in the Cosmic City." In K. Ierodiakonou (ed.), *Topics in Stoic Philosophy*. Oxford, Clarendon Press, 178-95.

Oliver, J. H. (1953) "The Ruling Power: A Study of the Roman Empire in the Second Century after Christ through the Roman Oration of Aelius Aristides." *Transactions of the American Philosophical Society* 43: 871-1003.

Paulus Orosius (2010). *Seven Books of History against the Pagans* 2.5.5; *PL* 31, 755; *Orosius: Seven Books of History against the Pagans*, trans. A. T. Fear. Translated Texts for Historians 54. Liverpool, Liverpool University Press.

Pétré, H. (1948) *Caritas: Étude sur le vocabulaire latin de la charité chrétienne*. Spicilegium Sacrum Lovaniense 22. Louvain, Spicilegium Sacrum Lovaniense.

Picard, J.-M. (2000) "*Princeps* and *principatus* in the Early Irish Church: A Reassessment." In A. P. Smyth (ed.), *Seanchas: Studies in Early and Medieval Irish Archaeology, History, and Literature in Honour of Francis J. Byrne*. Dublin, Four Courts Press, 146-60.

Pietri, C. (1961) "*Concordia apostolorum* et *renovation urbis* (culte des martyrs et propaganda pontificale)." *École Française de Rome: Mélanges d'Archéologie et d'Histoire* 73: 276-322.

Plumpe, J. (1939) "*Ecclesia mater*." *Transactions and Proceedings of the American Philological Association* 70: 535-55.

Plumpe, J. (1943) "*Mater ecclesia*": *An Inquiry into the Concept of the Church as Mother in Early Christianity*. Studies in Christian Antiquity 5. Washington, DC, Catholic University of America Press.

Ps-Clement (1868) *Letter to James*, trans. A. Cleveland Cox. Ante-Nicene Fathers 8. Buffalo, NY, Christian Literature Co.

Richter, D. S. (2011) *Cosmopolis: Imagining Community in Late Classical Athens and the Early Roman Empire*. Oxford, Oxford University Press.

Smit, J. W. (1971) *Studies on the Language and Style of Columba the Younger (Columbanus)*. Amsterdam, Adolf M. Hakkert.

Suelzer, M. J. (1947) *Julianus Pomerius: The Contemplative Life*. Ancient Christian Writers 4. New York, Newman Press.

Thiel, A. (ed.) (1867) *Epistolae romanorum pontificum genuinae et quae ad eos scriptae sunt: Tomus 1, a S. Hilaro usque ad Pelagium II.* Braunsberg, E. Peter.

Thorsteinsson, R. M. (2010) *Roman Christianity and Roman Stoicism: A Comparative Study of Ancient Morality.* Oxford, Oxford University Press.

Tilley, M. A. (2007) "When Schism Becomes Heresy in Late Antiquity: Developing Doctrinal Deviance in the Wounded Body of Christ." *Journal of Early Christian Studies* 15: 1–21.

Torti, G. (1970) "*Patriae sua gloria Christus*: Aspetti della Romanità cristiana di Prudenzio." *Rendiconti dell'Istituto Lombardo di Scienze e Lèttere* 104: 337–68.

Twomey, V. (1982) *"Apostolikos thronos"*: *The Primacy of Rome as Reflected in the Church History of Eusebius and the Historico-Apologetic Writings of Saint Athanasius the Great.* Münsterische Beiträge zur Theologie 49. Münster, Aschendorff.

Ullmann, W. (1972) "The Cosmic Theme of the *Prima Clementis* and Its Significance for the Concept of Jewish Rulership." *Studia Patristica* 11: 85–91; repr. as section 1 of W. Ullmann, (1975) *The Church and the Law in the Earlier Middle Ages: Selected Essays.* London, Variorum.

Van Rensburg, F. (1992) "The Church as the body of Christ." In P. G. Schrotenboer (ed.), *Catholicity and Secession: A Dilemma?* Kampen, J. H. Kok, 28–44.

Van Unnik, W. C. (1950) "Is 1 Clement Purely Stoic?" *Vigiliae Christianae* 4: 181–9.

Vogt, K. M. (2008) *Law, Reason, and the Cosmic City: Political Philosophy in the Early Stoa.* Oxford, Oxford University Press.

Volp, U. (2012) Review of *Roman Christianity and Roman Stoicism: A Comparative Study of Ancient Morality,* by R. M. Thorsteinsson. *Vigiliae Christianae* 66: 221–4.

Walker, G. S. M. (ed. and trans.) (1957) *Sancti Columbani Opera.* Scriptores Latini Hiberniae 2. Dublin, Dublin Institute for Advanced Studies.

Wright, N. (1997) "Columbanus's *Epistulae*." In M. Lapidge (ed.), *Columbanus: Studies on the Latin Writings.* Woodbridge, Boydell Press, 29–92.

PART II

The Insular Background

The Political Background to Columbanus's Irish Career

DÁIBHÍ Ó CRÓINÍN

The "traditional" account of Columbanus's early years (as recounted by his biographer, Jonas),[1] leading up to his decision to leave his native Leinster and take up the monastic life in the north of Ireland, at Bangor (Co. Down), under the tutelage of Abbot Comgall, presents his motivation as a purely religious one.[2] There are some grounds, however, for thinking that there may have been more to the episode than meets the eye.[3] Although Jonas was not himself an Irishman but an Italian from the Alpine town of Susa,[4] and for that reason probably offers only a very spare account of the saint's Irish background, he does preserve what appears to be some genuine details, for example, concerning the names of some of the disciples (twelve in number) who accompanied Columbanus on his continental mission.[5]

1. On Jonas and the *VC*, see Wood 1982: 63–80; Stancliffe 2001: 189–220; Diem 2007: 521–59; and O'Hara 2009: 126–53.
    2. For a new analysis of the episode, see chapter 4 in this volume, by Elva Johnston. The classic discussion is Charles-Edwards 1976: 43–59, repr. in Wooding 2000: 94–104. For an interesting critique of Charles-Edwards's theory, however, see Johnston 2016: ch. 2. For Columbanus's continental career, see Bullough 1997: 1–28.
    3. See O'Hara 2013: 89–124.
    4. Bullough 1997: 3.
    5. They are listed (in Latinized format) in *VC* I.9, 13, 17, 21 (ed. Krusch 1905: 168, 174, 183–5, 198) as *unus e fratribus, nomen et ipse Columbanus*, further described as *ex eodem genere quo et beatus Columbanus unoque comeatu et nomen ex Hibernia processerat*; Commininus, Eunocus, Equonanus, *ex Scottorum genere*, and a fourth as Breton (or Briton?): *quartumque Gurganum genere Brittonem*; Lua (struck by a boatman with an oar), Domoalis, Gallus, Libranus, and Deicolus. These clearly represent genuine Irish names (with the exception of the Breton, of course): *Colmán, Cuimmíne, Echu, Echaid, Gall, Lugaid* (*Lua* is the hypocoristic or "pet-name" version). The seventeenth-century Irish Franciscan historian John Colgan stated that Gallus and Deicolus were twin brothers (*geminos uterinos fratres*); see Jennings 1948: 117, n. 2. Aidus (*Áed*) is mentioned in Columbanus, *Ep.* 4.2 as having consecrated an altar at Luxeuil (*iuxta altare quod sanctus Aidus episcopus benedixit*). He too presumably accompanied Columbanus from Ireland; see, however, Walker 1957: 31, who remarks: "The alternative is to suppose that the altar was a portable stone, blessed in Ireland, and carried thence to France." It is interesting that bishop Áed is described as *sanctus* by Columbanus. Domoalis may represent Irish *Domnal* (the single final "l" would be an archaism; the name is usually spelled *Domnall* in later Irish sources; perhaps the MS. originally read *Domonalis*, with the n stroke omitted by later scribes?). These names cannot have been conjured up out of nothing by Jonas. On their affiliations see further below. See also Breen 2000.

It is Jonas also who records that Columbanus was by birth a Leinsterman (I.9);[6] there is no reason to doubt the fact.

The most significant political grouping in the southern half of the kingdom of Leinster in Columbanus's time, and the most serious claimants to the overkingship of the entire province, were the Uí Bairrche. Two of their kings, Muiredach Mo-Sníthech and Móenach mac Cáirthinn, were numbered among the provincial kings in an archaic (early seventh-century?) poem embedded in the earliest Leinster genealogies, a document that lists those earliest Leinster kings who also claimed to have ruled as "high kings" of Ireland (kings of Tara) in pre-Christian times.[7] The two are listed in the genealogies as son and grandson of the eponymous ancestor Dáire Barrach, and extravagant claims are made for them both; but we know nothing more about them, so their claims cannot be assessed.[8]

The most important Uí Bairrche ruler in the period considered here was Cormac mac Diarmata, who appears to have enjoyed an unusually long reign (though his death is not recorded in any of the annalistic collections). He figures prominently in the early Leinster hagiography, appearing both as patron and as enemy of various holy men in the saints' Lives.[9] The hagiography associated with rival population groups such as the Uí Cennselaig and Dál Cormaic depicts him as a harrier of their holy men and the principal impediment to their political ambitions. In the *Life of Fintan/Munnu* of Tech Munnu (Taghmon, Co. Wexford), for example, it is stated that Cormac was held captive for a time by one Colmán son of Cormac Camshrón of the Uí Cennselaig,[10] while the *Life of Abbán* (representing Cormac's other chief rivals, the Dál Cormaic) depicts him as a persecutor of that saint.[11] In much the same way, the *Life of Cainnech* of Achad Bó (Aghaboe, Co. Kilkenny) represents Cormac as a barbarian king,

---

6. *VC* I.3: 157: *Relicto ergo natali solo, quem Lagenorum terram incolae nuncupant.*

7. O'Brien 1962: 8–9, beg. *Nidu dír dermait*; see Ó Cróinín 1995: 54ff., 2005: 193–4; 2017: 76–7; and Smyth 1974–1975: 502–3, at 518–9.

8. The genealogists state that the kingship of Leinster descended in fact through the line of Fíacc, another son of Dáire, which is certainly the impression given by the surviving texts; see O'Brien, *Corpus*, 47 (*Ó Fiacc hUí Maíli-humae ₇ a quibus ind ríg*) ("from Fiacc are the hUí M-U, from whom are the kings"), compared with O'Brien, *Corpus*, 10–1. However, allowance must be made for the strong possibility that the earlier traditions were tampered with by later keepers of the *senchas*.

9. On the problem of dating the earliest Irish saints' lives, see Sharpe 1991.

10. See Plummer 1910: ii, 102–3: *Rex aquilonalium Laginensium, Colum filius Cormachi, habebat in vinculis Cormacum filium Diarmoda regis Hua Kennselach, id est australium Laginensium, uolens eum occidere, quem apprehendit in insidiis.* It is conceivable, of course, that a young Cormac may have been held as a political hostage for a time by the rival Uí Cennselaig kings.

11. Plummer 1910: i, 23: *Quodam tempore Cormacus filius Diarmoda, rex Hua Cennselach [sic], Camross, cellam sancti Abani, predauit, volens familiam eius de ea expellere, et villam ipsam in sua potestate habere.* For the Abbán material I have drawn on unpublished research of my own.

reflecting the image that his Osraige rivals would have liked to see.[12] But the most striking testimony of his actual success is the fact that later Uí Cennselaig propagandists resorted to the brazen fiction of claiming him as one of their own, despite the fact that the genealogies leave us in no doubt as to his Uí Bairrche affiliations. Clearly, then, Cormac was a formidable player in the political game,[13] and though we must be careful about rushing to conclusions about Leinster politics in the absence of any continuous and early annalistic record,[14] it does not seem unreasonable to assume that Cormac was a man to be reckoned with.

Not the least of his claims to distinction is the fact that he appears to have died in his bed (although there is no mention of his death in the annals) after retiring to the monastery of Bangor (Co. Down), the same monastery where Columbanus spent most of his formative years.[15] The choice of location seems surprising at first, but there are several early connections between Leinster and Ulster centering on the Uí Bairrche. Hence when Columbanus left his native Leinster to join the community of Comgall at Bangor, he may well have encountered Cormac mac Diarmata there—if indeed he had not met him before that—since they must have been near contemporaries. In fact, the Leinster genealogies state explicitly that Bangor possessed extensive properties in Uí Bairrche territory, granted, it is said, by Cormac.[16] The reason for Cormac's grants is not known,

12. Plummer 1910: i, 164: *Cum autem sanctus Cainnicus in australes partes Laginie, id est Hua Cennselaich, venisset, vbi erat curia magna apud regem Cormacum [filium Dyarmici], quidam puer paruulus ductus est ad mortem crudelem, id est gall-cherd. Videns hoc sanctus Cainnicus esse horribile opus, postulauit a rege puerum liberari; sed non inpetrauit. . . . Hic est Dolue Lachdere, quem rex Cormacus sanct Cainnico obtulit, cuius ciuitas dicitur Ceall Dolue.*

13. For the genealogical affiliations, see O'Brien 1962: 11 [117 a 49], 46 [121 a 52 and ab 49]; 52 [122 ab 24]; 53 [122 ab 44, 55; 122 ac 42]; 54 [122 ba 8, 19; 122 bb 7]; 340 [LL 316 a 51]. Strange to say, Cormac does not figure in the lists compiled by Byrne and Doherty 1989: 200, in which there is a large gap in the chronological list of early Leinster kings.

14. "The Húi Bairrchi find no mention in the annalistic record for the period prior to the seventh century, simply because Leinster at this time had no annals of its own." Smyth 1974–1975: 522.

15. According to Jonas (*VC* I.3: 156–8), Columbanus spent his initial years in the north with Sinlanus/Sillanus/Sinilis/Sinlán alias Mo-Sinu maccu Min, after which he moved to the monastery of Bangor itself; the site has been identified as Crannach Dúin Lethglaisse (Cranny Island, in the southwestern arm of Strangford Lough, a few miles from Downpatrick); see Ó Cróinín 1982: 281–95; repr. Ó Cróinín 2005: 35–47. Mo-Sinu is the hypocoristic form of the name; cf. Mo-Lua < Lugaid, and the form *Lua* given by Jonas as one of Columbanus's disciples. Cranny Island appears to have been a separate affiliation of Bangor. Mo-Sinu is listed fourth in the poem *in memoriam abbatum nostrorum* in the famous Antiphonary of Bangor; see Warren 1893– 95: 4, 33. There is no good evidence to support the idea that another Sinilis (Sinell of Cleenish, Co. Fermanagh) was the person with whom Columbanus spent those early years. See, however, chapter 5 in this volume, by Alex Woolf.

16. O'Brien 1962, 54: "Cormac [mac] Diarmata ro idpair Imblech Ech do Chomgall Bendchuir, is leo ó Beluch Forcitail co Bannai" ("It was Cormac m. D. who granted I. E. to Comgall of Bangor; to them belongs [the territory] from B. F. to the Bann". It is generally assumed that Imblech Ech was in Leinster; it is not clear, however, whether the other two sites named are in Leinster or in Ulster. The form *Bannai* may indicate the latter (i.e., in reference to the river Bann). Note the archaic form of Cormac's name

but the connection appears to have continued into the seventh century and beyond: the later foundation of Dísert Diarmata (Casteldermot, Co. Kildare) was regarded as a daughter-house of Bangor; its founder (after whom it was named), Diarmait ua Áedo Róin (d. 825), was the grandson of Áed Rón (d. 735), Dál Fiatach king of Ulster, whose father in turn was nicknamed Bécc Bairrche. The Dál Fiatach connection is noteworthy also, and we shall meet it again, but traces of such early contacts appear to have survived through later centuries as well; it has been suggested, for example, that the military and political connections between Ulster and Leinster kings in the eleventh century, during the reigns of Niall Mac Eochada and Diarmait Mac Maíl na mBó, may well be a continuation of such earlier alliances.[17] Thus the fact that Columbanus should have considered faraway Bangor as a possible location in which to advance his studies may not have been altogether fortuitous.

The close alliance of church and politics in Columbanus's time (end of the sixth century), is strikingly indicated by the fact that the opening section of the Uí Bairrche genealogies[18] gives the name of the eponymous founder, Dáire Barrach, followed by a list of the most prominent saints affiliated with the tribe. These included Tigernach of Clones (Co. Monaghan), Fiacc and Fiachra of Slébte (Sletty, Co. Carlow), Mac Táil in Old Kilcullen (Co. Kildare), Mac Cuill in the Isle of Man (*Manaind*) and Émíne in *Letha*.[19] Another important indication of early Uí Bairrche importance in the politico-ecclesiastical sphere is the fact that the dossier of historical materials relating to Saint Patrick preserved in the famous Book of Armagh (c. 800)[20]—some of it of very early origin, perhaps going back even beyond the sixth century—preserved a tradition that the first bishop in Leinster was an Uí Bairrche saint, Fiacc of Slébte.[21] The tradition proved too strong even for the later propagandists to eradicate and was

here; the son-father form, without intervening *mac* but with the father's name in the genitive case, is an early usage.

17. See Byrne 1973: 146.

18. O'Brien 1962: 46.

19. Presumably some location in Ireland, though the name is often used in early sources to denote Armorica. Is it conceivable that perhaps this Émíne preceded Columbanus to the Continent? It would go some way to explaining why Columbanus apparently opted for Brittany as his first port of call on the Continent; he certainly had at least one Breton companion among his followers, for example, Winioc (*VC* I.15, ed. Krusch 1905: 178, and *VC* I.17, ed. Krusch 1905: 182); a later abbot of Bobbio, Uorgustus, must almost certainly have been Breton also. A manuscript of his has survived. See Lowe 1947: no. 365: *De arca domni Vorgusti abbatis* (Turin, Archivo di Stato IB, II. 27, fol. 1v); see also John 1996: 239–43, pl. 19. On the Breton links see further Ian Wood, chapter 6 in this volume.

20. See Bieler 1979.

21. Bieler 1979: 92. *Dubthoch macc Lugir, poetam optimum, apud quem tunc temporis ibi erat quidam adoliscens poeta nomine Feec, qui postea mirabilis episcopus fuit, cuius reliquiae adorantur hi Sleibti* (Muirchú, *Vita Patricii*, I.19).

preserved in the *Vita Tripartita* (c. 900 or later), which records Uí Bairrche and Uí Cennselaig rivalry. The *Vita* states that Óengus mac Meicc Erca (a brother of the Sletty bishop) slew Crimthann mac Cennselaig (d. 483) as vengeance for the exile of his people at the hands of the Uí Cennselaig.[22] That there was some sub-stance to the tradition of animosity is supported by the fact that other traditions of Uí Bairrche expulsion and exile are also found in historical material relating to the Déisi of Munster.[23] Notwithstanding the lack of a contemporary annal-istic record for the province, mid-sixth-century Leinster politics have all the appearance of having been volatile, to say the least.

By the early decades of the seventh century, however, all this had changed, and with the rise of the Uí Dúnlainge in north Leinster and the Uí Cennselaig in the south, the fortunes of the Uí Bairrche began to wane; they were a spent polit-ical force by the end of the seventh century.[24] This decline in their fortunes may perhaps be explained by the fact that Cormac mac Diarmata was apparently ousted from his kingship of the Uí Bairrche and forced into political exile in the north of the country, and his successors appear not to have recovered from that setback. The Dál Fiatach affiliations noted previously may well have saved him from a bloodier fate. There is a hint of the dangerous political waters swirling around Cormac in a further remark of the genealogists, that one Rotha mac Óengusa (an internal political rival, to judge from the sources) slew an uniden-tified Áed "in spite of the king's protection" (*di muin Chormaic ind ríg*).[25] That Cormac eventually succumbed to the intrigues of his opponents seems more than likely. The pious belief that he might be numbered among those "kings that opted out,"[26] forsaking the rough-and-tumble of political rivalries and cutthroat politics for a quiet and reclusive life in a monastery, is scarcely credible.[27] He may have had no choice in the matter. Cormac's military defeat at this time would coincide exactly with the beginning of the period of political decline for the Uí Bairrche; it may also have coincided with the time of Columbanus's

22. Mulchrone 1939: 116–7; Smyth 1974–1975: 518.
23. See Meyer 1901: 101–35, at 106, 1907: 135–42, at 137.
24. For the later history of the Uí Bairrche, see Smyth 1982: esp. 60.
25. O'Brien 1962: 52. Another brother of this Rotha, Tadc mac Óengusa, is described as holding terri-tory *hi crích Úa mBairrchi Tíre* ("in the territory of the inland Uí Bairrche"), in O'Brien 1962: 53.
26. See Stancliffe 1983: 154–76.
27. There is a certain irony in the fact that the more cynical interpretation of the evidence (that Cormac was forced out after defeat in battle) was offered by the Jesuit Bollandist scholar Père Paul Grosjean 1963: 55: "Ni l'un ni l'autre des deux hagiographes ne note que la conversion de Cormac, fils de Diarmait, et sa retraite dans un monastère lointain aient eu pour occasion immédiate, sinon pour cause, sa défaite, conduisant à son exil; mais cette hypothèse ne manque pas de plausibilité" ("neither the one nor the other hagiographer has considered the possibility that Cormac's exile so far from home may have been brought about, immediately or otherwise, by his [military] defeat; but the hypothesis is not lacking in plausibility").

departure from his native Leinster, as recorded by his biographer, Jonas. What I am suggesting, in other words, is that Columbanus was not just a contemporary of Cormac mac Diarmata but had close personal and dynastic links to the king. There is no explicit reference by Jonas to Columbanus being of royal origin, though the absence of any such statement need not necessarily preclude such a connection. That Columbanus was put to study while still young may bear out such a surmise; contemporary Irish evidence suggests that younger male siblings were sometimes viewed as potential rivals in kingship by their older brothers (or their stepmothers!) and therefore consigned to the monastery.[28] Donald Bullough's argument,[29] that he was not of sufficiently aristocratic lineage to warrant his being given out in fosterage, is refuted by himself when he remarks that such an arrangement could be with a religious foster-father; in fact Columbanus undertook just such a fosterage when he joined the company of Sinilis (later abbot of Bangor).[30]

If it is the case that Columbanus came of Uí Bairrche royal stock, perhaps a member of a cadet branch that was perceived by political rivals to be too close for comfort to Cormac and his family, then he may have been forced by the political circumstances of his time to join his deposed relative in exile. Certainly his bearing when in Burgundy and later in Italy suggests that he was used to dealing with kings. There would be nothing unusual about the scenario; far from it. The history of the islands in the sixth and seventh centuries is littered with stories of just such political exile being forced on those, clerics and laymen, unfortunate enough to lose out in "the game of thrones."[31] That Cormac placed himself under the protection of a Dál Fiatach king in Ulster—as far away as possible on the island of Ireland as he could safely remove himself—can be explained by the contemporary politics of the Leinster province. That Columbanus placed himself under the rule of the chief Dál Fiatach monastery (though Comgall was himself of the Dál nAraidi)[32] may be another reflection of that tightly knit world

---

28. See Ó Cróinín 1995, 55: Fáelán mac Colmáin (d. 666?), later king of Uí Dúnlainge, spent time during his youth in the monastery of Glendalough while his older brother, Máel Umai, ruled. The narrative in the *Vita* of Kevin is explicit that the incarceration was for Fáelán's own protection; see Plummer 1910: i, 250ff.

29. Bullough 1997: 3.

30. Bullough 1997: 3: "It is clear, however, from early and reliable *uitae sanctorum*, including Adomnán's *Vita S. Columbae* III.2 (ed. Anderson, 184–85), that the *aite* (Latin *nutritor*) of a *dalta* (Latin *alumnus*) could be a priest or monk; and Jonas—unsurprisingly—could simply have failed to recognise a distinctively Irish social custom."

31. See Ó Cróinín 2004, 2007.

32. The rival ambitions of Dál nAraide and Dál Fiatach are well brought out in O'Rahilly 1946: 346–52. On relations between Comgall and other prominent religious contemporaries, see below. The subject is one that would merit a detailed study.

of Irish church and politics at the close of the sixth century, in which events in the political arena often had consequences in the religious sphere.

Of the sixty-two names in the Ulster king-lists, only ten belonged to the Dál nAraidi; the rest were Dál Fiatach kings.[33] One of these had good claim to be the most powerful king in early medieval Ireland. Báetán mac Cairill reigned for only nine years (572–581) and died in unexplained circumstances (the Annals of Ulster report his *mors*, but not a violent death, *iugulatio*), but in that short time he did much to restore the military power and prestige of the Ulaid. Having apparently succeeded his brother in the kingship in 572,[34] he is said to have exacted hostages from as far away as Munster (interestingly enough at Imblech Ibair, Emly, Co. Tipperary, not the later "traditional" capital of Cashel) and to have received tribute from the rest of Ireland and from Scotland at his fortress (Dún Báetáin) in Lethet (Knocklayd, Co. Antrim?).[35] He is also credited with having "cleared" the Isle of Man (*is leis glanta Manand*), perhaps meaning that he had expelled the Conailli Muirtheimne, whose main branch occupied territories in north Louth and south Down and one of whose grandees is commemorated on an ogam inscription on the Isle of Man.[36] Báetán seems also to have taken the opportunity offered by the Dál Riata settlement in western Scotland to force the Dál Riata king to pay homage at Islandmagee, County Antrim. There is a hint of these events in the various annalistic references to military activity in this area during Báetán's reign: an expedition (*periculum*) to Man in 577 by the Ulaid, followed by their retreat (*reuersio*) the following year. The annals also record a victory by the Dál Riata king Áedán mac Gabráin in another Man battle in 582, the year after Báetán's death. Báetán was succeeded in the overkingship of Ulster by the notorious Cruithin king, Áed Dub mac Suibni (Aidus Niger in Adomnán of Iona's *Vita Columbae*).[37] The annalists say that Man was abandoned by the Irish (Gáidil) two years after Báetán's death, and this undoubtedly

---

33. O'Rahilly 1946: 347.

34. For Demmán's genealogy, see O'Brien 1962: 322 [161 b 49]; the text is headed *Geneloige rí nUlad* ("The Genealogy of the Kings of Ulster"). Demmán's and Báetán's father, Cairell, is there said to be the man "who believed in Patrick" (*qui credidit Patricio*), a curious phrase. Bullough 1997: 3 speculated that "it is a reasonable inference from the scanty evidence that Columbanus was born shortly before or shortly before 550, into a landowning family of below the highest rank, *which may well have been first-generation christian*" (emphasis added). I have not seen the arguments regarding Columbanus's origins in de Vogüé 1988: 72.

35. O'Brien 1962: 406: *Is dó ro cét ic brith chísa Muman dó fothuaid* ("Of him it was sung while he brought tribute north from Munster"), followed by a verse from a poem recounting his epic deeds. The full text of the poem was published by Skene 1867: 127ff. and Dobbs 1930: 321 (references in Byrne 1965: 57, n. 74).

36. Byrne 1965: 56, n. 63.

37. Anderson and Anderson 1961: 278ff. (*Life of Columba* I.35).

signals the first resurgence of Dál Riata independence after the demise of their principal foe.

But a grudging respect for Báetán persisted even after his death; the Ulster tract reckoned seven prehistoric and early historical kings of the Ulaid as kings of Ireland as well, and Báetán's claim was still regarded as strong enough in the eleventh century to be taken seriously by the genealogists, who admitted him (alongside Brian Bóruma) as an exception to the "rule" that all post-Patrician high kings were of the Uí Néill.[38] It is against this political background that we should set the arrival of Cormac mac Diarmata in Ulster, and perhaps also that of Columbanus. Far from arriving into a placid and tranquil retirement, neither man can have been oblivious to the constant warfare and the seemingly endless military campaigns that were taking place around them during those years. Hence, when it came to negotiating the murderous rivalries of Merovingian kings, Columbanus would have been well versed in the necessary techniques.

Báetán mac Cairill's military exploits are symptomatic of a wider perspective in the period; the Irish were in close contact with all the other peoples of the British Isles—Picts, Angles, and Britons—and were deeply involved in their respective political tussles. The Annals of Ulster, for example, record a joint expedition to the Western Isles of the southern Uí Néill and the Dál Riata, while a northern Uí Néill prince,[39] Máel Umai mac Báetáin (described as Máel hUmai *herois*), fought alongside the Irish of Scottish Dál Riata against the northern English kingdom of Bernicia at the battle of Degsastan and lived to tell the tale; he died in 610.[40] He is described in the genealogies as *in rígfhéinnid* ("leader of the royal warrior-band"),[41] and he clearly earned his reputation: the Anglo-Saxon Chronicle and Bede (*Historia ecclesiastica* I. 34; *Recapit. chron.* s.a. 603) recorded the clash at Degsastan (possibly Dawston in Liddlesdale), in the north of England, as "The Battle of the Saxons" (*Cath Saxonum*),[42] in

---

38. *Et sciendum est quia non alicuius seminis nisi ex semine eiusdem post Patricium Hiberniam quis tenuit exceptis duobus, id est, Báetán et Brian.* However, they added: *Sed alii Bóetán apud magnos reges non numerant* ("but others do not reckon B. amongst the great kings"): O'Brien 1962: 123.

39. Unless there is a mistake in the texts and the genealogists have confused the various Báetáns and Máel hUmais of their sources. For another view of Báetán's family background, see chapter 5 in this volume, by Alex Woolf.

40. See Moisl 1983: 103–26. In fact, Moisl's account goes back into the sixth century.

41. O'Brien 1962: 135. It is difficult to know if there is any significance in the fact that immediately after Máel hUmai's description as *rígfhéinnid* there follows a reference to Colmán Rímid, Uí Néill claimant to the high kingship (d. AD 604), there described as "father of Fín, mother of Fland Fína son of Osuiu, king of the Saxons" (*athair Fína, máthair í-side Flaind Fína mic Ossu regis Saxonum*). On Fland Fína (alias Aldfrith), see Ireland 1999. Given the obvious involvement of both brothers in Anglo-Saxon (specifically Northumbrian) affairs in the opening years of the seventh century, there may have been some logic, after all, behind the attack on those Uí Néill territories in AD 684 by Ecgfrith, king of Northumbria.

42. Kirby 1991; 2nd rev. ed. 2000: 59.

which the chief protagonist was Áedán mac Gabráin, clearly at the head of an army of Scottish Dál Riata in alliance with the Northern Uí Néill, *ubi cecidit Eanfrith frater Etalfraich la Maeluma mac Baedan, in quo uictus erat* ("where Eanfrith, brother of Æthelfrith, fell at the hands of Máel Umai, in which he was defeated").[43] This marked the final stage in what had clearly been an ambitious military career on the part of the same Áedán. The sketchy details that we have of the period, however, suggest that Áedán may not have been the first Irish king to try his luck in neighboring Britain; he almost certainly was preceded in this policy by Báetán mac Cairill.

For some years before 600 the Irish of Scottish Dál Riata had been campaigning far beyond the frontiers of their western kingdom and making occasional forays into southern Pictland as far as the Anglian kingdom of Northumbria (Northumberland). In 598 Áedán's son Domangart was slain fighting the Angles of Bernicia, the northernmost part of that kingdom. Doubtless all these maneuverings were the result of Dál Riata involvement in the interdynastic rivalries among the neighboring Anglo-Saxon kingdoms in particular that saw "regime change" take place there on an almost regular basis. Fortune favored the Angles, however, in that it produced in Æthelfrith a man who brought together the previously separated and rival subkingdoms of Bernicia and Deira and led them to military and political hegemony in the region.[44] Bede thought of him as a Northumbrian King Saul, so great were his conquests of neighboring British territory[45] It appears certain, in fact, that it was Anglian advances into neighboring British territories that stirred initial disquiet among the Irish in Dál Riata. Many of the rulers of the small and vulnerable British kingdoms around the region of Strathclyde, with its capital at Dumbarton, must have felt threatened by the Bernicians. To the south of Strathclyde was the kingdom of Rheged, stretching along the Eden valley as far as the Solway. To the south of them again was the even smaller kingdom of Elmet (the name of which survives in place names of the West Riding in Yorkshire). Matters may have come to a head, however, when Dál Riata and Bernician ambitions began to converge on the territories bordering on the Forth. As the tiny British kingdoms fell each in turn to Bernician aggression, Áedán mac Gabráin may have felt that he had no alternative but to try to deliver a knockout blow (in alliance with the Uí Néill, it appears) to his Anglian rivals before their overweening ambition got the better of him and his people.

43. See Stokes 1993: 140–1. Note that the Anglo-Saxon Chronicle, in its report of the battle, stated that another brother of Æthelfrith's, Theodbald, was slain *cum comitatu suo*; see Whitelock 1955: 147; Whitelock, Douglas, and Tucker 1961: 15.

44. For what follows I have drawn principally on Kirby 2000: 58–62. Discussion also in Yorke 1992.

45. Bede, *HE* i.34: 71. See Johnson 1987: 5–17 (ref. in Kirby 2000: 205).

The Battle of Degsastan, however, proved disastrous for him and for Scottish Dál Riata. Columbanus would have been an observer of the political developments that took place in the decade or more leading up to these events and immediately prior to his own departure for the Continent. He cannot have been greatly surprised, therefore, by what he encountered in the Merovingian kingdoms.

That the political alliances among the Irish, Scottish Dál Riata, and smaller British kingdoms persisted after Degsastan is clear, however, from the Irish accounts of a later clash, the battle of Fid Eoin (in northern Ireland or in England?). The same Annals of Tigernach that reported on the Degsastan disaster present the following account for the year 628:

> The battle of Fid Eoin in which Máel Cáich mac Scandail, king of the Cruithin, was victor. Dál Riata were defeated. Connaid Cerr, king of Dál Riata, fell. And Dícuil mac Echach, king of a Cruithin people, fell and the grandsons of Aédán [mac Gabráin], that is, Rigullán mac Conaing and Fáilbe mac Echach and Osric son of Alfred, royal heir (*ætheling*) of the Saxons, along with a large slaughter of their own people.[46]

Two features stand out. First, this was a large encounter, with serious losses on both sides. Equally striking is the array of different political factions present; alongside the Cruithin of Ulster and a subgroup of Latharna (who gave their name to the Co. Antrim port town of Larne), led by their king Dícuil, the Dál Riata were also involved. But of the three names given after the *nepotes Aedan*, two are remarkable: Oisric son of Alfred must have been an Anglo-Saxon royal, "doubtless one of the Bernician princes who fled to the Dál Riata Scots during the reign of Edwin."[47] These exiled Northumbrians have been much discussed; Oisric was one of many such political asylum seekers who feature in Irish and Anglo-Saxon sources of the period.[48] Not previously noticed, however (to my knowledge), is the ethnic composition of the name Rígullán mac Conaing. Neither name is Irish; Rígullán must be an Irish rendering of the British name Riguallaun (Welsh Rhiwallon), while the patronymic Conaing must be derived from the Old English form *cyning* ("king").[49] Here, then, was an individual of

---

46. *Cath Fedha Eoin in quo Maelcaith mac Scandail rex Cruithniu uictor erat. Dal Riada cecidit. Condadh Cerr rí Dal Riada cecidit ₇ Dicull mac Eachach ri ceneoil Cruithne cecidit et nepotes Aedan ceciderunt, id est Rigillan mac Conaing ₇ Failbe mac Eachach ₇ Oisiricc mac Albruit rigdomna Saxan cum strage maxima suorum.* Cited in Moisl 1983: 105; there is a parallel account in the Annals of Ulster.

47. Byrne 1965: 47. See also Hunter Blair 1950: 245ff.; and Jackson 1964: 20–62, at 27–8. For the MS. see Hunter Blair 1959: fol. 128v. Discussion in Yorke 1992.

48. See esp. Moisl 1983: passim (esp. 105ff.); and Ó Cróinín 2007: passim. It is possible that the symbol for *id est* (.i.) as an & abbreviation in the annal.

49. See O'Rahilly 1946: 362–3. According to O'Rahilly "the earliest known bearer of the name is Conaing, son of Aédán [mac Gabráin]," with ref. to AU 621. Regarding the southern Uí Néill kingdom

probable mixed parentage, British and Anglo-Saxon, another victim of the merciless merry-go-round of dynastic rivalries that resulted in constant "regime change" in all the kingdoms in these islands. Clearly, the political ebb and flood tides of the period swept up all the different populations of the Irish Sea area at one stage or another. Some indeed were swept away.

There is a remarkable echo of these events in the deeds described in the bardic poems traditionally ascribed to the Welsh poets Aneirin and Taliesin, which record how four British kings, Rhydderch, Urbgen (Urien), Gwallawg, and Morcant all campaigned (toward the close of the sixth and into the early seventh centuries) against a series of Bernician kings.[50] Taliesin describes Urien as "Rheged's protector," while Gwallawg is portrayed as "judge over Elmet"; Morcant may have been a ruler of the Strathclyde Britons.[51] The poems speak of fierce fighting and severe losses among the Angles, and the campaign culminated in a siege of the Bernician citadel at Bamburgh. But jealousy of Urien's military prowess and renown on Morcant's part supposedly caused him to assassinate the commander of the British forces, with catastrophic consequences.[52] The northern British kingdom of Rheged never really recovered from the disaster.

There may be some connection between these events and similar ones recorded about Baétán's successor as overking of Ulster, Fiachna mac Báetáin of Dál nAraidi, who also claimed authority over Dál Riata and, like his predecessor, campaigned also in Scotland. Indeed, a list of saga texts (*prímscéla*) known to the medieval storytellers includes one (unfortunately lost) with the title *Sluagad Fiachna meic Báitáin co Dún nGuaire i Saxanaib* (The hosting of Fiachna mac Báetáin to Dún Guaire in the kingdom of the Saxons).[53] This may be the event recorded in the Annals of Ulster 623: *Expugnatio Ratho Guali* (The siege of Ráith

---

of Brega (Co. Meath), Francis John Byrne has remarked: "Anglo-Saxon influence in Brega itself seems attested by the tendency to alliteration on the letter *C* in the pedigree of the North Brega dynasty from the seventh to the ninth century, as well as by the appearance there of the name Conaing (the first to bear it being a king of Brega who died in 662), which is a borrowing of the Anglo-Saxon *cyning* 'king'" (1973: 111–2).

50. Williams 1938; Jackson 1969. Williams 1960; Caerwyn Williams 1968. On the vexed question of dating for these poems, see the essays by Marged Haycock, Nerys-Ann Jones, Philip Dunshea, Oliver Padel, Thomas Owen Clancy, and John Koch in Woolf 2013.

51. One of Áedán mac Gabráin's grandsons was called Morcant (AU 662), while another bore the name Artúr (Old Welsh Arthur < Latin Artorius), doubtless after the famous hero of British legend. Áedán himself appears to have had as a wife a daughter of the king of the Britons of Strathclyde; see O'Rahilly 1946: 361–2. I have in mind to publish a study of Arthurian traditions in Ireland elsewhere. For a useful summary of (then) recent research, see Dark 2000. Dooley 1993 is concerned principally with the evidence of later medieval Irish poetry.

52. On the historicity or otherwise of the poems, cf. Charles-Edwards 1978 and Dumville 1988.

53. Best, Bergin, O'Brien, and O'Sullivan 1954–1965, 1983: iv, 837.

Guali), and annals and saga text apparently refer to an expedition by Fiachnae against the citadel of the Northumbrian kings at Bamburgh Castle (called Dún Guaire, "Guaire's Fort," in Irish sources).[54] Clearly the fierce political rivalries of Irish, British, Pictish, and Anglo-Saxon kings had not been finally settled by the Northumbrian victory at Degsastan in 603.

Whether Fiachna's campaign was successful is not clear; there is no record of his siege of Bamburgh in any surviving English sources, while he himself fell in 626 and his Dál Fiatach successor followed him to the grave shortly afterward. Their early deaths and the long-fought campaigns against the Northumbrian Angles clearly sapped the resources of these Ulster kings, in turn bringing about a further contraction of Ulaid power to the point where the Isle of Man (previously under Irish control) was occupied by the Northumbrian king Edwin (possibly c. 620).

For Columbanus's time in the north of Ireland, however, Báetán mac Cairill's successes are perhaps best judged by the effect they had on his enemies, particularly the Uí Néill and Dál Riata. In order to establish a "Second Front" against him, Áedán mac Gabráin made an alliance with the Uí Néill; this alliance was forged through the good offices of Columba/Colum Cille, whose first cousin was the northern Uí Néill high king. The occasion of the agreement was the famous convention of Druim Cett, now Mullagh or Daisy Hill, near Limavady in County Derry, in 590;[55] this was a gathering of kings and clerics from Ireland and Scottish Dál Riata, with Colum Cille and others in attendance. The annals are singularly uninformative about the event, and Adomnán, who mentions it in passing in his *Life of Columba*, says nothing about its purpose.[56] As Francis John Byrne remarked:

> It is also rather remarkable (though it may be pure accident) that although Adomnán has so much to say about the north of Ireland and often mentions the Cruithin and their kings (many of whom, as we have seen, became kings of Ulster), he never once mentions the Ulaid by name nor any of the Dál Fiatach kings. Could it be that the memory of Báetán was too delicate a subject for the propagandist of the Uí Néill high-kingship?[57]

54. For discussion, see Jackson 1964: 20–62, at 27–8.

55. AD 590 (instead of AD 575) is the date proposed by Sharpe 1995: 27. It has been generally accepted.

56. Byrne 1965: 46. For a good discussion, see Bannerman 1974: 157–70. In the *Vita Columbae*, however, Adomnán appears to go out of his way to emphasize the close relations that existed between Columba and Comgell; see Anderson and Anderson 1961: 314–7 (*Vita Columbae* I.49) (Columba and Comgell together at Druim Cett), and ibid, 500: *Alio in tempore quattuor ad sanctum visitandum Columbam monasteriorum sancti fundatores de Scotia transmeantes in Hinba eum invenerunt insula, quarum inlustrium vocabula Comgellus mocu Aridi, Cainnechus mocu Dalon, Brendenus mocu Alti, Cormac nepos Leathain* (*Vita Columbae* III.17).

57. Byrne 1965: 46.

ǀ

Later Irish tradition presented the convention at Druim Cett as the occasion when Columba saved the poets of Ireland from disbandment. It seems more likely, however, that the convention settled the vexed question of the relationship between the Dál Riata and the Uí Néill, while cementing the military alliance against Báetán mac Cairill. With Báetán's (untimely?) death, however, Áedán mac Gabráin became the principal Irish player in these dangerous political games.

The arrangement arrived at between the Dál Riata and Uí Néill at Druim Cett survived intact for fifty years, a considerable achievement for the time. The events, as they subsequently played out, are neatly summarized by Columba's earliest biographer, Cumméne Find, seventh abbot of Iona (657–669), who depicts the saint strictly warning the Dál Riata against breaking this alliance with the Uí Néill, and for as long as they abided by his warning they were successful. But a shift in their political alignment caused them to reverse their previous hostility toward the Ulaid, and they joined in alliance with them against their recent allies. In the great battle of Mag Roth (Moyra, Co. Down) in 637 the Uí Néill king Domnall mac Áedo meic Ainmirech (the only seventh-century king to be accorded the title *rex Hiberniae* by the annalists) annihilated the Cruithin king Congal Clóen and his Dál Riata allies. The battle marked a turning point for the Ulaid and signaled the end of their hopes of restoring Ulster to its ancient prestige.[58]

"If the situation in the sixth century was much more fluid than has hitherto been supposed, the political divisions of the country nevertheless serve to highlight the peculiar cultural unity of Ireland both in the ecclesiastical and secular spheres."[59] By that time, however, Columbanus was long gone out of Ireland, while Cormac mac Diarmata and Báetán mac Cairill, the leading political figures of his time, north and south, had passed away. Whatever impact the careers of those two remarkable men may have had on him personally, we may be sure that Columbanus brought with him to the Continent not just a burning zeal for conversion and the spreading of the gospel, but also a deep-rooted understanding of how the worlds of politics and religion were inseparable, not just in his native Ireland but also in the new world in which he arrived in 590–591.

BIBLIOGRAPHY

Anderson, A. O., and M. O. Anderson (eds.) (1961) *Adomnan's Life of Columba*. Edinburgh, Thomas Nelson.

58. Ó Cróinín 1995,2nd ed. (2016): 74.
59. Byrne 1965: 52.

Bannerman, J. (1974) *Studies in the History of Dalriada*. Edinburgh, Scottish Academic Press.

Best, R. I., O. Bergin, M. A. O'Brien, and A. O'Sullivan (eds.) (1954–1965, 1983) *Lebar na Nuachongbála, Formerly the Book of Leinster*. 6 vols. Dublin, Dublin Institute for Advanced Studies.

Bieler, L. (ed.) (1979) *The Patrician Texts in the Book of Armagh*. Scriptores Latini Hiberniae 9. Dublin, Dublin Institute for Advanced Studies.

Breen, A. (2000) "Columbanus' Monastic Life and Education in Ireland." *Seanchas Ardmhacha* 23.2: 1–21.

Bullough, D. (1997) "The Career of Columbanus." In M. Lapidge (ed.), *Columbanus: Studies on the Latin Writings*. Woodbridge, Boydell Press, 1–28.

Byrne, F. J. (1965) "The Ireland of St Columba." In J. L. McCracken (ed.), *Historical Studies V: Papers Read to the 6th Irish Conference of Historians*. London, Bowes and Bowes, 37–58.

Byrne, F. J. (1973) *Irish Kings and High-kings*. London, Batsford.

Byrne, F. J., and C. Doherty (eds.) (1989). *A New History of Ireland*, vol. ix, *Genealogies and Maps*. Oxford, Oxford University Press.

Caerwyn Williams, J. E. (1968) *The Poems of Taliesin*. Dublin, Dublin Institute for Advanced Studies.

Carley, J. P., and F. Ruddy (eds.) (1993) *Arthurian Literature*, vol. XII. Woodbridge, Boydell.

Charles-Edwards, T. M. (1976) "The Social Background to Irish *Peregrinatio.*" *Celtica* 11, 43–59; repr. in Jonathan Wooding (ed.), *The Otherworld Voyage in Early Irish Literature: An Anthology of Criticism*. Dublin, Four Courts Press, 2000, 94–104.

Charles-Edwards, T. M. (1978) "The Authenticity of the *Gododdin*: An Historian's View." In R. Bromwich and R. B. Jones (eds.), *Astudiaethau ar yr Hengerdd: Studies in Old Welsh Poetry*. Cardiff, Gwasg Prifysgol Cymru, 44–71.

Dark, K. (2000). "A Famous Arthur in the Sixth Century? Reconsidering the Origins of the Arthurian Legend." *Reading Medieval Studies* 26: 77–95.

de Vogüé, A. (1998). "En lisant Jonas de Bobbio." *Studia Monastica* 30: 63–103.

Diem, A. (2007). "Monks, Kings and the Transformation of Sanctity: Jonas of Bobbio and the End of the Holy Man." *Speculum* 82: 521–9.

Dobbs, M. C. (1930). "The History of the Descendants of Ír." *Zeitschrift für Celtische Philologie* 13: 308–59.

Dooley, A. (1993) "Arthur in Ireland: The Earliest Citation in Native Irish Literature." In J. P. Carley and F. Ruddy (eds.), *Arthurian Literature*, vol. XII. Woodbridge, Boydell, 165–72.

Dumville, D. N. (1988) "Early Welsh Poetry: Problems of Historicity." In B. F. Roberts (ed.), *Early Welsh Poetry. Studies in the Book of Aneirin*. Aberystwyth, National Library of Wales, 1–16.

Grosjean, P. (1963) "Notes d'hagiographie celtiques 55." *Analecta Bollandiana* 81.1–2 : 271–7.

Hunter Blair, P. (1950) "The Moore Memorandum on Northumbrian History." In C. Fox and B. Dickins (eds.), *The Early Cultures of North-West Europe*. Cambridge, Cambridge University Press.

Hunter Blair, P. (1959) *The Moore Bede*. Early English Manuscripts in Facsimile 9. Copenhagen, Rosenkilde & Bagger,.

Ireland, C. (ed.) (1999) *Old Irish Wisdom Attributed to Aldfrith of Northumbria: An Edition of Bríathra Flainn Fhína maic Ossu*. Medieval & Renaissance Texts & Studies 205. Tempe, AZ, Arizona Center for Medieval & Renaissance Studies.

Jackson, K. (1964) "On the Northern British Section in Nennius." In N. Chadwick (ed.), *Celt and Saxon. Studies in the Early British Border*. Cambridge, Cambridge University Press, 20–62.

Jackson, K. H. (trans.) (1969) *The Gododdin: The Oldest Scottish Poem*. Edinburgh, Edinburgh University Press.

Jennings, B. (ed.) (1948) *The 'Acta Sanctorum Hiberniae' of John Colgan*. Coimisiún Láimhscríbhinní na hÉireann reflex facsimiles V. Dublin, Ordnance Survey.

John, J. J. (1996) "The *ex-libris* in *Codices Latini Antiquiores*." *Scriptorium* 50 : 239–43.

Johnson, A. (1987) "Bede and Aethelfrith of Northumbria." *Trivium* 22: 5–17.

Johnston, E. (2016) "Exiles from the Edge? The Irish Contexts of *Peregrinatio*." In R. Flechner and S. Meeder (eds.), *The Irish in Europe in the Early Middle Ages: Identity, Culture and Religion*. London, Palgrave, 38–52.

Kirby, D. P. (1991/2000) *The Earliest English Kings*. London and New York, Routledge.

Lowe, E. A. (1947) *Codices Latini Antiquiores*, vol. 4. Oxford, Oxford University Press.

Meyer, K. (1901) "The Expulsion of the Déssi." *Y Cymmrodor* 14: 101–35.

Meyer, K. (1907) "The Expulsion of the Déssi." *Ériu* 3.2: 135–42.

Moisl, H. (1983) "The Bernician Royal Dynasty and the Irish in the Seventh Century." *Peritia* 2: 103–26.

Mulchrone, K. (ed.) (1939) *Bethu Phátraic, the Tripartite Life of Patrick*, vol. i. Dublin, Dublin Institute for Advanced Studies.

O'Brien, M. A. (ed.) (1962) *Corpus genealogiarum Hiberniae*, vol. i. Dublin, Dublin Institute for Advanced Studies.

Ó Cróinín, D. (1982). "Mo-Sinu maccu Min and the Computus at Bangor." *Peritia* 1: 281–95; repr. Ó Cróinín, *Early Irish History and Chronology*. Dublin, Four Courts Press, 2003, 35–47.

Ó Cróinín, D. (1995) *Early Medieval Ireland, 400–1200*. London, Routledge. 2nd edition, 2017.

Ó Cróinín, D. (2003) *Early Irish History and Chronology*. Dublin, Four Courts Press.

Ó Cróinín, D. (2004) *The First Century of Anglo-Irish relations, AD 600–700*. O'Donnell Lectures 2003. Dublin, National University of Ireland.

Ó Cróinín, D. (ed.) (2005) *A New History of Ireland*, vol. I, *Prehistoric and Early Ireland*. Oxford, Oxford University Press.

Ó Cróinín, D. (2007) *The Kings Depart: The Prosopography of Anglo-Saxon Royal Exile in the Sixth and Seventh Centuries*. Quiggin Pamphlets on the Sources of Gaelic History 8. Cambridge, Department of Anglo-Saxon, Norse, and Celtic, University of Cambridge.

O'Hara, A. (2009) "The *Vita Columbani* in Merovingian Gaul." *Early Medieval Europe* 17: 126–53.

O'Hara, A. (2013) "*Patria, Peregrinatio*, and *Paenitentia*: Identities of Alienation in the Seventh Century." In W. Pohl and G. Heydemann (eds.), *Post-Roman Transitions: Christian and Barbarian Identities in the Early Medieval West*. Turnhout, Brepols, 89–124.

O'Rahilly, T. F. (1946) *Early Irish History and Mythology*. Dublin, Dublin Institute for Advanced Studies.

Plummer, C. (ed.) (1910) *Vitae sanctorum Hiberniae*. 2 vols. Oxford, Oxford University Press.

Sharpe, R. (1991). *Medieval Irish Saints' Lives: An Introduction to Vitae sanctorum Hiberniae*. Oxford, Oxford University Press.

Sharpe, R. (1995) *Adomnán of Iona, Life of St. Columba*. Harmondsworth, Penguin.

Skene, W. (1867) *Chronicles of the Picts and Scots*. Edinburgh, HM General Register House.

Smyth, A. P. (1974–1975) "Húi Failgi Relations with the Húi Néill in the Century after the Loss of the Plain of Mide." *Études Celtiques* 14: 502–23.

Smyth, A. P. (1982) *Celtic Leinster: Towards an Historical Geography of Early Irish Civilization AD 500–1600*. Dublin, Irish Academic Press.

Stancliffe, C. (1983) "Kings Who Opted Out." In P. Wormald (ed.), *Ideal and Reality in Frankish and Anglo-Saxon Society: Studies Presented to J. M. Wallace-Hadrill*. Oxford, Oxford University Press, 154–76.

Stancliffe, C. (2001) "Jonas' *Life of Columbanus and His Disciples*." In J. Carey, M. Herbert, and P. Ó Riain (eds.), *Studies in Irish Hagiography: Saints and Scholars*. Dublin, Four Courts Press, 189–220.

Stokes, W. (ed.) (1993). *Annals of Tigernach*. 2 vols. Felinfach, Llanerch Press.

Walker, G. S. M. (ed. & trans.) (1957). *Sancti Columbani Opera*. Scriptores Latini Hiberniae 2. Dublin, Dublin Institute for Advanced Studies.

Warren, F. E. (ed.) (1893/1895). *The Antiphonary of Bangor: An Early Irish Manuscript in the Ambrosian Library at Milan*. Henry Bradshaw Society Publications 4 and 10. London, Harrison and Sons.

Whitelock, D. (trans.) (1955) *English Historical Documents*, vol. 1. London, Eyre and Spottiswoode.

Whitelock, D., D. C. Douglas, and S. I. Tucker (trans.) (1961) *The Anglo-Saxon Chronicle: A Revised Translation*. London, Eyre and Spottiswoode.

Williams, I. (ed.) (1938) *Canu Aneirin*. Cardiff, Gwasg Prifysgol Cymru.

Williams, I. (ed.) (1960) *Canu Taliesin*. Cardiff, Gwasg Prifysgol Cymru.

Wood, I. N. (1982). "The *Vita Columbani* and Merovingian Hagiography." *Peritia* 1: 63–80.

Woolf, A. (ed.) (2013) *Beyond the Gododdin: Dark Age Scotland in Medieval Wales*. Proceedings of a conference held by the Committee for Dark Age Studies, St Andrews, University of St Andrews.

Yorke, B. (1992) *Kings and Kingdoms of Early Anglo-Saxon England*. London and New York, Routledge.

4

Movers and Shakers?

How Women Shaped the Career of Columbanus

ELVA JOHNSTON[1]

The Columbanus who stepped on Breton shores in 590–591 was no blank slate; his cultural identity had been forged in Ireland.[2] This extended beyond adherence to paschal particularities or apparently stubborn faithfulness to Irish ecclesiastical custom. These aspects of his thought and practice have received significant scholarly attention, and our understanding of Columbanus as abbot, politician, and theologian has been greatly enhanced, as has our appreciation of his position within Frankish and later, Lombard, elite society.[3] Throughout his career Columbanus keenly and pragmatically deployed identity politics; he emphasized his Irishness.[4] But the longer Columbanus was away from Ireland, the more he must have altered and adapted to his environment. This adaptation proved successful; Columbanus was plugged into elite patronage networks. He was simultaneously an outsider and an insider, a man from the earth's edge at the center of ecclesiastical and court politics. There is little doubt that for Columbanus, a dedicated *peregrinus*, a lifelong clerical exile, the prospect of deportation to Ireland following his expulsion from Burgundy in 610, was traumatic. The threat of it produced his most moving letter. [5] If it

---

1. I would like to thank the peer-reviewers and, in particular, the editor of this volume for their most helpful suggestions. This paper is all the better for them.

2. There is a substantial literature outlining the career of Columbanus, although his Irish context is the least explored. For example, Bullough 1997: 1–26 has relatively little on Ireland. Aspects of his Irish career are examined in Lapidge 1985: 104–16; Ó Cróinín 1982: 281–95, and 1995: 169–209; Charles-Edwards 2000: 344–90; and Breen 2011: 1–21, among others.

3. The essays in Clarke and Brennan 1981 are an important starting point. Fox 2014 deals with Columbanus and his legacy in detail. See also Wood 1994: 181–202. The Lombard context is less explored, with Richter 2008 being one of the few studies. His theological positions are examined in Gray and Herren 1994: 160–70 and Bracken 2002: 168–213, while his association with computistical works, likely and otherwise, is explored in Ó Cróinín 1997: 264–70. His importance to the practice of penance is analyzed in Meens 2014: esp. 37–69.

4. Representative examples include: *Epp.* 1.4: 6, 2.9: 22, 3.2: 24, 4.8: 34, and 5.3: 38. It is striking how Columbanus's Irishness is deployed in each one of the letters. The pragmatism of his position is emphasized in Bracken 2002: 175–80; Leso 2013: 362–68; and O'Hara 2013: 96–102.

5. The trauma is evident in *Ep.* 4.8: 34. Richter 1999: 110 points out that Columbanus is one of the few *peregrini* to explicitly refer to himself as such. Leso 2013: 368 notes that the word *peregrinus* and its derivatives appear ten times in the *Epistulae*. The context to his *peregrinatio* is discussed by Charles-Edwards 1976: 43–59 and Johnston 2016: 38–52.

had come to pass he would have returned a stranger to his native land; over the course of two decades he had been shaped by a multitude of cultural encounters with peoples and institutions, men and women. These molded his career and how it came to be perceived. Those involving women were particularly important; it is argued in this chapter that they played a prominent role, both for Columbanus and for later perceptions of him. These interactions were also at the jagged edge of his own cultural expectations, because the social positions of women in the Ireland that he had left differed, despite similarities, from what he subsequently encountered.

Our sources for these cultural encounters are rich, complex, and contradictory. Columbanus wrote extensively on a number of topics, but much has been lost. However, his extant writings, particularly the letters, provide an unmatched insight into his thoughts.[6] Yet our impressions of Columbanus have been just as profoundly shaped by the *Vita Columbani*, written by the monk Jonas between 639 and 643, a text that is regarded as one of the most important *vitae* of the seventh century.[7] Jonas became a monk of Bobbio within a few years of the death of Columbanus.[8] He was certainly well-traveled and well-informed, in many cases drawing on vibrant communal and personal memories of the saint. Nonetheless, as scholars have emphasized, the *Vita Columbani* is an agenda-driven text.[9] This is especially clear in Part II, which focuses on the network of monasteries that venerated Columbanus in the quarter century following the saint's death.[10] It is now accepted that the issues of common identity, central to Part II, also suffuse the depiction of Columbanus in Part I. For example, Jonas presents Columbanus as being in the tradition of the founder figures of monasticism, men such as Anthony of Egypt and Paul the Hermit.[11] At the same time, he omits all direct reference to the controversies to which Columbanus was committed, including the dating of Easter and the debate concerning the Three Chapters.

---

6. Lapidge and Sharpe 1985: 166–68 (nos. 639–42). The standard edition of Columbanus's writings is Walker 1957. Of the six letters, five are considered authentic, while there is doubt about *Ep.* 6. See Wright 1997: 29–92. The *Epistulae*, excluding 6, are considered together as a body of work in Leso 2013: 358–89. The rules are considered in Stevenson 1997: 203–16 and the penitential in Charles-Edwards 1997: 217–39. There is also a group of thirteen sermons whose authorship is debated, but at the least they originate in a Columbanian context. See Stancliffe 1997: 93–202.

7. The standard edition is Krusch 1905. See now O'Hara and Wood 2017.

8. Jonas joined between 616 and 618. Stancliffe 2001: 190 summarizes the evidence suggesting a 616–617 date. See also Charles-Edwards 2000: 351.

9. Wood 1982: 63–80 provides an important and nuanced analysis. Stancliffe 2001: 189–220 explores Jonas's intentions in detail. These are further considered in Diem 2007: 521–59.

10. *VC*: 228–94; Fox 2014: 219–51.

11. *VC*: 148–224; Wood 1982: 63–4; Diem 2007: 522–5.

Thus, it is necessary to distinguish between Jonas's representation of Columbanus and the saint's self-representation. Even the latter needs to be considered against the actual historical realities on which it was based, which it also attempted to shape. Separating the sources highlights crucial differences. For instance, women feature more in the *Vita Columbani* than in Columbanus's writings, something that is partly a function of genre difference. Columbanus was not composing an autobiography. Nonetheless, references to women are uncommon in his extant corpus, and these are generally, with an important exception, nods to the male ascetic attitude that women are sources of temptation.[12] These attitudes are central to this chapter, which has two related aims. It explores the extent to which Columbanus's Irish origins informed his views about gender and, in particular, women. Furthermore, it examines the role that women played in his career. The relationship between expectation and reality lies at the heart of key cultural encounters that contributed to Columbanus's self-presentation and Jonas's presentation of him. Working at the interface of text and representation, is it possible to reconstruct how Columbanus perceived a world inhabited by women as much as by men?

AGAINST THE GRAIN? A TALE OF TWO WOMEN

Columbanus grew up in a politically divided island that nevertheless exhibited a degree of social cohesion, at least among elites. These elites, comprising aristocrats and clerics, as well as professional groups such as poets and judges, were by the end of the sixth century deeply engaged in a process of cultural consolidation that emphasized shared customs and ancestry rather than political unity.[13] Columbanus is a witness to this; he deployed various ethnic labels to self-identify as Irish and clearly viewed this identity as involving membership of a distinct *gens*, inhabiting a distinct location at the ends of the earth. Admittedly, however, our sources for this sixth-century world are scant, although they include the earliest Irish chronicle and a body of penitential literature.[14] In addition, it is very likely that this period also saw the beginning of the project to codify the vernacular law tracts, culminating in the creation of a robust legal framework soon after the middle of the seventh century.[15] It would be highly reductionist

12. For example, *Epp.* 1.2: 2, 1.6: 8, and 2.8: 20, all of which are stereotypical in tone. Rosenwein 2006: 160–1 places Columbanus's attitudes within their broader context. The exceptional depiction of Theodelinda in *Epp.* 5.8: 44 and 5.17: 56 is discussed elsewhere in this chapter.

13. Johnston 2013: 79–89.

14. Hughes 1972: 99–159, followed by Evans 2010: 115–70. For a differing interpretation, see McCarthy 2008: 159–63. The penitential genre was of British origin but was introduced into Ireland in the sixth century. For an overview, see Meens 2014.

15. The best introduction to the law tracts is Kelly 1988. Breatnach 2011 argues that the *Senchas Már* was compiled between 660 and 680.

not to accept that the rich body of extant sources, which emerged in the two generations following the death of Columbanus, do not offer some insight into his formation. This is not to minimize differences. Bullough, for instance, has suggested that Columbanus's family may have been first-generation Christians, making his experiences distinct from those of later Irish writers.[16] Moreover, his Ireland was arguably still in a process of acculturation of native and Christian traditions and may not have enjoyed the same cultural solidity that is evident in seventh-century writings. This may well be one factor underlying Columbanus's rigorism, reported by Jonas, on issues such as marital custom.[17] The last point raises a further consideration: information about Columbanus's life in Ireland comes mainly from Jonas. While Columbanus is an invaluable witness to Irish identities and to ecclesiastical customs and learning, his remarks are firmly tied to the struggles in which he was involved. On the other hand, it has been shown that Jonas was reasonably knowledgeable. For instance, it is almost certain that the Sinilis identified by Jonas as Columbanus's teacher in scripture is Sillán, future abbot of Bangor, an impressive example of the *Vita Columbani* being independently verified in Irish sources.[18] However, Jonas's depiction of the island of Ireland is also characterized by romanticization, one compounded by genre convention and geographical distance.[19] Keeping these provisos in mind—the relative paucity of sixth-century Irish sources, alongside an awareness of the motivations of Jonas—what can be gleaned concerning the basic cultural biases that filled Columbanus's Irish years and influenced his earliest attitudes toward gender?

These attitudes were certainly grounded in the fundamental inegalitarianism of Irish society. Status was all-pervasive, carrying with it rights, responsibilities, and disabilities. In general, women's rights were greatly inferior to those of men within their social class, although it is worth highlighting that status was relative to class for both genders.[20] This was underpinned by an economic system in which those lower down the scale owed complex services and rents to those in power.[21] Indeed, Columbanus's claim that among the Irish a man's principles, not status, were what mattered, is fascinatingly against the grain of everything we know about his society, a point to which this chapter returns. [22] Given his access

16. Bullough 1997: 3. It is possible to interpret *VC* I.2: 154, *Natus ergo hic inter primordia fidei gentis illius*, in this light.

17. *VC* I.19: 187–88.

18. *VC* I.3: 157–8. See Ó Cróinín 1982: 281–95 for further details.

19. Note especially *VC* I.2: 152–4.

20. Kelly 1988: 7–16, 68–79.

21. Kelly 1988: 29–35; Johnston 2013: 76–7.

22. *Ep.* 6.11: 48 states: *non enim apud nos persona sed ratio ualet.*

to a literate education from his youth, at least according to Jonas, it is very likely that Columbanus came from the upper social echelons whose interconnections in Church and secular society were so influential.[23] He may even have been intended for the Church from the beginning. This Church cooperated and competed with its secular counterparts for power and resources. Ecclesiastics were highly successful, and major monasteries, such as Bangor, emerged as economically and politically powerful.[24]

However, the Church also faced challenges, especially in the area of social custom. Nowhere was this clearer than in the regulation of reproduction. Early Irish law placed great emphasis on the rights of agnatic kindreds, the fundamental blocks upon which the entire legal system was built. One of their major characteristics was the robustness of inheritance patterns that ensured the succession of a male heir, except in unusual circumstances.[25] The ready availability of divorce and remarriage, in conjunction with strategies that embraced access to multiple partners, combined with an unusually wide concept of legitimacy, meant that the most common outcome, even if a man died without sons, was the inheritance of a male heir from within the kindred.[26] It is very likely that this crucial aspect of social organization was contested among Irish elites in the sixth century. The central role of sexual regulation in the penitential literature is suggestive.[27] It is even possible that when Columbanus left Ireland he had already experienced the limits of Christianization in this area. This pattern was further intensified in royal succession. An adult male heir always emerged. Irish kingship is frequently categorized as weak. However, it is noteworthy that there were no boy kings and no need for regencies. Not a single one is recorded before the arrival of the Normans in the twelfth century.[28] As a result, women were much less likely to gain positions of direct political power than, for example, in Merovingian Gaul. This was ultimately an unintended consequence of the Irish Church's almost complete failure to recalibrate marital customs to anything approaching the indissoluble monogamous ideals of Augustine.

Despite this picture of relative female disempowerment within a society structured around agnatic kindreds, two women are particularly highlighted

23. *VC* I.3: 54. See Ó Cróinín, chapter 3 in this volume, which suggests that Columbanus may have been closely connected with the Leinster Uí Bairrche dynasty.

24. Johnston 2013: 59–65.

25. Ó Corráin 1995: 52–7.

26. Kelly 1988: 102–5; Ó Corráin 1995: 45–57; Ní Chonaill 2008: 9–10.

27. Pereira Farrell 2012: 116–51 is the fullest treatment of this material. The use of the term *adaltrach*, indicating a legal secondary wife, based on the Latin word for adulterer, is probably also indicative of clerical disapproval.

28. Ó Corráin 1971: 7–39; Jaski 2000: 143–70.

in Jonas's portrayal of the saint's formative years. These are his unnamed mother, his first nurturer, and the equally anonymous female ascetic who urges Columbanus to consider *peregrinatio*.[29] It is striking that Jonas emphasizes but does not identify these women. In contrast, he names the two men who structurally repeat their roles within the text, Sinilis, Columbanus's first ecclesiastical teacher, and Comgall, the abbot who finally allowed him to go on *peregrinatio*.[30] It is also striking that Columbanus's father is never mentioned, despite the fact that the patriline was of the utmost importance in Irish society. This material is by no means straightforward, but a number of interpretations seem likely. First of all, the climax of Book I of the *Vita Columbani* centers around the actions of the negatively portrayed Queen Brunhild (d. 613).[31] Throughout the first book of the *Life*, women play typecast roles: they are either opponents of the saint or the bearers of holy inspiration. This is apparent in Jonas's treatment of Columbanus's mother. For example, she receives a dream from heaven that foreshadows the future greatness of Columbanus, a hagiographical commonplace.[32] Her later, somewhat contradictory, attempt to stop him entering the religious life, by throwing her body across the threshold as he leaves their home, is another hagiographical cliché.[33] Yet not everything is so stereotyped. For instance, Jonas remarks that the saint's mother raised him herself, unwilling to entrust her son even to relatives.[34] This telling comment is likely a reference to the Irish institution of fosterage, which ensured that the children of aristocrats spent a large part of their childhood apart from their natal family, creating enduring affective, social, and political bonds in the process.[35] It is worth speculating that the prominence of Columbanus's mother in the *Vita Columbani* is grounded in the fact that she reared Columbanus, rather than sending him to another family to be fostered. Could this be related to her religious beliefs? As already outlined, sixth-century Irish society was still undergoing Christianization. In fact, Columbanus's reference to the spiritual leaders of his homeland fighting the Lord's battle might be more than rhetorical.[36] His family may well have seen themselves as set apart from others who were less Christian or even pagan. Perhaps significantly, the fear of a pagan fostering a Christian features in the

---

29. *VC* I.2–3: 154–7 (mother); I.3: 156–7 (female hermit).

30. *VC* I.4: 158–60.

31. *VC* I.18–9: 186–93. For the implications of this portrayal see Nelson 1986: 1–48.

32. *VC* I.2: 154. Rosenwein 2006: 149–50 remarks on the typological similarities drawn between Columbanus's mother and Brunhild.

33. *VC* I.3: 157; Breen 2011: 9–10.

34. *VC* I.2: 154.

35. Mulchrone 1939: 187–205 remains indispensable. See also Kelly 1988: 86–90; Charles-Edwards 1993: 78–82; and Ní Chonaill 2008: esp. 10–30.

36. *Ep.* 6.8: 44.

early *Life* of Brigit, known as the *Vita Prima*, although here a miraculous solution is found.[37]

The other major female figure in this part of the *Vita Columbani*, the female hermit, has received more attention, primarily because her speech about *peregrinatio* has become the classic description of the ideal and practice for many scholars.[38] The assumption that there were two distinct grades of *peregrinatio*, an internal one within Ireland and an external, superior, one abroad, is largely based on this passage written by Jonas. There can be little doubt that Jonas's words echo, in large measure, Columbanus's own understanding and practice of *peregrinatio*, although the latter never specifically mentions the existence of two grades.[39] Moreover, the legal position of a *peregrinus* or *deorad dé* in Irish law was a very high one. *Peregrini* were members of the elite, and even women may have gained a degree of freedom through the practice.[40] However, what is less remarked is that the episode is clothed in the same language of female attachment to the world already seen in the depiction of Columbanus's mother. For example, Columbanus encounters the female ascetic after suffering the attention of sexually aggressive young women. She warns him against temptation, quoting a charged list of sinful Old Testament women, including Eve and Delilah, a clear foreshadowing of the later condemnation of Brunhild as a Jezebel.[41] There appears to be as much Jonas as memories of Columbanus in this passage. Nonetheless, it is worth stressing that there is no reason to believe that the female ascetic was an invention of Jonas. She was, in all likelihood, an actual inspiration for Columbanus's desire to become a *peregrinus*. In structural terms, Jonas has Columbanus repay his debt to her through Burgundofara, who dedicates herself to the religious life under his influence, founding Faremoutiers after the saint's death.[42] However, the voice of the unnamed ascetic has been conflated with that of the hagiographer.

A conflation of the experiences of the saint with the agenda of Jonas runs through the entire section of the *Life* devoted to Ireland. Despite this, several details have a strong claim to be rooted in the reality of Columbanus's Irish

---

37. There is no modern edition of this text. Scholars still rely on Colgan's seventeenth-century edition. See Colgan 1647: § 10, 528, for the episode.

38. See Charles-Edwards 1976 and Richter 1999: 41–7. An assumption of Jonas's accuracy underpins most scholarly writings on *peregrinatio*.

39. Johnston 2016: 41–7 stresses the importance of sources other than Jonas.

40. Charles-Edwards 1976: 43–59 shows that *peregrini* expected and received high status in Ireland. O'Hara 2013: 97–9 explores the implications of this expectation for Columbanus. Women as hermits feature in a wide variety of hagiographical texts. A useful example is Canir, discussed in Johnston 2001: 308–10.

41. *VC* I.3: 157, I.18: 187 (Brunhild).

42. *VC* II.7–10: 240–57. Her importance is discussed by Wood 1982 and Stancliffe 2001: esp. 197–99.

experience. For example, Columbanus was almost certainly of high status. It seems that he grew up in a strongly Christian environment, where he experienced the formative influence of women, especially that of his mother and, at a later point, that of the female hermit. The former relationship may well have been intensified if, as has been argued, Columbanus was not fostered but was raised within his biological family until adulthood. On a more general level, negotiations between secular and religious elites were still in the process of shaping society during this era. In some areas, such as marital custom, secular practice eventually won out; in others, such as patronage and learning, the Church was successful. The Columbanus who landed in Brittany was a product of all these contexts: emotional, political, and institutional.

Crossing Boundaries? The Saint and the Wicked Woman

Columbanus landed on his feet, quickly identifying the levers of power and patronage. With the support of the Merovingian family, he founded new monastic communities in Annegray, Luxeuil, and Fontaine.[43] Luxeuil, in particular, brought him into contact with Brunhild. She was the queen who effectively ruled Austrasia and Burgundy for years, a powerbroker who corresponded with a pope and emperor,[44] the woman who was killed horrifically at the orders of her opponent, Chlothar II († 629), and an example of a type of female empowerment that was impossible in Ireland. Scholars have long recognized that Merovingian queens, through a combination of owning dowry land, the exercise of a managerial role within the royal household, and their control of at least part of the royal treasure, had the potential to exert an unusual amount of influence and patronage.[45] This was heightened if the queen's husband died leaving her with a son or sons too young to rule in their own right. Unlike in Ireland, minorities were relatively common, and queens could become regents, governing for their sons.[46] Nonetheless, as Nelson has noted, the agency of

---

43. Fox 2014: 2–9 provides a useful contextualization. The political and social contexts of these foundations are analyzed in O'Hara 2015: 143–70.

44. Nelson 1986: 1–48 carefully distinguishes the historical queen from her various representations and subsequent vilification. She is assessed within the contexts of Merovingian queenship and reproductive strategies by Dailey 2015: 141–60. Gillett 2010: 141–80 provides the fullest examination of Brunhild's Austrasian letters. Wood 1994: 128–31 provides a broad political context.

45. Wemple 1981: 58–70 considers aristocratic women, although impressionistically. Stafford 1983: 93–174 gives a broad overview of the political and economic resources deployed by Merovingian queens. Dailey 2015: 101–17 provides an in-depth analysis, focusing in particular on the role of marital customs.

46. See the comments in Nelson 1986: 8–9 about the rival claims of a male *nutritor* to be regent to a minor, a role adopted on occasion by mayors of the palace.

Merovingian queens should not be overemphasized. Their position was not an institutional one and depended almost entirely on personal circumstances.[47] However, there is still an arresting contrast with the far more limited authority exercised by royal women in early medieval Ireland. Columbanus would literally never have come across a woman like Brunhild before and certainly not one as obviously powerful. Moreover, Brunhild and her family were central to Columbanus's career. For example, it is arguable that her son Childebert II (d. 596) was the saint's patron of Luxeuil, granting him the site on which to establish his second principal monastery, although his identity is suppressed by Jonas and replaced with that of his father, Sigibert I (d. 575), presumably to minimize any suggestion that either Brunhild or her descendants helped Columbanus.[48] Jonas even claims that Sigibert died as a result of Brunhild's maneuverings, an apparently groundless accusation.[49] Moreover, Brunhild's downfall was momentous, placing all the Columbanian communities, bar Bobbio, within lands owing allegiance to Chlothar II, her enemy. Practically, Chlothar's triumph led to the growth of a second wave of loosely connected Columbanian foundations, establishing the broader monastic *familia* for whom Jonas wrote the *Vita Columbani*.[50]

It is no exaggeration to stress that Brunhild is the most memorable character in the *Vita Columbani*. She is presented extremely negatively by Jonas as a second Jezebel, embodying the worst aspects of women.[51] His account of her persecution of Columbanus was widely recapitulated in other texts, serving to further blacken the dead queen's memory.[52] Brunhild's grandson, Theuderic II (d. 613), is presented as weak and ineffectual, despite his own better instincts.[53] He never escapes his grandmother's sway, sealing his future failure. Fortunately, other sources, written while Brunhild was alive, balance Jonas's sensationalist post-mortem portrait. For example, the queen corresponded amicably with Gregory the Great (d. 604) and is portrayed positively by Gregory of Tours (d. 594), the latter a grateful recipient of her patronage.[54] In contrast, Jonas's account of the

---

47. Nelson 1986: 44–8.

48. Bullough 1997: 9–11 outlines the chronological difficulties. See O'Hara 2015: 144–47. See also Wood, chapter 6 in this volume, on King Guntram as the possible first patron of Columbanus and his role in the foundation of Annegray.

49. *VC* I.18: 186.

50. Fox 2014: 31–4 explores the dynamics. See also Rosenwein 2006: 131–5. Chlothar is, unsurprisingly, positively portrayed by Jonas in *VC* I.24, in which Columbanus foretells his victory over Theuderic.

51. The Jezebel comparison is made in *VC* I.18: 187. Nelson 1986: esp. 29–31 provides the classic analysis.

52. *VC* I.18–9: 186–93. The implications of the conflict are outlined in Wood 1982: 70–71 and Nelson 1986: 28–30. See also Diem 2007: 531 and O'Hara 2009: 128–34.

53. *VC* I.18: 187.

54. Gregory the Great corresponded with her, particularly on church reform. The context is

struggle between Brunhild and Columbanus is artificially loaded, drawing on conventional depictions of saints in conflict with rulers.[55] It may come as a surprise, then, to realize that Columbanus never once mentions Brunhild or his dealings with her and Theuderic in his extant writings.[56] Stancliffe has compellingly argued that Brunhild functions as a clever decoy in the *Vita Columbani*. The real source of difficulty lay between Columbanus and the Gallic bishops.[57] For example, Columbanus declined to attend a council at Chalon-sur-Saône in 603, despite being summoned. The major issues appear to have been the dating of Easter and the independence of the fledgling Columbanian *familia* from episcopal control.[58] Columbanus's enforced exile from Burgundy turned, to a great extent, on these tensions. However, it is also likely that the fallout of Chalon-sur-Saône meant that Columbanus did find himself in difficulty with Brunhild and Theuderic, who, after all, were major patrons of the Gallic episcopacy. Arguably Jonas has simply omitted the controversial roots of the events of 609–610, weighting the role of Brunhild and, as a result, blaming her for ecclesiastical hostility toward Columbanus, a strategy more successful than wholesale invention.[59] Does this reweighting of events obscure the actuality of Columbanus's dealings with Brunhild, or does reality break through?

In Jonas's account, these dealings revolve around two disputes: Columbanus's refusal to bless Theuderic's illegitimate sons, Brunhild's great-grandsons, and Theuderic's related attempt, incited by Brunhild, to enter the heart of Luxeuil.[60] In both instances, it is possible to detect influence from Columbanus's Irish background, although Jonas's bias is always apparent. The first conflict is straightforward enough. Theuderic had four sons, all the children of concubines. This was not an unusual situation, as concubinage was practiced among the Merovingian family, especially from the sixth century onward; the sons of concubines had every chance of royal succession, despite the lower status of their mothers.[61] For example, Brunhild's estranged grandson, Theudebert II, king of Austrasia (d. 612), was the child of a concubine.[62] Royal blood had the potential to

discussed by Wood 1994: 130–1. See also Nelson 1986: 12–3. Dailey 2015: 141–60 explores the extent to which Gregory of Tours was personally indebted to Brunhild.

55. Diem 2007: 538–42 usefully explores several likely models.

56. In *VC* I.19: 189, Jonas claims that Columbanus addressed a letter to Theuderic on his sinful ways. However, no other evidence of it survives.

57. Stancliffe 2001: 201–4; Charles-Edwards 2000: esp. 367–8; Flechner and Meeder 2016b: 197–9.

58. These issues are fundamental to understanding *Epp.* 2: 12–22 and 3: 22–4.

59. Stancliffe 2001: 201–9 convincingly identifies this pattern in the *Vita Columbani*. In nearly every case of controversy, whether it be paschal observance or the harshness of the rule, Jonas omits rather than invents. He blames Brunhild for ecclesiastical opposition to Columbanus in *VC* I.19: 189–90.

60. *VC* I.19: 187–93.

61. Stafford 1983: 35–38, 62–71; Nelson 1986: 4–5; Dailey 2015: 108–17.

62. Nelson 1986: 15; Stafford 1983: 64. See also Wood 1994: 132.

trump legitimacy. However, as time passed the inheritance of the children of concubines became a contested issue, and a rigorist position, such as that articulated by Desiderius of Vienne (d. 607), became more common.[63] This gained traction because while practices of polygyny and divorce were not unknown in Gaul, they took place within a framework in which the boundaries of ideal monogamy were emphasized.[64] This contrasts sharply with Ireland, where these boundaries were ultimately rejected in favor of the multitude of reproductive unions acknowledged in customary law. This decisive rejection may not yet have taken firm hold in Columbanus's time, although it was cemented soon after the middle of the seventh century when the vernacular laws began to take written form.[65] It is reasonable, therefore, to suggest that Columbanus was already familiar with the dizzying array of reproductive unions accepted among the Irish aristocracy, unions that he opposed. He brought this opposition with him to the Merovingian kingdoms. Significantly, Columbanus expresses strong disapproval of sexual practices among the Gallic clergy in his first letter, citing Gildas and his Irish teachers in support of his purist position. [66] It is not much of a stretch to imagine him being equally hostile to any request from Brunhild that he recognize the rights of her great-grandsons. As hindsight shows, Columbanus ended up on the right side of history in Gaul and, in the generation following his death, his views would not have seemed especially unusual.[67]

The second source of conflict, Theuderic's attempt to enter Luxeuil, arguably triggered a similarly strong response. Once again, Brunhild is presented as the perpetrator, although it is Theuderic who acts.[68] This is best approached by first considering the immediately foregoing incident in the *Life* in which the saint travels to Theuderic's residence and awaits the king outside the palace. Theuderic sends food to Columbanus, which the saint refuses. Several broken dishes later, Brunhild and Theuderic promise to mend their ways.[69] It is tempting to see here the influence of an Irish legal custom, the ritual hunger strike known as *troscad*. This was a weapon of public shaming used by individuals who sought redress from their social superiors. The injured party fasted outside the residence of their opponent, usually from sunrise to sunset. It is a commonplace

63. Wood 1982: 70.

64. Stafford 1983: 71–92.

65. Breatnach 2011 dates the compilation of the *Senchas Már* to between 660 and 680. Knowledge of the materials is likely to have predated their written forumulation. Note also his warnings against characterising Irish marital custom as polygynous, although multiple and concurrent reproductive unions did occur. See Breatnach 2016: 1–29.

66. *Ep.* 1.6: 8.

67. Wemple 1981: 75–96.

68. *VC* I.19: 189–90 specifically blames Brunhild.

69. *VC* I.19: 188–9.

in Irish hagiography; saints are frequently shown fasting against kings, just like Columbanus against Theuderic.[70] Ian Wood has stated that any search for Irish elements in the *Vita Columbani* is "doomed to failure," but it seems apparent that echoes of the historical saint do reverberate through the *Life*, bringing with them an Irish freight.[71] This freight is even clearer in subsequent events. In a complex passage Theuderic accuses Columbanus of violating the customs of the land, especially in his refusal to allow him entry to the *septa secretiora* of Luxeuil.[72] The context shows that the *septa* was a part of the monastic enclosure reserved for monks. The laity could enter other parts of the complex, but not the *septa*. Columbanus's stance does, of course, carry political weight, and it very neatly reverses the previous passage in which he had resisted going under Theuderic's roof. Jonas contrasts the sinful space of the palace with the pure space of the *septa*.[73] However, there is more to it than Jonas's rhetorical artistry. It is almost certain that Columbanus's recalcitrance was grounded in Irish practice. While scholars have suggested various possible continental influences for the *septa*, the most likely inspiration is a direct one.[74] Delimiting space according to a hierarchy of purity was a core feature of Irish ecclesiastical foundations,[75] one that fit well in a society dominated by differences of grade and status. This management of space is well-attested in Hiberno-Latin writings from the seventh century onward; they draw on a variety of biblical and early Christian texts, creating something distinctive in the process.[76] The *Collectio Canonum Hibernensis* is very clear. It identifies the innermost space of a monastery as being one in which only religious can enter; it is *sanctissimus*. Intriguingly, the *Hibernensis* stresses the exclusion of women, although it also prohibits entry to the laity in general.[77] This is remarkably similar to Jonas's account.

70. Kelly 1988: 182–3. Binchy 1982: 165–78.

71. Wood 1982: 72.

72. *VC* I.19: 190.

73. De Jong 2001: 297.

74. Markus 1990: 139–55 discusses, generally, the holy place in early Christianity. Klingshirn 1994: 151–9 explores Caesarius's idea of a holy space, while Diem 2007: 535–8 suggests possible continental models for Columbanus, including Caesarius. None, however, is as close as those underpinning Irish practice. For the latter, see Picard 2011: esp. 55–60. The theological perspectives that are foundational to Irish texts are explored in Jenkins 2010.

75. Picard 2011: 54–63 gives an excellent analysis of the evidence, particularly that concerning the laity. Herity 1984: 105–16 provides an archaeological perspective. See also Swift 1998: 105–25. Rosenwein 1999: 70–3 discusses Jonas's influence.

76. Picard 2011: 54–63.

77. *Collectio Canonum Hibernensis* 44.5: 202 states: *Duos uel tres terminos circa locum sanctum debent fieri: primus in quem praeter sanctos nullum introire permittimus omnino, quia in eum laici non accidunt et mulieres, nisi clerici*. It is possible that *mulieres* here refers to women in general and may not include the specific category of virgins.

Without doubt, this is keyed to Jonas's wider strategy of blaming all of Columbanus's Merovingian woes on a forceful Brunhild and an ineffectual Theuderic. The latter is no more than a pawn of the wicked queen. This allows the hagiographer to present the saint as entirely the victim of a jealous old woman, whitewashing other problems. It must be remembered, however, that this tack was effective because Brunhild really was a powerful queen. She played the game of thrones for three decades before finally succumbing, spectacularly, to her enemies. So, given the pervasiveness of Jonas's approach, is there anything left of the real Columbanus? What can be suggested is that his Irish origins may well have predisposed him to act in particular ways that put him at odds with Brunhild. It is unlikely, however, that these were primarily based on attitudes toward gender, although they certainly had serious ramifications for the role of women within the family. Columbanus's ideology concerning the organization of reproduction, forged amid the rival values of his homeland, did bring him into direct conflict with one of the major sources of agency for many a Merovingian queen, an influence over the reproductive destiny of her male offspring, a path through which she could hope to exercise and maintain power. In this sense, Brunhild's support for Columbanus's communities must always have been contingent upon his acknowledging, even if through silence, the precarious realities of her position.

MOTHER AND CHILD: COLUMBANUS AND THE CATHOLIC QUEEN

Columbanus eventually arrived in Italy in 612–613, where he received the patronage of Agilulf (d. 616) and Theodelinda (d. 628), king and queen of the Lombards.[78] Oddly, given that Bobbio was his final foundation and resting place, its establishment is not treated in detail by Jonas.[79] He names Agilulf and notes that Arianism was present in the region, further remarking that Columbanus composed a learned work against the heresy.[80] He is very careful not to say that the king himself was an Arian and briefly acknowledges his role as a patron of Bobbio. Significantly, however, he never mentions Theodelinda at all. Instead, Part I of the *Life* ends by emphasizing Columbanus's relationship with Chlothar II. Yet Theodelinda is the only historical woman to feature in the entirety of

---

78. The key sources for the career of Theodelinda are analyzed in detail by Balzaretti 1999: 183–207. In chapter 14 of this volume Gasparri discusses Agilulf's importance as a patron. Evidence of near-contemporary sources for this period of Lombard history is usefully discussed by Borri 2014: 43–54.

79. *VC* I.30: 230–32. O'Hara 2015: 168–9 analyzes Jonas's description.

80. This may be a reference to *Ep.* 5: 36–58, although to describe it as primarily an anti-Arian work is disingenuous.

Columbanus's extant writings.[81] Moreover, it is worth stressing that this letter is among our earliest sources for the career of Theodelinda.[82] Her apparently good relationship with the saint is in marked contrast with the enmity dividing Columbanus and Brunhild, an enmity that Jonas, for political reasons, had stressed so strongly. Moreover Theodelinda, as a largely successful example of a powerful queen, does not appear to have matched the hagiographer's agenda. However, her importance to Columbanus offers an invaluable insight into his attitudes toward women, rulership, and the family, particularly when placed within the religious and familial dynamics of the Lombard royal family.

Theodelinda's position was defined by religious belief, marriage, and mother-hood.[83] She was the wife of two successive Lombard kings, Authari (d. 590) and Agilulf. Under Lombard law women had limited rights, but the legal situation was fluid and Theodelinda may well have benefited from the influence of late Roman law, which gave far more extensive rights to women in areas such as property holding. The Romanizing tendencies of Agilulf's court make this an attractive proposition, although these tendencies should not be overemphasized in what was a complex cultural milieu.[84] Indeed, it has been shown that Roman legal influences helped shape Lombard law, making any strict dichotomy of Roman and barbarian questionable.[85] However, Theodelinda certainly established a powerful presence and was instrumental in bolstering a Catholic influence among the Arian and pagan Lombards.[86] This was achieved visibly through her role as ecclesiastical patron and relic enthusiast.[87] Like Brunhild, she received correspondence from Gregory the Great.[88] Moreover, she remained influential throughout her life. Following the death of Agilulf she reigned as regent alongside her son Adaloald (d. 628), continuing her activities as patron.[89] For example, in one of his diplomas Adaloald specifies a small property that was intended for Bobbio by Theodelinda.[90] When Adaloald was deposed in 626,

81. *Epp.* 5.8: 44, 5.17: 56.

82. Balzaretti 1999: 186.

83. See Stafford 1983: 110, 137–8. She had previously been intended for Brunhild's son Childebert.

84. The Romanizing tendencies of Agilulf's court are discussed in Wickham 1981: 33–4. Their potential benefit to Theodelinda is touched on in Stafford 1983: 137–8. However, it must be pointed out that this can be over-romanticized. Borri 2014: 39–42 offers a necessary corrective.

85. Borri 2014: 60–1.

86. Borri 2011: esp. 252–4 demonstrates Theodelinda's likely role in shaping perceptions of her image through the *Chronicle* of Secundus. These lay the foundation for her largely favorable image in sources such as the *Historia Langobardorum* of Paul the Deacon.

87. Trout 2005: 131–50.

88. The religious identity of the Lombards is unclear; it is likely many were still pagan in the early seventh century. See Wickham 1981: 33–8. The importance of Theodelinda's correspondence in showing her influential role is highlighted in Balzaretti 1999: 186–8.

89. Stafford 1983: 161–2.

90. Balzaretti 1999: 189; see also Gasparri, chapter 14 in this volume.

he was succeeded by Arioald (d. 636), the husband of Theodelinda's daughter Gundeberga.[91] She in turn married his successor, Rothari (d. 652). The role of women, especially Theodelinda and Gundeberga, in maintaining continuity in Lombard rulership is striking.[92]

Thus, when Columbanus first encountered Theodelinda in Milan he met a woman who wielded considerable power, a Catholic queen alongside her Arian husband. Her importance was arguably intensified by the divisions of faith within the royal family; these gave her a distinct political identity apart from Agilulf, enhancing her position as the Catholic voice at court. Furthermore, their young son, Adaloald, was also a Catholic, following his mother's faith. However, to complicate matters, she belonged to a branch of the Church that had split from the mainstream, owing to the condemnation of particular theological writings known as the Three Chapters.[93] The so-called Three Chapters controversy remained a concern in Italy until the end of the seventh century and became wrapped in issues of politics and identity. Columbanus's fifth letter, addressed to Pope Boniface IV (d. 615), was written in 613 from Milan and was an attempt at mediation between the papacy and royal family. [94] Fascinatingly, this attempt is partly presented through intriguingly rich verbal portrayals of the royal family, particularly of Theodelinda. In three related and remarkable passages he meditates on Theodelinda as queen, wife, mother, and, implicitly, a representation of the unity of the Church. The importance of unity is, of course, a theme throughout his letters.[95] It is especially emphasized here because of the theological divisions affecting the Church, which, as was commonplace, is imagined as a mother. The result is that this letter has more female imagery in it than any other, strongly underpinning Theodelinda's meaning for Columbanus within the framework of the conflict.[96] She is more than a queen; she is a living embodiment of the Church itself and of its potential for unity.

The first reference to Theodelinda is in the context of Agilulf's request that Columbanus express his concerns to the pope.[97] The king is worried about the division of the people (*schisma populi*), on account of his queen (*pro regina*) and his son (*pro filio*) and maybe also for himself (*pro se ipso*). Columbanus

---

91. Borri 2014: 61–2 suggests that Adaloald's fall may, in part, have been a reaction to Theodelinda's policies.

92. Theodelinda's interest in female genealogy is explored in Pohl 2004: 37–9.

93. For a useful introduction to the Three Chapters controversy see the collection of essays gathered in Chazelle and Cubitt 2007.

94. *Ep.* 5: 36–56. The context of the letter is discussed in Gray and Herren 1994: 160–70 and Leso 2013: 378–89.

95. Emphasized by Bracken 2002: 168–213.

96. See especially *Ep.* 5.12–13: 50–2.

97. *Ep.* 5.8: 44. Agilulf's request is repeated in 5.14: 52 and 5.17: 54.

has chosen his words carefully and emphasizes Theodelinda's royal status. She is the *regina*. The division between faiths in the family is mirrored by the division of the country. Solving one mends the other. In this passage Agilulf's role is predominant, although he is grouped slightly apart from Theodelinda and Adaloald. The queen gains more significance as the letter progresses, a significance underscored by the most sustained use of gendered imagery in the writings of Columbanus. [98] The passage begins with a consideration of the pope's responsibilities as successor of Peter, before moving on to the sorrows of the Church, the common mother (*communis matris*) of all Christians. Furthermore, this Church, compared to the biblical Rebecca, is a mother torn apart by discord among her sons.[99] The only solution is to turn back to the Son of God. This image of a pope divided from his Church and from Jesus is a daring parallel to the Lombard king, the queen, and their son. They are introduced in identical sequence: king (pope), queen (the Church/ Rebecca), and son (Jesus). The pope, like Agilulf, stands slightly apart from the other figures. Theodelinda is implicitly identified with the Church, and her motherhood links her to both Rebecca and the Virgin Mary. The latter's theological importance is referenced in the next passage, which continues to deploy the imagery of motherhood.[100] These themes are brilliantly brought together in the letter's conclusion. Once again, the king and queen are mentioned side by side, asking for unity. Columbanus then refers back to his earlier trope of Church as mother and finishes with a rhetorically effective vision of a world at peace.[101]

There can be little doubt that the theological content of the letter, which turned on debates about the divinity of Christ, is the primary reason for Columbanus's extensive use of strongly gendered imagery. It could be argued that Theodelinda's function is subordinate to the basic argument of the letter, and this would, in part, be true. However, there is more to her role than rhetoric. Columbanus need not have mentioned her so prominently; he could have focused entirely on Agilulf's request.[102] By placing Theodelinda at Agilulf's side, Columbanus is stressing her influence and importance. His recognition of her title, a complete contrast with Jonas, who refuses to acknowledge Brunhild as a queen, is telling. The fact that Theodelinda is a mother is underscored by maternal imagery and references to her son. Intriguingly, it is never made explicit, unlike her queenship. It is likely that this emphasis on Theodelinda as queen

---

98. *Ep.* 5.12: 50. I am not considering here the short verse *In Mulieres*, ascribed to Columbanus. It is only four lines long and is not definitely of his authorship. It is edited and translated in Walker 1957: 214–5.

99. For further discussion on this rhetoric, see Bracken, chapter 2 in this volume.

100. *Ep.* 5.13: 52.

101. *Ep* 5.17: 54–6.

102. This is particularly clear in *Epp.* 5.14: 52 and 5.17: 54.

reflected the reality that Columbanus encountered in Milan. Theodelinda was powerful. Her influence continued long after the deaths of her husband and Columbanus. It is also worth noting that at no point does Columbanus condemn her for being married to a heretic.[103] On the contrary, her marriage was of the type that he approved, a husband and wife joined together in a monogamous union that had produced a legitimate son. Here, in Ambrose's city, toward the end of his life, he finally found the Christian marriage that had been under threat in Ireland and Burgundy.

CONCLUSIONS

Returning to the question with which this chapter began: Is it possible to discern the role women and perceptions of them played for Columbanus? How did they shape his career? Answers are by no means straightforward, particularly as it is so easy to confuse Columbanus with his influential biographer. Without a doubt women are an important force for Jonas's Columbanus. There is a strong pattern of female support and opposition running throughout the *Vita Columbani*. But, as has been argued, this is driven by ideology. For example, Brunhild is so encrusted in stereotype that it is difficult to detect the historical queen beneath layers of vilification. On the other hand, memories of the real Columbanus are scattered throughout the *Life*, especially in the opening section devoted to Ireland. Used with extreme care, they are helpful in reconstructing the saint's cultural background. However, they must be constantly tested against Columbanus's own writings and contemporary and near-contemporary Irish sources. The plausible picture that emerges suggests that Columbanus came from a distinctively Christian background, one where his mother was an important and, possibly, enduring influence. The female ascetic who inspired him to *peregrinatio* was also significant. Together these two women played a formative role. Without them Columbanus's career would never have taken the path that it did. Furthermore, Columbanus grew to maturity in a society where the Church was struggling to establish itself against the norms of customary law, some of which ran counter to core Christian teachings. The regulation of reproduction is by far the most blatant example of this, and it is an area in which the Irish Church eventually failed. It is also one that inevitably deeply concerned women. Therefore, it is not difficult to imagine that a request from Brunhild to bless her great-grandsons would have touched a nerve, bound up as it was in her need for maintaining power as against Columbanus's adherence to the strictures of

---

103. Columbanus never explicitly calls Agilulf an Arian, although it is strongly implied in *Ep.* 5.8: 44, and he describes him as a *rex gentilis* in 5.14: 52.

Christian marriage. Indeed, Columbanus was in many ways a man who worked against the grain. It is unlikely that he accepted a deviation from the Christian ideal either in Ireland or on the Continent. Finally, and fortunately, the voice of Columbanus does break free from the shackles of Jonas in his fifth letter. His invaluable references to Theodelinda show a man at ease with an empowered queen. However, this empowerment was bolstered by a Christian identity and a marriage more ideal than those that he had previously encountered in the Merovingian kingdoms or, indeed, Ireland. Arguably, Columbanus's perception of Theodelinda hints at something more. His Ireland could not have produced a female ruler wielding her type of direct influence. When he first arrived on the Continent the existence of powerful queens must have seemed strange to Columbanus. Moreover, he never lost that sense of difference, of being a foreigner and outsider. And yet at the end of his tumultuous career he was more at the heart of events than ever, and his relationship with the Lombard queen was a central factor. It may well be significant that Jonas chose not to foreground this connection. After all, it would have militated against his powerfully simplistic presentation of female royal power as wicked. Of course, Columbanus's perceptions of women are, in many respects, unknowable. Nonetheless, an examination of his writings does suggest that he was far more than the angry firebrand of Jonas's colorful fulminations.

BIBLIOGRAPHY

Balzaretti, R. (1999) "Theodelinda, 'Most Glorious Queen': Gender and Power in Lombard Italy." *Medieval History Journal* 2: 183–207.

Binchy, D. A. (1982) "A Pre-Christian Survival in Medieval Irish Hagiography." In D. Whitelock, R. McKitterick, and D. Dumville (eds.), *Ireland in Early Medieval Europe: Studies in Memory of Kathleen Hughes*, Cambridge, Cambridge University Press, 165–78.

Borri, F. (2011) "Murder by Death: Alboin's Life, End(s), and Means." *Millennium 8/2011: Jahrbuch zu Kultur und Geschichte der ersten Jahrtausends n. Chr.*, 223–70.

Borri, F. (2014) "Romans Growing Beards: Identity and Historiography in Seventh-Century Italy." *Viator* 45.1: 39–71.

Bracken, D. (2002) "Authority and Duty: Columbanus and the Primacy of Rome." *Peritia* 16: 168–213.

Breatnach, L. (2011) "The Early Irish Law Text *Senchas Már* and the Question of its Date." E. G. Quiggin Memorial Lectures 13. Cambridge, Department of Anglo-Saxon Norse and Celtic.

Breatnach, L. (2016) "On Old Irish Collective and Abstract Nouns. The Meaning of *Cétmuinter*, and Marriage in Early Medieval Ireland." *Ériu* 66: 1–29.

Breen, A. (2011) "Columbanus' Monastic Life and Education in Ireland." *Seanchas Ardmhacha* 23.2: 1–21.

Bullough, D. (1997) "The Career of Columbanus." In M. Lapidge (ed.), *Columbanus: Studies on the Latin Writings*. Woodbridge, Boydell, 1–29.

Collectio Canonum Hibernensis (1885). In *Die irische Kanonensammlung*, ed. Hermann Wasserschleben. Leipzig.

Charles-Edwards, T. M. (1976) "The Social Background to Irish *Peregrinatio.*" *Celtica* 11: 43–59.

Charles-Edwards, T. M. (1993) *Early Irish and Welsh Kinship.* Oxford, Clarendon Press.

Charles-Edwards, T. M. (1997) "The Penitential of Columbanus." In M. Lapidge (ed.), *Columbanus: Studies on the Latin Writings.* Woodbridge, Boydell, 217–39.

Charles-Edwards, T. M. (2000) *Early Christian Ireland.* Cambridge, Cambridge University Press.

Chazelle, C., and C. Cubitt (eds.) (2007) *The Crisis of the Oikoumene: The Three Chapters and the Failed Quest for Unity in the Sixth-Century Mediterranean.* Turnhout, Brepols.

Clarke, H. B., and M. Brennan (eds.) (1981) *Columbanus and Merovingian Monasticism.* Oxford, British Archaeological Reports International Series (B.A.R.).

Colgan, J. (ed.) (1647) *Triadis Thaumaturgae seu Divorum Patricii Columbae et Brigidae, Trium Veteris et Maioris Scotiae, seu Hiberniae, Sanctorum Insulae, Communium Patronorum Acta.* Louvain.

Dailey, E. T. (2015) *Queens, Consorts, Concubines: Gregory of Tours and Women of the Merovingian Elite.* Leiden, Brill.

de Jong, M. (2001) "Monastic Prisoners or Opting Out? Political Coercion and Honour in the Frankish Kingdoms." In M. de Jong, F. Theuws, and C. van Rhijn (eds.), *Topographies of Power in the Early Middle Ages.* Leiden, Brill, 291–329.

Diem, A. (2007) "Monks, Kings, and the Transformation of Sanctity: Jonas of Bobbio and the End of the Holy Man." *Speculum* 82.3: 521–59.

Evans, N. (2010) *The Present and the Past in Medieval Irish Chronicles.* Woodbridge, Boydell.

Flechner, R., and S. Meeder (eds.) (2016a) *The Irish in Europe in the Early Middle Ages: Identity, Culture and Religion.* London, Palgrave.

Flechner, R., and S. Meeder (eds.) (2016b) "Columbanus and Ethnic Tensions." In R. Flechner and S. Meeder (eds.), *The Irish in Europe in the Early Middle Ages: Identity, Culture and Religion.* London, Palgrave, 195–213.

Fox, Y. (2014) *Power and Religion in Merovingian Gaul: Columbanian Monasticism and the Frankish Elites.* Cambridge, Cambridge University Press.

Gillett, A. (2010) "Love and Grief in Post-Imperial Diplomacy: The Letters of Brunhild." In B. Sidwell and D. Dzino (eds.), *Studies in Emotions and Power in the Late Roman World: Papers in Honour of Ron Newbold.* Piscataway NJ, Gorgias Press, 141–80.

Gray, P. T. R., and M. W. Herren (1994) "Columbanus and the Three Chapters Controversy— A New Approach." *Journal of Theological Studies* 45: 160–70.

Hen, Y. (2007) *Roman Barbarians: The Royal Court and Culture in the Early Medieval West.* London, Palgrave.

Herity, M. (1984) "The Layout of Early Irish Christian Monasteries." In P. N. Chatháin and M. Richter (eds.), *Ireland and Europe: The Early Church.* Stuttgart, Klett-Cotta, 105–16.

Hughes, K. (1972) *Early Christian Ireland: An Introduction to the Sources.* Cambridge, Cambridge University Press.

Jaski, B. (2000) *Early Irish Kingship and Succession.* Dublin, Four Courts Press.

Jenkins, D. (2010) *"Holy, Holier, Holiest": The Sacred Topography of the Early Medieval Irish Church.* Turnhout, Brepols.

Johnston, E. (2001) "Powerful Women or Patriarchal Weapons? Two Medieval Irish Saints." *Peritia* 15: 302–10.

Johnston, E. (2013) *Literacy and Identity in Early Medieval Ireland.* Woodbridge, Boydell.

Johnston, E. (2016) "Exiles from the Edge? The Irish Contexts of *Peregrinatio.*" In R. Flechner and S. Meeder (eds.), *The Irish in Europe in the Early Middle Ages: Identity, Culture and Religion.* London, Palgrave, 38–52.

Kelly, F. (1988) *A Guide to Early Irish Law.* Dublin, Dublin Institute for Advanced Studies.

Klingshirn, W. E. (1994) *Caesarius of Arles: The Making of a Christian Community in Late Antique Gaul*. Cambridge, Cambridge University Press.

Lapidge, M. (1985) "Columbanus and the 'Antiphonary of Bangor.'" *Peritia* 4: 104–16.

Lapidge, M. (ed.) (1997) *Columbanus: Studies on the Latin Writings*. Woodbridge, Boydell.

Lapidge, M., and R. Sharpe (eds.) (1985) *A Bibliography of Celtic-Latin Literature 400–1200*. Dublin, Royal Irish Academy.

Leso, T. (2013) "Columbanus in Europe: The Evidence from the *Epistulae*." *Early Medieval Europe* 21.4: 358–89.

Markus, R. A. (1990) *The End of Ancient Christianity*. Cambridge, Cambridge University Press.

McCarthy, D. (2008) *The Irish Annals: Their Genesis, Evolution and History*. Dublin, Four Courts Press.

Meens, R. (2014) *Penance in Medieval Europe, 600–1200*. Cambridge, Cambridge University Press.

Mulchrone, K. (1939) "The Rights and Duties of Women with Regard to the Education of their Children." In R. Thurneysen et al. (eds.), *Studies in Early Irish Law*. Dublin, Royal Irish Academy, 187–205.

Nelson, J. L., (1986) "Queens as Jezebels: Brunhild and Balthild in Merovingian History." In J. L. Nelson (ed.), *Politics and Ritual in Early Medieval Europe*. London, Hambledon Press, 1–48.

Ní Chonaill, B. (2008) "Child-Centred Law in Medieval Ireland." In R. Davis and T. Dunne (eds.), *The Empty Throne: Childhood and the Crisis of Modernity*. Cambridge, Cambridge University Press, 1–31.

Ó Corráin, D. (1971) "Irish Regnal Succession: A Reappraisal." *Studia Hibernica* 11: 7–39.

Ó Corráin, D. (1995) "Women and the Law in Early Ireland." In M. O'Dowd and S. Wichert (eds.), *Chattel, Servant or Citizen: Women's Status in Church, State and Society. Papers Read before the XXIst Irish Conference of Historians*. Belfast, Institute of Irish Studies, 45–57.

Ó Cróinín, D. (1982) "Mo-Sinnu moccu Min and the Computus of Bangor." *Peritia* 1: 281–95.

Ó Cróinín, D. (1995) *Early Medieval Ireland 400–1200*. London, Longman.

Ó Cróinín, D. (1997) "The Computistical Works of Columbanus." In M. Lapidge (ed.) *Columbanus: Studies on the Latin Writings*. Woodbridge, Boydell, 264–70.

O'Hara, A. (2009) "The *Vita Columbani* in Merovingian Gaul." *Early Medieval Europe* 17.2: 126–53.

O'Hara, A. (2013) "*Patria, Peregrinatio* and *Paenitentia*: Identities of Alienation in the Seventh Century." In W. Pohl and G. Heydemann (eds.), *Post-Roman Transitions: Christian and Barbarian Identities in the Early Medieval West*. Turnhout, Brepols, 89–124.

O'Hara, A. (2015) "Columbanus *ad Locum*: The Establishment of the Monastic Foundations." *Peritia* 26: 143–70.

O'Hara, A. and I. Wood (trans.) (2017) *Jonas of Bobbio: Life of Columbanus, Life of John of Réomé, and Life of Vedast*. Translated Texts for Historians 64. Liverpool, Liverpool University Press.

Pereira Farrell, E. (2012) "Taboos and Penitence: Christian Conversion and Popular Religion in Early Medieval Ireland." PhD dissertation, University College Dublin.

Picard, J.-M. (2011) "Space Organization in Early Irish Monasteries: The *Platea*." In C. Doherty, L. Doran, and M. Kelly (eds.), *Glendalough: City of God*. Dublin, Four Courts Press, 54–63.

Pohl, W. (2004) "Gender and Ethnicity in the Early Middle Ages." In L. Brubaker and J. M. H. Smith (eds.), *Gender in the Early Medieval World: East and West, 300–900*. Cambridge, Cambridge University Press, 23–43.

Richter, M. (1999) *Ireland and Her Neighbours in the Seventh Century.* Dublin, Four Courts Press.

Richter, M. (2008) *Bobbio in the Early Middle Ages: The Abiding Legacy of Columbanus.* Dublin, Four Courts Press.

Rosenwein, B. H. (1999) *Negotiating Space: Power, Restraint and Privileges of Immunity in Early Medieval Europe.* Ithaca, NY, Cornell University Press.

Rosenwein, B. H. (2006) *Emotional Communities in the Early Middle Ages.* Ithaca, NY, Cornell University Press.

Stafford, P. (1983) *Queens, Concubines and Dowagers: The King's Wife in the Early Middle Ages.* London, Batsford.

Stancliffe, C. (1997) "The Thirteen Sermons Attributed to Columbanus and the Question of their Authorship." In M. Lapidge (ed.), *Columbanus: Studies on the Latin Writings.* Woodbridge, Boydell, 93–202.

Stancliffe, C. (2001) "Jonas's *Life of Columbanus and His Disciples.*" In J. Carey, M. Herbert, and P. Ó Riain (eds.), *Studies in Irish Hagiography: Saints and Scholars.* Dublin, Four Courts Press, 189–220.

Stevenson, J. (1997) "The Monastic Rules of Columbanus." In M. Lapidge (ed.), *Columbanus: Studies on the Latin Writings.* Woodbridge, Boydell, 203–16.

Swift, C. (1998) "Forts and Fields: A Study of 'Monastic Towns' in Seventh- and Eighth-Century Ireland." *Journal of Irish Archaeology* 9: 105–25.

Trout, D. (2005). "Theodelinda's Rome: 'Ampullae,' 'Pittacia,' and the Image of the City." *Memoirs of the American Academy in Rome* 50: 131–50.

Walker, G. S. M. (ed.) (1957) *Sancti Columbani Opera.* Scriptores Latini Hiberniae 2. Dublin, Dublin Institute for Advanced Studies.

Wemple, S. (1981) *Women in Frankish Society: Marriage and the Cloister 500 to 900.* Philadelphia, University of Pennsylvania Press.

Wickham, C. (1981) *Early Medieval Italy: Central Power and Local Society 400–1000.* London and Basingstoke, Macmillan.

Wood, I. N. (1982) "The *Vita Columbani* and Merovingian Hagiography." *Peritia* 1: 63–80.

Wood, I. N. (1994) *The Merovingian Kingdoms 450–751.* London, Longman.

Wood, I. N. (2001) *The Missionary Life: Saints and the Evangelisation of Europe 400–1050.* London, Longman.

Wright, N. (1997) "Columbanus's *Epistulae.*" In M. Lapidge (ed.), *Columbanus: Studies on the Latin Writings.* Woodbridge, Boydell, 29–92.

5

Columbanus's Ulster Education

ALEX WOOLF

Columbanus was born in Leinster and made his career on the Continent, but despite Jonas's reticence on the topic, it is clear that his training as both a monastic leader and a theologian was the product of his sojourn in Ulster. While the chronology is inexact and somewhat confused, our subject's monastic profession and training are clearly said to have taken place at the monastery of Bangor under the headship of its founder, Comgall (abbot c. 559–602). At the end of book I, chapter 4, of the *Vita Columbani* we are told that Columbanus left Bangor for the Continent at the age of twenty. This seems a very early age for leading his own mission and is almost certainly an error by either Jonas or an early copyist. It is highly unlikely that Comgall would have approved one so young as the leader of a band of pilgrims setting out overseas; it is much more likely that either Jonas's method of calculation is awry, perhaps reflecting his belief that the saint had arrived in Gaul during the reign of Sigibert (c. 561–575), or that at some point a period of twenty years as a professed monk was confused with carnal age. One intriguing possibility that suggests itself is that this is a very early example of confusion between Columbanus and Columba, since the latter seems to have left Ireland in 563, the former's twentieth year and the second year of King Sigibert's reign. Jonas, of course, frequently refers to his subject simply as "Columba," and the saint himself used this form in his correspondence. It is easy to see how such confusion might have arisen.

At the end of the previous chapter of the *Vita*, Jonas had introduced his readers to a venerable man and teacher, Sinilis, with whom Columbanus studied before entering into monastic profession at Bangor. Sinilis has been identified in the modern scholarship with a future Bangor abbot, Mo Sinu moccu Min (d. 610).[1] An alternative identification, however, may be the Sinell (d. 603)[2] who became bishop of Moville in succession to Uinnianus in 579.[3] In either case this phase of the saint's training also took place in Ulster. The purpose of this chapter

---

1. Ó Cróinín 1982, following Charles-Edwards 1976, at 44. Obituary at AU 610.2. Bullough 1997: 4 preferred to identify Sinillis with the saint of Clóeninis–Cleenish Island in Lough Erne, but for whom we are reliant on much later sources. Cf. Ó Cróinín, chapter 3 in this volume.
2. AU 603.4.
3. AU 579.1.

is to look at the context of this Ulster education and to discuss why Columbanus might have been drawn to the region in the later sixth century.

The term "Ulster" is used here to denote *not* the modern province of Northern Ireland, but the late antique kingdom of the Ulaid. In the period under discussion this kingdom of Ulster stretched, roughly, from the mouth of the Boyne north to the southern shore of Belfast Lough, largely, though not precisely, corresponding to modern Counties Louth and Down.[4] Bangor lies at the extreme northern end of this district, and it is perhaps not a coincidence that its founder, Comgall, was said to have been born among the Cruithni, whose collection of kingdoms stretched north and west beyond Belfast Lough, in the direction of Lough Foyle.[5] Six or seven kilometers south of Bangor lay Moville, which seems to have been an episcopal see, or quite possibly the chief episcopal see, for the Ulaid during the period in question. The Irish annals record the obituaries of three bishops of Moville: Uinnianus in 579, Sinell in 603, and Sillan in 619.[6] After the death of Sillan the local episcopal see seems to have moved to Nendrum, on an island in Strangford Loch, about ten kilometers farther south.[7] Obituaries for three bishops based here are found for the period between 639 and 659.[8]

The Ulstermen became famous in the literature of medieval Ireland, and claims were made for their early domination of the whole of the North, but it is worth noting that their seventh-century extent was broadly similar to the region attributed to the "Woluntioi," from whom their name is derived, in Ptolemy's second-century map.[9] This part of Ireland also appears, on the basis of the current evidence, to have been one of the main areas into which E-ware, the distinctive pottery produced in what is now western France, was imported between the mid-sixth and the very early eighth centuries.[10] The fortress at Scrabo Hill, about three kilometers southwest of Moville, has produced such finds. This site, which sits atop the 540-foot hill, is described "as oval in shape, 90m x 37m.

---

4. Though now somewhat dated, the most useful general discussion remains Byrne 1973: 106–29.

5. Adomnán, *Vita Columbae*, I.49.

6. AU.579.1; 603.4; and for Sillan an obituary at AU 619.2 as abbot but as bishop at AFM 619.

7. Moville (modern Movilla in Co. Down), Nendrum, and Bangor are all located in the territory of the later cantred of Uí Blaithmeic, which is said to have been named from an eighth-century Ulster dynast. The territory was also known by the name Duibthrian. See MacCotter 2008: 232–3. If Moville and Nendrum were not the chief episcopal sees of the Ulaid as a whole in our period, then they must at least have dominated this area. Dendrochronology has recently dated the construction of the horizontal mill at Nendrum to the year 619, the precise year of our last episcopal obituary from Moville (McErlean and Crothers 2007: 80). This may simply be coincidence, but possibly the appropriation of episcopal tithes from Moville at this point increased the volume of grain being processed at the site.

8. AU 639.4, 643.2, 659. For Nendrum's position as the principal see of the Ulaid, see Charles-Edwards 2000: 260.

9. Freeman 2001: 77–80.

10. Campbell 2007: 46.

It consists of a badly mutilated stone-cored earthen bank with a ditch on the inside which is now filled in."[11] Ewan Campbell has speculated that it may have been the political center of the region, from which other items of E-ware were distributed to the surrounding area. Unlike Downpatrick, at the southern end of Strangford Loch, however, Scrabo has no recognized textual attestation.[12] The provenance of E-ware is as yet uncertain, but the favored hypothesis seems to be that it originated in either the lower Loire basin or that of the Charente—which provides a pleasing parallel with Jonas's evidence for the point of departure for ships to Ireland.[13]

It is notable that the territory of the Ulaid, and certainly County Down, does not seem to have participated in the earlier phase of Mediterranean trade that saw late Roman amphorae, known as B-ware, being imported to parts of Britain and Ireland.[14] The late sixth-century appearance of Ulster on the archaeological map coincides with the appearance in textual records of the episcopal see at Moville and with its first known incumbent, Uinnianus. Whether Uinnianus should be seen as a moving agent in the development of the Ulaid or merely as another manifestation of the development is unclear.

Uinnianus is likely to have established himself at Moville when the Ulaid were ruled by Demmán and Báetán, the sons of Cairell mac Muiredaig, who between them seem to have ruled from 557 to 581, and the younger of whom, Báetán, seems to have been a major player who extended his influence beyond the Ulaid heartland.[15] Uinnianus is best known to us through the pages of Adomnán's *Vita Columbae*, in which he is presented as the saint's last teacher and in which a number of forms of his name are used: Finnbar, Finnio, and Uinniau. The last form makes it clear that we are dealing here with a Briton, the forms with initial 'F' indicating a natural gaelicization of the pronunciation by the late seventh century.[16] As "Uinnianus," the bishop is also well-known

11. http://archaeologydataservice.ac.uk/archsearch/record.jsf?titleId=2601817.

12. Campbell 2007: 110.

13. See Campbell 2007; and now Loveluck and O'Sullivan 2016. Both build on Wooding 2002.

14. Campbell 2007: 14–26.

15. Byrne 1973: 109–11, much of which is recapitulated by Ó Cróinín in this volume. It is interesting to note that the late Old Irish tale *Scél Tuáin meic Chairill* has our bishop meet on arrival in Ulster with a cleric, Tuán son of Cairell, who claims to have inherited from his father the lands between Mag nÍtha and the Benna Bairche—that is, the valley of the Foyle and the Mountains of Mourne (the extent of the combined kingship of the Cruithni and the Ulaid in the ninth and tenth centuries after most of Louth had been lost to the Uí Néill). Tuán is clearly intended to be a brother of Demmán and Báetan. The text is edited by Carey 1984.

16. For a full, though perhaps overly skeptical, discussion see Dumville 1984. Sharpe 1984: 198 and Charles-Edwards 2000: 290–3 take, in my view, a more balanced approach. The possible confusion between a Finnian of Moville (d. 579) and a Finnian of Clonard (d. 549) within some of our source material cannot be ignored, but the identification of the saint of Moville, but not Clonard, as a bishop and the proximity of Moville to Bangor, as well as the form "Uinnianus" used in his annalistic obituary, in my

from the correspondence of Columbanus.[17] Bishop Uinnianus may well have been the main attraction for both Columba and Columbanus when they chose the land of the Ulaid for their higher education.[18] Jonas does not mention Uinnianus as one of Columbanus's educators, but since he died in 579, when, according to the standard chronology, Columbanus was in his midthirties, it seems likely that he had a part to play, if only as the line manager or teacher of Sinilis. That Columbanus cites Uinnianus's correspondence is suggestive that he may have spent time in Moville, where the bishop's archive would have been maintained. It lay only a short walk from Bangor, so we need not hypothesize a long period of residence there. This line of reasoning may strengthen the case for identifying Sinilis with Uinniau's successor Sinell rather than with Mo Sinu moccu Min.

In *Epistula* 1.7 Columbanus cites Uinnianus's correspondence with Gildas, and it is generally agreed that the so-called *Fragmenta Gildae* were compiled in part, or as a whole, from Gildas's reply.[19] Uinnianus appears to have been asking about the procedure to follow when a monk wished to leave his monastery to seek a stricter discipline.[20] Such a question would make most sense coming from a bishop, since he would most likely be the arbitrator in such a dispute. As bishop of Moville, Uinnianus would have had at least two major monasteries in his diocese, Nendrum and Bangor, and possibly others. It is tempting to imagine a specific incident that might have triggered such a question.

Adomnán, in the *Vita Columbae*, never identifies the monastery at which his subject took his vows, nor does he identify his monastic teacher; the three teachers named—Cruithnechán, Gemmán, and Uinnianus—are none of them said to be in monastic orders. Throughout the *Vita*, however, particular respect is paid to Comgall of Bangor, who is mentioned more than any abbot other than Columba himself, and the Iona chronicle appears to have noted the death of every single Bangor abbot.[21] Bearing in mind the proximity of Moville, where Columba's final teacher was based, we might speculate that when Columba left Ireland for Britain in 563, he and his companions may have been leaving Comgall's Bangor and seeking out a more austere calling in the islands of the ocean. Part of Gildas's response to Uinnianus appears to have been that "a laxer

---

view make it almost beyond doubt that it is he we are dealing with in the careers of both Columba and Columbanus.

17. Columbanus, *Ep.* 1.7.
18. Charles-Edwards 2000: 290–3.
19. Sharpe 1984; Herren 1990. The *Fragmenta* have been edited by Winterbottom 1978, text at 143–5 and translation at 80–2. On Columbanus's interest in Gildas, see Wood, chapter 6 in this volume.
20. For a detailed discussion of this passage, see Sharpe 1984: 196–8.
21. Smyth 1972: 33–43.

abbot should not hold one of his monks back if he is inclined to stricter ways, for priests and bishops have a terrible judge; it is his task, not ours, to judge them in both worlds."[22] It is interesting to note that Gildas's alleged visit to Ireland took place just two years after Columba's departure for Britain.[23] It is probably a little fanciful to suggest that Uinnianus's original letter to Gildas had specifically asked for advice on the question "How do you solve a problem like Columba?," but this example has the potential to illustrate the kind of situation that might have prompted the bishop's inquiry. Why he should write to Gildas in particular is another interesting point.

There was a strand of genealogical thinking in the Middle Ages that attributed to Gildas a son named Uinnianus or some variant of the name. While the "Finnio Gildae" of *Corpus Genealogiarum Sanctorum Hiberniae*, lacking the patronymic, is ambiguous, the Gwynnog ap Gildas of *Bonedd y Sant* and *Achau'r Sant* is not.[24] This may simply be coincidence, but a biological relationship is not out of the question. Gildas was already in middle age but not yet in monastic orders when he penned *De Excidio*, so he may have fathered sons (a Naiton is also recorded). Alternatively, a father-son relationship may have been construed from an earlier tradition of a master-pupil relationship. Whatever the truth of the matter, as Sharpe and Herren have argued, Gildas was regarded as a leading figure in the development of the British and Irish churches and in particular with that of monasticism. This should hardly surprise us.

Although we tend to focus on the achievements of the Irish Church in the early Middle Ages, due to the nature of the surviving material, it should not be forgotten that this Church was itself an offshoot of the British Church.[25] By the late eleventh century even the Britons seem to have forgotten this and often have their early saints sent to Ireland for training, but the reality was the reverse.[26] Columba and Columbanus were part of the first generation of Irish churchmen to go abroad following a phase of monastic reform or foundation by British fathers. In later literature Uinnianus was renowned as a scholar who had brought the law of Moses or the gospels to Ireland in a number of texts dating from the ninth century or later.[27] More securely Uinnianus is generally accepted

22. *Fragmenta* § 6.
23. Gildas's voyage to Britain is noted in *Annales Cambriae* C, s.a. 565. This date fits with his meeting with Ainmere mac Sétnai in the Ruys *Life*; Williams 1899: § 12. I have suggested elsewhere (Woolf 2007: 6) that a Hiberno-Latin source may lie behind parts of this text. Gildas's obituary s.a. 570 appears to have been part of the original *Chronicle of Ireland*, and I see no reason to doubt it; cf. Stancliffe 1997: 179–81.
24. O'Riain 1985: 145; Bartrum 1966: 63 and 70.
25. See also chapter 6 in this volume for the prior influence of British monks on the Continent.
26. O'Riain 1981.
27. Such as *Scél Tuáin*, discussed above, Carey 1984; or *Félire Oengus* under September 10.

as the author of *Penitentialis Uinniani*. Since this appears to be the principal un-
acknowledged source for Columbanus's own penitential, it seems likely that this
should be attributed to our Uinnianus.[28] This sixth-century text is very much in
the tradition of British penitentials and stands at the beginning of the distinctly
Irish tradition, thus supporting the contention that Uinnianus was himself a
vector for bringing this British monasticism to Ireland. It develops the mode
of thought first seen in the text known as the *Praefatio Gildae de Poenitentia*,
also thought to be sixth century and British.[29] Despite its ascription to Gildas,
and Gildas's evident influence upon Uinnianus, modern scholarship has been
skeptical of the attribution.[30] Herren argues that the author of the *Fragmenta*
cannot be the same as the author of the *Praefatio* because *Fragmenta* 2 states that
"[a]bstinence on bodily food is useless without charity. Those who do not fast
unduly or abstain over much from God's creation, while being careful in the sight
of God to preserve within them a clean heart (on which, as they know, their life
ultimately depends), are better than those who do not eat flesh or take pleasure
in food of this world, or travel in [vehicles] or on horseback,[31] and so regard
themselves as superior to the rest of men: to these death has entered through the
windows of their pride,"[32] while the *Praefatio* extensively recommends putting
monks on short rations as a form of penance. In Herren's words: "It is difficult
in the extreme to believe that the author of the *Fragments*, who regards fasts
and vigils as largely the activity of the vainglorious and hypocritical, would
then proceed to write a penitential work in which going without supper was
the most common punishment for minor transgressions and vigils for more
serious ones."[33] It could be argued, however, that Herren confuses form with
substance. The vainglorious faster chooses abstinence to set himself above his
fellows, whereas the penitent brother humbly submits to his abbot's prescription
of abstinence. Since the *Penitentialis Uinniani* also depends on fasts and vigils
as penances, it seems not out of line with the school of thought represented by
Gildas and Uinnianus and later by Columbanus.

What else might have been on the curriculum at Moville or Bangor? In a recent paper on Columbanus's monastic inspiration,[34] Clare Stancliffe draws our
attention to the fact that not all of those works penned in Europe or Asia that
influenced Columbanus need necessarily have been encountered by him after he

---

28. Bieler 1975: 3–4; 75–95. For a fuller commentary, see de Vogüé 1989.
29. Bieler 1975: 60–5.
30. Herren 1990: 66–71.
31. This calls to mind Aidan of Lindisfarne as described by Bede in *HE* III.5.
32. Winterbottom 1978: 80; text at 143.
33. Herren 1990: 70.
34. Stancliffe 2011.

left Ireland.[35] Columbanus describes having encountered the works of Faustus of Riez while still a young monk,[36] presumably in Ireland. Lapidge has argued that the hymn *Precamur patrem*, preserved in the Antiphonary of Bangor, was the product of Columbanus's pen while he was still based in Ireland. The manuscript of the Antiphonary dates to around 700. *Precamur patrem* shows familiarity with Rufinus's Latin translation of Gregory of Nazianus's *Orationes*, Virgil, the Gospel of Nicodemus, and Cassian's *Institutes*,[37] as well as Sulpicius Severus, Venantius Fortunatus, and Jerome.[38] Stancliffe also draws attention to the evidence provided by *Amra Choluimb Chille*, an elegy to Columba of Iona that appears to have been composed almost immediately after his death.[39] This poem claims that Columba applied the Rule of Basil and loved the books of Cassian. If the poem does date to 597–598, it strongly suggests that these works were available in the northern Gaelic world at the time Columbanus left for the Continent, and it is not stretching the evidence much further to suggest that they may have formed part of the curriculum that Uinnianus established in his diocese, which included Comgall's Bangor.

A further issue is brought to mind by Stancliffe's chapter in this volume (see chapter 7), which emphasizes "shunning" and the ideology based on Ezekiel 33, which saw the Godly as watchmen (*speculatores*) set by God to warn the sinful among the powerful, both lay and ecclesiastical. This is, of course, a major feature of Gildas's *De Excidio* and is also evident, as Stancliffe discusses in depth, in Columbanus's own work. Echoes of it can also be seen in Adomnán's portrayal of Columba, in particular with his dealing with kings and his refusal to have polluted laymen on Iona. Was this part of Uinnianus's curriculum, and might it, perhaps be connected more widely to the changes happening in the Church in Ireland in this period?

In this chapter I have focused perhaps more on Uinnianus than might have been expected, but the extreme proximity of the churches of Duibthrian, the episcopal see at Moville, and the monastic houses at Bangor and Nendrum, neither more than an hour's journey by foot or boat from it, suggest to me that we should picture this area as a unified ecclesiastical province whose clerics interacted with one another on an almost daily basis. It is tempting as well to

---

35. Stancliffe 2011: 26–8.
36. Columbanus, *Instructiones* 2.1; for discussion see Stancliffe 1997.
37. Lapidge 1997: 261–2.
38. Stancliffe 1996.
39. Stancliffe 2011: 27. For the *Amra*, text and translation are available in Clancy and Márkus 1995: 96–128. Doubts about the early date of the *Amra* have recently been raised by Bisagni 2009, but my reading of his work suggests that the evidence for late forms depends on a handful of readings in the latter part of the poem that might simply reflect problems of transmission.

suggest that the fact that Columba and Columbanus share a name in religion, the Latin word for "dove", may reflect Uinnianus's spiritual direction. The vernacular form of the name, Colmán, has been shown to derive from a British rather than an Irish coinage, despite the name being confined almost exclusively to Gaelic-speaking milieus.[40] The name springs into being in the historical record in the later sixth century, and in moments of whimsy one might be tempted to imagine that Uinnianus may have called all his students, secular and clerical, by the same name. Certainly Jonas of Bobbio, in both his name, from the Hebrew for "dove", and his writing, continued to pun on this idea of doves, and it is difficult to believe that Columba's island was transformed from Í to Iona purely by a slip of the pen.[41] Like some new Noah, Uinnianus repopulated the world with his spiritual sons. It may even be the case that this tradition has its origins with Gildas. In *De Excidio* Gildas describes Maglocunus's monastic vocation, after a military career, as follows: "Where you had been a raven, you had become a dove [*ex corvo Columbam*]: as though you were stoutly cleaving the hollow air with your whirring glide and avoiding sinuous twists the savage talons of the swift hawk, you came swiftly and in safety to the caves and consolations of the saints that you can trust so well."[42]

BIBLIOGRAPHY

Anderson, A. O., and M. O. Anderson (eds.) (1961) *Adomnán's Life of Columba*. London, Nelson.
Bartrum, P. C. (ed.) (1966) *Early Welsh Genealogical Tracts*. Cardiff, University of Wales Press.
Bieler, L. (ed.) (1975) *The Irish Penitentials*. Dublin, Dublin Institute for Advanced Studies.
Bisagni, J. (2009) "The Language and Date of Amra Choluimb Chille." In S. Zimmer, ed., *Kelten am Rhein: Akten des dreizehnten Internationalen Keltologiekongress*. Mainz, Bonner Jahrbücher, 1–11.
Bullough, D. (1997) "The Career of Columbanus." In M. Lapidge (ed.), *Columbanus: Studies on the Latin Writings*. Woodbridge, Boydell, 1–28.
Byrne, F. J. (1973) *Irish Kings and High Kings*. London, Batsford.
Campbell, E. (2007) *Continental and Mediterranean Imports to Atlantic Britain and Ireland, AD 400–800*. CBA Research Report 157. York, Council for British Archaeology.
Carey, J. (1984). "Scél Tuáin meic Chairill." *Ériu* 35: 93–111.
Charles-Edwards, T. M. (1976). "The Social Background to Irish *Perigrinatio*." *Celtica* 11: 43–59.
Charles-Edwards, T. M. (2000) *Early Christian Ireland*. Cambridge, Cambridge University Press.
Clancy, T. O., and G. Márkus (eds.) (1995) *Iona: The Earliest Poetry of a Celtic Monastery*. Edinburgh, Edinburgh University Press.

40. Thurneysen 1933: 209; Jackson 1953: 509.

41. The standard view is that the modern form "Iona" drives from a misreading or miscopying of "Ioua"—the genitive and ablative forms of "Io" used by Adomnán. See Anderson and Anderson 1961: 154–5.

42. *DEB* 34.15–9.

de Vogüé, A. (ed.), (1989). *Saint Colomban: Règles et Pénitentiels monastiques*, Bégrolles-en-Mauges, Abbaye de Bellefontaine.

Dumville, D. N. (1984) "Gildas and Uinniau." In M. Lapidge and D. N. Dumville (eds.), *Gildas: New Approaches*. Woodbridge, Boydell, 207–14.

Freeman, P. (2001) *Ireland and the Classical World*. Austin, University of Texas Press.

Herren, M. (1990) "Gildas and Early British Monasticism." In A. Bammesberger and A. Wollman (eds.), *Britain 400–600: Language and History*. Heidelberg, C. Winter, 65–78.

Jackson, K. H. (1953) *Language and History in Early Britain*. Edinburgh, Edinburgh University Press.

Lapidge, M. (1997) *"Precamur patrem"*: An Easter Hymn by Columbanus?" In M. Lapidge (ed.), *Columbanus: Studies on the Latin Writings*. Woodbridge, Boydell, 255–63.

Loveluck, C., and A. O'Sullivan (2016) "Travel, Transport and Communication to and from Ireland, c. 400–1100: An Archaeological Perspective." In R. Flechner and S. Meeder (eds.), *The Irish in Early Medieval Europe: Identity, Culture and Religion*. London, Palgrave, 19–37.

MacCotter, P. (2008) *Medieval Ireland: Territorial, Political and Economic Divisions*. Dublin, Four Courts Press.

McErlean, T. C., and N. Crothers (2007) *Harnessing the Tides: The Early Medieval Tide Mills at Nendrum Monastery, Strangford Lough*. Belfast, Stationery Office.

Ó Cróinín, D. (1982) "Mo-Sinnu moccu Min and the Computus of Bangor." *Peritia* 1: 281–95.

Ó Riain, P. (1981) "The Irish Element in Welsh Hagiographical Tradition." In D. Ó Corráin (ed.), *Irish Antiquity*. Cork, Tower Books, 291–303.

Ó Riain, P. (ed.) (1985) *Corpus genealogiarum sanctorum Hiberniae*. Dublin, Dublin Institute for Advanced Studies.

Sharpe, R. (1984) "Gildas as a Father of the Church." In M. Lapidge and D. N. Dumville (eds.), *Gildas: New Approaches*. Woodbridge, Boydell, 193–205.

Smyth, A. P. (1972). "The Earliest Irish Annals." *Proceedings of the Royal Irish Academy* 72C: 1–48.

Stancliffe, C. (1996) "Venantius Fortunatus, Ireland, Jerome: The Evidence of *precamur patrem*." *Peritia* 10: 91–97.

Stancliffe, C. (1997). "The Thirteen Sermons Attributed to Columbanus and the Question of Their Authorship." In M. Lapidge (ed.), *Columbanus: Studies on the Latin Writings*. Woodbridge, Boydell, 93–202.

Stancliffe, C. (2011) "Columbanus' Monasticism and the Sources of His Inspiration: From Basil to the Master?" In P. Russell and F. L. Edmonds (eds.), *Tome: Studies in Medieval Celtic History and Law in Honour of Thomas Charles-Edwards*. Woodbridge, Boydell, 17–28.

Thurneysen, R. (1933) "Colmān mac Lēnēni und Senchān Torpēist." *Zeitschrift für celtische Philologie* 19: 193–209.

Vogüe, A. de, (1989), *Saint Colomban règles et Pénientiels monastiques*, Erreur Perimes, Abbaye de Bellefontaine.

Williams, H. (ed.) (1899) *Two Lives of Gildas by a Monk of Ruys and Caradoc of Llancarfan*. Cymmrodorion Record Series. London, The Honourable Cymmrodorion Society.

Winterbottom, M. (ed.) (1978) *Gildas: The Ruin of Britain and Other Documents*. Chichester, Phillimore.

Wooding, J. (2002) "Trade as a Factor in the Transmissions of texts between Ireland and the Continent in the Sixth and Seventh Centuries." In P. N. Chatháin and M. Richter (eds.), *Ireland and Europe in the Early Middle Ages: Texts and Transmission*. Dublin, Four Courts Press, 14–26.

Woolf, A. (2006) *Where Was Govan in the Early Middle Ages?* Govan, Friends of Govan Old.

PART III

The Frankish World

6

Columbanus in Brittany

IAN WOOD

From the account of Jonas of Bobbio we can deduce that Columbanus landed in what is now called Brittany when he first arrived on the Continent.[1] Most scholars have thought that the saint disembarked near the eastern corner of the north coast; traditionally the landing place was regarded as being near Saint-Coloumb, at the mouth of the Rance, where the name is thought to commemorate his arrival.[2] There is, however, no early medieval evidence for the place name or the church dedication. In any case Jonas is explicit about where the Irishman landed: it was on the *sinus Brittanicus*.[3] Although he does not identify the place in his description of the saint's journey to the Continent, he uses the same phrase to describe the region from which Columbanus was supposed to have departed, when Theuderic II exiled him from Luxeuil and Francia in 610.[4] Here we can be absolutely certain that Jonas was referring to territory to the west of Nantes. Moreover, Columbanus himself talks of being *in vicinia Brittonum* just before his intended deportation.[5] In other words, we can be certain that for Jonas the *sinus Britannicus* was in what is now southeast Brittany. The supposition that Columbanus landed on the north coast is thus fallacious.

If we wish to be more specific about Columbanus's landing place we have to resort to hypothesis. Here it is worth looking carefully at the term *sinus*, which in classical Latin means a curve, and, by extension, a bay, bight, or gulf.[6] We should therefore be looking for a distinctive part of the coast to the west of Nantes, dominated by a bay. A site that most obviously fits the description is the Golfe de Morbihan, an identification that was made at least as far back as 1915, although it has fallen from academic consciousness.[7] As we will see, this is a very attractive identification, even if it can be no more than a suggestion.

---

1. *VC* I.4: 160.
2. Giot, Giognon, and Merdrignac 2003: 120.
3. *VC* I.4–5: 160–1.
4. *VC* I.21: 198. See also *Brittanica arva*, in *VC* I.20: 196.
5. *Ep.* 4.9: 36–7.
6. Lewis and Short 1879: 1709–10.
7. Concannon 1915: 299.

It is worth asking why the land to the west of Nantes, arguably the Golfe de Morbihan, was known as the *sinus Brittanicus*. Fortunately we know a little about the Britons who dominated the Vannetais, the province of Vannes, which is part of the Morbihan, and indeed lies at the head of the Golfe, since they appear relatively frequently in the *Histories* of Gregory of Tours. I use the terms "Britons" and "British" because, when talking about the fifth, sixth, and seventh centuries, it is impossible to make any ethnic distinction between the Britons of the island of Britain and the Bretons of Brittany.[8] In book IV, chapter 4, which relates to the late 540s, Gregory tells how a *comes* of the Britons, Chanao, wished to kill his brothers and succeeded in disposing of three of them. A fourth, called Macliaw, escaped to the protection of another *comes*, Conomor, who hid him in a grave mound. Having survived, Macliaw went to Vannes, where he took ecclesiastical orders and was elected bishop. After Chanao's death, however, he renounced his position, rejoined his wife, and seized his brother's lands.[9] The next time we meet Macliaw is in c. 569. According to Gregory, he had entered into an agreement with another British *comes*, Bodic, that whichever of the two lived longer would act as guardian for the other's offspring. When Bodic died, however, Macliaw drove his son Theuderic from his lands; the boy gathered a group of followers and succeeded in killing Macliaw, who himself left a son, Waroch.[10]

It is Waroch who is of most interest to us, for he was alive at the time of Columbanus's arrival in the *sinus Brittanicus*. He makes a remarkable number of appearances in Gregory's works, and not just in the *Histories*, for one of his retainers, named Britto, is the villain of a chapter of the *Liber in Gloria Martyrum*. Britto tried to take a belt that had been placed as an offering on the altar of the church of saint Nazarius, near Nantes, only to bash out his brains against the lintel of the church porch as he tried to ride away. His master, shaken by the course of events, made reparations to the church.[11]

Although Gregory tells us that after the death of Clovis the Britons were always subject to the Franks and were therefore ruled by *comites* and not *reges*,[12] it is clear that Waroch was a ruler of some importance; he was surely more powerful than many of the Irish kings whom Columbanus had encountered. He makes his first major appearance in the *Histories* in c. 578, around ten years after his father's death. Having managed to destroy the Saxon contingent in a motley

---

8. Charles-Edwards 2013: 1–2.
9. *DLH* IV.4: 137–8. See Smith 1992: 21; Charles-Edwards 2013: 63.
10. *DLH* V.16: 214.
11. *Liber in Gloria Martyrum*, 60: 79–80 (trans. Van Dam: 84–5).
12. *DLH* IV.4: 137–8.

army sent against him by the Frankish king Chilperic, which also contained men of Touraine, Poitou, the Bessin, Maine, and Anjou, Waroch came to terms with the king, agreeing to pay tribute in return for recognition of his right to the city of Vannes. However, he almost immediately reneged on the payments, sending the bishop of Vannes, Eunius, to announce his decision, much to the king's fury.[13] Just under ten years later Waroch made another appearance, when he and an otherwise unknown Vidimaclis were forced by the Merovingian king Guntram to acknowledge that their cities were subject to the Franks. This agreement did not stop him from seizing the vineyards of Nantes.[14] Such plunder seems to have been a regular occurrence.[15]

It is Gregory's next reference to Waroch that is of most importance for the student of Columbanus. In 590 the Breton *comes* and his son Chanao were causing problems in the valley of the Vilaine, in other words around Rennes and Nantes. To put a stop to this, Guntram sent an army led by his generals Beppolen and Ebrachar. The latter, however, for personal reasons was not prepared to work with the former, who was also disliked by the Merovingian dowager queen, Fredegund, mother of the young Neustrian king Chlothar II.[16] Gregory provides us with the backstory for Fredegund's hostility to Beppolen. Initially he had been a general of Fredegund's husband, Chilperic, who sent him to deal with problems in the region of Angers and Vannes.[17] After the king's murder Beppolen initially supported the widowed queen, but in 586, feeling that he was not getting the promotion that he deserved, he transferred his allegiance to Guntram, who sent him against the cities of Rennes and Angers, which had belonged to Chilperic and which ought to have passed to his son, Chlothar II.[18] Then in 590 Beppolen and Ebrachar were sent to deal with Waroch.[19] At this moment Fredegund, intent on destroying Beppolen, ordered the Saxons of Bayeux to disguise themselves as Britons and to join Waroch's men. In the resulting conflict Beppolen was killed. Ebrachar then marched against Waroch, who failed to escape with his treasure to the islands off the coast, presumably those of the Golfe de Morbihan, and had to make terms. The Frankish general headed to Vannes, where the bishop, Regalis, explained that he and his city had been unable to fulfill their obligations to the Merovingian king because they had been subject to British control, and they took an oath of allegiance to Guntram.

---

13. *DLH* V.26: 232–3.
14. *DLH* IX.18: 431–2.
15. *DLH* V.31: 236.
16. *DLH* X.9: 491–4. On this episode, see Charles-Edwards 2013: 57, 70.
17. *DLH* V.29: 234–5.
18. *DLH* VIII.31, 42: 398, 408.
19. *DLH* X.9: 491–4.

Having apparently re-established Frankish authority in the region, Ebrachar set off for Burgundy. Waroch, however, directed his son Chanao to launch an attack across the Vilaine, where the latter took large numbers of prisoners, many of whom were subsequently manumitted by Waroch's wife using the ritual of taper and tablet. One detachment of the Frankish army was attacked by the locals at Angers, while the main body plundered the region of Tours as it returned home. Upon reaching Guntram's court Ebrachar and his colleague, Wiliachar, were accused of having done a deal with Waroch. According to Gregory, Wiliachar went into hiding. Fredegar adds the information that Ebrachar was subsequently dispossessed of his wealth and left destitute.[20]

Waroch, then, was the dominant Briton in the region of the *sinus Brittanicus* at the time of Columbanus's arrival, so much so that he gave his name to the district. The later Breton name Broërec, which is applied to the Vannetais and the Morbihan, means nothing other than the "Land of Waroch."[21] The Britons of the *sinus Brittanicus* can therefore be identified first and foremost as members of the family of Waroch and their followers. This may help us to understand why the territory was regarded as British; however, it does not help us understand why Columbanus landed there. One simple answer to this question is clearly that boats moved between Ireland and the mouth of the Loire; indeed, Columbanus was sent to Nantes to make just such a crossing.[22] Yet we may be able to go further than this.

Admittedly we are only in the realm of hypothesis, but it is worth remembering that in later tradition it was to this region, and specifically to St.-Gildas-de-Rhuys in the Morbihan, that Gildas retired. The *Life of Gildas*, although it seems only to have reached its present form in the eleventh century, apparently contains information that has been argued on linguistic grounds to be a good deal earlier, reflecting sixth-century reality.[23] Interestingly, according to the *Life*, not only did Gildas settle in the Morbihan, but there he came into contact with a *princeps* called Waroch.[24] He may, of course, be the figure in Gregory's *Histories*, who has been borrowed anachronistically by the hagiographer. But since we know that names did recur in this British family—there are, for example, unquestionably two figures called Chanao[25]—we might guess that there was a Waroch who was active in the middle of the sixth century, at the time of Gildas's arrival, and that he was the father of Macliaw and Chanao I. If the British ecclesiastic did indeed

---

20. Fredegar, IV.12: 10.
21. Giot, Giognon, and Merdrignac 2003: 96, 116. See also Davies 2005: 258–60, 262.
22. *VC* I.23: 205–6.
23. Breeze 2008: 347–50; Breeze 2010: 131–8.
24. *Vita Gildae auctore monaco Ruiensi*, 44–53.
25. Charles-Edwards 2013: 63.

travel to the Continent, it would in all probability have been in the generation prior to the conflict between the two brothers, if one accepts David Woods's identification of the dense cloud referred to in the *De Excidio Britonum* as an allusion to that caused by a volcanic eruption in the southern hemisphere in 536–537.[26] Gildas could well have been in the Morbihan in the 540s.

If we accept that Gildas did indeed settle in southeastern Brittany, in the territory dominated by the family of Waroch, we may be able to identify a reason for Columbanus's decision to move from Ireland to the *sinus Brittanicus*. It is absolutely clear from the Irishman's first letter that Gildas was a figure for whom he had the utmost respect, for he refers to him as *auctor* and cites his opinions.[27] Did Columbanus travel to the Morbihan because of its association with Gildas, or if not with the British ecclesiastic himself perhaps with his disciples? This would certainly provide an explanation for the Irishman's chosen point of arrival. It may also explain the fact that he clearly gathered a number of British followers, who would later travel with him to the Vosges and would be exiled with him in 610.[28] Jonas names Gurgan as being *genere Brittonum*,[29] while on the strength of their names, Autiernus, Comininus, and Eunocus have been identified as British.[30]

The presence of Gildas may explain Columbanus's decision to leave Ireland for the Vannetais. We should not, however, lose sight of Waroch. It has been a point of disappointment that Gregory of Tours says nothing of the arrival of Columbanus or of his establishment in the Vosges, even though the Irishman may well have visited the shrine of Saint Martin on his journey to Burgundy, just as he did in the course of his later deportation to Nantes.[31] The bishop of Tours may, however, shed more light on Columbanus's early years on the Continent than has been realized. We know that the Irishman left the *sinus Brittanicus* in 590 or thereabouts. In the second of his surviving letters, addressed to the Gallic bishops, which can be dated to 603, he states that he had already spent twelve years among them.[32] Jonas, moreover, claims that the saint had spent twenty years in Burgundy, before he was driven out in 610.[33] Thus, we can be certain that the Irishman arrived in the heartland of Guntram's kingdom in c. 590–591.

---

26. *DEB* 93, 3: 70, 133. Woods 2010: 226–34.
27. *Ep.* 1.6–7: 8–9.
28. *VC* I.20: 196.
29. *VC* I.13: 172–4.
30. Kerlouégan 1995: 189–206, at 193. See Wood 2017 for a fuller discussion of this issue, with some reservations about Kerlouégan's argument.
31. *VC* I.23: 200–3.
32. *Ep.* 2.6: 16–19.
33. *VC* I.20: 197.

This, it should be noted, does not date his arrival on the Continent. Jonas states that he had stayed for a little (*paulisper*) in the *sinus Brittanicus*.[34] It is not clear how much time is indicated by this word, but it is likely to be months or a limited number of years, rather than days or weeks, and indeed Jonas uses the same word to describe the length of time that the saint spent in Bregenz before entering Italy.[35]

It would seem, then, that Columbanus left the *sinus Brittanicus* for Burgundy in 590 or possibly 591. That is, his journey took place within months of the campaign of Beppolen and Ebrachar directed against Waroch. Moreover, since, as we have seen, the *sinus Brittanicus* can plausibly be identified with the Morbihan, which was part of the territory controlled by Waroch, or at least to which he laid claim, we can conclude that Columbanus was living in exactly the region attacked by Guntram's generals in 590. There is surely a strong likelihood that his transfer to Burgundy was in some way connected with the return of Ebrachar to the East. This suggests a number of possibilities. On the one hand, Columbanus may have been too closely associated with Waroch for the liking of the Franks, and he may have been forced to accompany Ebrachar's army back to Burgundy. Equally, since we are told by Gregory that complaints were leveled against Ebrachar and Wiliachar, it may be that Columbanus and his monks represented those who had suffered at the hands of the Frankish army and who complained to Guntram.[36] A third possibility is that the arrival of Beppolen and Ebrachar drew Columbanus's attention to the advantages of living somewhat nearer to the royal court. Overlapping with all these possibilities is the point that the Vannetais was a war-torn region both before and after 590, and however attractive the Golfe de Morbihan may have appeared to someone at the Irish monastery of Bangor, in reality it can scarcely have been conducive to the monastic life. This list is obviously no more than a set of possibilities; we can only guess at the reasons for Columbanus moving eastward, even if we can be reasonably certain that the context of the move was the arrival of Beppolen and Ebrachar; the attack on Waroch, the leader of the Britons in the *sinus Brittanicus*; and the return of Ebrachar to Burgundy.

Gregory springs one further surprise. The chapter following the account of the campaign against Waroch seems totally unconnected. The bishop recounts that on discovering that an aurochs had been killed in the forest of the Vosges—something that was deemed illegal—Guntram asked who had perpetrated the act. The royal *cubicularius* Chundo was accused of the crime by the forester, and

34. *VC* I.4: 164.
35. *VC* I.27: 213.
36. *DLH* X.9: 493–4.

when he denied it, Guntram ordered a trial by battle. Chundo was represented by his nephew, who, along with his accuser, died in the contest. Seeing this, Chundo fled for sanctuary, but before he could reach the church of St. Marcellus, he was caught, tied to a stake, and stoned—an act that Guntram immediately repented: *multum se ex hoc deinceps rex paenitens.*[37]

The story of Chundo is well known and is often cited in discussions of the history of trial by battle.[38] In Gregory's narrative, however, it seems somewhat freestanding. Gregory's habit of juxtaposing stories, which is a distinctive feature of his writing, often leads him to place apparently unrelated material side by side in order to direct the reader to interpret the information in one way or another.[39] It is not obvious, however, that there was any purpose behind the juxtaposition of the histories of Waroch and Chundo. On the other hand, the placing of the two stories exactly echoes the move of Columbanus from the *sinus Brittanicus* to the Vosges. Moreover, Annegray would have been a perfect center for royal hunting.[40] Although it can certainly be no more than speculation, it is worth asking whether there is any connection between the establishment of Columbanus's first monastery at Annegray and the king's penitence for the death of Chundo. Gregory's precise words, *multum se ex hoc deinceps rex paenitens*, may be of some interest here. Although historians have been rather inclined to overlook the evidence for the development of penitential thought in the sixth century, before the arrival of Columbanus, it is true that there are relatively few comments on penance in Gregory's *Histories*, other than in the accounts of the notoriously criminal bishops Salonius and Sagittarius, the revolt of the nuns of Poitiers, and Gregory the Great's sermon in 590.[41] The use of the word *paenitens* would seem, therefore, to indicate some major penitential act.[42] Annegray was established almost immediately after Columbanus's move to Burgundy, in 590–591. Although Jonas wrongly names the king at the time as Sigibert (or in one manuscript Childebert),[43] Columbanus's initial patron was surely Guntram.[44] Was Annegray founded to assuage the king's guilt over Chundo's execution?

37. *DLH* X.10: 494.
38. See, for example, Wood 1986: 7–22, at 18.
39. Wood 1993: 253–70.
40. O'Hara 2015: 143–70.
41. On Salonius and Sagittarius, *DLH* V.20, 27: 228, 233. On the nuns of Poitiers, *DLH* IX.39–41, X.15–6. 463, 366, 469, 502–6. On the sermon of Gregory I, *DLH* X.1: 478–9. Other references to *paenitentia* are *DLH* I.20, 44; III.28; V.25; VI.5; VII.16; VIII.20, 46; and IX.33: 17, 29, 125, 231, 271, 338, 386, 412, 453.
42. *DLH* X.10: 494.
43. *VC* I.6: 162.
44. Wood 1998: 99–120, at 105–6

And if this were the case, it might explain Gregory's juxtaposing the tales of Waroch and Chundo. We know that Columbanus was accompanied by Britons when he arrived in Burgundy. They had presumably joined Columbanus while he was in the *sinus Brittanicus*. Moreover, the Britons who were still with him in 610 were told that they could, or should, leave the Vosges.[45] Columbanus's British companions in 590 could have sent news back to the *sinus Brittanicus* following the foundation of Annegray—and any message sent from the Vosges to the Morbihan surely passed through Tours, where Gregory would have heard the news. Moreover, Columbanus's British disciples were not the only Britons in the Vosges; there is the mysterious Carantoc of the monastery of Salicis,[46] who might also have had contacts with the *sinus Brittanicus*.

All this is to pile hypothesis on hypothesis: that Gildas really did settle in the Morbihan, that Columbanus headed for the region because of its association with Gildas, that he moved to the Vosges in the context of Ebrachar's campaign against Waroch, and that he was settled in Annegray by Guntram in expiation for the unjust execution of Chundo. These hypotheses, however, are attached to much harder facts. Columbanus did not land near Saint-Coloumb, on the north coast of Brittany, but in or near the Morbihan, the *sinus Brittanicus*, a region dominated by the British family of Waroch, about whose activities in the region we have a considerable amount of information. Moreover, chronologically Columbanus's moves from the *sinus Brittanicus* to Burgundy and subsequently to the Vosges, coincide with the conclusion of the campaign of Beppolen and Ebrachar against Waroch. Gregory of Tours, in other words, provides us with the context for Columbanus's time in the *sinus Brittanicus* and move eastward. His narrative sheds more light, perhaps a good deal more, on Columbanus's initial career on the Continent than has generally been recognized.

Bibliography

Breeze, A. (2010) "Gildas and the Schools of Cirencester." *The Antiquaries Journal* 90: 131–38.

Breeze, A. (2008) "Where Was Gildas Born?" *Northern History* 45: 347–50.

Charles-Edwards, T. M. (2013) *Wales and the Britons, 350–1064*. Oxford, Oxford University Press.

Concannon, H. W. (1915) *The Life of St. Columban (St. Columbanus of Bobbio): A Study in Ancient Irish Monastic Life*. Dublin, Catholic Truth Society of Ireland.

Davies, W. (2005) "The Celtic Kingdoms." In P. Fouracre (ed.), *The New Cambridge Medieval History*, vol. I, *c. 500–c. 700*. Cambridge, Cambridge University Press, 232–62.

45. *VC* I.20: 196.
46. *VC* I.7: 164–6.

Giot, P.-R., P. Giognon, and B. Merdrignac (2003) *Les premiers Bretons d'Armorique*. Rennes, Presses Universitaires de Rennes.

Gregory of Tours (1885) *Liber in Gloria Martyrum*, ed. B. Krusch. MGH, *Scriptores rerum Merovingicarum*, I, 2. Hannover, 1885; *Gregory of Tours, Glory of the Martyrs*, trans. R. Van Dam. Liverpool, Liverpool University Press, 1988.

Kerlouégan, F. (1995) "Présence et culte des clercs irlandais et bretons entre Loire et Monts Jura." In J.-M. Picard (ed.), *Aquitaine and Ireland in the Middle Ages*. Dublin: Four Courts Press, 189–206.

Lewis, C. T., and C. Short (1879) *A Latin Dictionary*. Oxford, Oxford University Press.

O'Hara, A. (2015) "Columbanus *ad Locum*: The Establishment of the Monastic Foundations." *Peritia* 26: 143–70.

Smith, J. M. H. (1992) *Province and Empire: Brittany and the Carolingians*. Cambridge, Cambridge University Press.

Vita Gildae auctore monaco Ruiensi Vita Gildae auctore monaco Ruiensi, ed. H. Williams. Cymmrodorion Record Series. London, 1899.

Wood, I. (1986) "Disputes in Late Fifth- and Sixth-Century Gaul: Some Problems." In W. Davies and P. Fouracre (eds.), *The Settlement of Disputes in Early Medieval Europe*. Cambridge, Cambridge University Press, 7–22.

Wood, I. (1993) "The Secret Histories of Gregory of Tours." *Revue Belge de Philologie et d'Histoire* 71: 253–70.

Wood, I. (1998) "Jonas, the Merovingians, and Pope Honorius: *Diplomata* and the *Vita Columbani*." In A. C. Murray (ed.), *After Rome's Fall. Narrators and Sources of Early Medieval History. Essays presented to Walter Goffart*. Toronto, University of Toronto Press, 92–120.

Wood, I. (2017) "Columbanus, the Britons and the Merovingian Church." In L. Olson (ed.), *St Samson of Dol and the Earliest History of Brittany, Cornwall and Wales*. Woodbridge, The Boydell Bress, 103–14.

Woods, D. (2010) "Gildas and the Mystery Cloud of 536–7." *Journal of Theological Studies* 61: 226–34.

7

Columbanus and Shunning

The Irish *peregrinus* between Gildas, Gaul, and Gregory

CLARE STANCLIFFE

When one thinks of the encounters between Columbanus and those with whom he came into contact on the Continent, two words spring to mind: confrontation and controversy. This reflects one important aspect of Columbanus's relations with leading figures whom he engaged with. Yet it is surely not the only aspect; otherwise it is hard to see how he could have been so successful as a monastic founder and lasted for some twenty years in Gaul. The perception of Columbanus as engaged in confrontation and controversy arises because of the nature of our sources. Of the four letters that survive from his time in Gaul, three are directly concerned with the Easter controversy, and the fourth was written to his family of monks after Columbanus himself had been exiled. Jonas, author of the *Life of Columbanus and His Disciples*, does provide us with stories about Columbanus's monastic role; but he says nothing of his dealings with bishops, and little about those with royalty or aristocrats until we reach the chapters detailing the events leading up to his exile. Given the patchiness of our sources, this chapter proceeds not just by interrogating the few that we have, but also by trying to place these in context and understand the issues surrounding them. First, it seeks to investigate Columbanus's relationship with Gregory the Great as fully as possible, setting alongside each other all the scraps of available evidence and seeing what emerges. One issue that this approach throws up, which has hitherto attracted little attention, is that of "shunning," or withholding oneself from relations with Christians one perceives as sinful, although they have not been excommunicated. The Insular background to this is investigated in the second section, before turning back in the third section to Columbanus's dealings with the Merovingians in the events leading up to his exile, using our new awareness of shunning as a way of re-reading Jonas's account of how relations between Columbanus and the royal court soured, ending in his exile.

Columbanus's Relationship with Gregory the Great

When we seek to explore Columbanus's relationship to Gregory the Great, an initial assumption may be that we have only one source of evidence, Columbanus's *Epistula* 1, addressed to that pope.[1] Recent scholarship, however, has elucidated that this is just the sole survivor of an unknown number of letters.[2] The loss of others is very understandable given that even Columbanus's five principal letters (addressed to various people) that we have today survived only by the slender thread of two seventeenth-century copies from perhaps the same Bobbio manuscript.[3] If, however, we seek to understand the full extent of Columbanus's relationship with Gregory, then there are additional sources that we can use. For clarity's sake, I shall first set out what the evidence consists of; we may then proceed to a discussion of how the various pieces of evidence might be assessed in relation to each other.

We begin with the letters which Columbanus addressed to Gregory. As mentioned, *Epistula* 1 is the sole survivor. This letter, after introductory remarks, plunges straight into questioning the practice of celebrating Easter on the twenty-first or twenty-second days of the moon, something that was a feature of the Easter tables of Victorius of Aquitaine which were at that time followed throughout Gaul and probably also in Rome.[4] The letter calls upon Gregory to suppress this practice, asserting that Victorius had not been accepted by Irish computistical scholars, and asking for Gregory's support for Columbanus's stance, "for the quelling of this storm that surrounds us"; he had been criticized by the Gallic bishops for celebrating Easter on the fourteenth day of the moon on the grounds that "we ought not to hold Easter with the Jews." After three sides (in Walker's edition) devoted to the Easter controversy, he then turns more briefly to a second question on which he seeks Gregory's ruling, that of whether he should be in communion with bishops who were guilty of simony or who had marital relations with their wives after being ordained as deacons. Thirdly, again briefly, he asks Gregory's advice on monks who abandoned the monastery where they had taken their monastic vows. In relation to both the second and the third questions Columbanus adduces the teaching of Gildas and other Insular authorities. These issues once covered, he then expresses his desire to

---

1. To avoid confusion, I consistently refer to the texts edited by Walker as *Epp.* 1, 2, 3, and 4, using terms like "first letter" to refer to the hypothesised letter that preceded it but has not survived.

2. Charles-Edwards 2000: 359 n. 66 and 368–71; Leso 2013: 360–2; Dubreucq 2015: 105–11, 126. I would like to thank Alain Dubreucq warmly for giving me a copy of his paper before publication.

3. Walker 1957: xxxv; Bieler 1957: lxxiii–lxxv; Dubreucq 2015: 105–7.

4. Papal usage is inferred from Cummian's account and Pope Honorius's apparent recommendation of Victorius's tables to the Irish c. 630: Walsh and Ó Cróinín 1988: 28; cf. Wallis 1999: lx.

visit Gregory in person if such were possible; praises his *Regula Pastoralis,* which he has read; and asks Gregory for copies of his exegetical works on Ezekiel, the Song of Songs, and Zechariah. Finally Columbanus asks Gregory's pardon for his outspokenness; commends *meos,* presumably his monks who were acting as his letter bearers; and ends with a brief return to the Easter question: he has heard from Candidus, Gregory's representative in Gaul since September 595, the pope's reply "that what has been confirmed by long passage of time cannot be changed" but reminds him that "truth has always stood longer."

While this is the only letter of Columbanus to Gregory to have survived, we know of others from references in two of Columbanus's subsequent letters. In his *Epistula* 2, addressed to the bishops assembled in synod at Chalon-sur-Saône c. 603, Columbanus writes: "As I have noted in the *tomo* of my reply, which I have now sent you, though it was written three years ago, all the churches of the entire West do not consider that the resurrection should take place before the passion . . . For the rest, I have informed the holy father in three *tomos* of their [i.e. the western churches'] opinions upon Easter."[5] If we may interpret Columbanus's use of the word *tomus* to denote a substantial letter containing reasoned argument,[6] then the implication would be that by 603 he had written three such letters to the pope on the Easter question. Was one of these the *tom[us] responsionis meae* that he was enclosing for the bishops at Chalon along with *Epistula* 2? That is plausible, since if it had originally been composed for one of the Burgundian bishops, then presumably the bishops at Chalon would already have had access to it, but we cannot rule out other interpretations. Further evidence of Columbanus's correspondence with Gregory comes in *Epistula* 3, written during a vacancy of the Roman see. Here, Columbanus writes that "once and again Satan hindered the bearers of our letters once written to Pope Gregory of blessed memory and annexed to this." These "are forwarded" (note the plural) along with *Epistula* 3. This means that two of the letters which Columbanus had written to Gregory did not get through. It does not tell us how many he had written in toto, but if we put the evidence of both letters together, we may deduce that by 603 he had written three letters to Gregory on the western churches' position on Easter. Presumably one of these is *Epistula* 1, but we should not automatically assume that this was the one written in 600 and forwarded to Chalon in 603, as Walker posited.[7]

---

5. *Ep.* 2.5.

6. Walker 1957: 17, n. 1 implicitly adopts this interpretation when he suggests identifying the *tom[us] responsionis meae* with Columbanus's *Ep.* 1. Cf. also Leo I's famous *Tomus ad Flavianum,* for the Council of Chalcedon, alias his *Ep.* 28.

7. Walker 1957: 17, n. 1.

The collection of Gregory's letters as it survives today is incomplete and does not contain any replies to Columbanus's letters to him. It may in any case be that Gregory found it more diplomatic not to reply in writing, but rather to send verbal messages via letter bearers, or, from 595, via Candidus.[8] Among Gregory's letters written to other correspondents, however, there are two that mention a priest, Columbus. The first of these, written in November 594, is a letter to Venantius, bishop of Luni. It states that Gregory is sending a manuscript of his *Regula Pastoralis* to *domno Columbo presbytero* by the same letter bearers as are bringing Gregory's letter to Venantius and asks him not to hold it back, as another copy will be sent soon for his own use.[9] The second letter is addressed to Conon, abbot of Lérins, and dated to October 600. It commends to him "our son, the priest Columbus."[10] Is Gregory's "Columbus" our Columbanus, who normally wrote his own name in his letters as "Columba?"[11] Although the names are not identical, giving the name a masculine termination would have been an understandable alteration to make, particularly as Gregory had another male correspondent (an African bishop) called Columbus, while the only Columba to feature in his letters was a woman.[12]

A third source of information is the record of a meeting between Columbanus and Laurence, one of Gregory's missionaries to England, who became bishop of Canterbury after Augustine's death. It appears in a letter sent in the names of bishops Laurence, Mellitus, and Justus to the Irish Church, which survives only in an excerpt from its opening paragraphs given by Bede. Its significance for our topic has been demonstrated by Roy Flechner, who dates it between 605 and 615 (inclusive).[13] Since its precise wording is important for us, it is quoted here verbatim:

> The apostolic see . . . directed us to preach to the heathen in these western regions, and it was our lot to come to the island of Britain; before we knew them we held the holiness both of the Britons and of the Irish in great esteem, thinking that they walked according to the customs of the universal Church: but on becoming acquainted with the Britons, we still thought that the Irish would be better. But now we have learned from Bishop Dagan when he came to this island and from Abbot Columbanus when he

8. Charles-Edwards 2000: 370. Columbanus's wording in *Ep.* 1.10 (*Rescribere te persuadet caritas*) might be read as begging for a written reply from Gregory.

9. Gregory, *Reg.Ep.* V.17, noted by Walker 1957: 11, n. 2.

10. Gregory, *Reg.Ep.* XI.9.

11. So in the opening salutations of *Epp.* 1, 2, 3, and 4. In *Ep.* 5.1 he punned upon his name by utilizing a different word for a pigeon, Palumbus. In general, see Flechner 2005: 72–4.

12. E.g., *Reg.Ep.* IV.35 (of July 594) and XII.2; index, Norberg 1982: 1132.

13. Flechner 2005: esp. 68–71.

came to Gaul that the Irish do not differ from the Britons in their way of life. For when Bishop Dagan came to us he refused to take food, not only with us but even in the very house where we took our meals.[14]

These three groups of sources, all of them letters, and contemporary or nearly so, comprise our main evidence for probing Columbanus's relationship with Gregory. In addition, two somewhat less precise types of evidence may contribute something. One consists of other letters of Gregory that concern his perception of the moral failings of the Gallic episcopate and his desire for these to be addressed in a synod. When these are set alongside Columbanus's comments in his *Epistulae* 1 and 2, there is a degree of convergence which suggests that their criticisms are not independent of each other. This issue has been raised recently in a paper by Alain Dubreucq[15] and will be discussed further below. The second type of evidence is dedications, and here the chief problem is that these are not attested until much later. The most interesting dedication is that of Columbanus's third monastery, Fontaine, to Saint Pancras, who was a Roman martyr. This dedication is only attested in the fourteenth century, but it is rare in France, and the most plausible context for such a dedication is arguably that of Columbanus's original mission.[16] This hypothesis is strengthened by the likelihood that the Roman mission to Kent, sent by Gregory the Great, also founded a church dedicated to Saint Pancras. Again, the dedication is not attested until the fourteenth century, but the ruins of the Anglo-Saxon church still stand some three hundred feet east of Augustine's original monastery of Saints Peter and Paul (later Saint Augustine's), and the most probable context for this dedication is that of the original mission to Kent.[17] It seems, then, a plausible hypothesis that both dedications originated with gifts of relics of Saint Pancras sent from Rome when these two churches were founded, and in the case of Fontaine, that was during the pontificate of Gregory. Gregory is known to have involved himself with this martyr cult. He had removed the Roman church of Saint Pancras from its negligent priests in March 594, replacing them with a monastic community, and he had acceded to a request of the bishop of Milan for relics of Saints Paul, John, and Pancras in July 599.[18] We might also note that both the

14. Bede, *HE* II.4.
15. Dubreucq 2015: 118–9.
16. O'Hara 2015: 160–1; Bully 2015: 57.
17. Cambridge 1999: 211–6 and n. 53. Cambridge argues that the surviving church might belong to a "second generation" of church buildings, albeit still early in the seventh century, but the evidence is so fragmentary that this is somewhat hypothetical.
18. *Reg.Ep.* IV.18 and IX.184.

monastic church at Luxeuil and that at Bobbio bore dedications to Saint Peter,[19] although that is obviously a common dedication, so less significant.

Let us now seek to put this information together. First, as already recognized,[20] the argument for identifying Gregory's "Columbus" with our Columbanus is a strong one, given the explicit reference to Gregory's sending him a copy of his *Cura Pastoralis* and the fact that Columbanus had already read this text when he wrote *Epistula* 1. For Gregory, the normal route to Gaul lay along the coast (whether travelling by ship or road) via Liguria and Provence, and then up the Rhone valley, as we can see from the route that Augustine and his companions took.[21] The Lombard disruptions in northern Italy had rendered the inland routes too hazardous, which means that the coastal route was probably also the one favoured by Columbanus's letter bearers. Further, continental scholars have drawn attention to the network of islands with hermitages and monasteries along this coastline, thus linking Gorgonia and Capraria, southwest of Luni, with Lérins, and making the link between the Columbus mentioned in Gregory's letter to the bishop of Luni and that mentioned in his letter to the abbot of Lérins highly plausible.[22] The argument for identifying Gregory's Columbus and our Columbanus would be further strengthened if we were to regard the *tom[us] responsionis meae* of 600 as having originally been sent to Gregory, as suggested above, as this would then tally with the date of Gregory's letter to Conon commending "Columbus" to him. The details dovetail neatly. Even better, if we look at table 7.1, which sets out the Easter data for the *Latercus* followed by Columbanus side by side with those of Victorius of Aquitaine followed by the Gallic Church,[23] we can see why Columbanus would have been in trouble with the Gallic bishops in 600: he would have celebrated Easter on April 3 that year, which according to their calendar meant that he was celebrating on Luna 14—precisely the point for which they attacked him.[24]

If, then, we regard it as likely that one of Columbanus's letters to Gregory was written in 600, when were his other letters to that pope written? On the evidence of Gregory's letter to the bishop of Luni, Columbanus probably first made contact with the pope in 594. We might surmise that Columbanus had written to Gregory earlier in the year, but that his letter bearers had wanted to

---

19. According to Jonas, the Bobbio dedication preceded Columbanus: *VC* I.30.

20. Walker 1957: 11, n. 2; Flechner 2005: 72–4.

21. Blair 1970: 49–51.

22. Judic 2000: 97–8; Dessì and Lauwers 2009: 231–4.

23. I gratefully acknowledge my debt to Dr. Eric Graff, then of the National University of Ireland, Galway, for a table providing the full Easter data for the *Latercus* eighty-four-year cycle, Victorius, and Dionysius in parallel columns alongside AD dates, from which this is a very small selection.

24. *Ep.* 1.4.

Table 7.1. The Easter Dates of the *Latercus* and of Victorius of Aquitaine

AD	*Latercus* Easter	*Latercus* Luna age at Easter	Victorius's Easter	Victorius's Luna age at Easter
591	April 15	18	April 15	16
592	March 30	14	April 6	18
593	April 19	16	March 29	21
594	April 11	18	April 11 or 18	15 or 22
595	March 27	14	April 3	19
596	April 15	14	April 22	19
597	April 7	17	April 7 or 14	15 or 22
598	March 30	20	March 30	18
599	April 12	14	April 19	19
600	April 3	16	April 10	21
601	March 26	19	March 26	17
602	April 15	20	April 15	18
603	March 31	16	April 7	21

return to Gaul before the weather became too bad. They had thus left Rome, while Gregory had a copy of his *Regula Pastoralis* made and sent to Columbanus with his own letter bearer via Luni in November 594. There is, however, one major problem about accepting that the relationship between Columbanus and Gregory originates as early as 594: in that case, about the Irish Church differing in certain respects from "the customs of the universal church," as Laurence's letter puts it, when they left Rome in 596? The problem of squaring the evidence of our different sources is a real one, but it is not insurmountable. If we look at the Easter data for 594 (see table 7.1), we can see that it is not a year in which the Gallic bishops are likely to have worried about Columbanus celebrating Easter on his date of April 11, since it was one of those years in which Victorius gave alternatives that included that date. On the other hand, Columbanus himself might well have objected to them celebrating as late as April 18, Luna 22. This is precisely his main objection to Victorius's tables in his *Epistula* 1.3. *Epistula* 1 itself cannot have been the letter that Columbanus wrote in 594 because it mentions Candidus, who was only appointed to Gaul in 595, but it may repeat some of the same arguments. I would thus suggest that although the topic of Easter already figured in Columbanus's first letter to Gregory, as we can see from Gregory's reply as transmitted by Candidus,[25] Columbanus raised the issue in the form of an attack on Victorius's Easter, rather than as a defence or an exposition of his own Easter practice. That would have meant that in 596, when the

25. *Ep.* 1.12.

missionaries were setting out for England, they (or at least Gregory) might have known that Columbanus objected to an Easter as late as Luna 22, but might not have grasped how his own Easter cycle functioned and the fact that in most years it meant that he celebrated Easter on a different date.

In addition, we have no means of knowing how significantly the Easter question figured in Columbanus's first letter to the pope. It might perhaps have taken second place to the issue of the failings of the Gallic bishops and the question of how Columbanus should relate to them. Initially, while he was at his first foundation of Annegray and a relative newcomer to the area, it is possible that neither Easter nor the need to relate to the Gallic bishops caused serious problems. But when Columbanus founded Luxeuil, probably between 593 and 596,[26] he was establishing his main monastery in a place with an existing Christian population and church, either within or immediately outside a functioning *castellum*.[27] This would have brought Columbanus into direct contact with the existing church structures, which would have made discordant Easter dates far more problematic. It might also have brought him into contact with bishops who, in his eyes, were leading sinful lives. As we shall see, this issue had worried Gildas, who had given somewhat conflicting rulings on it, probably at different phases of his life. That could well have left Columbanus unsure about how he should interact with Gallic bishops, about whose personal lives or payment of money for office he may well have heard rumours while also receiving information in his role as a confessor. The likelihood that the issue of episcopal immorality, as well as Easter, was raised in his first letter to Gregory is suggested by the fact that part of Gregory's response was to send Columbanus a copy of his *Regula Pastoralis*. This was Gregory's treatise on the responsibilities of the bishop's role and the qualities required for such a weighty calling. After all, we do need to find a reason why Gregory privileged sending a copy of his work to Columbanus, a mere priest, when he had not yet managed to get sufficient copies made to send it to his bishops, for whom it was primarily intended.

If these—admittedly hypothetical—suggestions are allowed, then what occurred in 594 was Columbanus consulting the pope about problems that he saw with the Gallic Church—not problems that the Gallic bishops had raised with him. That means that this first letter may not even have counted as one of the three in which Columbanus informed the pope of the Western Churches' opinions about Easter.[28] It also means that Columbanus would initially have

---

26. Charles-Edwards 2000: 368 and n. 112.
27. VC I.10; Bully 2014; cf. O'Hara 2015: 143–60 and 169–70.
28. *Quod quidem illi sentiunt de Pascha sancto papae per tres tomos innotui: Ep. 2.5.*

struck Gregory as a kindred spirit, objecting to the very faults that Gregory himself found so intolerable in many bishops.[29]

Indeed, one might go further and suggest that Columbanus was one of the sources from whom Gregory learned of the widespread failings of the Gallic episcopate. Luce Pietri has shown that Gregory initially had very few contacts in Gaul and knew little of it, and then emerged in August 595 with a much better grasp of its problems and a plan for combating them.[30] "I have learned from certain informants (*quibusdam . . . narrantibus*) that in the lands of Gaul and Germany, no one may obtain holy orders without handing over a payment," he wrote to Vergilius, bishop of Arles, in August 595.[31] Who else might his informants have been? Assuredly not the bishops themselves, nor King Childebert (who had asked the pope to make Vergilius the papal vicar in Gaul), all of whom were implicated in the practice. It may well have been Columbanus's no doubt forthright comments in 594, looking with the eyes of a newcomer, that first made Gregory aware of the scale of the problem, though the pope will presumably have made wider enquiries, talking to Gallic pilgrims who came ad limina.[32]

Particularly striking is the common ground between Columbanus's comments and a later letter of Gregory to the four leading bishops of Burgundy, Syagrius of Autun, Etherius of Lyon, Vergilius of Arles, and Desiderius of Vienne; it was written in July 599.[33] Here, Gregory begins by urging them to give heed to the *patrum regulis et praeceptis dominicis* and expel avarice, and he then broaches the topic of simony in Gaul, which is denounced as a sin and a heresy. Next he passes to the problem of laymen who are precipitately catapulted into the role of bishop with no prior formation. He then turns to rumours that women are living with those in holy orders. Finally, he urges upon the bishops the summoning of synods as a remedy against dissension and to promote discussion on ecclesiastical observance. If circumstances do not permit the holding of synods twice a year, as enjoined by previous synods, then at least they should meet once a year. Gregory trusts that the synod, which he urges one of the bishops[34] to hold alongside his own trusted

---

29. See Neil 2013: 17.
30. Pietri 1991: 109–15.
31. *Reg.Ep.* V.58, lines 29–31.
32. Alongside simony, Gregory adduces the problem of laymen suddenly raised to episcopal office (*Reg.Ep.* V.58), which is not mentioned in Columbanus's surviving *Ep.* 1.
33. *Reg.Ep.* IX.219.
34. The text of *Reg.Ep.* IX.219, line 186 reads Aregius, but comparison with lines 194–5 and with the following letter written to Aregius himself implies that this is a slip for Syagrius; see *Reg.Ep.* IX.220, lines 54–6. Aregius, though bishop of the unimportant see of Gap, is charged with attending the synod and reporting back on it to Gregory: *Reg.Ep.* IX.220, lines 54–62.

representative, will ban everything that is opposed to the sacred canons: there should be no payments made for sacred orders, no precipitate promotions of laymen to bishoprics, and no women living with priests (except for those close relatives allowed by earlier canons). Now four of the five topics covered here are found in Columbanus's letters: the issues of simony and marital relations in *Epistula* 1.6, and the need for stricter observance of Christ's and the apostles' teaching, approval of the holding of a synod (even if it cannot be held once or twice every year, according to the canons), and hopes that such a synod might be used to promote stricter observance of the gospel religion and apostolical tradition, in *Epistula* 2.[35] Alain Dubreucq has recently suggested that Columbanus's denunciations of the Gallic bishops' sins in *Epistula* 1 may be related to Gregory's remarks against simony and the problem of clerical relations with women in this papal letter to the leading bishops of Burgundy.[36] There certainly appears to have been a close relationship between the ideas of the two churchmen on the besetting sins of the Gallic bishops and the idea of a synod to remedy them. Presumably Columbanus was one of Gregory's informants on the Gallic bishops, while the idea of a synod originated with Gregory. Columbanus might have received a letter from Gregory that was later lost; more plausibly, Candidus might have mediated Gregory's plans for a reforming synod to him.[37]

It is not possible to unpick all the details of the relationship between Gregory and Columbanus because so much of the correspondence is lost. We may conclude, however, that it developed over at least six years, and perhaps longer, extending from 594, when it probably began, to 600 (or beyond). Whether there were one or two letters between these dates depends on whether one regards the lost letter of 594 as constituting one of the three *tomi* which Columbanus wrote to Gregory about the Western Churches' views on Easter. Can we place the surviving *Epistula* 1 in this sequence? The fact that Columbanus there spends considerable space combating the holding of Easter on Luna 21 or 22 might suggest that it was written in a year when that had occurred in Gaul, either 597 or 600 (see table 7.1).[38] The year 600 is obviously an attractive option since we have deduced, independently, that Columbanus probably wrote to Gregory that

---

35. Columbanus, *Ep.* 2.2 and 2.6.

36. Dubreucq 2015: 118–9. Since he accepts Walker's date of 600 for Columbanus's *Ep.* 1, he is not thinking of this letter as the direct source of Gregory's remarks.

37. The *Life of Sadalberga* claims that Gregory *melliflua remisit scripta* to Columbanus, but this may mean simply that Gregory sent Columbanus some of his works: Kerlouégan 1986: 589 and 595, n. 3. If Gregory had written a letter to Columbanus, one would expect his monks to have preserved that carefully and Columbanus to have cited it in his subsequent letters.

38. 594 is ruled out because Candidus only took up his post in September 595.

year. Yet 600 seems very late for Columbanus to be asking Gregory's opinion on how he should relate to the Gallic bishops, since Luxeuil was probably founded by 596 at the latest, and 597 is unlikely because in that year his Easter date of April 7 would have been acceptable to the Gallic bishops, whereas when he wrote he was under attack for "hold[ing] Easter with the Jews."[39] My suggestion is therefore that *Epistula* 1 was sent in 596, when his Easter would have fallen on *Luna* 14 for the second year running, thus explaining his trouble with the bishops, while the Gallic Church would have celebrated Easter on what, for him, was Luna 21 (see table 7.1). Whether or not it reached Gregory, we cannot know, but if not, then presumably some of the same issues about the moral failings of the Gallic episcopate were repeated in a subsequent letter.

Although many uncertainties remain, some important conclusions can be reached. First, it was an extensive relationship that developed over at least six years; it was not the case of Columbanus writing a single letter to Gregory. Secondly, the Easter question was not the only issue raised; the moral failings of the Gallic episcopate certainly figured, and other topics may well have been explored, including, perhaps, a request from Columbanus for relics for the dedication of his new church at Fontaine. We should also note Columbanus's warm response to Gregory's literary works; these left their mark on his own later writings, including both his letters and his sermons.[40] Thirdly, the relationship probably did not start with Columbanus appealing to Gregory because he was in trouble over the Easter question. It appears to have begun in 594, very probably with Columbanus asking Gregory's advice on how to deal with Gallic bishops who were, in his eyes, guilty of serious sins, as well as his attacking Victorius's readiness to celebrate Easter on Luna 21 or 22. Even *Epistula* 1, which was later than this letter of 594, reads more like a fraternal consultation rather than a formal appeal to the pope. Finally, what emerges from putting Columbanus's approaches to Gregory side by side with Gregory's own concerns is the extent of the common ground between them. At its deepest level this arises from the fact that both of them genuinely strove to be disciples of Christ. They were both monks; they both took the injunctions of the New Testament seriously; and they both belonged to the ascetic tradition in the church, which regarded the calling to the priesthood as a heavy responsibility. There is thus much to be said for regarding Gregory's own views as closer to those of Columbanus than to those of the Gallic episcopate.

---

39. *Ep.* 1.4; Stancliffe 2006: 205–7.
40. See Kerlouégan 1986: 589; Wright 1997: 78–9; Stancliffe 1997: 110–1; Stancliffe 2009: 15.

Columbanus and the Insular Tradition of Shunning

If we move away from regarding Columbanus's correspondence with Gregory simply as a means of extricating himself from the hostility of the Gallic bishops over his Easter dating, then it makes sense to explore more deeply other issues raised in *Epistula* 1: What, from Columbanus's viewpoint, were his problems with the Gallic bishops, and why did he raise these with Gregory? He writes: "Concerning those bishops, however, who ordain uncanonically, that is for hire, I ask what you decree; Gildas the writer (*auctor*) set them down as simoniacs and plagues. Are we really to communicate with them? For many, which is too serious a matter, are known to be such in this province." Similarly, he asks for Gregory's ruling on those who had committed secret adultery as deacons, whether such men could later become bishops; "yet I mean adultery committed with their partners (*cleantillis*); which among our teachers is reckoned to be of no less guilt."[41] Thirdly, he asks Gregory about monks who go against their vows in fleeing the monastery where they have made their monastic profession, and, against their abbot's wishes, "either relapse or flee to the deserts. Finnian the writer (*Vennianus auctor*) questioned Gildas about them, and he sent a most polished reply; but yet through the zeal for learning anxiety grows ever greater."[42] The final topic obviously relates to Columbanus's responsibilities as an abbot and is not considered here; but it, like the questions over bishops' morals, reveals Columbanus as standing in an Insular tradition in which both Gildas and Finnian were regarded as authorities, this being the implication of the use of the word *auctor* to describe them. What is more, we possess sizable excerpts of Gildas's response to Finnian, as it was regarded as authoritative teaching by the early Irish Church.[43] We also possess the text of Finnian's *Penitential*, in which we find the ruling about a cleric fathering a child with his wife after they have taken a vow precisely as Columbanus reports it: "it is not less than if he . . . had sinned with a strange girl"; and Columbanus reproduces this ruling in his own *Penitential*.[44]

These references to Insular authorities have not gone unremarked. The most extreme line was taken by Joseph Kelly, who noted a number of seemingly insulting comments and puns in Columbanus's *Epistula* 1, addressed to a pope known for his regard for gravitas, and interpreted it as Columbanus deliberately asserting to Gregory the purity of the Western Churches over against the

---

41. *Ep.* 1.6; but "partners" is my translation; cf. Bieler 1963: 82–3 and 243–4, n. 12.
42. *Ep.* 1.7.
43. Sharpe 1984: esp. 196–9.
44. Cf. *Penitentialis Vinniani* § 27 and *Paenitentiale Columbani* § 8.

corruption of the established Church. Columbanus wanted Gregory to accept his point of view; he did not seek to win him over. Columbanus's citation of "an obscure British monk who died barely a generation ago" was all part of this campaign "not to convince Gregory but to assert to him, again, the importance of the Western, Celtic Christians."[45] That Columbanus knowingly wrote an offensive letter to the pope[46] is implausible, given his sincerity in wanting to live his whole life as a disciple of Christ, coupled with his warm appreciation of Gregory's own writings. But a less extreme version of Kelly's views has recently been put forward: Columbanus would surely have realized "how out of place the reference to Gildas would be in the context of *Epistula I*," but included it "to assert . . . the importance of 'western Christianity.'"[47]

I suggest an alternative approach: Columbanus specifically cited Gildas because he had been formed in a tradition that regarded Gildas's views as authoritative and because those views were strikingly pertinent to the situation in which Columbanus found himself, but he had good reason to seek clarification because Gildas's views appeared self-contradictory and also at variance with the norms of the Church in Gaul. The earlier of Gildas's works known to Columbanus was his *De Excidio Britonum*, of c. 535.[48] This is an excoriation of the rulers of Britain, both kings and also the clerical establishment. Gildas attacks simony, which appears to have been rife, and the failure to set a good example—both topics of concern to Columbanus.[49] Gildas's work would have seemed particularly apt to Columbanus because the great majority of the British churchmen of Gildas's day were very comparable to those of Gaul as depicted by Gregory of Tours. There were many churchmen seeking bishoprics from ambition and enjoying the status and power that the position gave, while paying scant heed to the ideals set out in the New Testament epistles.[50] But Gildas also insists that even those bishops who are themselves leading a good life are at fault because they do not denounce evildoers, but rather associate with them.[51] It was precisely because of this lack of speaking out and warning people about the consequences of their sins on the part of the bishops—the *rectores* and *speculatores*—that Gildas felt it was incumbent on him to take on this role, though he was not even a priest.[52] He draws attention to the role of the watchman (*speculator*) in Ezekiel, who must

---

45. Kelly 1991; quotation at 219.
46. Kelly 1991: 222.
47. Leso 2013: 365.
48. On the dating see Stancliffe 1997: 179–81.
49. *DEB* 67 and 107.3–4. For the latter cf. Columbanus, *Ep.* 2.3–4.
50. *DEB* 66–7, 108.3–109. Cf. Davies 1968: 140–1.
51. *DEB* 69.1–3, 110.1.
52. *DEB* 1, esp. § 14; cf. 65.

warn the wicked or else he himself will be held responsible for their fate.[53] One can see that the words and example of Gildas would have prompted Columbanus likewise to speak out about the shortcomings of the Gallic bishops, though he was but a priest himself; for many in the watchman tradition, this role was not restricted to bishops, and that includes the first part of Jerome's *Commentary on Isaiah*, which Columbanus certainly knew.[54]

As regards the specific question raised by Columbanus in *Epistula* 1.6, that of whether he should be in communion with simoniac bishops, Gildas's approach in *De Excidio* was clear: it was incumbent upon all true bishops and priests not just to be personally chaste and good, but actively to castigate evildoers and stop them from sinning, remembering how Eli's own failure to correct the shameful practices of his sons had resulted in his being punished by God along with them, despite his own refusal to participate.[55] In relation to persistent evildoers who refused to mend their ways, one must refuse to associate with them, as we see from Gildas's criticism of contemporary British clergy:

> Which hated the counsel of evil-wishers and refused to sit with the impious . . . ? Which of them refused to admit into the ark of salvation (now, the church) anyone who was God's adversary, as did Noah in the time of the flood, so as to make it quite clear that only the innocent and most worthy repenters should be present in the house of the Lord?[56]

In the same vein, Gildas elsewhere cites Saint Paul's condemnation of the gentiles given over to every wickedness together with those consenting thereto, "not only those who do these things, but those who consent to their doing,"[57] and he shortly passes on to I Corinthians 5:11, where Paul turns to the problem of nominal Christians who are behaving unacceptably, calling upon the Christian community to shun them: "I meant you not to mix with anyone who is called a brother but is in fact a fornicator or greedy or idolatrous or blasphemous or drunken or rapacious, and not even to take bread with them."[58]

What is confusing, however, is that in the fragmentary reply of Gildas's response to Finnian's inquiry, directly alluded to by Columbanus in *Epistula* 1.7, Gildas takes a totally different line.

53. *DEB* 91.
54. Jerome, *Commentarii in Hiezechielem* I.iii.21, *speculator magisterque*; knowledge of it attested in Columbanus, *Ep.* I.9. See further Mohrmann 1977; Smit 1971: 40–5, 50.
55. *DEB* 69.1–3, 76.
56. *DEB* 69.2–3.
57. *DEB* 97–98.1, citing Rom. 1.25–6, 28–32, and explicitly commenting on its application to his contemporary Christian priests and people.
58. *DEB* 100.3.

On excommunication Gildas says: Noah did not wish to keep his son Ham, teacher of the magic art, away from the ark or from sharing his table. . . . Isaac did not forbid Abimelech and Ahuzzath and Phichol, leader of the army, to share his table: but they swore oaths to each other after eating and drinking. . . . Our Lord Jesus Christ did not avoid eating with publicans, so as to save all sinners and whores.[59]

Even more important in the present context is Fragment 7:

> It is better for fellow bishops and abbots, and also fellow subjects, not to judge each other. But let them gently and patiently reprove those in bad odour for some ill report, rather than openly accuse them; as far as they can in conscience, they should avoid them as suspect (without excommunicating them like truly guilty ones and keeping them from their table or the peace), unless it is absolutely necessary to meet and talk to them. . . . But as for persons we know without doubt to be fornicators, we keep them from the peace and table, unless they do penance in the legitimate manner, as it [is written]: "If any man is called a brother, and he is a fornicator . . ." and the rest [I Cor. 5:11]. We ought to exclude our brothers from communion of the altar and of the table when times demand it for no other reason than in well proven cases of the principal sins.[60]

Juxtaposition of these passages, all ascribed to Gildas, enables us to see why Columbanus might well have wanted to get clarification from Gregory. It was not just that the Bible, and even the New Testament, included teaching and stories that pointed in diametrically opposite directions. Even more confusing, we find Gildas using the example of those whom Noah admitted to the ark first to justify exclusion from the Church, then as an example of inclusivity, and first citing I Corinthians 5:11 as teaching to be followed as regards fellow Christians who failed to live up to the expected standard of morality, then hedging this around with conditions. It is possible that Columbanus was mistaken in thinking that the letter to Finnian was by the same person as the *De Excidio*; but given that Gildas was highly regarded by the early Irish Church and had probably died only about twenty years before Columbanus left Ireland for Gaul, it is more plausible to regard the letter as genuine, but the product of a later period and different circumstances than the *De Excidio*.[61] A likely

---

59. *Fragmenta* 1.
60. *Fragmenta* 7, with some changes to Winterbottom's translation.
61. Stancliffe 1997: 181.

hypothesis is that his earlier work had had a significant impact on the British Church and sparked an ascetic revival, but that this had spawned a rigorist approach which Gildas now regarded as rather unhelpful because it focused too much on taking pride in one's own ascetic practices at the expense of showing Christian charity to others.

Excommunication at that period is a highly complex topic, not least because the language used is imprecise, its meaning is frequently not spelt out, and it is used in different contexts with different implications. For instance, it is sporadically used in monastic contexts as early as the Rule of Basil, and more systematically in the Master and Benedict. Here, it denotes the abbot temporarily suspending a monk from the communal regime, so focusing on meals (*mensa*) or the office (*oratorium*), or both, until he makes amends.[62] In the Church at large, however, it is a sanction regulated by episcopal synods and applied by a bishop, and its primary implication is suspension from the Eucharist. This might take the form of putting the sinner on a similar footing to a catechumen, when he would have to leave the church building along with the catechumens after the first part of the Eucharist, or the more serious step of excluding him from the whole Christian community. The latter would entail exclusion from attending any part of the Eucharist or even entering the church building, and also from sharing meals with Christians.[63] In the Insular world there may have been crossover in the usage of excommunication from the monastic to the wider pastoral sphere, thanks to the extension of monastic penitential practices to laypeople.[64] This is particularly significant for our consideration of Columbanus, since his penitential shows that he expected laypeople to aspire to the same standards as monks: he lays down penances for laypeople not just for serious sins like killing, sodomy, and fornication, but even for masturbation, drunkenness, and desiring—but not committing—adultery.[65]

In addition to this potential in Insular circles for blurring the distinction between excommunication in a monastic setting and in the wider Church, Insular churchmen also differed from those on the Continent by practising a lesser form of exclusion, that of shunning. We see this in Gildas's Fragment 7, quoted above, in which he draws a distinction between formal excommunication, on the one hand, and withdrawing oneself from the company of morally dubious persons, on the other. Gildas recommends this practice of shunning where there

---

62. Rosé 2015.
63. Vogel 1952: 59–67, 175–81; Mathisen 2009: 539–52; Bührer-Thierry 2015: 11–3; Péricard 2015: 21–3. For an example of the less serious kind, see Gregory of Tours, *Vita patrum* XVII.2.
64. Cf. Meens 2014: 45–6; Körntgen 1993: 35–7.
65. *Paenitentiale* B, §§ 15–7, §§ 22–3. Meens 2014: 55–7.

is uncertainty about someone's guilt or their sins are relatively minor. Flechner has also noted that it is appropriate where a minority is critical of a majority that it regards as sinful, but is in no position to excommunicate.[66] This practice of shunning was widely recognized by the British Church, and at this date seemingly by the Irish Church also: witness the example of the Irish Dagán, who, according to Laurence's letter quoted above, had refused even to eat in the same house as the Roman missionaries—presumably on the grounds that the latter were associating with pagan or loose-living Anglo-Saxons.[67] Those recommending such shunning could look back not just to Saint Paul but also to the example of Saint Martin, who had been extremely reluctant to eat with the Emperor Maximus (who had blood on his hands), or to communicate with those bishops who were implicated in the execution of Priscillian, an allegedly heretical Spanish bishop; and also that of Saint Patrick, who had called on all "holy and humble men at heart" to recognize that Coroticus and his men, who had massacred some and carried off others of Patrick's Irish converts, should be excluded from the community; no one should fawn upon them, take food or drink with them, or receive alms from them till they repented.[68] In addition to these precedents, Gildas may have been influenced by Pelagian views, which insisted that all baptized Christians should be holy in deed, not just name, and "should live, humble and gentle by the example of Christ, shunning the company of all evil men to the extent that you do not take *food with fornicators or the covetous or detractors or drunkards or the grasping.*"[69]

We do not find on the Continent the same official recognition of the practice of shunning, although Saint Paul's recommendations and the incident involving Saint Martin would have been known. The closest parallel known to me occurred during the trial of Bishop Praetextatus, when Gregory of Tours records that he himself had spoken out against the bishops being cowed into silence by King Chilperic, and had recalled to them both the words of Ezekiel about the responsibility of the watchman to speak out and the example of Saint Martin and the Emperor Maximus. King Chilperic had demanded that Gregory come to see him on his own and first threatened him, then tried to win him over, offering

---

66. Flechner 2005: 76. On the need to excommunicate only when guilt is clear-cut, see Péricard 2015: 23–5.

67. To the evidence discussed by Flechner 2005: 74–7 and Herren and Brown 2002: 130–6, one can add the case of King Judicael of Brittany, who refused to eat with Dagobert because he was *relegiosus et temens Deum ualde*: Fredegar IV.78.

68. Sulpicius Severus, *Vita Martini* 20, esp. § 2, and *Dialogi* III.11–13; Patrick 1993: esp. 7.

69. *De virginitate* 7, based on the translation of Herren and Brown 2002: 132, but italicizing the quotation from I Cor. 5.11. Note that this passage from *De virginitate* comes immediately after the sentence from there that is quoted with approval by Gildas in *DEB* 38.2.

COLUMBANUS AND THE MEROVINGIANS

If the Insular background to the shunning of sinners was in Columbanus's mind as he wrestled with how to relate to simoniac Gallic bishops, it was equally in his mind when he faced the question of how to deal with the royal family. This is a crucial topic, since it began with Columbanus being welcomed by the king and granted land for establishing his monasteries, but ended in his being driven into exile at the royal command. Why should the Merovingians originally have been keen to patronize Columbanus, but then turned against him? We have only one of Columbanus's letters from this period, so depend largely on Jonas's *Life of Columbanus and His Disciples*. This was clearly written for a specific audience and agenda c. 640, and the question of how far it can be trusted will be discussed below. First we must see how Jonas tells the story;[73] his details and the precise wording are often important for us.

Jonas briefly sets the scene by sketching how royal power passed after Sigibert's death to Childebert, and then to his two sons, Theudebert and Theuderic, along with their grandmother, the dowager queen Brunhild (Sigibert's widow). Theuderic succeeded in Burgundy and was initially delighted to have Columbanus within his kingdom, visiting him often. Columbanus urged him to abandon his mistresses and take a wife so as to father legitimate offspring; but at this the devil entered into Brunhild, who is equated with the wicked queen Jezebel in the Bible: she feared that she would be displaced as queen if her grandson took a legitimate wife. So one day, when Columbanus was visiting Brunhild, she produced Theuderic's sons born of mistresses and demanded: "These are the king's sons: strengthen them with your blessing." Columbanus refused: "You should know that these will never wield the royal sceptre, for they have come out of brothels." Brunhild was furious and issued an order that none of Columbanus's monks should go outside the monastery's bounds, nor should any support be given to the monks. Thus threatened, Columbanus sought the court, then at Époisses, letting the king know that he was at his door but refusing to enter. Theuderic tried to propitiate him by sending a royal feast out to him, but Columbanus cursed (*abominatus*) it, saying, "It is written: *the Most High rejects the gifts of the wicked*; for it is not fitting for the lips of God's servants to be polluted by the food of one who refuses the servants of God entrance not only to their own dwelling places, but also to those of others."[74] The dishes slipped from the nerveless grasp of the servants and shattered on the ground as they ran to tell the king what had transpired. Columbanus spent the night outside the king's house, and at first light Theuderic and Brunhild came and asked his pardon, promising to put things right.

But their good intentions did not last, and the king returned to his mistresses. Columbanus responded with a critical letter, threatening the king with excommunication if he did not mend his ways. This angered Brunhild, who inflamed the king against Columbanus. She stirred up the court and magnates to turn Theuderic against Columbanus, while also working on the bishops, disparaging

---

73. *VC* I.18–9. Wallace-Hadrill's translation and notes to Fredegar IV.36 are also useful.

74. *VC* I.19, italicizing Ecclesiasticus 34:23. Cf. also Prov. 15:8: *victimae impiorum abominabiles Domino.*

Columbanus's *religio* and the character of his monastic rule. As a result Theuderic went to Luxeuil and asked Columbanus "why he differed from the customs of others in the kingdom, and would not allow entrance to the inner enclosure to all Christians." Columbanus responded "that it was not his custom to lay open the dwelling places of God's servants to laymen, outsiders in religion (*saecularium hominum et relegione alienis*), but that he had convenient and suitable places ready where guests could be received." The king insisted that if Columbanus wished to receive royal gifts and support, he should admit all comers to all parts of the monastery. Columbanus hit back that if the king chose to violate his rule, he would accept none of his gifts, and he prophesized that if Theuderic had come to destroy the monastery and its rule, then "your kingdom shall speedily crumble and you with all your family shall be destroyed." Theuderic responded that "if he continued to defy the conventions of the country he should go back whence he had come. At the same time all the courtiers cried out that they had no desire to have there a man who would have nothing to do with them." The story continued with Columbanus and his Irish and British monks eventually being forced into exile.

Two questions concern us here regarding Jonas's narrative. How far should this be taken as a historical account of what may actually have happened in 610 and the preceding years, as opposed to reflecting the story that Jonas wished to spin c. 640? And how does the Insular background on shunning help us to interpret it?

Contemporary scholars are agreed that Jonas had an agenda when writing c. 640, which we need to take into account when assessing his work.[75] He wrote after the overthrow of Columbanus's original Merovingian patrons by Chlothar II and after significant changes had been made to Columbanus's original Rule and religious observances, including the computation of Easter. By pinning all the blame for the events leading up to Columbanus's exile on Brunhild, and to a lesser extent on Theuderic, Jonas was able to present their supplanter, Chlothar II, in a favourable light and also to exonerate the bishops and magnates who had been involved in attacking Columbanus's practices. Linked to this, Jonas also covered up the fact that Columbanus had run into trouble with the bishops earlier in his life, never mentioning the Easter controversy and implying that problems arose only shortly before he was exiled, and that these were due to Brunhild's machinations rather than originating with the bishops. Nonetheless, Jonas was in a position to be well informed about the events leading up to Columbanus's expulsion in 610; given the emotional angst and existential threat

---

75. Wood 1994: 194–7; Charles-Edwards 2000: 345–6, 350–71; Stancliffe 2001.

to Columbanus's foundations that this caused, these events are likely to have been well remembered. Where his account tallies with what can be gleaned from other sources or from what we know of Columbanus's Insular background, we should not reject it.

A general point is that Jonas has used hagiographer's license to order his material to some extent thematically, rather than chronologically. He has thus grouped Columbanus's dealings with the royal family into book I, 18–19, with the concomitant (and doubtless deliberate) effect that the many years of royal support (probably including land for the foundation of his monasteries) are passed over rapidly, while the emphasis falls on the final quarrel.[76] Turning now to this, if we exclude the prophecies put into Columbanus's mouth by Jonas, we find that overall his account is plausible, as far as it goes. Jonas does not explicitly mention Theuderic's marriage to a Visigothic princess, Ermenberga, but what he says of Columbanus's remonstrations with the king about the need to produce "royal offspring from an honourable queen" clearly fits with this marriage, which is attested in Fredegar's Chronicle as having taken place in 607. Fredegar further tells us that the marriage was never consummated because "the talk of Brunechildis his grandmother and of his sister Theudila poisoned him against his bride."[77] That Brunhild followed this up by putting Columbanus on the spot by asking him to bless the king's bastards is possible, though not else-where attested.[78] In any case, Columbanus's forthright opposition to Theuderic's mistresses and advocacy of marriage turned Brunhild against Columbanus, and she determined to get rid of him. As Ian Wood has shown, the role here attributed to Brunhild gains credibility by tallying with what can be deduced about her from elsewhere. He has shown that Brunhild's opposition to having a younger queen threaten her position at court can be supported by her op-position in a parallel instance; that Brunhild is attested in the hagiography about Desiderius of Vienne as persecuting another churchman who had urged Theuderic to take a wife and father legitimate sons; and that Brunhild can be shown to have persecuted other churchmen for their perceived opposition to her family, being ready to exile or kill them if it suited her.[79] Charles-Edwards, however, regards the role attributed to Brunhild in the breakdown of Theuderic's marriage as implausible, because Brunhild had been in favour of an earlier marriage alliance between her daughter and Hermenigild, son of the Visigothic king Leovigild, and because her own empathy with her sister's brutal death at

---

76. Charles-Edwards 2000: 352–6; cf. Wood 1994: 194–7, and Wood, 1998.
77. Fredegar IV.30.
78. Johnston, chapter 4 in this volume; cf. Charles-Edwards 2000: 360–3.
79. Wood 1994: 130–6 and cf. 194–7; also Nelson 1978.

the hands of an earlier Merovingian would have rendered her sympathetic to the plight of Ermenberga.[80] But what Brunhild cared about was her own family, not a general Visigothic alliance,[81] and there was no stable Visigothic dynasty. In fact Witteric, Ermenberga's father, had the last king of Leovigild's dynasty "deposed, mutilated and then murdered in 603."[82] This makes Brunhild's hostility to Witteric's daughter plausible; and in the context of Merovingian society, in which a queen whose husband had died was in a vulnerable position, Brunhild's ruthless attempts to remain in power are entirely explicable.

Nonetheless, while we should not reject Jonas's story, it is likely enough that he focused on just one aspect of a complex set of circumstances that together led to the outcome of Columbanus's exile. This means that Charles-Edwards's discussion as to why Theuderic eventually exiled Columbanus should be given due weight: it is thorough and acute.[83] The most significant points that he makes are, first, that the Easter controversy remained a running sore between Columbanus's foundations and the bishops from 600 (or earlier) right through to the aftermath of the Synod of Mâcon in 626–627; it was not settled as a result of Columbanus's exile. Secondly, he draws attention to the factionalized nature of the Burgundian court and nobility, on the one hand, and on the other to Columbanus's position as a controversial figure who had long since alienated a majority of the Gallic bishops over his refusal to change his Insular Easter reckoning, thereby showing his refusal to accept the authority of the Gallic bishops. What had hitherto preserved Columbanus from being disciplined or driven out was a combination of his obvious Christian commitment, which led to his being respected as a holy man, together with his appeal to the papacy. The former won him respect from the royal family and from at least some of the aristocracy and bishops, while the latter meant that he could be given the benefit of the doubt as long as he retained the support of the court. All this is plausible; I disagree only regarding the timing and the reasons for his losing such royal support. Charles-Edwards thinks that he retained this up to 610, when political weakness led Theuderic to exile him because he was a source of division. I suggest a more drawn-out process, one that incorporates Jonas's story: that Columbanus lost the support of Brunhild c. 607, when Theuderic appeared to be listening to his (and others') advice rather than hers over his marriage to the Visigothic princess.

---

80. Charles-Edwards 2000: 359–60. His further point about Arigius's role in the embassy asking for Ermenburga's hand is rendered less significant when we recall that Arigius, as metropolitan bishop of Lyons, was the most important churchman in Burgundy (Mathisen 2000: 288), which would explain his role.

81. Nelson 1978: 39–45; Wood 1994: 135.

82. Collins 1983: 57.

83. Charles-Edwards 2000: 356–9, 367–71.

This is dated to 607 and comes just a year after the killing of Brunhild's closest ally at court, Protadius. At this point her power weakened, giving an opening to magnates who had a different agenda. But in the event Brunhild fought back to reassert her dominance at the Burgundian court. She did this by eliminating her political opponents, while also seeking to counteract Columbanus's influence with Theuderic.[84] In Jonas's account of Columbanus's visit to Époisses, it is Theuderic who wants to mollify Columbanus, not Brunhild. But Brunhild was successful in preventing Ermenberga from taking her position as Theuderic's queen, and Theuderic returned to his mistresses. Krusch's date of c. 607–608 for this is plausible, and the whole drama that Fredegar assigned to a single year was in reality spread out over at least three years.[85]

It was when Columbanus subsequently threatened Theuderic with excommunication that Brunhild went out of her way to build a coalition against him and above all to work on Theuderic to change his mind about Columbanus. At this point, Columbanus's adoption of an Insular hard-line approach played into her hands. At Époisses, what Columbanus had been doing was "shunning" the court: he had refused to enter it, and had refused to accept the king's food. There are three points to note here. First, Columbanus was shunning the court even though the king had not been excommunicated. As we saw above, this behaviour tallies with Insular teaching; but it would have seemed harsh and inappropriate in Gaul, where shunning was not recognized, and even in cases of excommunication there was often no ban on eating with the sinner. In general, exclusion from sharing meals with a sinner appears to have been a much commoner practice in Ireland and Britain than it was on the Continent.[86] A second point arises from Bonnie Effros's study of the significance of feasting together in Merovingian Gaul. She draws attention to its role in forging *amicitia*, bonds of friendship and alliances, not least between the lay and the ecclesiastical worlds. Indeed, it was all the more important for churchmen since other avenues were closed to them.[87] This means that at a time when Columbanus should have been seeking to gather support for the hard line that he was taking on Theuderic's adulterous behaviour after his marriage, he was boycotting one of the most valuable sources of such support. This left the way open for Brunhild to play on their sense that Columbanus was being too demanding of the king, and on their feelings of exclusion from his holy circle—something that was reinforced when Columbanus refused to admit laypeople to the inner enclosure of his monastery,

---

84. Fredegar IV.24–32; Wood 1994: 131–3.
85. Fredegar IV.36; cf. *VC* I.19.
86. Meens 2015; Flechner 2005: 69, 74–7.
87. Effros 2002: 25–37.

as the king demanded. Note the courtiers' comment: "They had no desire to have somebody in these places who would not associate with everyone."[88] As regards access to the inner enclosure, it may also have been the case that those who were most concerned (although Jonas does not let on to this) were the bishops, who found themselves excluded; for Columbanus refused episcopal oversight over his monasteries.[89] Thirdly, by holding himself aloof from the court Columbanus was running the risk of appearing politically disloyal. On top of that, he openly rejected the king's gifts. Since we are here dealing with a culture of gift and countergift, this was probably read by the court as signifying that he would no longer pray for the king—prayer being the countergift for Theuderic's material support.[90] It is small wonder that at this point he lost Theuderic's favour.

One aspect of Jonas's story requiring further consideration is Columbanus's defence of monastic purity against contamination by a sinful ruler. Mayke de Jong skilfully presented this as focused on the boundaries between monastic space and royal space, and the interdependence between them, with both monasteries and kings deriving benefit from a positive relationship—and thus as a topic for Jonas's own time.[91] This was taken further by Albrecht Diem, who rejected the historicity of this event and argued that the idea of the inner monastic enclosure as "holy space" was an invention by Jonas, drawing on Caesarius of Arles's *Regula ad virgines*.[92] Their ideas are interesting but do not take account of all the evidence. First, the quarrel was not focused just on maintaining holy space; rather, this was part of a wider attempt by Columbanus to maintain his and his monks' purity from the polluting effects of the sinful king and his court. This is shown by the story of Columbanus rejecting the king's food, together with the words that Jonas puts into his mouth on that occasion. Nor was this concern with purity an innovation of Jonas's time. Columbanus himself specified confession every day and also seems to have been concerned to maintain sacred boundaries as regards both eating (note the requirement to bless spoons) and space.[93] Further, a desire to maintain monastic purity from polluting influences

---

88. *VC* I.19: 191.

89. *Ep.* 3.2. Cf. Stancliffe 2001: 202.

90. Charles-Edwards 2000: 382–3; cf. Angenendt 2008: the general principle of *pro animo* gifts was understood in Columbanus's lifetime, though not yet tariffed in any precise way. Columbanus's *Regula monachorum* 7 actually alludes to prayer for one's enemies, as well as for almsgivers and for peace between kings, as occurring during the daily office, but he would probably not have offered a mass for a sinful king; cf. *Praefatio Gildae* canon. 23.

91. De Jong 2001: 307–12, 327–8.

92. Diem 2007: 524, 531–42; his claim that Jonas modelled his account of Columbanus and Theuderic on that of Nicetius of Trier in Gregory of Tours's *Vita patrum* lacks convincing evidence. Diem 2011: 63.

93. Columbanus, *Regula coenobialis* §§ I–III; cf. *Regula monachorum* VI on the importance of inner purity, and *Ep.* 2.8 on the need for physical seclusion from the world.

may well have derived from Columbanus's Irish roots. An anonymous *Life of Brigit* tells how Saint Brigit vomited the food of an "impure" (*immundus*) druid; instead she had to be given milk from a cow milked by a Christian virgin.[94] Again, concern to maintain an inner sacred enclosure free from the pollution of sinful laity may well reflect Columbanus's background in Ireland, which drew on both native and biblical ideas of holy places in relation to the ordering of ecclesiastical sites.[95] Secondly, de Jong and Diem were unaware of the Insular concept of shunning. That, however, is precisely what Columbanus was doing at Époisses. It may also, as Johnston suggests, be an example of Irish *troscad*;[96] but, as we have seen, it is certainly an example of Columbanus refusing to associate with someone who, though not excommunicated, was a fornicator—but one with whom he needed to treat. The issues raised in Columbanus's letter to Gregory, the high sexual standards demanded even of laypeople in his penitential, and the teaching of Gildas all fit with Jonas's account here. This interpretation is further strengthened when we look at the language that Columbanus used when objecting to Theuderic's desire to open Luxeuil's inner enclosure to men who were *saeculares* and *religione alieni*. *Saeculares* of course denotes laymen, but it carries overtones of people still immersed in the *saeculum*, which candidates forswore at baptism,[97] while ecclesiastical synods regularly used terms such as *habeatur alienus* as a synonym for excommunication.[98] Conversely, *religionis virtus* is precisely what Jonas had identified as lacking in the Gaul to which Columbanus came, despite its being nominally Christian.[99] The Insular tradition that strove to hold all forms of worldly contamination at bay by avoiding intercourse with anyone suspected of slipshod Christianity explains much about the way in which Jonas portrays Columbanus's dealings with Frankish Gaul, and it makes it likely that Jonas is here reflecting Columbanus's own practice. The vagueness of the term *religio*, together with its generally positive meaning, will have suited Jonas's purpose. As we have seen, Brunhild is depicted as stirring up the bishops against Columbanus by disparaging his *religio* and besmirching the status of his monastic rule; Theuderic's critical visit to Luxeuil follows shortly

94. *Vita I Brigitae* ch. 10. Cf. Meens 1995: 15–6.

95. Cf. Doherty 1985: esp. 57–9; Picard 2011; Charles-Edwards 2000: 358; Johnston, chapter 4 this volume.

96. See chapter 4 in this volume.

97. Cf. *Abrenuncias Satanae, pompis ejus, luxuriis suis, saeculo huic?* from the Bobbio Sacramentary (Duchesne 1949: 324, n. 4) with *VC* I.10 on the children of the nobility entering Luxeuil *ut, exspreta faleramenta saeculi et praesentium pompam facultatum temnentos, aeterna praemia caperent.*

98. E.g., *Synodus I S. Patricii* canons. 7, 21, 24, 31; Tours (461) canons 2, 3, and 9, as cited by Mathisen 2009: 542; Lyon II (567–70) canons 2 and 4 (*Concilia* II); Vogel 1952: 176, 178.

99. *VC* I.5.

thereafter. Columbanus's Easter practice is probably subsumed within the catch-all *religio*,[100] and I suggest that shunning was included also.

CONCLUSION

A combination of the scantiness and the nature of our sources poses a challenge to historians seeking to understand Columbanus's career on the Continent and his relationships with the people he encountered there. This chapter has sought to show that advances in our knowledge are still possible; we can gain a more nuanced understanding of his relationship with Gregory the Great, and fresh insight into how relations with the Merovingian court turned sour. Intriguingly, it turns out that there is a thread that links the two, and which leads back also to Gildas. That is, the question of how to behave towards those wielding power who were sinful. This chapter has brought out Columbanus's reluctance to associate with them. He himself had the highest Christian standards: one should aim at perfection. Yet those in power in Gaul, both bishops and the king, did not just fall short; they were guilty of what the Christian tradition regarded as serious sins. Unlike Gregory the Great, Columbanus was not by nature a diplomat. Rather, he sought to confront people with their sins; if this was impossible or got him nowhere, his inclination was to shun them. We have seen this in his reluctance to be in communion with sinful bishops in the 590s, and the same practice played a significant role in developing the rift between himself and Theuderic over the years 607–610. In this, he shows the indelible impression left on him by the tradition of Gildas and of his native Ireland.

BIBLIOGRAPHY

Angenendt, A. (2008) "*Donationes pro anima*: Gift and Countergift in the Early Medieval Liturgy." In J. R. Davis and M. McCormick (eds.), *The Long Morning of Medieval Europe: New Directions in Early Medieval Studies*. Aldershot, Ashgate, 131–54.

Bieler, L. (ed.) (1963) *The Irish Penitentials*. Scriptores Latini Hibernici 5. Dublin, Dublin Institute for Advanced Studies.

Bieler, L. (1957) "Notes on the Text Tradition and Latinity of St Columban's Writings", in *Sancti Columbani Opera*, ed. G. S. M. Walker, pp. lxxiii–lxxxii.

Blair, P. H. (1970) *The World of Bede*. London, Secker and Warburg.

Bührer-Thierry, G. (2015) Introduction to *Exclure de la communauté chrétienne: sens et pratiques sociales de l'anathème et de l'excommunication (IVe–XIIe siècle)*, ed. G. Bührer-Thierry and S. Gioanni. Turnhout, Brepols, 7–18.

---

100. Charles-Edwards 2000: 358.

Bührer-Thierry, G., and S. Gioanni (2015) *Exclure de la communauté chrétienne: Sens et pratiques sociales de l'anathème et de l'excommunication (IVe–XIIe siècle).* Turnhout, Brepols.

Bully, S. (2015) "Le monastère de Fontaine." In *Colomban et l'Abbaye de Luxeuil au cœur de l'Europe du haut moyen âge.* Archéologie en Franche-Comté, 5. Besançon, Direction régionale des affaires culturelles de Franche-Comté—Service régional de l'archéologie, 56–57.

Bully, S., et al. (2014) "Les origines du monastère de Luxeuil (Haute-Saône) d'après les récentes recherches archéologiques." In M. Gaillard (ed.), *L'empreinte chrétienne en Gaule du IVe au IXe siècle.* Culture et société médiévales 26. Turnhout, Brepols, 311–55.

Cambridge, E. (1999) "The Architecture of the Augustinian Mission." In R. Gameson (ed.), *St. Augustine and the Conversion of England.* Thrupp, Stroud, Sutton Publishing, 202–36.

Charles-Edwards, T. M. (2000) *Early Christian Ireland.* Cambridge, Cambridge University Press.

Collins, R. (1983) *Early Medieval Spain: Unity in Diversity, 400–1000.* London and Basingstoke, Macmillan.

Concilia = Les Canons des conciles mérovingiens (VIe-VIIe siècles) (1989) Latin text of C. de Clercq, with French translation, introduction, and notes by J. Gaudemet and B. Basdevant. 2 vols. Sources Chrétiennes 353–54. Paris, Éditions du Cerf.

Davies, W. H. (1968) "The Church in Wales." In M. W. Barley and R. P. C. Hanson (eds.), *Christianity in Britain, 300–700.* Leicester, Leicester University Press, 131–50.

De Jong, M. (2001) "Monastic Prisoners or Opting Out? Political Coercion and Honour in the Frankish Kingdoms." In M. de Jong, F. Theuws, and C. van Rhijn (eds.), *Topographies of Power in the Early Middle Ages.* Leiden, Brill, 291–328.

De virginitate (1866) In C. Halm (ed.), *Sulpicii Severi Opera.* Corpus Scriptorum Ecclesiasticorum Latinorum 1. Vienna, appendix, 224–50.

Dessì, R. M., and M. Lauwers (2009) "Désert, église, île sainte: Lérins et la sanctification des îles monastiques de l'antiquité à la fin du moyen âge." In Y. Codou and M. Lauwers (eds.), *Lérins, une île sainte de l'antiquité au moyen âge.* Turnhout, Brepols, 231–79.

Diem, A. (2007) "Monks, Kings, and the Transformation of Sanctity: Jonas of Bobbio and the End of the Holy Man." *Speculum* 82: 521–59.

Diem, A. (2011) "Inventing the Holy Rule: Some Observations on the History of Monastic Normative Observance in the Early Medieval West." In H. Dey and E. Fentress (eds.), *Western Monasticism ante Litteram: The Spaces of Monastic Observance in Late Antiquity and the Early Middle Ages.* Turnhout, Brepols, 53–84.

Doherty, C. (1985) "The Monastic Town in Early Medieval Ireland." In H. B. Clarke and A. Simms (ed.), *The Comparative History of Urban Origins in non-Roman Europe.* Oxford, British Archaeological Reports, International Series 255. 1:45–75.

Dubreucq, A. (2015) "L'Œuvre épistolaire de Colomban et les échanges épistolaires de son temps." In F. Schnoor et al. (eds.), *Gallus und seine Zeit: Leben, Wirken, Nachleben.* Monasterium Sancti Galli 7. St. Gallen, Stiftsbibliothek St. Gallen, 101–27.

Duchesne, L. (1949) *Christian Worship, Its Origin and Evolution: A Study of the Latin Liturgy up to the Time of Charlemagne,* trans. M. L. McClure. 5th edition; repr. London, Society for Promoting Christian Knowledge, 1919.

Effros, B. (2002) *Creating Community with Food and Drink in Merovingian Gaul.* New York and Basingstoke, Palgrave Macmillan.

Flechner, R. (2005) "Dagán, Columbanus, and the Gregorian Mission." *Peritia* 19: 65–90.

Gildas (1978a) *De Excidio Britonum.* In M. Winterbottom (ed. and trans.), *Gildas: The Ruin of Britain and Other Works.* Chichester, Phillimore, 13–79.

Gildas (1978b) *Fragmenta*. In M. Winterbottom (ed. and trans.), *Gildas: The Ruin of Britain and Other Works*. Chichester, Phillimore, 80–82, 143–88.

Gregory of Tours (1937) *Decem Libri Historiarum*. ed. B. Krusch and W. Levison. Scriptores, *Scriptores rerum Merovingicarum* 1/1. MGH. Hanover.

Gregory of Tours (1885) *Vita patrum*. In B. Krusch (ed.), *Scriptores rerum Merovingicarum* 1/2. MGH. Hanover; new edition 1969, 211–94.

Herren, M. W., and S. A. Brown (2002) *Christ in Celtic Christianity*. Woodbridge, Boydell Press.

Jerome (1964) *Commentarii in Hiezechielem*, ed. F. Glorie. Corpus Christianum Series Latina 75. Turnhout, Brepols.

Judic, B. (2000) "L'influence de Grégoire le Grand dans la Provence du VIIe siècle." In C. de Dreuille (ed.), *L'Église et la mission au VIe siècle: La mission d'Augustin de Cantorbéry et les églises de Gaule sous l'impulsion de Grégoire le Grand*. Paris, Éditions du Cerf, 89–120.

Kelly, J. F. (1991) "The Letter of Columbanus to Gregory the Great." In *Gregorio Magno e il suo tempo*. Studia Ephemeridis "Augustinianum" 33. Rome, Institutum Patristicum "Augustinianum," 1:213–23.

Kerlouégan, F. (1986) "Grégoire le Grand et les pays celtiques." In J. Fontaine, R. Gillet, and S. Pellistrandi (eds.), *Grégoire le Grand*. Paris, Éditions du Centre National de la Recherche Scientifique, 589–96.

Körntgen, L. (1993) *Studien zu den Quellen der frühmittelalterlichen Bussbücher*. Sigmaringen, Thorbecke Verlag.

Krusch, B. (ed.) (1905) *Ionae Vitae Sanctorum Columbani, Vedastis, Iohannis*. MGH, *Scriptores rerum Germanicarum in usum scholarum separatim editi*. Hanover and Leipzig.

Leso, T. (2013) "Columbanus in Europe: The Evidence from the *Epistulae*." *Early Medieval Europe* 21: 358–89.

Mathisen, R. W. (2000) "Syagrius of Autun, Virgilius of Arles, and Gregory of Rome: Factionalism, Forgery, and Local Authority at the End of the Sixth Century." In C. de Dreuille (ed.), *L'Église et la mission au VIe siècle: La mission d'Augustin de Cantorbéry et les églises de Gaule sous l'impulsion de Grégoire le Grand*. Paris, Éditions du Cerf, 260–90.

Mathisen, R. W. (2009) "Les pratiques de l'excommunication d'après la législation conciliaire en Gaule (Ve–VIe siècle)." In N. Bériou, B. Caseau, and D. Rigaux (eds.), *Pratiques de l'eucharistie dans les Églises d'Orient et d'Occident (Antiquité at Moyen Âge)*. Collection des Études Augustiniennes, Série Moyen Âge et Temps Moderne 45. Paris, Institut des Études Augustiniennes, 1:539–60.

Meens, R. (1995) "Pollution in the Early Middle Ages: The Case of the Food Regulations in the Penitentials." *Early Medieval Europe* 4: 3–19.

Meens, R. (2014) *Penance in Medieval Europe 600–1200*. Cambridge, Cambridge University Press.

Meens, R. (2015) "The uses of Excommunication in Missionary Contexts (Sixth–Eighth Centuries)." In G. Bührer-Thierry and S. Gioanni (eds.), *Exclure de la communauté chrétienne: Sens et pratiques sociales de l'anathème et de l'excommunication (IVe-XIIe siècle)*. Turnhout, Brepols, 143–56.

Mohrmann, C. (1977) "Episkopos—Speculator." In C. Mohrmann, *Études sur le latin des chrétiens*, vol. 4, *Latin chrétien et latin médiéval*. Storia e Letteratura 143. Rome, Edizioni di Storia e Letteratura, 231–52.

Neil, B. (2013) "The Papacy in the Age of Gregory the Great." In B. Neil and M. Dal Santo (eds.), *A Companion to Gregory the Great*. Leiden and Boston, Brill, 3–27.

Nelson, J. L. (1978) "Queens as Jezebels: The Careers of Brunhild and Balthild in Merovingian History." In D. Baker (ed.), *Medieval Women*. Studies in Church History, Subsidia 1. Oxford, Blackwell for the Ecclesiastical History Society, 31–77.

O'Hara, A. (2015) "Columbanus *ad Locum*: The Establishment of the Monastic Foundations." *Peritia* 26: 143–70.

Paenitentiale = Columbanus's *Penitential* (1957) In G. S. M. Walker (ed.), *Sancti Columbani Opera*. Scriptores Latini Hiberniae II. Dublin, Dublin Institute for Advanced Study, 168–180.

Patrick (1993) *Ep. ad milites Corotici*. In L. Bieler (ed.), *Libri Epistolarum Sancti Patricii Episcopi*. Royal Irish Academy Dictionary of Medieval Latin from Celtic Sources, Ancillary Publications 4 = Clavis Patricii 2. Dublin, The Royal Irish Academy.

Penitentialis Vinniani.(1963) In L. Bieler (ed.), *The Irish Penitentials.*Scriptores Latini Hibernici 5. Dublin, Dublin Institute for Advanced Studies, 74–95.

Péricard, J. (2015) "L'excommunication dans le royaume franc: Quelques remarques sur le législation canonique et ses contournements (Ve–IXe siècle)." In G. Bührer-Thierry and S. Gioanni (eds.), *Exclure de la communauté chrétienne: Sens et pratiques sociales de l'anathème et de l'excommunication (IVe–XIIe siècle)*. Turnhout, Brepols, 21–37.

Picard, J.-M. (2011) "Space Organization in Early Irish Monasteries: The *Platea*." In C. Doherty, L.Doran, and M. Kelly (eds.), *Glendalough: City of God*. Dublin, Four Courts, 54–63.

Pietri, L. (1991) "Grégoire le Grand et la Gaule: Le projet pour la réforme de l'Église Gauloise." In *Gregorio Magno e il suo tempo*. Studia Ephemeridis "Augustinianum," 33. Rome, Institutum Patristicum "Augustinianum," 1:109–28.

Praefatio Gildae de poenitentia (1963). In L. Bieler (ed.and trans.), *The Irish Penitentials*. Scriptores Latini Hibernici 5. Dublin, Dublin Institute for Advanced Studies 60–5.

Regula coenobialis (1957) In G. S. M. Walker (ed.), *Sancti Columbani Opera*. Scriptores Latini Hiberniae II. Dublin, Dublin Institute for Advanced Study, 142–68.

Regula monachorum (1957) In G. S. M. Walker (ed.), *Sancti Columbani Opera*. Scriptores Latini Hiberniae II, Dublin, Dublin Institute for Advanced Study, 122–42.

Rosé, I. (2015) "Exclure dans un monde clos? L'*excommunicatio* dans les règles monastiques du haut Moyen Âge." In G. Bührer-Thierry and S. Gioanni (eds.), *Exclure de la communauté chrétienne: Sens et pratiques sociales de l'anathème et de l'excommunication (IVe–XIIe siècle)*. Turnhout, Brepols, 119–42.

Sharpe, R. (1984) "Gildas as a Father of the Church." In M. Lapidge and D. Dumville (eds.), *Gildas: New Approaches*. Studies in Celtic History 5. Woodbridge, Boydell Press, 193–205.

Smit, J. W. (1971) *Studies on the Language and Style of Columba the Younger (Columbanus)*. Amsterdam, Hakkert.

Stancliffe, C. (1997) "The Thirteen Sermons Attributed to Columbanus and the Question of Their Authorship." In M. Lapidge (ed.), *Columbanus: Studies on the Latin Writings*. Woodbridge, Boydell Press, 93–202.

Stancliffe, C. (2001) "Jonas's *Life of Columbanus and His Disciples*." In J. Carey, M. Herbert, and P. Ó Riain (eds.), *Studies in Irish Hagiography: Saints and Scholars*. Dublin, Four Courts Press, 189–220.

Stancliffe, C. (2006) "Columbanus and the Gallic Bishops." In G. Constable and M. Rouche (eds.), *Auctoritas: Mélanges offerts à Olivier Guillot*. Paris, Presses de l'Université Paris-Sorbonne, 205–15.

Stancliffe, C. (2009) "Creator and Creation: A Preliminary Investigation of Early Irish Views and their Relationship to Biblical and Patristic Traditions." *Cambrian Medieval Celtic Studies* 58: 9–27.

Sulpicius Severus (1967) *Vita Martini*, ed. J. Fontaine. *Sulpice Sévère, Vie de saint Martin*, vol. 1. Sources Chrétiennes 133. Paris, Éditions du Cerf.

Sulpicius Severus (2006) *Dialogi*, ed. J. Fontaine. *Sulpice Sévère, Gallus: Dialogues sur les "vertus" de saint Martin*. Sources Chrétiennes 510. Paris, Éditions du Cerf.

Synodus I S. Patricii (1963). In L. Bieler (ed. and trans.), *The Irish Penitentials*, Dublin, Dublin Institute for Advanced Study, 54–9.

Vita I Brigitae (1647), ed. J. Colgan. *Trias Thaumaturga*. Louvain, 527–42.

Vogel, C. (1952) *La discipline pénitentielle en Gaule des origines à la fin du VIIe siècle*. Paris, Letouzey et Ané.

Walker, G. S. M. (ed.) 1957. *Sancti Columbani Opera*. Scriptores Latini Hiberniae II. Dublin, Dublin Institute for Advanced Study.

Wallis, F. (1999) *Bede: The Reckoning of Time*. Translated Texts for Historians 29. Liverpool, Liverpool University Press.

Walsh, M., and D. Ó Cróinín (1988) *Cummian's Letter De controversia paschali and the De ratione conputandi*. Toronto, Pontifical Institute of Mediaeval Studies.

Wood, I. (1994). *The Merovingian Kingdoms 450–751*. Harlow, Longman.

Wood, I. (1998). "Jonas, the Merovingians, and Pope Honorius: *Diplomata* and the *Vita Columbani*." In A. C. Murray (ed.), *After Rome's Fall: Narrators and Sources of Early Medieval History; Essays Presented to Walter Goffart*. Toronto, University of Toronto Press, 99–118.

Wright, N. (1997) "Columbanus's *Epistulae*." In M. Lapidge (ed.), *Columbanus: Studies on the Latin Writings*. Woodbridge, Boydell Press, 29–92.

8

Orthodoxy and Authority

Jonas, Eustasius, and the Agrestius Affair

ANDREAS FISCHER

Meeting the *gentes* meant encountering diversity in seventh-century Europe, in a variety of ways including in a religious sense. Like other wandering monks and missionaries, Columbanus experienced a world that was shaped by paganism and multifarious manifestations of Christianity in Gaul and Europe, including religious deviance of all kinds, such as different forms of syncretism and heresies, but also social practices devoid of their former religious connotations.[1] According to the *Vita Columbani*, which Jonas of Bobbio wrote between 639 and 643, the endeavor for orthodoxy and orthopraxy was an integral part of the Irish monk's missionary activities.[2] The text reports that Columbanus planned to preach the gospel throughout the Merovingian kingdoms, after having realized the lack of *penitentiae medicamenta* on the Continent upon his arrival.[3] He also wanted to use sermons in his fight against the "perfidious Arian heresy" that existed in Milan and its surroundings, that is, in the realm of the Lombards.[4] Through preaching, the Irish monk obviously intended to safeguard Christian faith in the regions he crossed.

However, evangelization within and beyond the borders of the Frankish realm was reserved for the next generation, for the followers of the Irish monk rather than for the master.[5] Jonas nevertheless attributed the origins of their missionary activities, which also included the conversion of heretics, to Columbanus himself. In a section dedicated to Eustasius, the abbot of Luxeuil, an order of the master, a *preceptum magistri*, prompted the protagonist's efforts to nourish "the neighbouring peoples [. . .] with the sustenance of faith."[6] Consequently,

---

1. On which see Hen 2016: esp. 233, 249; Wood 2013: 3–4.

2. For the *VC* and its structure, see Berschin 1988: 26–8 with n. 59 and 37–8; Rohr 1995: 235–44; Stancliffe 2001: 192–201; Wood 1998: esp. 100–1, 1982: 63; for the role of Columbanus's orthodoxy and intended missionary activities in the text see Wood 1982: 63–4 and 75.

3. *VC* I.5: 161; cf. Brown 2013: 252 and also below p. 146 with n. 21. For the situation in Gaul at Columbanus's arrival, see Wood 1998: 112, Wood 2015: 189–93; O'Hara and Wood 2017: 4–15.

4. *VC* I.30: 220–1. Cf. O'Hara and Wood 2017: 166–67 with n. 384.

5. See Wood 2001: 31–9. For Jonas's general interest in correcting errors and fighting against heresies, see *VC, Ep.*: 146 and the *praefatio* in *VC* I.1: 152.

6. *VC* II.8: 243; for the translation see O'Hara and Wood 2017: 191. For the phrase *vicinae gentes* used here, cf. also *VC* I.2 and 27: 153 and 211; for the translation of *gens* in general, see also O'Hara and Wood 2017: 156–7 with n. 335.

the latter started his work as a missionary first among the Warasqui, a group steeped in different syncretistic practices and heretical beliefs, before he turned to the Bavarians to promote their evangelization. Jonas's description of the life of Eustasius, however, also shows that the missions and the question of orthodoxy redounded upon the abbot and the community itself. After his return to Luxeuil, Eustasius had to face the rebellion of a wayward monk and former notary of Theuderic II named Agrestius, in which both the rival claims for missions among the *gentes* and allegations of heresy connected with the interpretation of the Columbanian community's religious practices played a major role.[7] As Jonas's description of the events that took place in the 620s suggests, the conflict between the two opponents, Eustasius and Agrestius, shifted the focus on the movement's orthodoxy: what had been an external problem to be solved through the evangelization of the peoples became an internal one.

Recent research has shed light on the link between the conflict with Agrestius and the different factions in Burgundy. The accusations against Eustasius have been analyzed against the backdrop of the politically motivated machinations of a circle that centered on the Burgundian *maior domus*, Warnachar, and the bishop of Geneva, Abbelenus, a relative of the rebel monk.[8] At the time Jonas wrote the section dedicated to Eustasius and Luxeuil, the major protagonists in the conflict were dead, although other witnesses of the affair were certainly still alive, which undoubtedly contributed to a continued interest in the episode in the 640s.[9] Yet the concentration on the issue of heresy, the peculiar connection of the missionary fight against heretics outside and the allegations of heresy brought up in the quarrel about the rule and doctrine inside the monastic community in the 620s, which also included a discussion of Columbanus's orthodoxy, in Jonas's text still lacks a satisfactory explanation. Why was it so important for the author to draw the readers' attention to Eustasius's efforts in his struggle against heresy, both on his missions and in his role as the leader of the monastic community in Luxeuil at the beginning of the 640s? The fact that Jonas did not tacitly gloss over the theological implications of the debate, as he did with Columbanus's controversy with the Gallic bishops about the Easter cycle, leaves us to wonder whether an explanation in primarily political terms lives up to contemporaries' view of the events.[10] Why the issue of orthodoxy still mattered fifteen years after the conflict was settled is an open question.

---

7. For an overview over this episode, see Stancliffe 2001: 205–7; Dumézil 2007: 136–8; Kreiner 2014b: 83–4; Fox 2014: 92–7.

8. Dumézil 2007: esp. 149; Fox 2014: 33–4 and 92-7, esp. 94 and 96.

9. As emphasized by Stancliffe 2001: 209; Stansbury 2012: 68–9; cf. also Dumézil 2007: 136.

10. For this issue see below pp. 152–3.

To find an answer the text has to be read against the backdrop of the wider worries about orthodoxy in the seventh century. A closer analysis of both (1) the crucial parts of the *Vita Columbani*, that is the section dedicated to Eustasius and Luxeuil (which Bruno Krusch had merged with other chapters in book II), and (2) their historical context, will illuminate how the missions among the *gentes* and the role of allegations of heresy in the internal conflicts of the Columbanian community in the generation after its founder became entangled. In the separate analysis this section requires, specific attention is given to the protagonists of the conflict and the way Jonas presented them in his narrative, starting with the abbot of Luxeuil.[11]

Jonas's report on Eustasius in the second book of the *Vita Columbani* begins with a cross reference to an episode at the end of the first book dedicated to a meeting between the Irish saint and the abbot of Luxeuil in Italy. The latter had been sent there by Chlothar II, the new ruler of the Merovingian kingdoms, to ask Columbanus to return to Gaul.[12] His biographer played on this situation to stress the good relationship between the Merovingian King and the abbot with his monastery, but he first and foremost seized the opportunity to present Eustasius as the one in charge to remember the saint's efforts and to teach the brothers, building a "community of many."[13] On his way back from Italy, Eustasius cured Burgundofara, the daughter of the nobleman Chagneric, from blindness, thus emulating Columbanus himself, who had blessed the young girl during his stay at the nobleman's house years before.[14] Since the miraculous healing eventually allowed Burgundofara to enter a nunnery founded on family land,[15] the abbot of Luxeuil here appeared to accomplish what the saint had begun, just as the contemporary readership might have expected from Columbanus's direct successor.

Jonas then carried on with his presentation of Eustasius as the true heir of the Irish monk; what follows the Burgundofara episode is the aforementioned order of the master, which the abbot of Luxeuil was ready to execute, that is, to evangelize the neighboring peoples.[16] Eustasius took even the suggestion of vicinity seriously and began his activity among the Warasqui who lived near the monastery of Luxeuil in a part of the old *provincia Sequanorum* on the banks of the Doubs. There he met members of the people prone to worshipping idols,

---

11. The structure of Krusch's edition justifies a separate analysis of the Eustasius section; see Berschin 1988: 26; Rohr 1995: 243–4; Wood 1998: 101 with n. 9.
12. *VC* II.7: 240–1, referring to *VC* I.30: 222–3.
13. *VC* I.30: 223, trans. by O'Hara and Wood 2017: 168–9.
14. *VC* II.7: 241–2, referring back to *VC* I.26: 209.
15. *VC* II.7: 243.
16. See above p. 143 with the references in n. 6.

while others were, according to Jonas, "stained with the error of Photinus and Bonosus."[17] After he had converted them, Eustasius turned to the Bavarians. According to Jonas, the abbot evangelized many of them himself, but left it to unnamed wise men to continue his work after awhile and set out for Luxeuil.[18] On his way back to the monastery he cured another girl, named Sadalberga, who had gone blind, and he also healed Agilus, the future abbot of Rebais, who had been his companion during the mission in Bavaria.[19]

After the abbot's arrival in Luxeuil, the monastery saw Eustasius resolutely bringing the "remedies of penance" (*medicamenta paenitentiae*) to bear inside and outside of its walls, while he tried to excite Christian vigor among the neighboring *populi* and the *plebs*, that is the monks, within the abbey.[20] In his description of these efforts Jonas picked up the wording he had chosen for the first steps of Christianization that Columbanus himself had undertaken upon his arrival in Gaul, as mentioned previously.[21] In so doing, the author put emphasis on the heritage that the current abbot of Luxeuil apparently felt obliged to preserve. The mission continued even after Eustasius had returned from the lands of the pagans and heretics. Christian faith, as it was interpreted by the abbot, still needed to be enforced and realigned according to a norm, even among the members of the community in Luxeuil. At the same time, Eustasius seemed to insist on a specific hierarchy within the monastery and his position at the top of it. Jonas has Romaric submit to the *monarchiae instituta* upon his arrival in Luxeuil, and since this is the only time in the whole text he uses the term *monarchia* in connection with the rule in a monastery, it represents a unique feature attributed to Eustasius. One can assume Jonas used it to substantiate a claim of absoluteness with regard to the abbot's authority.[22] Both Romaric and Amatus felt the effects of this even after they left the monastery. As Jonas tells it, they were sternly reprimanded due to their interpretation of the

---

17. *VC* II.8: 243–4, trans.by O'Hara and Wood 2017: 191. For the location of the Warasqui, see the Merovingian *Vita Sadalbergae* 7, ed. Krusch: 54; for the dating of the text, see Hummer 2003; for its textual dependency on the *VC*, see O'Hara 2009: 130–2; cf. Fox 2014: 141–50. See also Hardt 2003: 449–50.

18. *VC* II.8: 244. Cf. Wood 1982: 75.

19. *VC* II.8: 244–5.

20. *VC* II.8: 245, trans. by O'Hara and Wood 2017: 193. For the meaning of *plebs* in the *VC*, see O'Hara and Wood 2017: 202, n. 602.

21. See above p. 143 with n. 3; for the use of *medicamenta paenitentiae*, see also *VC* I.5, I.10, II.1, II.8, II.15, II.19, and II.25: 161, 170, 232, 245, 265, 273 and 290; cf. Wood 1982: 73 and Stancliffe 2001: 217; on the occasional reference of the phrase to monastic life, see Wood 2016a: 200, 2016b: 90, 92–3; and Meens 2016: 136–7. For its use in earlier texts, see O'Hara and Wood 2017: 13 and 106 with n. 98.

22. *VC* II.10: 252. While de Vogüé 1988: 94 prefers another reading of this passage (referring to "monks," *monachi*, rather than to *monarchia*), we follow Krusch's edition and the understanding of other modern readers, such as O'Hara and Wood 2017: 199, who translate *monarchiae instituta* as "the customs of absolute rule". Cf. also note 36 below.

rule when they were honorable members of a group affiliated with Luxeuil in Remiremont.[23] Whether this reproach has to be seen against the backdrop of the major changes the rule of Columbanus underwent at some time after the saint's death, which could well have happened during the abbacy of Eustasius, cannot be ascertained.[24] However, seen together, both entries in the same passage suggest the author of the *Vita Columbani* drew a line between the abbot's regime and the admonition of Romaric and Amatus. But rather than reading the lines as an acknowledgment of the well-founded implementation of the movement's rules, they should be understood as a reference to the authoritarian assertion of strictness by Eustasius himself: he personally represented the *monarchia* that controlled Luxeuil and that exerted its power elsewhere.

On the whole, Jonas does not seem to have shared the abbot's rigidity, and he drew a much more positive picture of other followers of Columbanus, an aspect we return to below. In the conflict with Agrestius, however, he clearly sided with Eustasius. His narrative continues after the description of the latter's efforts in and around Luxeuil. Agrestius offered an object lesson in religious deviance and behavioral aberration. In a posture deemed arrogant by Jonas, the monk asked for permission to preach to the *gentes*.[25] Eustasius, who did not regard the novice as fully prepared, declined. Finally, however, he let him go. Agrestius set off to the Bavarians, only to learn that the fruits of missionary labor were difficult to harvest. According to Jonas his efforts were not successful.[26] Agrestius moved on to Aquileia, where he made contact with those who had broken off communion with the Holy See during the Three Chapters controversy.[27] There he also seems to have adopted their position; in Jonas's words he "at once joined the schismatics. Having broken from communion with the See of Rome, and separated from communion with the whole world (*totius orbis*), he condemned all those who remained joined to the Roman See, maintaining that orthodox faith was retained in Aquileia alone."[28] Agrestius also got in touch with the court of the Lombard king Adaloald (616–626), himself a Catholic, and convinced one of his notaries to hand over a letter he had written to Athala, the abbot of Bobbio.[29] Jonas reports that Athala, having read the letter, considered it

---

23. *VC* II.10: 252. For Romaric, Amatus, and Remiremont see Fox 2014: 90–9. For the connections between Romaric and Eustasius, see also *Vita Sadalbergae* 9, ed. Krusch: 54. Cf. Fox 2014: 147–8.

24. For this see Wood 1982: 66. Stancliffe 2001: 213–4 dates the changes to the time after the Council of Mâcon, which could indeed have inspired them. See also Charles-Edwards 2000: 385; Fox 2014: 233–4.

25. For this and the following see *VC* II.9: 246–7.

26. Cf. Hardt 2003: 450.

27. For the Aquileian stance in the controversy, see Gray and Herren 1994: 162 and 167.

28. *VC* II.9: 247, trans. by O'Hara and Wood 2017: 195.

29. On Athala's concerns about heresy, see Wood 1998: 109.

ridiculous, but gave it to him in order to preserve it. Jonas kept it for many years, but finally, by his own account, lost it through his own negligence.[30] Agrestius, however, directly turned to Eustasius and tempted him "with the prods of schism" in order to corrupt his "sane mind with his insanity."[31] In response to this, the latter unavailingly admonished the monk for a long time, but finding no antidote against the contagion that had infected Agrestius's mind, Eustasius finally decided to debar him from the community, fearing that his error might spread among the other members.[32]

Agrestius sought allies. He found one in his relative Abbelenus, the bishop of Geneva, who supported him by trying to win over other bishops nearby.[33] Treticus of Lyon joined the circle around the monk, as did the Burgundian *maior domus*, Warnachar, who according to Jonas sided with Agrestius due to his enmity against Eustasius.[34] The *Vita* suggests that some of the bishops even tried to persuade Chlothar II to turn to their faction, but all the king did, trusting in Eustasius's authority and doctrine, was order an examination of the case at a synod that was eventually held in Mâcon in 626/627.[35] It dealt with the accusations against the abbot of Luxeuil; Eustasius had to face the charges against the holy rule of Columbanus, the *regula, disciplina*, and *instituta* that he as the abbot of Luxeuil represented.[36] In the assembly Agrestius made different allegations, such as the making of the sign of the cross over a vessel used for drinking and the fact that people entering or leaving any building within the monastery should ask for a blessing. Finally, he accused Columbanus himself of being responsible for practices deviating from the *mores* and for the multiplication of prayers among other superfluous things that, according to Agrestius, "together with their author, should be detested, as if they were heretical traditions."[37]

The charge of heresy represented the culmination and the turning point of the conflict in Jonas's narrative. The author put Eustasius's response in direct speech and made the abbot rebut the accusations in a long objection interspersed

---

30. The passage is seen as evidence for Jonas being in charge of the community's archive in Bobbio; see Wood 1998: 109 and O'Hara and Wood 2017: 195, n. 566.

31. VC II.9: 248, trans. by O'Hara and Wood 2017: 195. For the possibly deliberate allusion to *Aquilegensis* hidden in the word "sting" (*aculeus*), see 195, n. 567.

32. VC II.9: 248. For the background of this decision, see Dumézil 2007: 141 with n. 32.

33. On him see Dumézil 2007: 145.

34. VC II.9: 248. For Warnachar see Ebling 1974: 235–8 no. 309, Fox 2014: 33–34, and Dumézil 2007: 146; for Treticus see Dumézil 2007: 149.

35. VC II.9: 248–49. For the dating see Dumézil 2007: 138; for the council cf. also Halfond 2010: 51–2 and 237.

36. VC II.9: 249. For the *disciplina* see VC II.10: 251; for the *instituta* see 251 and 255. The latter term can certainly be interpreted as meant to suggest a fixed, approbated rule; Stancliffe 2001: 213 with n. 105, cf. 217.

37. VC II.9: 249–50, trans. by O'Hara and Wood 2017: 197.

with quotations from the Bible.[38] Further criticism that Agrestius brought forward concerning the shape of the tonsure that differed from the customs was countered by Eustasius in another speech which ended with the prophetic allusion to the monk's untimely death within a year.[39] Some of the episcopal supporters of Agrestius were frightened and alarmed by the announcement. Everyone on the council voted for the conclusion of a peace that eventually was sealed with a kiss.[40] Agrestius, after having concluded only a "pretended peace" (*simulata pax*), continued his machinations even after the council. While he could not succeed in persuading Burgundofara of his position, he managed to include Romaric and Amatus in Remiremont in his network of intrigues, which in Jonas's view was aimed at the contempt of the *regula Columbani*.[41] In a quick response to their behavior, divine punishment descended on the convent of Remiremont. Many nuns died, and Agrestius was killed by a servant he himself had freed. Jonas reports rumors that the monk had been involved with the murderer's wife but refrains from confirming them in the text.[42] With Eustasius's prophecy fulfilled and some of Agrestius's supporters such as Warnachar already dead,[43] both Romaric and Amatus reconciled with the abbot of Luxeuil. The former adversaries among the bishops and even Abbelenus strove to back up the *regula* of Columbanus, while Eustasius himself sought to correct the wrongdoers and "decided to accommodate" them "to his peace," as Jonas put it. The conflict was over, the movement flourished, and many new monasteries were founded.[44] Jonas concluded his account with Eustasius's death after thirty days of severe infirmity, which was meant to cure "what the passage of past years had not purged with diverse afflictions."[45]

At first sight, this report appears to present the untroubling solution of a conflict that was caused by an individual member of the community having gone rogue and that ended in a predictable result. To be sure, Jonas took pains in his narrative to present the debate at the synod as a nearly effortless and clear victory for the abbot of Luxeuil. By claiming that the discussion dealt with negligible points, he obviously also tried to downplay the accusations Agrestius brought forward at the assembly in Mâcon, which might well have had a deeper

---

38. *VC* II.9: 250.
39. *VC* II.9 and 10: 251. For the accusations and Eustasius's response, cf. Wood 1982: 72–3; Dumézil 2007: 142–3; and Fox 2014: 92–3 and 228.
40. *VC* II.10: 251–2. For this and the following, cf. Dumézil 2007: 144.
41. *VC* II.10: 252–3. For the Burgundofara episode, see Fox 2014: 201; for the *Regula Columbani* in the *Vita*, see Diem 2002: 67–71, esp. 68–9.
42. *VC* II.10: 253–4.
43. Fredegar IV.54, ed. Krusch: 148; *VC* II.10: 249.
44. *VC* II.10: 255–6, trans. by O'Hara and Wood 2017: 201–3.
45. *VC* II.10: 256–7, trans. by O'Hara and Wood 2017: 203.

theological nature.[46] All the same, his sketchy account creates doubts about the completeness of the issues taken under scrutiny by the bishops. Eustasius's performance might well have been not that adroit in the wake of different allegations, and if so, Jonas certainly had no interest in bringing up both the accusations and the abbot's reaction in his text. Finally, the description of the discussion's ending and the resulting conclusion bespeaks a narrative embellishment in favor of Eustasius. While Agrestius had to be pushed by his followers to reconcile according to the text, Jonas presented the abbot as the complaisant winner of the debate who was willing to agree to a peaceful conclusion. The author of the *Vita* even labeled this as *sua pax* in a later passage; in so doing, he turned his protagonist into the honest negotiator that the rebellious monk with his *simulata pax* only pretended to be.[47] At the same time, however, he also made him the creator of an order that was rooted in the peace terms of Mâcon, which other dissenters finally had to accept. But despite all these efforts, Jonas could not ignore the fact that the bishops had the lead in the process. It was they who demanded a proper response to Agrestius's accusations from Eustasius, and it was the whole council, not only some of Agrestius's supporters, who forced the opponents to reconcile. The opponents had to comply with a public conclusion of peace that was sealed with a kiss due to episcopal authority.[48]

And there was even more behind the story. Despite the smooth description of the outcome, which seemed to suggest the whole episode was just a marginal phenomenon that only briefly disturbed the otherwise stable and cohesive Columbanian network, Jonas could not hide the fact that the community was cut to the quick.[49] Since the opposition against Eustasius included monks such as Amatus, who was brought from Agaune to Luxeuil by the abbot himself before he went to Remiremont, the disruptions caused by the quarrel certainly affected the community more severely than Jonas could pretend only fifteen years after. That Agrestius was supported by a number of bishops at the instigation of his relative, Abbelenus of Geneva, also attests to the wide extent of the rebellion. It might well have been even a broader movement than the one the author of the *Vita* outlined in his text.

Moreover, the opposition against Eustasius and the interpretation of Columbanian monasticism he stood for seems not to have been swiftly finalized by the council's decision. Even after the death of his antagonist Warnachar and the end of the assembly, Eustasius had to bring remaining opponents to terms.

46. Cf. Wood 1982: 65.
47. *VC* II.10: 252 and 256.
48. See Charles-Edwards 2000: 364.
49. See also Fox 2014: 33 and 241.

Here again Jonas made an effort to present the abbot of Luxeuil as the winning party: the reference to *sua pax* was certainly meant to underline that Eustasius had set up the framework to accommodate the remainder of the opposition to a peaceful ending of the conflict.[50] However, whether the integration of the opponents was indeed an act of grace based on the abbot's conditions, as the text suggests, seems to be open to question. The description here does not match with the interpretation of Eustasius's submission to the judgment of the bishops in general and his compliance with the episcopal demand to come to terms with Agrestius. What is more, the subsequent passages in the text itself seem to indicate a certain weakness of the abbot's position in the wake of the council. First of all, Jonas mentioned that many monasteries were founded in the neighborhood, which were, as he told, organized and built not by Eustasius, but by his successor, Waldebert.[51] Second, the text continues with the abbot's imminent death and his purgation through the infirmity of the body that, according to Jonas, was a result of the sentence of the Just Judge. Contrary to many other protagonists that the author portrayed in the *Vita Columbani*, Eustasius's life did not end in a *felix exitus* that was announced in visions to prepare the addressees for their blissful passage to the afterworld;[52] rather, the abbot was confronted with the inescapable prospect of being punished instead. The only favor granted to him was to choose the measure and duration of the pain that was in the offing for him. In this respect the abbot of Luxeuil stands out among his colleagues who figure in Jonas's text. The author of the *Vita* made Eustasius pay for misdemeanors, even accept the harder punishment, but left it to the reader to clarify what he might have done. With the account of the abbot's life in mind that was dominated by the Agrestius affair, it certainly was difficult to think of something other than Eustasius's attitude and conduct in this matter. As mentioned previously, Jonas did not appreciate the abbot's rigidity, and his portrait of him doing penance for his unspecified sins at the end of the passage dedicated to his life could be understood as a telling way to distance himself from Eustasius and his line of action.

This reading understands Jonas's report of the events as being somewhat reticent. It also suggests that Eustasius's behavior had disturbed the community's freedom in the long run, with effects that were still present in his biographer's days. The reason for the estrangement that the narrative conveys has mostly been attributed to the political implications of the quarrel. Indeed, people like

---

50. *VC* II.10: 256.

51. For Waldebert see Fox 2014: 106–8 and Stansbury 2012: 74.

52. Cf. especially the description of abbot Athala's death in *VC* II.6: 238–40. On this issue see Kreiner 2014a: esp. 116–7, cf. 125–8.

Warnachar, Abbelenus, and other bishops certainly had their interests in the conflict, supporting the one or the other side, although the wider ramifications and the roots thereof remain obscure. As a matter of fact, each of Eustasius's antagonists seems to have had connections to Burgundian factions that had formed in earlier conflicts. Warnachar's enmity against the abbot of Luxeuil, for example, could actually have been the result of the latter's intercession on behalf of one of the Burgundian conspirators against Chlothar II, whom the *maior domus* had supported in establishing the *monarchia trium regnorum* and to whom he owed his position.[53] But since he died before the council started, and his son Godinus fell from grace with the king and was killed shortly thereafter,[54] one might doubt whether Warnachar's role in 626/627 motivated Jonas's narrative in the first place. That the Burgundians seized the opportunity of his death to ask Chlothar not to replace Warnachar with another *maior domus* also puts into question the continuity of the factions that certainly existed in the realm before the council of Mâcon.[55] Times had changed, and Jonas seems to have been troubled more by other aspects of the Agrestius affair in the 640s than by a Burgundy-rooted factionalism.

That the affair and its implications nevertheless still concerned him when he wrote the *Vita* is suggested by Jonas's reference to the letter Agrestius had sent to Athala of Bobbio. It seems remarkable that the hagiographer took pains to describe the letter's whereabouts;[56] had it not been lost due to his, Jonas's, negligence, it could have been an important testimony to the theological stance of Agrestius. As matters stood, even though the document was lost, it served to underline Jonas's authority on the issue. The wording he chose to reassure the reader that he actually had seen the letter and recognized the monk's writing certainly was meant to guarantee the authenticity of his version of the events. After the other witnesses of Agrestius's theological statement, Athala and Eustasius, had died, only Jonas was able to bear testimony to the doctrinal implications of Agrestius's letter. Its contents appear to indicate what had still been an issue in the Columbanian community at the time Jonas wrote the *Vita*, although we do not know why and to what extent. The affair obviously had an afterlife that prompted him to dedicate his description of Eustasius's life nearly completely to this topic.

53. For Eustasius's support of Leudemund of Sion, see Fredegar IV.44, ed. Krusch: 142–3. Cf. Dumézil 2007: 146.

54. See Fredegar IV.54, ed. Krusch: 147–8; cf. Ebling 1974: 237; Dumézil 2007: 146–7; Scholz 2015: 190–1.

55. Fredegar IV.54, ed. Krusch: 148.

56. *VC* II.9: 247–8.

The fact that Chlothar commissioned and authorized a synod to solve the problem also shows that it was primarily an ecclesiastical issue that was at stake, while political intrigues seem to have played only a secondary role.[57] The final decision of the bishops, purged from Jonas's effort to embellish Eustasius's role, also suggests that they regarded the conflict as an internal ecclesiastical dispute on the one hand. On the other hand, however, it was they who benefited from the course of events: they settled the conflict in the end, arranged the terms for the reconciliation, and underlined their decisive authority in questions of doctrine and theological issues like heresy. And it was most probably the latter that really mattered, as Jonas's report strongly suggests. Brought up as an accusation by Agrestius in the narrative, the allegation of heresy formed the peak of Jonas's life of Eustasius and was rejected at length by the abbot. It was also an issue during the first mission ascribed to the latter, which had taken place in a nearby area south of Luxeuil, still in northern Burgundy. And even in the rest of the abbot's *Vita*, worries about orthodoxy were a factor that lent cohesion to the narrative: the term itself was mentioned in a negative sense when the text described Agrestius's affiliation with the Aquileians, as an antipode to the orthodoxy represented by the Roman See and those in communion with it.[58] The report about the reinforcement of the rule, as Eustasius defined it, in the monastery and the revival of Christianity in its surroundings after the abbot's return from Bavaria are also related to the notion of being orthodox:[59] the people were realigned according to a norm. And deviations from there seem to have been on Jonas's mind while he wrote his text.

What is more, the concept of religious deviance from a norm also became manifest in the language the author used: the *Vita* of Eustasius is tinged with metaphors that refer both to orthodoxy and heresy, such as the often-cited phrase *sana mens* and its counterpart, *vesania*.[60] Moreover, the repetitive use of the phrase *medicamenta paenitentiae* points to a language of remedy that was and remained typical in the context of religious deviance in earlier and later times. It corresponded with the aforementioned metaphors related to illness, while it also suggested a call for doctors who provided the sick with therapy. In

---

57. For the relationship between king and bishops in connection with the Merovingian councils, see Hen 2016: 243–4; for Chlothar II and the bishops, see Scholz 2015: 191–3.

58. *VC* II.9: 247.

59. *VC* II.8: 245.

60. *VC* II.7, 9 and 10: 241, 248, and 252 (*sana mens*); II.9 and 10: 248, 252, and 253 (*vesania*); cf. also II.24: 287 (*vesanior*). It is interesting to see that, apart from the latter term *vesanior*, all the evidence for *sana mens* and *vesania* concentrates in the life of Eustasius. *Vesania* as a characteristic of heretics also appears in the letter Martin I sent to Amandus; *Vita Amandi II auctore Milone*, ed. Krusch: 456, line 6; *Concilium Lateranense*, ed. Riedinger: 424, line 16.

this context drastic measures could be taken; like other texts related to heretics, the *Vita* furthermore elaborates on medical metaphors such as the sword, which was meant to cut off rotten limbs in order to separate the healthy parts from the sick ones. Jonas made Columbanus himself refer to the sword of the gospel as an instrument to protect orthodoxy in the text, and he also put preaching and the spoken or written word at the center of his description of Eustasius's life, culminating in the verbal exchange at the council of Mâcon.[61]

In fact, the author of the *Vita Columbani* had many reasons to worry about the issue of heresy. The founder of the monasteries, Columbanus himself, had nourished reservations about the orthodoxy of the community. There was his struggle with the bishops about the Easter cycle, in which even the papacy got involved. For other micro-Christendoms in peripheral areas like the British Isles, this was still a matter of dispute in the mid-630s. Jonas chose not to mention it at all, probably because he wanted to deliberately omit any aspect that could put Columbanus's orthodoxy into question.[62] This might also apply to the treatment of other doctrinal issues the Irish founder of the movement had touched upon, such as the Three Chapters controversy. To be sure, the author of the *Vita Columbani* was not outspoken about it. However, he left a clear trail in his text when he was referring to Agrestius's sojourn in Aquileia and the ensuing theological implications in the letter sent to Athala. Contrary to the conflict about Easter, therefore, the Three Chapters controversy mattered to an extent that prevented Jonas from passing over it in silence at the time he wrote his text.

As a matter of fact, the discussion on the nature of Christ continued in the seventh century, and controversies like the one on the condemnation of the Three Chapters had not yet been settled. Resistance to the vague papal stance on this lingered not only in northern Italy, but also in Gaul.[63] In 597 Gregory the Great had complained about the presence of schismatics in the Merovingian kingdoms.[64] Sixteen years later Columbanus expressed his sorrow about a possible tendency of the Holy See toward heresy, in a letter sent to Pope Boniface IV that was prompted by Rome's position on the decision made on the Three Chapters.[65] The Council assembled at Clichy in 626/627, shortly after the bishops

---

61. *VC* I.30: 221 and II.9–10: 249–52.

62. For the Easter cycle (or the lack thereof in Jonas's text), see Schäferdiek 1982 : 189 and 200; Schäferdiek 1983: 364–9; also Bullough 1997: 14, n. 44; Charles-Edwards 2000: 365, 368–9; Stancliffe 2001: 201–16; Dumézil 2007: 143; Stansbury 2012: 68 and 71; Fox 2014: 93. For the term "micro-Christendoms" see Brown 2013: 15 and 359.

63. For the situation in northern Italy, see Sotinel 2007; for the one in Gaul, see Wood 2007; Kreiner 2014a: 125–8.

64. Gregory, *Reg.Ep.* 8.4: 518–21, esp. 520–1; cf. Wood 2007: 230 and 238.

65. *Ep.* 5, ed. Walker: 36–57; see Bracken 2002: esp. 175–82, 189–90, 196–7, and 211–13; Wood 2007: 238; see also Gray and Herren 1994; Charles-Edwards 2000: 372, 375–7; Leso 2013: 378–85.

had come together to deal with the allegation of heresy in the Agrestius affair, commanded the members of the clergy to search and convert heretics to secure the Catholic faith that prevailed in Gaul.[66] The canon explicitly referred to the Bonosians, that is, to the group of heretics Eustasius had evangelized on his mission to the Warasqui. Since they, like the Photinians, whom the *Vita Columbani* mentioned in its description of the abbot's voyage to northern Burgundy, denied Christ's divinity and in doing so argued about the two natures within his person, they were exactly in line with the current trends in contemporary theological dispute, a mainstream heresy, after all. That Jonas referred to them clearly indicates the abiding importance of the theological question of the two natures.

Indeed, heresy also concerned his contemporaries in the 640s, when Monothelitism spread from the East. Originally meant to solve the problem posed by the debate on the two natures of Christ, this new doctrine had recently arisen in Byzantium, where it was backed by imperial policy. It made a noticeable impact in the West at the end of the 640s, when the papacy tried to ward off what was seen as a heresy. In 649 Pope Martin I sent a letter to Amandus in Gaul in which he promoted the fight against Monothelitism,[67] but it could be that the shockwaves of the conflict about the doctrine had reached the Merovingian kingdoms even before that.[68] At the beginning of the decade a heretic from *partibus transmarinis* arrived in Autun and spread his *nefanda dogmata*, before he was condemned by a synod assembled in Orléans.[69] We do not know anything about the theological message the man was conveying in Gaul, but if we can assume that the anonymous stranger did indeed come from the Mediterranean area, he might well have preached the tenor of Monothelitism.

However, around the same time, at the end of the 640s or the beginning of the 650s, a council in Chalon-sur-Saône delegated Wandregisel, the abbot of Fontenelle, to travel to Rome, most probably to learn more about the papal standpoint on the issue of Monothelitism.[70] As with the assembly in Orléans, the

---

66. *Concilia Galliae a. 511–a. 695*, ed. de Clercq: 290–7, at 292 no. 5. For the council in Clichy, see Scholz 2015: 191–5, esp. 193; Halfond 2010: 237 and refer to the index.

67. The letter of Martin I is inserted in the *Vita Amandi II auctore Milone*, ed. Krusch: 452–6; cf. its most recent edition in *Concilium Lateranense*, ed. Riedinger: 422–4. For the letter in general see Scheibelreiter 1992; Borias 1987: 54, 58–9; Wood 1994: 245–6, 2007: 239–40.

68. Frankish churchmen also knew about the Three Chapters controversy very soon after it became an issue in the East; Wood 2007: 223, cf. 238 for an earlier knowledge of Columbanus about the Three Chapters controversy. For the flow of information from the Mediterranean East to Gaul in Late Antiquity and the early Middle Ages, see Wood 2014 and Fischer 2014: esp. 71–72.

69. *Vita Eligii* I.35, ed. Krusch: 691–2; cf. *Concilia Galliae a. 511–a. 695*, ed. de Clercq: 301. Cf. Borias 1987: 61.

70. *Vita altera Wandregisili* II.10 and 11: 275; for the Council see *Concilia Galliae a. 511–a. 695*, ed. de Clercq: 302–10. Cf. Borias 1987: esp. 49, 61, 63; Wood 1994: 246, 2007: 240.

council thus testifies to the assumption that religious deviance and the debates about it still flourished in the middle of the seventh century. It also clarifies who was regarded as the authority one had to turn to in a case like this. In the eyes of contemporaries the papacy was the center of orthodoxy, as it had been for Columbanus.[71] The sources attest to an increasing number of contacts of the Christian peripheries with Rome, which had been stimulated by papal initiatives on the one hand and the growing need for clarification of theological matters on the other. In times of insecurity about the papal position, however, people seem to have turned to other hallmarks of orthodoxy, such as the acts of the Councils of Nicea and Chalcedon. The first canon of the Council of Chalon-sur-Saône, for instance, defined the *norma fidei* explicitly according to the one given by these two assemblies.[72] This position was not new, in particular for members of the Columbanian circle. The Irish monk himself seems to have referred to the council of Chalcedon in a letter sent to Pope Boniface at the beginning of the seventh century when he pointed out that the Aquileians accused Pope Boniface of having favored heretics such as "Eutyches, Nestorius, and Dioscorus."[73] The vague, if not ambivalent, stance of the papacy in the Three Chapters controversy had nourished doubts about Rome's position back then. People feared that a condemnation of the Three Chapters entailed an acceptance of the heretics who had been condemned in 451, which strengthened the supporters of the former. Columbanus's following appeal to the pope to purge himself from the allegation by anathematizing Eutyches and Nestorius, who had been condemned at the synod in 451, could therefore be understood "as a call to reaffirm the council of Chalcedon."[74] In fact, this council figured prominently among the other synods, due to the authority of Pope Leo the Great and his *Tomus*. The text, basically a long letter, addressed the issue of Christ's nature and represented the hallmark of orthodoxy in the West during the following centuries.[75] In 557 a papal letter related to the Three Chapters, which appealed to Childebert to extirpate heresy in his realm, referred to Leo's *Tomus*. And the pope continued to figure prominently in Frankish-papal relations in the seventh century. That Wandregisel received a piece of Leo's knee as a relic from Pope Martin I during his stay in

---

71. To him it represented the "chief see of the orthodox faith" (*fidei orthodoxae sedem principalem*); *Ep.* 5.9, ed. Walker: 46–7. For the background see Bracken 2002: esp. 182.

72. *Concilia Galliae a. 511–a. 695*, ed. de Clercq: 303 no. 1; cf. Borias 1987: 59–60.

73. *Ep.* 5.10, ed. Walker: 46–7; cf. Gray and Herren 1994: 165; Brown 2013: 249, who also notes that it is difficult to assess how much Columbanus knew exactly about the theological implications of the discussion of the issue in the East. How much Columbanus knew exactly about the theological implications of the discussion of the issue in the East is difficult to assess; see Brown 2013: 249.

74. Wood 2007: 232; cf. Bracken 2002: 197.

75. Gray and Herren 1994: 161. See also the reference to the *Tomus* next to the condemnation of Nestorius, Dioscorus, and Eutyches in Chalcedon in Gregory, *Reg.Ep.* VI.2, ed. Norberg: 370–1.

Rome could be seen against the backdrop of the latter's advocacy for an orthodoxy based on his predecessor's theological statements.[76] There is even evidence
for the contemporary use of the *Tomus* in the Merovingian kingdom. On his
deathbed Amatus, the companion of Romaric in Remiremont, who had been
scolded so badly by Eustasius, asked one of the bystanders to read out the *Tomus*
because it contained "the fullest principle of the Catholic Faith (*plenissima racio
fidei catholice*)." He then recited the creed in front of his fellow brothers, including his belief in the Holy Trinity, just to prove his orthodoxy in all respects,
as his seventh-century *Vita* put it.[77]

The case of Amatus leads us back again to Jonas and his account of the
Agrestius affair. Although Amatus was closely connected to Eustasius, he and
Romaric chose to support Agrestius in the conflict with the abbot of Luxeuil.
Jonas's report seems to suggest that they sided with the rebellious monk because earlier admonitions of Eustasius had offended them.[78] But there was certainly more to it. Amatus passed away in 628 or 629, shortly after the council
of Mâcon.[79] The deathbed scene described in the *Vita Amati* might have been
authentic or made up by the author of this text. Either way it was meant to
emphasize the saint's orthodoxy, which seems to have been doubted during
the Agrestius affair.[80] It is only in this context that this evidence makes sense.
The depiction of the last hours of Amatus strongly suggests that the reference to Leo's *Tomus* was rather an act of defiance than a purely defensive re-
affirmation of orthodoxy. The author of the *Vita* insisted that the saint always
(*semper*) phrased his sentences according to his creed, a creed that referred to
Chalcedon.[81] This seems to be a reflex to an orthodoxy called into question;
we can therefore assume that Amatus was also accused of religious deviance
during the Agrestius affair, and since he shared the position of the rebel in
his conflict with Eustasius and later reaffirmed his Chalcedonian orthodoxy,
Agrestius might also have put the council of 451 in first place. He probably did
so to insist on the condemnations of the heretics Eutyches and Nestorius, just as
Columbanus had done in his letter to Pope Boniface IV. Scholars generally agree
on the assumption that Agrestius had been much closer to Columbanus than
his other followers.[82] The possible similarity in their attitude toward Chalcedon

76. Borias 1987: esp. 63–4.
77. *Vita Amati* 12, ed. Krusch: 220, esp. l.11 and 1.18. Cf. Wood 1994: 245; Dumézil 2007: 141; Fox
2014: 242. For the *Vita* and its dating see Goullet 2001: 50–6; cf. Heinzelmann 2010: 78; Wood 1982: 70.
78. See above pp. 146–7.
79. See Gauthier 1980: 284.
80. Cf. Wood 1994: 245, 1982: 65–6; Gauthier 1980: 176–8 and 280–3; Goullet 2001: 55.
81. *Vita Amati* 12, ed. Krusch: 220 l. 17–8: *Per universas sententias suam semper aptabat confessionem,
scilicet ut vir sanctus se in omnibus orthodoxum comprobaret.*
82. Wood 1998: 101; Dumézil 2007: 140.

and the Three Chapters corroborates this belief. Nevertheless, Jonas depicted Agrestius in a negative way, using a derogatory rhetoric to belittle him when he referred to his words as *microloga*.[83] Even his name could have been used for this purpose, if we read it as a form of the Latin word *agrestis*, which means "wild," but could also be translated as "uneducated," "raw," or "brute." These possible translations match the characterization of the rebel so well that one wonders whether the name was real or made up, the more so because Jonas could expect his contemporary audience to know whom he had in mind in any case.[84]

However, Agrestius's negative depiction in the *Vita Columbani* at the beginning of the 640s does not blend well with both the peace imposed on the opponents at the council of Mâcon and the critical nuances in Jonas's portrait of Eustasius. His description of the protagonists, which staged Agrestius as the perpetrator but also criticized the abbot of Luxeuil for his conduct, bespeaks general reservations: for him the whole situation seems to have been an issue. The conflict had exposed the Columbanian community to the arbitration and authority of the bishops at the council, and with it, to their will and secular interests. They decided what was orthodox and what was not. That the episcopacy intervened in what originally had been an internal monastic discussion certainly appeared to be a convenient solution in a time when no other entity could rule on the matter with unquestioned authority. The papacy's expertise in the field of orthodoxy and orthopraxy had been challenged in the wake of the second Council of Constantinople in 553. Columbanus alluded to this issue when he referred to Pope Vigilius in his correspondence with Rome at the beginning of the seventh century and when he asked Pope Boniface IV in the same letter to defend the faith and to convene a synod in order to clear the charges the Aquileians had pressed. The pope was meant to take the lead in this matter. Columbanus seems, as the letter's phrasing suggests, to have regarded a synod as compulsory if the pontiff wanted to clear himself from the charges and deprive his opponents of any lawful argument. In doing so, the Irish monk on the one hand credited the pope together with the assembly with the legitimate and indubitable power to decide about being orthodox or heretic. On the other hand, the request for a synod also highlights his view of the extent of the current doubts that had been cast on papal authority in doctrinal issues: the pope had to dispel them within and through an assembly.[85]

---

83. *VC* II.10: 251; cf. Kreiner 2014b: 107. Interestingly enough, Columbanus had used the term *micrologus* for himself to express his humility toward his respective papal addressee in two of his letters; cf. *Epp.* 1.2 and 5.1, ed. Walker: 2–3 and 36–7. For this see also Dumézil 2007: 150; O'Hara and Wood 2017: 198, n. 585.

84. This issue will be addressed in another essay. For now see de Vogüé 1988: 94.

85. *Ep.* 5.4, ed. Walker: 40–1.

But the papacy's standing in issues of faith became invigorated in the eyes of contemporaries over the following decades, and what was regarded as an enfeeblement of its reputation very much in line with Columbanus's argument in 626/627 was certainly seen in a different light by the time Jonas wrote his *Vita Columbani*. As Monothelitism loomed large on the horizon and heresies flourished in Gaul and elsewhere, the papacy had taken a much firmer and clearer stance on the issue of religious deviance, culminating in the preparations of the Lateran Council in Rome in 649 and Pope Martin I's exile. Moreover, the Columbanian movement had committed itself even more to the Roman See in the meantime. In 628, one or two years after Mâcon, Bobbio had received a privilege from Pope Honorius I exempting the monastery from the bishop's power, a privilege that became a model for later monastic immunities in Gaul.[86] Jonas himself was part of the group that went to Rome. Without a doubt he was aware of the importance of this privilege for the community. To him it must have seemed obligatory to follow the papal line, not just for the sake of orthodoxy. The close association with Rome appeared to be even more necessary against the backdrop of the privileges that saved the Columbanian movement and its foundations from episcopal interference. At the beginning of the 640s, when Jonas was writing the *Vita Columbani* including the life of Eustasius, Luxeuil appears to have received such a privilege on behalf of the papacy, and Bobbio seems to have benefited from a similar one that granted greater freedom from episcopal intervention than the one dedicated to the abbey in 628.[87] Even more than back then, the papacy in Rome had become the authoritative anchor for the Columbanian monasteries. This could have been the reason why Jonas saw the need to stress the importance of remaining in communion with the papacy by the frequent reiteration of the lack thereof in his report about the Aquileians and Agrestius's affiliation with them. That he did not have Eustasius refer to the papacy as an authority in his account of the assembly in Mâcon does not disprove this interpretation.[88] Probably the audience, so close to the events, was too well-informed to be deluded by the author about an appeal to Rome that actually had never taken place.[89] Many people might well have known that in the end the bishops had decided and that there had been no plea to Rome to prevent the council's judgment. However, the members of the community seemed to have

---

86. Wood 1998: 117–20; Wood 2016a: 192.

87. *Diplomata*, ed. Pardessus: 67–9 no. 299 (Luxeuil), and *Codice diplomatico*, ed. Cipolla: 104–12 no. 13 (Bobbio). Cf. Ewig 2009: esp. 561, 565 (for restrictions on episcopal intervention) and 543–4 and 566–7 (privilege for Bobbio). Cf. Wood 1982: 78–9, 2016a: 192.

88. The lack thereof is taken into consideration by Stancliffe 2001: 213, n. 100.

89. See Stancliffe 2001: 215; for the audience of the *Vita* in general, see also Charles-Edwards 2000: 367 and Wood 2001: 116–7.

learned their lesson from the episode. It has been suggested that the quest for the papal privilege in 628 was triggered by the Agrestius affair and the events in Mâcon.[90] Conversely, it might also be possible that the current need for papal support or the community's obligation to be grateful for the privileges they already had received determined Jonas's version of the episode at the beginning of the 640s.

All the same, there had been even more at stake in the conflict between the rebellious monk and the abbot of Luxeuil than the freedom of the community and its alliance with the papacy. The issue of orthodoxy and heresy had put the missionary efforts into question. Their success—that is, the acceptance of former and future Christianization of certain areas—depended on the orthodoxy of the missionaries. And Rome knew exactly who was in charge, as the letter Pope Martin I addressed to Amandus clearly shows. What is more, Jonas again was personally involved. He wrote the *Vita Columbani* while he was working with Amandus on the Scheldt River close to Elnone (modern Saint-Amand-les-Eaux).[91] The sojourn doubtless left a deep impression on him and is certainly the reason that missionary activities figure so prominently in his text. From this perspective, his criticism of both Agrestius and Eustasius is also comprehensible. The former was not prepared to evangelize, although he, Agrestius, assumed himself to be so, and the fact that he lapsed into heresy later corresponded with his failure on the mission. Eustasius on the contrary was successful, because he was orthodox, but deserved to be scolded because his rigidity had put so much at risk: the concord of the community itself and the support of the papacy that would no longer grant privileges to a monastic movement arguing about heretics among its own members.[92]

Recent research has identified Jonas's account of the Agrestius affair as "a deliberate piece of obfuscation."[93] Indeed, the author tried hard not to impugn the abbot's stance in terms of content. Although he did not call Eustasius to account for what had happened, he was critical of his conduct before and during the affair. Jonas's portrait, including the fact that he narrowed down his protagonist's term as abbot to this issue, suggests the episode represented a narrative constructed with hindsight.[94] However, the text certainly was not meant to be a general appeal to treat conflicts between abbots and monks in

90. Stancliffe 2001: 207.
91. *VC, Ep.*: 145. Cf. O'Hara and Wood 2017: 36.
92. For the issue of discord in the *Vita Columbani*, see Wood 1982: 66–7; cf. also Stancliffe 2001: 203–8.
93. Wood 1994: 197. Cf. also Dumézil 2007: 136, referring to "l'art subtil de déformation."
94. For a possible connection between the Agrestius affair and the *Regula cuiusdam patris*, which deals with the solution of conflicts in a monastic community, see Diem 2016: 74–6 and chapter 15 in this volume.

the cloisters as internal matters. Rather, the narrative seems to have been deter-mined by situational needs that occupied the Columbanian community in ge-neral and Jonas in particular when he wrote the *Vita*. As the contextual evidence found in other late Merovingian hagiographic works suggests, Jonas's report represented a tribute to the critics of Eustasius's behavior; whether followers of Amatus in Remiremont were among them is unclear, but the fact that the *Vita* of the saint broached the issue of orthodoxy testifies to the continuing discussion about the topic, as does the version of the events in the *Vita Sadalbergae*.[95] Even though the latter strongly relied on the *Vita Columbani* in its description of what happened during the Agrestius affair, the text clearly shows that religious devi-ance still mattered decades after Jonas picked it out as a central theme. In times of uncertainty concerning theological issues, when opaque discussions haunted Christians in Europe, people seem to have been particularly nervous, as the evidence from the seventh century shows. In their conflict, both Agrestius and Eustasius had opened the Columbanian community's orthodoxy to criticism and episcopal arbitration, and both were to blame and to be punished for it just because they had brought the issue up. It seems that Jonas's text was very much inspired by this theological dimension. His report reminded the monastic com-munity of the authority and the instruments it could resort to in challenging situations: the papacy and the *medicamenta penitentiae* provided the resources for being orthodox in a world of deviance.

ACKNOWLEDGMENTS

The research this chapter is based on received funding from the European Research Council under the European Union's Seventh Framework Programme (FP7/2007–2013)/ERC grant agreement No. 269591. I am grateful to Thomas Gobbitt, Francesco Borri, and Max Diesenberger for reading and commenting on earlier versions of this paper.

BIBLIOGRAPHY

Berschin, W. (1988) *Biographie und Epochenstil im lateinischen Mittelalter, Bd. II, Merowingische Biographie: Italien, Spanien und die Inseln im frühen Mittelalter*. Quellen und Untersuchungen zur Lateinischen Philologie des Mittelalters 9. Stuttgart, Anton Hiersemann Verlag.

Borias, A. (1987) "Saint Wandrille et la crise monothélite." *Revue Bénédictine* 97: 42–67.

Bracken, D. (2002) "Authority and Duty: Columbanus and the Primacy of Rome." *Peritia* 16: 168–213.

95. *Vita Sadalbergae* 8, ed. Krusch: 54.

Brown, P. (2013) *The Rise of Western Christendom: Triumph and Diversity, A.D. 200–1000*. 10th edition. Malden, MA, Wiley-Blackwell.

Bullough, D. (1997) "The Career of Columbanus." In M. Lapidge (ed.), *Columbanus: Studies on the Latin Writings*. Studies in Celtic History 17. Woodbridge, Boydell Press, 1–28.

Charles-Edwards, T. M. (2000) *Early Christian Ireland*. Cambridge, Cambridge University Press.

Codice Diplomatico del Monastero di S. Colombano di Bobbio fino all'anno.MCCVIII (1918), ed. C. Cipolla, vol. 1. Fonti per la Storia d'Italia 52. Roma, Tipografia del Senato.

Concilia Galliae a. 511–a. 695 (1963), ed. C. de Clercq. Corpus Christianorum Series Latina 148A. Turnhout, Brepols.

Concilium Lateranense a. 649 celebratum (1984), ed. R. Riedinger. Acta Conciliorum Oecumenicorum Series Secunda 1. Berlin, Walter de Gruyter.

de Vogüé, A. (1988) "En lisant Jonas de Bobbio: Notes sur la vie de Saint Colomban." *Studia Monastica* 30: 63–103.

Diem, A. (2002) "Was bedeutet *regula Columbani*?" In W. Pohl and M. Diesenberger (eds.), *Integration und Herrschaft: Ethnische Identitäten und soziale Organisation im Frühmittelalter*. Forschungen zur Geschichte des Mittelalters 3. Wien, Verlag der Österreichischen Akademie der Wissenschaften, 63–89.

Diem, A. (2016) "Columbanian Monastic Rules: Dissent and Experiment." In R. Flechner and S. Meeder (eds.), *The Irish in Early Medieval Europe: Identity, Culture and Religion*. London and New York, Palgrave Macmillan, 68–85 and 248–49.

Diplomata, chartae, epistolae, leges aliaque instrumenta ad res Gallo-Francicas spectantia (1849), ed. J. M. Pardessus, vol. II. Paris, Typographeum Reipublicae.

Dumézil, B. (2007) "L'affaire Agrestius de Luxeuil: Hérésie et régionalisme dans la Burgondie du VIIe siècle." *Médiévales* 52: 135–52.

Ebling, H. (1974) *Prosopographie der Amtsträger des Merowingerreiches von Chlothar II. (613) bis Karl Martell (741)*. Beihefte der Francia 2. Munich, Wilhelm Fink Verlag.

Ewig, E. (2009) "Bemerkungen zu zwei merowingischen Bischofsprivilegien und einem Papstprivileg des 7. Jahrhunderts für merowingische Klöster." In id., *Spätantikes und fränkisches Gallien: Gesammelte Schriften (1974–2007)*, ed. by M. Becher, T. Kölzer, and U. Nonn, vol. 3, *Beihefte der Francia 3/3*. Ostfildern, Jan Thorbecke Verlag, 539–73.

Fischer, A. (2014) "Rewriting History: Fredegar's Perspectives on the Mediterranean." In A. Fischer and I. Wood (eds.), *Western Perspectives on the Mediterranean: Cultural Transfer in Late Antiquity and the Early Middle Ages, 400–800 AD*. London, Bloomsbury, 55–75 and 135–43.

Fox, Y. (2014) *Power and Religion in Merovingian Gaul. Columbanian Monasticism and the Frankish Elites*. Cambridge Studies in Medieval Life and Thought Fourth Series 98. Cambridge, Cambridge University Press.

Gauthier, N. (1980) *L'évangélisation des pays de la Moselle: La province romaine de Première Belgique entre Antiquité et Moyen-Âge (IIIe–VIIIe siècles)*. Paris, E. de Boccard.

Goullet, M. (2001) "Les saints du diocèse de Toul (SHG VI)." In M. Heinzelmann (ed.), *L'hagiographie du haut moyen âge en Gaule du Nord: Manuscrits, textes et centres de production*. Beihefte zur Francia 52. Stuttgart, Jan Thorbecke Verlag, 11–89.

Gray, P. T. R., and M. W. Herren (1994) "Columbanus and the Three Chapters Controversy—A New Approach." *Journal of Theological Studies NS* 45: 160–70.

Halfond, G. I. (2010) *Archaeology of Frankish Church Councils, AD 511–768*. Medieval Law and Its Practice 6. Leiden and Boston, Brill.

Hardt, M. (2003) "The Bavarians." In H.-W. Goetz, J. Jarnut, and W. Pohl (eds.), *Regna and gentes: The Relationship between Late Antique and Early Medieval Peoples and Kingdoms in the Transformation of the Roman World*. The Transformation of the Roman World 13. Leiden and Boston, Brill, 429–61.

Heinzelmann, M. (2010) "L'hagiographie mérovingienne: Panorama des documents potentiels." In M. Goullet, M. Heinzelmann, and C. Veyrard-Cosme (eds.), *L'hagiographie mérovingienne à travers ses réécritures*. Beihefte der Francia 71. Ostfildern, Jan Thorbecke Verlag, 27–82.

Hen, Y. (2016) "The Church in Sixth-Century Gaul." In A. C. Murray (ed.), *A Companion to Gregory of Tours*. Brill's Companions to the Christian Tradition 63. Boston and Leiden, Brill, 232–55.

Hummer, H. (2003) "Die merowingische Herkunft der Vita Sadalbergae." *Deutsches Archiv für Erforschung des Mittelalters* 59: 459–93.

Kreiner, J. (2014a) "Autopsies and Philosophies of a Merovingian Life: Death, Responsibility, Salvation." *Journal of Early Christian Studies* 22: 113–52.

Kreiner, J. (2014b) *The Social Life of Hagiography in the Merovingian Kingdom*. Cambridge Studies in Medieval Life and Thought Fourth Series 96. Cambridge, Cambridge University Press.

Leso, T. (2013) "Columbanus in Europe: The Evidence from the *Epistulae*." *Early Medieval Europe* 21: 358–89.

Meens, R. (2016) "The Irish Contribution to the Penitential Tradition." In R. Flechner and S. Meeder (eds.), *The Irish in Early Medieval Europe: Identity, Culture and Religion*. London and New York, Palgrave Macmillan, 131–45 and 255.

O'Hara, A. (2009) "The *Vita Columbani* in Merovingian Gaul." *Early Medieval Europe* 17: 126–53.

O'Hara, A., and I. Wood (trans.) (2017) *Jonas of Bobbio, Life of Columbanus, Life of John of Réomé, and Life of Vedast*. Translated Texts for Historians 64. Liverpool, Liverpool University Press.

Rohr, C. (1995) "Hagiographie als historische Quelle: Ereignisgeschichte und Wunderberichte in der Vita Columbani des Ionas von Bobbio." *Mitteilungen des Instituts für Österreichische Geschichtswissenschaften* 103: 229–64.

Schäferdiek, K. (1982) "Columbans Wirken im Frankenreich (591–612)." In H. Löwe (ed.), *Die Iren und Europa im früheren Mittelalter*. Stuttgart, Klett-Cotta. Bd. 1, 171–201.

Schäferdiek, K. (1983) "Der irische Osterzyklus des sechsten und siebten Jahrhunderts." *Deutsches Archiv für Erforschung des Mittelalters* 39: 357–78.

Schäferdiek, K. (1985) "Bonosius von Naissus, Bonosus von Serdika und die Bonosianer." *Zeitschrift für Kirchengeschichte* 96: 162–78.

Scheibelreiter, G. (1992) "Griechisches—lateinisches—fränkisches Christentum: Der Brief Martins I. an den Bischof Amandus von Maastricht aus dem Jahre 649." *Mitteilungen des Instituts für Österreichische Geschichtsforschung* 100: 84–102.

Scholz, S. (2015) *Die Merowinger*. Stuttgart, W. Kohlhammer.

Sotinel, C. (2007) "The Three Chapters and the Transformations of Italy." In C. Chazelle and C. Cubitt (eds.), *The Crisis of the "Oikoumene": The Three Chapters and the Failed Quest for Unity in the Sixth-Century Mediterranean*. Studies in the Early Middle Ages 14. Turnhout, Brepols, 85–120.

Stancliffe, C. (2001) "Jonas's *Life of Columbanus and His Disciples*." In J. Carey, M. Herbert, and P. Ó Riain (eds.), *Studies in Irish Hagiography: Saints and Scholars*. Dublin, Four Courts Press, 189–220.

Stansbury, M. (2012) "Agrestius et l'écriture de Luxeuil." In *Autour du Scriptorium de Luxeuil. Les Cahiers Colombaniens 2011.* Luxeuil-les-Bains, Enseignes Monnier, 68–75.

Vita altera S. Wandregisili abbatis Fontanellensis (1868). In *Acta Sanctorum*, vol. 32. Paris and Rome, Victor Palmé, 272–81.

Vita Amandi episcopi II auctore Milone (1910). In B. Krusch (ed.), *Scriptores rerum Merovingicarum* 5. Hanover and Leipzig, Hahnsche Buchhandlung, 450–83.

Vita Amati (1902). In B. Krusch (ed.), *Scriptores rerum Merovingicarum 4.* MGH. Hanover and Leipzig, Hahnsche Buchhandlung, 215–21.

Vita Eligii episcopi Noviomagensis (1888). In B. Krusch (ed.), *Scriptores rerum Merovingicarum* 4. Hanover, Hahnsche Buchhandlung, 634–741.

Vita Sadalbergae abbatissae Laudunensis (1910). In B. Krusch (ed.), *Scriptores rerum Merovingicarum* 5. MGH. Hanover and Leipzig, Hahnsche Buchhandlung, 40–66.

Wood, I. (1982) "The Vita Columbani and Merovingian Hagiography." *Peritia* 1: 63–80.

Wood, I. (1994) *The Merovingian Kingdoms, 450–751.* Harlow et. al., Longman.

Wood, I. (1998) "Jonas, the Merovingians, and Pope Honorius: *Diplomata* and the *Vita Columbani.*" In A. C. Murray (ed.), *After Rome's Fall. Narrators and Sources of Early Medieval History. Essays in presented to Walter Goffart,* Toronto et al., University of Toronto Press, 99–120.

Wood, I. (2001) *The Missionary Life: Saints and the Evangelisation of Europe, 400–1050.* Harlow et al., Longman.

Wood, I. (2007) "The Franks and Papal Theology, 550–660." In C. Chazelle and C. Cubitt (eds.), *The Crisis of the "Oikoumene": The Three Chapters and the Failed Quest for Unity in the Sixth-Century Mediterranean.* Studies in the Early Middle Ages 14. Turnhout, Brepols, 223–41.

Wood, I. (2013) "The Pagans and the Other: Varying Presentations in the Early Middle Ages." *Networks and Neighbours* 1: 1–22.

Wood, I. (2014) "The Burgundians and Byzantium." In A. Fischer and I. Wood (eds.), *Western Perspectives on the Mediterranean: Cultural Transfer in Late Antiquity and the Early Middle Ages, 400–800 AD.* London, Bloomsbury, 1–15 and 107–11.

Wood, I. (2015) "The Irish in England and on the Continent in the Seventh Century: Part I." *Peritia* 26: 171–98.

Wood, I. (2016a) "The Irish in England and on the Continent in the Seventh Century: Part II." *Peritia* 27: 189–214.

Wood, I. (2016b) "Columbanian Monasticism: A Contested Concept." In R. Flechner and S. Meeder (eds.), *The Irish in Early Medieval Europe: Identity, Culture and Religion.* London and New York, Palgrave Macmillan, 86–100 and 250–1.

9

Columbanus and the Mission to the Bavarians and the Slavs in the Seventh Century

HERWIG WOLFRAM

The German archaeologist Hermann Dannheimer found and excavated the remains of a seventh-century monastery on the island of Herrenchiemsee, Bavaria, and the late Austrian historian Heinz Dopsch was the first to provide a provisional historical interpretation of the finds.[1] The discovery of Herrenchiemsee, the oldest monastic site in Bavaria, is spectacular, even more so as Dannheimmer also found there the remains of a stone church, which he dated to c. 680/700.[2] But as is often the case with such discoveries,[3] they can leave the historian in the dark due to the lack of other historical sources. This would have been the case with Herrenchiemsee if it were not for Jonas's near-contemporary *Vita Columbani*.

The monastic site is situated on an island in Lake Chiemsee, which would have been geographically at the center of the early medieval Agilolfing duchy of Bavaria. Dannheimer discovered the remains of two three-nave buildings made of wood and orientated west to east. The older building was built around 620, the younger after 650. The assumption that these buildings were churches is supported by comparison with other finds and the fact that two obviously high-ranking ecclesiastics were buried here. The graves excavated on the site contain nothing but skeletons, which is typical of clerics. Grave 108 contained the skeleton of a man who died in his early thirties around 650. Splinters of mid-seventh-century pieces of ceramic found in the grave support this date. Grave 109 contained the skeleton of a somewhat older man who died about a century later. When he was buried people took care not to disturb the earlier grave. They must have known who the incumbent of this grave was and acted in respectful memory of him. Dannheimer and Dopsch assume that the man who died around 650 was the leader or even the abbot of the Luxeuil missionaries, who founded Herrenchiemsee. Indeed, Jonas ends his report about Eustasius in Bavaria with the words: "When he had stayed there for sometime he sent wise

---

1. See Dannheimer 2011: 21–50; Dopsch 2011: 51–72.
2. The publication is forthcoming.
3. See Štih 2010: 94, 117, and 151; and Wolfram 2013: 30 about the nameless eighth-century monastery of Molzbichl, Carinthia, the oldest monastery in the Slavic world.

men, who could tire themselves carrying out the work that had been begun; he took care to return to Luxeuil."[4] Furthermore, Dannheimer excavated more than a dozen skeletons that still await an anthropological examination. According to Dannheimer and Dopsch, the man in the second grave could have been Bishop Dub-dá-chrích, an Irishman who followed his master Virgil to the Continent via Quierzy to Salzburg. Here he administered the sacraments until Virgil was ordained bishop of Salzburg in June 749.[5] Afterward Dub-dá-Chrích became abbot of Herrenchiemsee and seemingly stayed there until the end of his life. After the second burial the two graves were clearly and distinctly marked for posterity to remember. Recent isotopic investigation, however, has showed that the man in the second grave was not of Insular but of continental origin. Whatever the identity of this person, he was clearly someone of importance for the community. Irish-type styli and *rasoria*/scrapers for wax dypticha of the seventh century were also discovered on the site, which are important because of their origin and date.

It is very likely that these finds are related to the so-called Luxeuil mission to Bavaria during the first half of the seventh century.[6] This was not a mission of evangelization in the strict sense, since early medieval Bavaria was not and had never been a thoroughly pagan land. When in 589 Theodelinda, the daughter of the Bavarian duke Garibald I, came to Italy to marry the Lombard king Authari, she was a Catholic.[7] At least four if not seven late Roman saints were continuously venerated, especially in those areas of Bavaria where Christian Roman communities had survived or at least were in a strong minority. After the return of Eustasius and his followers to Luxeuil the Burgundian monastery began to venerate Afra and Florian. So the memory of two of the Bavarian saints had traveled with the missionaries back to Burgundy.[8] As Eustasius fought heresies, syncretism, and more or less isolated pagan rites with the neighboring Warasci, he set out to correct the Bavarians "with the remedy of faith."[9] He worked within the borders of the former Roman Empire and must have cooperated with an already Christian Bavarian duke who stood for the conversion of his people(s). If Eustasius went to Bavaria soon after Columbanus had died in 615 this duke could have been Garibald II. If the mission started about a decade later we are at a loss for a name.[10] But it is safe to assume that Herrenchiemsee was a ducal

---

4. Wood 2001: 36; *VC* II.8: 214.
5. Wolfram 2013: 62, 102, 106, and 120. See also Wolfram 1995b: 450, s.v. Dobdagrecus.
6. Prinz 1965: 357–62. See further Fischer, chapter 8 in this volume.
7. Wolfram 1995a: 77, 100, and 342; Pohl 2005: 412.
8. Wolfram 2017, nn. 181–3.
9. *VC* II.8: 243 sq.; Haubrichs 2006: 258–61.
10. Cf. Wolfram 1995a: 79 and Dopsch 2011: 51–3 do not completely exclude the validity of Aventin's

monastery from the beginning and had close ties to the Agilolfings. So Eustasius aimed at "inner mission" and re-Christianization of former Roman territory, which remained under the overlordship of Frankish kings who tried to expand, consolidate, and intensify their power in the region. Chlothar II (584/613–629) was one of four Frankish kings whom the prologue of the *Lex Bavariorum* praises as royal lawgivers who Christianized and thus improved their laws. It was Chlothar II in particular who strongly supported Eustasius and his engagement in Bavaria.[11]

A mission to the Slavs, however, meant that these peoples had to be converted *ab origine*. Their conversion had to start from scratch and was a mission in the full sense of the word—in theory. In reality, it was thoroughly impossible to convert the still fragmented Slav societies.[12] Many Slavic tribes were under the sway of the Avars, whose heathendom was part of their core identity, as Walter Pohl has shown.[13] Despite, or rather because of, Samo, "the first king of the Slavs,"[14] there was no power to guarantee Christianization from top down, as Bishop Amandus (who died around 675) experienced firsthand. The Slavs did not know what to do with this Western missionary; they did not even care to kill him.[15] So it was wise of Columbanus that he gladly accepted angelic advice to leave the Slavic world alone, since there was nothing but wilderness and disorder there.[16] Obviously for top security reasons the angel did not mention that at the same time the Avars had launched a very successful offensive against Friuli and defeated the Bavarians near Aguntum/Lienz.[17] It took Bishop Virgil of Salzburg (746/747–784), another Irish exile, in the following century (after a decisive defeat of the Avars) to organize a successful mission to the Carantanians, who became the first Christianized Slavonic people, but only after having been united under the sway of a single ruler who wanted their conversion. In the eastern Alpine region, the former Roman province of Noricum, conversion from the top down was then effective.[18] The question, however, of whether or not it was worthwhile and desirable to send missionaries beyond the pales of the former Roman Empire had a telling aftermath in the ninth century. When

remark that a duke Tassilo made Eustasius establish Herrenchiemsee as a double monastery for men and women.

11. *Lex Baiowariorum*, Prologus: 200–3.
12. Cf. Stancliffe 1980 on the difficulties faced in Ireland by Bishop Patrick in leading a mission to a politically fragmented country without consistent royal support.
13. Pohl 2002: 205.
14. Wolfram 2013: 115–7 and 310–4.
15. Wood 2001: 39–42; Wolfram 1995a: 400, n. 181; *Vita Amandi* 16: 439.
16. Wood 2001: 34; *VC* I.27: 216.
17. Wolfram 1995a: 79.
18. Wolfram 2013: 109–65.

in 862 the Moravian prince Rastislav sent messengers to Constantinople to ask for teachers and a bishop, Emperor Michael III called his advisers to discuss the topic. A considerable number of them raised sincere doubts and were opposed to the demands, since Moravia was situated beyond the boundaries of the former Roman Empire.[19] It might have been due to his lack of pragmatism that "Amandus brought together ideas of Columbanus, on the *peregrinatio pro Christo*, and Gregory the Great, particularly on the evangelization of the English, to create a notion of mission to all nations," as Ian Wood has noted.[20]

Despite the fact that the writing utensils discovered on Herrenchiemsee were of Irish type, the mission to Bavaria was largely a Frankish affair. Eustasius, abbot of Luxeuil (c. 614–629), and Agilus, his only follower whose name is recorded, were aristocratic Franco-Burgundians. Jonas made his audience believe, however, that Columbanus was the driving force behind the mission to the Bavarians and indirectly the Slavs. His disciple Eustasius did allegedly nothing but fulfill "the command of the master."[21] On the other hand, Jonas could not hide the fact that his saint was anything but enthusiastic about going afield himself and visiting pagan peoples in their wild habitat. Ian Wood speaks of "Columbanus's half-hearted missionary work."[22] Needless to say, Columbanus was a religious genius and charismatic leader. He attracted followers of both Irish and Frankish origins and left behind a lasting religious and spiritual legacy.[23] But following his banishment from Luxeuil in 610 and his arrival in Alamannia, Columbanus did not choose to work among pagan *gentes* beyond the sphere of Frankish influence after hearing about their apparent "coolness."[24]

The Frankish king Theudebert II (596–612) initiated and supported Columbanus's visit to the Alamannian *gentes* in what is now Switzerland and the westernmost part of Austria.[25] These peoples lived at the periphery of Theudebert's kingdom but again still inside the boundaries of the former Roman Empire. After a short and unsuccessful interlude near Lake Zurich (not discussed by Jonas), Columbanus and his followers went to Bregenz on the eastern banks of Lake Constance. This somewhat rundown place, which Columbanus did not like when he arrived, was still considered an *oppidum*, located by Jonas in Germania. There lived Christians, baptized heathens, and outright pagans, Romans and Alamanni side by side. Columbanus restored

---

19. Wolfram 2013: 24.
20. Wood 2001: 39, after Wolfgang H. Fritze.
21. *VC* II.8: 243.
22. Wood 2001: 38.
23. Cf., e.g., *VC* I.26: 209 and II.25: 289–94.
24. See Wood 2001: 31; as to Columbanus, *Ep.* 4: 167.
25. See further the contributions by Fox and Dörler, chapters 12 and 13 in this volume.

a church dedicated to Saint Aurelia, cleansed it of three pagan idols, chased out demons and devils, and almost against his will got involved in converting and baptizing the locals.[26] It thus seems more accurate to speak of a Hiberno-Frankish (Burgundian) mission when defining Luxeuil's engagement in Bavaria.

The history of mission is also a history of refusal and failure, as becomes apparent when we consider the case of the troublemaker Agrestius. He was a former notary of Theuderic II who became a monk at Luxeuil and asked Eustasius to be sent as a missionary to the Bavarians. At first the abbot declined Agrestius's petition on the grounds of his being "still untrained in religion," but finally gave in. Agrestius failed in his missionary efforts in Bavaria and became a follower of the Aquileian position in the Tricapitoline schism. He went to Aquileia and then turned against the Columbanian movement itself. Jonas wanted to hide the fact that Agrestius took the same stance as Columbanus in the schism, and as he was not overly interested in what Agrestius did in Bavaria, he did not transmit any details of his stay there. The only information that we may infer from his report is the time period. It must have been sometime before 629 or, rather, 626 at the latest.[27]

Even less can be learned about the Bavarians through the contact with the region of Bishop Amandus, the itinerant missionary bishop with whom Jonas worked in northern Francia. Amandus came from Aquitaine, was forced by royal command to become a bishop without a see before 629, and did a lot of missionary work among the pagans in the southern as well as the northern periphery of the Frankish kingdom. He is considered the "apostle of the Belgians." Amandus also wanted to convert the Slavs. In order to reach them he had to cross the Danube. This is the only hint to where he went and means that he traveled along the Danube through Bavaria until he probably met the Slavs in what is now northeastern Lower Austria. If the assumption is correct that this happened during the reign of King Dagobert I (623–639), Amandus set out for his endeavor when the Central European Slavs under Samo had shaken off Avar dominance.[28] But Jonas does not mention Samo or anything else about Bavaria. It took another two or three generations for the Bavarian duke Theodo (c. 696–717/718) to be strong enough to invite Frankish bishops to reform the Church in Bavaria and lay the foundations for the work of the Anglo-Saxon Boniface to organize the Bavarian church in 739.[29]

---

26. Wood 2001: 32–4; Schäferdiek 1982: 175 (Swiss interlude); *VC* I.27: 211–7. See also O'Hara 2015 on Columbanus's period in Bregenz.

27. Wolfram 1995a: 400 n. 179.

28. Wood 2001: 39. As to Samo, see Wolfram 2013: 310–4.

29. Wolfram 1995a: 105–11.

Finally, there is the Woden story as told by Jonas, which is also the subject of two detailed contributions in this volume (see chapters 10 and 11). When the locals around Bregenz prepared a sacrifice for Woden, Columbanus destroyed the large vat of beer that was dedicated to the pagan god, which was, as Jonas notes, possessed by the devil. Jonas obviously liked the story of the broken cask so much that he used it also in his account of Bishop Vedast of Arras, though in a slightly different form.[30] But what does the Woden story mean in the context of the *Vita Columbani*? Was it really due to Jonas's geographical ignorance that he placed Bregenz within Germania instead of Raetia? A man who had traveled widely throughout the Frankish kingdom and experienced its Germanic periphery before he started writing the *Vita Columbani*[31] must have known better. And indeed, Jonas did know better. He was familiar with the ancient geographical terminology, from which he borrowed the notion that Germania bordered on the right bank of the Rhine,[32] and he was interested in Germanic language and ethnology. As Gregory of Tours, if in a wrong context, realized that the Suebi and the Alamanni were the same people,[33] Jonas speaks of Suaevi when he means Alamanni. Also, Woden and Germania fit perfectly well together,[34] and not only since Bede, who knew that Woden, "from whose stock sprang the royal house of many Anglo-Saxon provinces," was the great-great-grandfather of Hengist and Horsa, the *duces* of those peoples who came from Germania.[35] Instead, the *Vita Columbani* contains not only the oldest equation of Woden with the Roman god Mercury but also the oldest datable literary evidence of Woden in the historical record. It is not certain whether the famous contemporary fibula of Nordendorf, which bears a runic-Alamannian inscription mentioning Woden and Thor, is a dedication to, or a curse on, the pagan gods. The Alamanns, however, did not venerate Woden as their premier god. Instead, they were Ziuvari, Ziu's/Tyr's men; Alamannian Augsburg was also called Ciesburg, Ziu's/Tyr's castle; and even today the Swabians say Ziestag for Tuesday.[36]

Jonas had knowledge not only of the vernacular name of the Germanic god Woden first recorded by him, but also of the Germanic name for the Slavs. It is true that the author wrote the Latin form Veneti. But it was also Jonas who for the first time expressly equated them with the Slavs and used a Germanism. Originally, the Veneti were an Indo-European group of peoples who were

30. Wood 2001: 38; *VC* I.27: 213.
31. Wood 2001: 38.
32. *VC* I.16: 179 (also in connection with a beer story) and I.27: 211.
33. Gregory of Tours, *DLH* II.2: 39.
34. *VC* I.27: 213.
35. Bede, *HE* I.15.
36. However, cf. Maier's comments in chapter 10 in this volume.

widespread all over Europe. Veneti lived in Gaul along the Channel. Venice and Venetia derive their names from the Veneti. Lake Constance was Lacus Venetus. The Veneti east of the Vistula River seem to have been the strongest group of these peoples. They used to be the eastern neighbors of the Germanic peoples.[37] When these eastern Veneti disappeared and were succeeded by the Balts and Slavs, the Germanic peoples transferred their name as Wends/Winds/Windisch to all Slavic peoples. Even today there are still some towns and villages in Austria whose names start with Windisch, such as Windischgarsten, Windisch-Bleiberg, Windisch-Baumgarten, Windisch-Minihof.

Jonas perhaps became interested in the Germanic vernacular as he realized its importance for a successful mission and convincing preaching to those Germanic peoples whom Columbanus and his disciples encountered. So he had the master call upon Gallus for preaching to the people of Bregenz, since the disciple was both excellent in Latin and fluent in the local "barbarian vernacular," which he could have learned during his time in the Vosges, adjacent to Suebian territory. (Jonas even mentions Suebian bandits near Luxeuil.)[38] Was this one reason for Gallus to stay behind in Alamannia when Columbanus and his followers continued on to Italy? But how did it come about that Gallus spoke a Germanic language like a native speaker? The late Johannes Duft explains the name Gallus as an ethnic nickname like Franciscus/Francesco and assumes that his father could have been a Frank.[39] The language problem caused an even greater impediment to the mission to the Slavs. As far as is known, neither Columbanus nor Amandus could rely on a Slavic-speaking interpreter, let alone a preacher. Only Adalram, the second archbishop of Salzburg (821–839), is praised for having been able to preach to Slavic peoples in their own language. He was also the first and for a long time the last high-ranking ecclesiastical official who went to the Slavic Far East, and he consecrated a church at Nitra (now in Slovakia) in the early 820s.[40] Instead, Constantinople sent Konstantinos/Cyrill and Methodios, who were born and raised in bilingual Thessalonike, created a Slavic literary language, were supported by regional lords, and met in the long run with lasting success. One of these princes called Chozil "loved the Slavic characters so much that he learned them himself" and ordered that this script be taught to a group of young people.[41] But how was it possible that the ecclesiastics from Salzburg were successful in Carinthia? The same mechanism

37. Wenskus 1977: 228–34. See, e.g., Jordanes, *Getica*: 166, s.v. *Venethi*; or Fredegar IV.48.
38. Wetti, *Vita Galli* 6: 260; Walahfrid Strabo, *Vita Galli* I.6: 289.
39. Duft 1974: 16.
40. Wolfram 2013: 185.
41. Wolfram 2013: 20; *Vita Constantini* 15.

worked again: when in the 750s the Salzburg clerics started their mission to the Carantanians, they were invited by a strong regional lord and first sent mostly Bavarian Romans. So they obviously responded to the fact that a Roman vernacular was a kind of second language of the Carantanians. It was only during one of the last missions in the mid-770s that the Irish Dublittir joined the Salzburg mission.[42] Two of the three oldest Carantanian mother churches were founded in or near former Roman cities. The late Roman saint Nonnosus was continuously venerated in the neighborhood of former Teurnia, the *metropolis Norici* of the *Life of Severinus*.[43] Even today many Carantanian toponyms and hydronyms remember the Romans once living in this Slavic principality, which until the 740s had to accept Bavarian overlordship. The area where the ruins of Teurnia are located is still called Auf der Läschitz, a Slavo-Germanic hybrid that literally means "at the Romans." On the western slopes of the Hemmaberg there is a little village called Kršna Vas, "village of the baptized" (i.e., Roman Christians as opposed to the pagan Slavs). In Old Slovene, after its speakers had long since been Christianized, a maiden was still called *krščenica*, which etymologically meant a baptized female. But the Salzburg mission to the Carantanians is another story.[44]

BIBLIOGRAPHY

Dannheimer, H. (2011) "Das Kloster im Frühen und Hohen Mittelalter." In W. Brugger (ed.), *Herrenchiemsee: Kloster—Chorherrenstift—Königsschloss*. Regensburg, Verlag Friedrich Pustet, 21–50.

Dopsch, H. (2011) "Vom Mönchskloster zum Kollegiatstift: Die frühe Geschichte nach dem Befund der Schriftquellen 7.–9. Jahrhundert." In W. Brugger (ed.), *Herrenchiemsee: Kloster—Chorherrenstift—Königsschloss*. Regensburg, Verlag Friedrich Pustet, 51–72.

Duft, J. (1974) "Irische Einflüsse auf St. Gallen und Alemannien." In A. Borst (ed.), *Mönchtum, Episkopat und Adel zur Gründungszeit des Klosters Reichenau*. Sigmaringen, Thorbecke, 9–35.

Eugippius (1898) *Vita Severini*, ed. T. Mommsen. MGH, *Scriptores*. Berlin.

Haubrichs, W. (2006) "Warasci." In *Reallexikon der Germanischen Alterumskunde* 33, Berlin, de Gruyter.

Jordanes (1882) *Getica*, ed. T. Mommsen. MGH, *Auctores antiquissimi* 5, 1. Berlin.

Lex Baiowariorum (1926), ed. E. von Schwind. MGH, *Leges* 5, 2. Hanover.

O'Hara, A. (2015) "Columbanus *ad locum*: The Establishment of the Monastic Foundations." *Peritia* 26: 143–70.

---

42. Wolfram 2013: 32.
43. Eugippius, *Vita Severini* 21.2.
44. Wolfram 2013: 126–57. Cf. Wood 2001: 168–71.

Pohl, W. (2002) *Die Awaren: Ein Steppenvolk in Mitteleuropa, 567–822 n.Chr.* Munich, C. H. Beck.

Pohl, W. (2005) "Theodelinde." In *Reallexikon der Germanischen Alterumskunde* 30, Berlin, de Gruyter.

Prinz, F. (1965) *Frühes Mönchtum im Frankenreich: Kultur und Gesellschaft in Gallien, den Rheinlanden und Bayern am Beispiel der monastischen Entwicklung (4. bis 8. Jahrhundert).* Munich, Oldenbourg.

Schäferdiek, K. (1982) "Columban's Wirken im Frankreich (591–612)." In H. Löwe (ed.), *Die Iren und Europa im früheren Mittelalter.* Stuttgart, Klett-Cotta, 171–201.

Stancliffe, C. (1980) "Kings and Conversion: Some Comparisons between the Roman Mission to England and Patrick's to Ireland." *Frühmittelalterliche Studien* 14: 59–94.

Štih, P. (2010) *The Middle Ages between the Easern Alps and the Northern Adriatic: Select Papers on Slovene Historiography and Medieval History.* Leiden, Brill.

Vita Amandi (1910). In B. Krusch (ed.), *Scriptores rerum Merovingicarum* 5. MGH, Hanover and Leipzig, , 395–485.

Vita Constantini = Žitje Konstantina (1967) In R. Vercerka (ed.), *Magnae Moraviae fontes historici* 2. Brno, Universita J. E. Purkyně, 57–115.

Walahfrid Strabo (1902). *Vita Galli.* In B. Krusch (ed.), *Scriptores rerum Merovingicarum* 4. MGH. Hanover, 280–337;

M. Joynt (trans.), *The Life of St. Gall.* London, 1927; repr. in M.-A. Stouck (ed.), *Medieval Saints: A Reader.* Peterborough, ONT, Broadview Press, 1997, 223–49.

Wenskus, R. (1977) *Stammesbildung und Verfassung: Das Werden der frühmittelalterlichen gentes.* Cologne and Vienna, Böhlau Verlag.

Wetti, Vita Galli (1902). In B. Krusch (ed.), *Scriptores rerum Merovingicarum* 4. MGH. Hanover, 256–80.

Wolfram, H. (1995a) *Grenze und Räume: Geschichte Österreichs vor seiner Entstehung.* Vienna, Ueberreuter.

Wolfram, H. (1995b) *Salzburg, Bayern, Österreich: Die Conversio Bagoariorum et Carantanorum und die Quellen ihrer Zeit.* Vienna, Munich, Oldenbourg.

Wolfram, H. (2002) *Die Germanen.* Munich, C. H. Beck.

Wolfram, H. (2013) *Conversio Bagoariorum et Carantanorum: Das Weißbuch der Salzburger Kirche über die erfolgreiche Mission in Karantanien und Pannonien mit Zusätzen und Ergänzungen.* Ljubljana, Hermagoras.

Wolfram, H. (2017) "Die frühmittelalterliche Romania im Donau- und Ostalpenraum." In W. Pohl, I. Hartl, and W. Haubrichs (eds.), *Walchen, Romani und Latini: Variationen einer nachrömischen Gruppenbezeichnung zwischen Britannien und dem Balkan.* Forschungen zur Geschichte des Mittelalters 21/Denkschriften der philosophisch-historischen Klasse 491. Vienna, Austrian Academy of Sciences Press, 27–57.

Wood, I. (2001) *The Missionary Life: Saints and the Evangelisation of Europe, 400–1050.* Harlow, Routledge.

PART IV

On the Fringe

Columbanus and Gallus in Alamannia

Between the Devil and the Deep Lake Constance

Jonas of Bobbio, *interpretatio Christiana*, and the Pagan Religion of the Alamanni

BERNHARD MAIER

One of the most recent accretions to the numerous legendary traditions about Columbanus, apparently first attested in the present century, seems to be the assertion that he coined the phrase: "It is my design to die in the brew-house; let ale be placed to my mouth when I am expiring, so that when the choirs of angels come, they may say, 'Be God propitious to this drinker.' "[1] Obviously the lines are only a slight modification of the quatrain beginning *Meum est propositum in taberna mori* from the twelfth stanza of the Archpoet's *Confession*, which in its turn has been shown to consist of a conflation of a few lines from Ovid's *Amores* and two verses from Luke's Gospel, poking fun at the sacrament of penance.[2] While it is difficult to know who first ascribed the modified version of these lines to Columbanus, there can be little doubt that the Irish champion of asceticism could only come to be depicted as the author of a stanza in praise of drinking because Jonas of Bobbio in his *Vita Columbani* credited him with three miracle stories connected with beer (*VC* 16, 17, and 27). To appreciate the significance of these stories, it is worth looking at Jonas's narrative in some detail.

The first miracle story in chapter 16 of the *VC* relates how the cellarer of the monastery of Luxeuil had once drawn the plug of the vat containing beer for the monks, when he was suddenly called away, absentmindedly taking the plug with him instead of putting it back into the vat. When he returned, expecting that nothing would be left in the vat, he found to his amazement that all the beer

---

1. The saying is ascribed to Columbanus in Cian Molloy, *The Story of the Irish Pub: An Intoxicating History of the Licensed Trade in Ireland* (Dublin: Liffey Press, 2002), 11; Christopher Mark O'Brien, *Fermenting Revolution: How to Drink Beer and Save the World* (Gabriola Island, Canada: New Society Publishers, 2006), 42; and Jess Lebow, *The Beer Devotional: A Daily Celebration of the World's Most Inspiring Beers* (Avon, MA: Adams Media, 2010), 167. Further examples may be found on the Internet; the almost identical English wording and apparent lack of any German or French equivalents suggests that all of the resources be based on a single source.

2. See Dronke 1997: 91–2.

had run into a jar and not the least drop had fallen outside. The second story in chapter 17 of the *VC* relates how Columbanus once went to the monastery of Fontaine, where the hard-working monks working in the fields had only two loaves of bread and very little beer. Raising his eyes to heaven, Columbanus asked Christ to multiply the loaves and the beer, upon which all were satisfied and each one drank as much as he wished. The third story is connected with the saint's sojourn among the pagan Alamanni in the area around Lake Constance. Jonas tells us:

> While he was staying there and was going among the inhabitants of this place, he discovered that they wished to perform a profane sacrifice. They had a large cask that they call a cupa, which held about twenty measures. It was full of beer and had been placed in their midst. When the man of God approached it he asks what they wanted to do with it. They tell him that they want to make an offering to their God, Woden, whom, as others say, they affirm to be Mercury. When Columbanus hears about this pestilential work, he blows into the cask. Astonishingly, it breaks with a crash and pieces shatter everywhere, and the great force of the explosion causes the beer to spill out. Then it is clear that the Devil had been concealed in the cask and that he ensnared the souls of the participants with the profane drink. When the barbarians see this they are stunned and say that the man of God had a great deal of puff to split a well-bound cask in that manner. Columbanus rebukes them with the words of the Gospel so that they would stop performing these sacrifices and commands them to return to their homes. Many were then converted to the faith of Christ through the preaching and teaching of the blessed man and were baptized. And like a good shepherd he led others, who had already been baptized, but who were held in profane error, back to the observance of the Gospel teaching and the bosom of the Church. [3]

Obviously the second of these three episodes is modeled on the first of the two stories about Christ feeding the multitude that are found in the canonical gospels. This is confirmed by Jonas making Columbanus himself refer to the five loaves and five thousand people in the desert that are mentioned in Matthew 14:13–21, Mark 6:30–44, Luke 9:10–17, and John 6:5–15, Jonas's two loaves (*duo panes*) and a little beer (*paulolum cervisae*) having replaced the canonical five loaves and two fishes. The first and the third of the three miracle stories related by Jonas might be said to complement each other, the one making Columbanus

---

3. Jonas of Bobbio, *VC* I.27, trans. O'Hara and Wood 2017: 159–60.

prevent the spilling of beer to be used in a monastery, and the other making him spill the beer that was meant to be used in a pagan ritual. In modern scholarship the first miracle has been interpreted as an edifying story calculated to extol the virtue of monastic submission: as the spilling of beer is specifically mentioned among the offenses for which Columbanus's *Regula monachorum* stipulates a severe punishment, the miracle wrought by the saint ensured that the cellarer would not suffer on account of his unhesitating obedience.[4] The third miracle might also be taken to have served an edificatory purpose, extolling Columbanus's missionary skills. However, it has also been quoted and interpreted as evidence for the pagan religion of the Alamanni. To see whether this use of the episode related by Jonas is justified, let us consider both the history of scholarship on Alamannic paganism and the literary and archaeological sources on which our knowledge of it is based.[5]

As may be inferred from both literary and archaeological sources, the Alamanni had begun to move into the formerly Roman territories to the east of the Rhine and to the north of the Danube, present-day Baden-Württemberg or Southwest Germany, in the second half of the third century AD. From what is known of their material culture, it may be surmised that the newcomers had migrated from and were still maintaining links with regions farther to the northeast, the area around the rivers Elbe and Saale. From around 500, the predominantly pagan Alamanni had to bow to the neighboring Franks, who had converted to Christianity before them, later tradition telescoping this development into the story of the battle of Tolbiac, according to which the Frankish king's vow to embrace Christianity is said to have resulted in the immediate intervention of heavenly hosts and the death of the Alamannic king.

In Germany the modern interest in the ancient Alamanni may be said to have begun in 1803, when the vernacular poet Johann Peter Hebel (1760–1826) published his *Allemannische Gedichte* (Alamannic poems), imbued with the spirit of romanticism. For a long time this romantic spirit made itself felt in an antiquarian enthusiasm for Alamannic paganism, which tended to be colored by a good deal of wishful thinking. Thus scholars were prone to gloss over the inherent shakiness of the evidence, as there was so little material that even questionable pieces of information were felt to be indispensable. Moreover, scholars tended to start from the romantic assumption of a fundamental continuity in

---

4. Nelson 2005: 93 and 160.

5. For recent surveys of Alamannic history and civilization from the third to the mid-eighth centuries, see Geuenich 2005; Krapp 2007; Ade et al. 2008; and Morrissey 2013. For the first three centuries of Alamannic history, see also Drinkwater 2007. I have been unable to consult Philip A. Shaw, "Uses of Wodan: The Development of His Cult and of Medieval Literary Responses to It" (PhD thesis, University of Leeds 2002), which is referred to in Yaniv Fox, chapter 12 in the present volume.

matters of religion, inferring the religious conditions at the time of Columbanus from those that were believed to have prevailed among the reputed ancestors of the Alamanni in the Elbe-Saale area or from those that were thought to be reflected in documents dating from a much later period. Thus the designation of the Suebi/Alamanni as Cyuuari in a ninth-century manuscript was taken to characterize them as "followers of Ziu," and the name Ciesburc, found in a twelfth-century manuscript to designate the town of Augsburg, was thought to contain the same element as that found in Alamannic Ziestag (Tuesday or *dies Martis*).[6] The hypothetically reconstructed Alamannic god Ziu, supposed to be the equivalent of the Norse god Týr, was then declared to be identical with the anonymous supreme god (*regnator omnium deus*) of the first-century Semnones tribe mentioned by Tacitus (*Germania* 39.2).[7] In point of fact, however, it is only the Alamannic designation of the Tuesday as Ziestag that stands up to critical scrutiny, whereas both Cyuuari and Ciesburc may represent scribal errors, the identity of Tacitus's *regnator omnium deus* remaining questionable.[8]

Looking for contemporaneous written evidence for Alamannic paganism at the time of Columbanus, a convenient starting point is a much-quoted description from the Byzantine historian Agathias of Myrina around the middle of the sixth century:

> They have their own traditional way of life too, but in matters of government and public administration they follow the Frankish system, religious observance being the only exception. They worship certain trees, the waters of rivers, hills and mountain valleys, in whose honour they sacrifice horses, cattle and countless other animals by beheading them, and imagine that they are performing an act of piety thereby. But contact with the Franks is having a beneficial effect and is reforming them in this respect too; already it is influencing the more rational among them and it will not be long, I think, before a saner view wins universal acceptance.[9]

From this passage it appears that by the middle of the sixth century Alamannic society was still predominantly, though by no means exclusively, pagan.

6. Cf. Wolfram, chapter 9 in this volume.

7. See, e.g., Meyer 1903: 339: "Die Semnonen aber brachten südwärts wandernd den Kultus ihres göttlichen Stammvaters aus der Mark Brandenburg ins Schwabenland, wo man Cyuuari d. h. Ziuverehrer kannte und eine Hauptstadt, das heutige Augsburg, mit echt deutschem Namen Ziesburc hieß. Im deutschen Südwesten gilt ja noch heute der Zistag oder Zistig statt des Dienstags."

8. For the interpretation of *Cyuuari* and *Ciesburc*, see Rübekeil 2002: 388–92 and Reitzenstein 2013: 39–42. For suggestions about the identity of the *regnator omnium deus*, see Lund 1986: 80–1 and Timpe 1992: 476–7.

9. Agathias 1975: 15. For a critical study of the possible sources of Agathias's description of Alamannic paganism, see Gottlieb 1969.

Archaeologically, Agathias's reference to the beheading of animals may be linked to the well-attested decapitation of horses in Alamannic burial rites, yet his overall description of the pagan religion is rather stereotyped, reproducing typically classical, biblical, and Christian clichés.[10] There are similar problems with a passage in the writings of Ammianus Marcellinus, who relates how the Alamanni once missed a favorable opportunity to attack the Romans, speculating that this may have been because their auguries were inauspicious. As Greek and Roman ethnographers were always quick to attribute this kind of reasoning to barbarian nations, it is not difficult to suggest a number of possible models for the passage in question.[11]

Turning to archaeology, we are faced with a conspicuous lack of evidence for Alamannic paganism, as there are no sanctuaries or sacrificial sites comparable to those that we find in northern Germany or southern Scandinavia. Several iron objects discovered in Münchhöf-Homberg near Constance in 1938 are thought to be the remnants of a weapon sacrifice, but we know neither the people who offered up this sacrifice (if it was a sacrifice) nor the deity to which it was addressed.[12] Thus most of what we do know about the religion of the pagan Alamanni is based on inferences drawn from graves and grave goods.[13] One class of objects is thought to indicate a belief in the efficiency of charms and amulets, and possibly the idea that the dead were particularly in need of them. Food placed in graves is also thought to be characteristic of pagan ideas, as we may infer from the gradual abandonment of this custom in the wake of Christianization.[14] Yet another indication of pagan ideas is the existence of multiple burials in a single grave and horse burials.[15]

Only rarely do we find depictions of religious or mythological conceptions, such as the carvings of two-headed snakes on the lids of wooden coffins excavated in a burial field at Oberflacht near Tuttlingen.[16] Interestingly, this type of snake appears to have had an Irish cousin, for in the Old Irish *Saltair na Rann*

10. For a comprehensive discussion of the worship of trees and waters attributed to contemporary pagans in the early Middle Ages, see Krutzler 2011: 76–154.

11. See Krutzler 2011: 154–214, who refers to Tacitus, *Germania* 10, and Caesar, *De Bello Gallico* 1.50.4–5 and 1.53.7, in his discussion of the early medieval evidence for divinatory practices in Germanic paganism.

12. See Quast 1997. For a recent general survey of the archaeological evidence relating to Alamannic paganism, see Behrens 2012.

13. For a recent survey of funerary rituals in the early Middle Ages, see Brather-Walter and Brather 2012.

14. For a recent general survey, see Blaich 2009.

15. For multiple burials, see the recent survey in Schneider 2008 and the comprehensive study in Lüdemann 1994. For a comprehensive study of Merovingian horse burials, see Oexle 1984.

16. See Paulsen 1992.

we find *in béist imamnas imchenn*, "the very fierce, two-headed beast" as a designation of the devil.[17] The fact that this refers to a snake with two heads on either side of the body, as in the Oberflacht depictions, is shown by the expression *nathair imchenn*, which in the Middle Irish treatise *Auraicept na nÉces* is used to designate a palindrome, that is to say a line of Ogam writing that can be read in the same way both from top to bottom and from bottom to top.[18] In other instances, Alamannic depictions can profitably be compared with similar finds from adjacent areas of the early Germanic world, as is thought to be the case with an embossed golden disc found at Pliezhausen.[19] This shows a mounted warrior who is just riding over his fallen enemy, aided by a presumably supernatural figure gripping the shaft of his spear. A rather similar depiction is known from a helmet plate found in one of the seventh-century Valsgärde graves near Uppsala, where we also see a supernatural being guiding the spear of a mounted warrior riding over his fallen enemy. Likewise, an Alamannic sword sheath found at Gutenstein depicts what looks like a warrior dressed up as a wolf in a fashion similar to the depiction on a helmet plate matrix found at Torslunda in Sweden.[20] Sometimes it is assumed that we may identify individual deities also known from written sources, such as for instance in a bronze disk found in a grave at Hailfingen, where the central figure surrounded by eagles has been taken to represent the god Woden.[21] All these identifications, however, are ultimately conjectural, based on inferences that are not always made transparent.

What, then, do we make of the story about Columbanus and the beer sacrifice to the god Woden "whom others call Mercury"? In the article "Mithras and Wodan," published in 1978, Hilda Ellis Davidson speculated that the reference to the Irish saint's "strong breath" might be significant. Pointing out that there is a strong connection between the Old Norse god Óðinn and poetic inspiration, she suspected that Columbanus might have been "represented as deliberately outdoing Wodan at his own game."[22] The correct interpretation of this detail, however, emerges when we compare the story of Columbanus and the Alamanni with a very similar episode in the *Vita Vedastis*.[23] In this episode, Vedast is said to have once been invited to a dinner with some Frankish nobles. Entering the house, he saw several vessels, filled with beer according to the

17. See Stokes 1883: 17, line 1130.
18. See Carey 1990: 37–9.
19. See Böhner and Quast 1994; Quast 1997: 436.
20. Quast 1997: 437.
21. Quast 1997: 438.
22. Ellis Davidson 1978: 107.
23. See Nelson 2005: 89–90.

pagan custom (*conspicit gentile ritu vasa plena cervisiae domi adstare*).[24] In response to his question, he was told that some of these vessels had been offered up by Christians, others by pagans. As soon as Vedast made the sign of the cross over all the vessels, invoking the name of God and giving a blessing, those vessels that had been offered up in accordance with the pagan custom burst into pieces, and all the beer they contained spilled onto the floor. Obviously the breathing in the *Vita Columbani* is the direct equivalent of the sign of the cross in the *Vita Vedastis*, and instead of considering a special connection with the figure of Woden, we should probably view this detail as another instance of exsufflation, common in Christian liturgy and hagiography.[25]

As early Christian and later Muslim references to ritual blowing against demons among Egyptians, Phoenicians, and Arabs suggest, ideas connected with the potency of the breath appear to have been widespread in the ancient Near East. In the Bible, this is reflected in passages implying the life-giving force of God's breath (Gen. 2:7, Ezek. 37:9, John 20:22), but also in those that reflect the belief in its destructive power (Job 4:9, Ezek. 21:31, 2 Thess. 2:8). As early as the late second century AD, Tertullian (in *De idolatria* 2) mentions *despuere* and *exsufflare* as means by which Christians express their abhorrence of demons. Based on the above-mentioned biblical antecedents and such popular notions, rites of exsufflation as a means of exorcising demons began to form part of the liturgies of baptism and the catechumenate from at least the fourth century. At around the same time, the motif also entered Christian hagiography, as Saint Anthony was reported to have made a demon who had tried to tempt him vanish by blowing against him (*Vita Antonii* 40).[26] In the Latin West, it was Sulpicius Severus who established the tradition of holy men casting out demons by blowing at them, making Saint Martin expel a demon by merely breathing at him (*exsufflans*) from a distance (*Dialogus* 3,8).

As Jonas of Bobbio is known to have consciously modeled his *Vita Columbani* on the *Vita Martini*, his story of the Irish saint using exsufflation to oppose a god of the pagan Alamanni may well reflect the model supplied by Sulpicius Severus. This may be important in yet another respect, as Sulpicius Severus also claimed that the devil used to appear to Martin as Jupiter, Venus, and Minerva, but most often as Mercury (*Vita Martini* 22; cf. *Dialogi* 2.13.6 and 3.6.4). Could it not be that it was precisely this passage that prompted Jonas to identify an anonymous pagan god opposed by Columbanus with the Germanic equivalent of Mercury,

---

24. Jonas of Bobbio, *Vita Vedastis* 7 in O'Hara and Wood 2017: 272–4.

25. For what follows, see the classical study by Dölger 1909: 118–30.

26. For the influence of the *Vita Antonii* on Jonas of Bobbio, see most recently O'Hara 2015 and literature cited therein.

Woden?[27] Needless to say, the whole story hardly looks like a factual account, and Jonas's statement that the pagans finally realized that it was the devil who had been present in the casket appears to credit them with a negative reflection of a Christian idea, namely the notion that their god was present in the beer to be sacrificed, just as Christians believed that their God was present in the wine of the Eucharist.[28] In view of these parallels, I argue that the true significance of Jonas's story about Columbanus and the pagan Alamanni does not lie in its preservation of any authentic details of Alamannic ritual, but rather in the fact that this is the oldest instance of *interpretatio Christiana* in the Germanic-speaking world.[29] That is to say, this is the first time that a Germanic god known by his proper name was directly identified with the devil, following the precedents established by early Christian demonology. But obviously, *interpretatio Christiana* tends to blur the picture of pagan deities rather than bring it out in any detail, for if one assumes that all the gods are only manifestations of the one devil, it stands to reason that details are of no consequence.

The limits that *interpretatio Christiana* impose on the source value of hagiographic texts may also be illustrated by the example of the goddess Diana, who in the Roman imperial period was identified not only with the Greek goddess Artemis, but also with such native Celtic deities as Abnoba and Arduinna.[30] In the ninth century the anonymous author of the *Passio Kiliani* invokes her name in connection with the pre-Christian religion in the area of Würzburg, making one of the pagan Franks there declare that, unless the Christian God would manifest his superior power, he and his people would rather serve "the great Diana." On the basis of this detail, it has repeatedly been suggested that the oldest church on the Marienberg at Würzburg had replaced a pagan sanctuary and that the great Diana might be identified with a figure of Germanic mythology. However, as Knut Schäferdiek demonstrated, the phrase "the great Diana" clearly indicates that the author of the *Passio Kiliani*, who was writing several generations after the events that he described, had been influenced by the description of the confrontation between the Pauline mission and the cult of Diana at Ephesus, as related in the Acts of the Apostles.[31] As Schäferdiek points out, "Diana" had become a sobriquet of Christian demonology as early as the sixth century, and there is some evidence that the members of the Frankish

---

27. As pointed out by Karl Helm (1953: 253), Jonas may have known the cult of Woden from Lombard Italy and may have used the name in this context rather arbitrarily to identify a god whose name he did not know.

28. Thus Achterberg 1930: 22.

29. Achterberg 1930: 17.

30. For a summary, see Bauchhenss 1984.

31. See Schäferdiek 1994.

nobility with whom Kilian had to deal in the area around Würzburg were in fact Christians rather than pagans. Conceding with Schäferdiek that the Church was hardly ever interested in the details of pagan cults, we may suspect that this holds also for the case of the Alamannic Woden, who remains an elusive figure, despite Jonas's memorable story.

In conclusion, let us consider the significance of the fact that it was beer (rather than any other liquid or solid substance) that was offered up as a sacrifice by the pagan Alamanni. On the one hand, this may well reflect a genuine cultic practice, but in the context of Jonas's narrative, as we have seen, it also serves to contrast Columbanus's uncompromising opposition to beer used in a pagan ritual with his unqualified approval of beer used in Christian monasteries. As Max Nelson pointed out in his comprehensive history of beer in ancient Europe, by the Roman imperial period both Greeks and Romans had come to regard beer as "the barbarian's beverage," inferior to wine and characteristic of such peoples as Celts, Germans, Scythians, and Illyrians.[32] Unsurprisingly, this is the view that also prevailed among the Church Fathers, Christian writers who extolled wine and denigrated beer, including Sextus Iulius Africanus (*Cesti* 1.19.17–23), Eusebius (*Commentarius in Isaiam Prophetam* 1.75), and Jerome (*Commentarius in Isaiam Prophetam* 7.19.5–11).[33] Ireland, however, was different in this respect, for just as beer had been common in Roman Britain and in the British Church, it continued to be widely used in Irish monasteries. Even there, however, opinions were divided: on the one hand, there was a widespread belief in the medicinal qualities of beer, but on the other hand, there was the traditional denigration to be found in the writings of the Church Fathers, its rejection as interfering with asceticism, and last but not least its well-known association with pagan cultic practices. Thus Maelruain, the founder of the Irish monastery of Tallaght, is credited with prohibiting his monks from drinking beer, even on feast days.[34] Columbanus, however, was obviously much more favorably disposed toward the use of beer in monasteries, and one may suspect that the prominent place the controversial beverage holds in the miracle stories related in the *Vita Columbani* was meant not least to champion his view in an ongoing debate, namely that beer was fine as long as it was used in a monastic context, even if it had to be destroyed when used in a pagan ritual. Thus it could be argued that the three miracles related in the *Vita Columbani* are meant to drive home a message of discrimination that the author of the *Vita Vedastis* managed to compress into a single miracle. In the end, it was the view of Columbanus

---

32. Nelson 2005. Cf. Lund 1986: 82–5 and Tacitus 1990: 193–5.
33. Nelson 2005: 74–6.
34. Nelson 2005: 93.

rather than that of Maelruain that prevailed, not only in Ireland but also in Continental Europe. Thus, although Columbanus can hardly be credited with anything like the phrase quoted at the beginning of this chapter, he probably did make a substantial contribution to popularizing the beverage that later came to be regarded as a hallmark of Central and Northern European drinking cultures.

BIBLIOGRAPHY

Achterberg, H. (1930) *Interpretatio Christiana: Verkleidete Glaubensgestalten der Germanen auf deutschem Boden*. Form und Geist: Arbeiten zur germanischen Philologie Band 19. Leipzig, Hermann Eichblatt.

Ade, D., B. Rüth, and A. Zekorn (eds.) (2008) *Alamannen zwischen Schwarzwald, Neckar und Donau*. Stuttgart, Theiss.

Agathias (1975) *The Histories*, ed. and trans. J. D. Frendo. Corpus fontium historiae Byzantinae, vol. 2a. Berlin and New York, W. de Gruyter.

Bauchhenss, G. (1984) "Diana in den nordwestlichen Provinzen." *Lexicon Iconographicum Mythologiae Classicae* 2: 849–55.

Behrens, F. (2012) "Spuren vorchristlicher Religion im archäologischen Fundmaterial der Merowingerzeit in Süddeutschland." In N. Krohn and S. Ristow (eds.), *Wechsel der Religionen—Religion des Wechsels*. Hamburg, Kovac, 193–222.

Blaich, M. C. (2009) "Bemerkungen zur Speisebeigabe im frühen Mittelalter." In O. Heinrich-Tamaska, N. Krohn, and S. Ristow (eds.), *Dunkle Jahrhunderte in Mitteleuropa? Tagungsbeiträge der Arbeitsgemeinschaft Spätantike und Frühmittelalter*. Hamburg, Kovac, 27–44.

Böhner, K., and D. Quast (1994) "Die merowingerzeitlichen Grabfunde aus Pliezhausen, Kreis Reutlingen." *Fundberichte aus Baden-Württemberg* 19: 383–419.

Brather-Walter, S., and S. Brather (2012) "Repräsentation oder Religion? Grabbeigaben und Bestattungsrituale im frühen Mittelalter." In N. Krohn and S. Ristow (eds.), *Wechsel der Religionen—Religion des Wechsels*. Hamburg, Kovac, 121–44.

Carey, J. (1990 "Vernacular Irish Learning: Three Notes: Nathair imchenn, compóit mérda, brisiud cend for mac fri clocha." *Éigse* 24: 37–44.

Dölger, F. J. (1909) *Der Exorzismus im altchristlichen Taufritual: Eine religionsgeschichtliche Studie*. Paderborn, Schöningh.

Drinkwater, J. F. (2007) *The Alamanni and Rome 213–496 (Caracalla to Clovis)*. Oxford, Oxford University Press.

Dronke, P. (1997) *Sources of Inspiration: Studies in Literary Transformations, 400–1500*. Roma, Edizioni di storia e letteratura.

Ellis Davidson, H. (1978) "Mithras and Wodan." In *Études mithriaques*. Acta Iranica 17, Première Série, Actes de Congrès IV. Leiden, Brill, 99–110.

Geuenich, D. (2005) *Geschichte der Alemannen*, vol. 2. überarbeitete Auflage. Stuttgart, Kohlhammer.

Gottlieb, G. (1969) "Die Nachrichten des Agathias aus Myrina über das Christentum der Franken und Alamannen." *Jahrbuch des Römisch-Germanischen Zentralmuseums Mainz* 16: 149–58.

Helm, K. (1953) *Altgermanische Religionsgeschichte: Zweiter Band, Die nachrömische Zeit, Teil II, Die Westgermanen*. Heidelberg, Carl Winter.

Krapp, K. (2007) *Die Alamannen: Krieger—Siedler—Frühe Christen*. Stuttgart, Theiss.

Krutzler, G. (2011) *Kult und Tabu: Wahrnehmung der Germania bei Bonifatius*. Vienna, LIT.

Lüdemann, H. (1994) "Mehrfach belegte Gräber im frühen Mittelalter: Ein Beitrag zum Problem der Doppelbestattungen." *Fundberichte aus Baden-Württemberg* 19: 421–589.

Lund, A. (1986) "Zum Germanenbegriff bei Tacitus." In H. Beck (ed.), *Germanenprobleme in heutiger Sicht*. Berlin, de Gruyter, 53–88.

Meyer, E. H. (1903) *Mythologie der Germanen, gemeinfasslich dargestellt*. Strassburg, Trübner.

Morrissey, C. (2013) *Alamannen zwischen Bodensee und Main: Schwaben im frühen Mittelalter*. Karlsruhe, G. Braun.

Nelson, M. (2005) *The Barbarian's Beverage: A History of Beer in Ancient Europe*. London and New York, Routledge.

Oexle, J. (1984) "Merowingerzeitliche Pferdebestattungen—Opfer oder Beigaben?" *Frühmittelalterliche Studien* 18: 122–72.

O'Hara, A. (2015) "Columbanus *ad locum*: The Establishment of the Monastic Foundations." *Peritia* 26: 143–70.

O'Hara, A., and I. Wood (trans.) (2017) *Jonas of Bobbio: Life of Columbanus, Life of John of Réomé, and Life of Vedast*. Liverpool, Liverpool University Press.

Paulsen, P. (1992) *Die Holzfunde aus dem Gräberfeld von Oberflacht und ihre kulturhistorische Bedeutung*. Stuttgart, Theiss.

Quast, D. (1997) "Opferplätze und heidnische Götter: Vorchristlicher Kult." In Archäologisches Landesmuseum Baden-Württemberg (ed.), *Die Alamannen*. Stuttgart, Theiss, 433–40.

Reitzenstein, W.-A., Freiherr von (2013) *Lexikon schwäbischer Ortsnamen*. Munich, C. H. Beck.

Rübekeil, L. (2002) *Diachrone Studien zur Kontaktzone zwischen Kelten und Germanen*. Vienna, Verlag der Österreichischen Akademie der Wissenschaften.

Schäferdiek, K. (1994) "Kilian von Würzburg: Gestalt und Gestaltung eines Heiligen." In H. Keller and N. Staubach (eds.), *Iconologia Sacra: Mythos, Bildkunst und Dichtung in der Religions- und Sozialgeschichte Alteuropas. Festschrift für Karl Hauck zum 75. Geburtstag*. Arbeiten zur Frühmittelalterforschung 23. Berlin, de Gruyter, 313–40.

Schneider, T. (2008) "Mehrfachbestattungen von Männern in der Merowingerzeit." *Zeitschrift für Archäologie des Mittelalters* 38: 1–32.

Stokes, W. (ed.) (1883) *Saltair na Rann*. Anecdota Oxoniensia I, 3. Oxford, Clarendon Press.

Tacitus (1990) *Germania*. Lateinisch und deutsch von G. Perl. Schriften und Quellen der Alten Welt 37, 2. Berlin, Akademie-Verlag.

Timpe, D. (1992) "Tacitus' Germania als religionsgeschichtliche Quelle." In H. Beck, D. Ellmers, and K. Schier (eds.), *Germanische Religionsgeschichte: Quellen und Quellenprobleme*. Berlin, de Gruyter, 434–85.

11

Drinking with Woden

A Re-examination of Jonas's *Vita Columbani* I.27

FRANCESCO BORRI

During his long journey across the borders of post-Roman Europe, Columbanus reached the town of Bregenz, a place on Lake Constance, which Jonas locates *intra Germaniae terminus*.[1] Columbanus decided to remain there for a while to Christianize its dwellers. Not far from the town he encountered the Suebi, one of the many *gentes* he met during his *peregrinatio*. The following story has become famous among historians. Columbanus discovered that the inhabitants of the place were about to officiate a *sacrificium profanum*. They must have gathered in a circle, because Jonas reports that in the middle there stood a large vat full of beer. Upon being asked the purpose of keeping such a a big receptacle, the barbarians responded that they wanted to offer it (*litare*) to their god Woden (*deo suo Vodano nomine*), called Mercury by some (*quem Mercurium, ut alii aiunt*). Columbanus decided to put an end to this hideous practice (*pestiferum opus*), so he blew on the vessel, shattering it to pieces, and the beer spilled out. The devil, we are told, was lurking inside the vat, with the intention of deceiving the barbarians through the blasphemous drink. Columbanus was unusually benevolent with the Suebi, merely rebuking them and sending them home. After this experience, some of the ritual imbibers were subsequently baptized, while the ones who had already been evangelised found the right path again.

The most striking element in this short story is Woden, who is mentioned here for the first time in a narrative source.[2] Woden is no stranger to historians, and generations of scholars have sought to follow the tracks of this fascinating character. Many scholars, not always in a methodologically sound approach, stretched the Scandinavian Óðinn back to the primeval forests of Germany to enrich the seventh-century Woden with much later witnesses. It was therefore tempting to see in Jonas's short entry the one-eyed high god of the Germanic pantheon, the lord of war and kingship, the keeper of the runes, and the watcher

---

1. *VC* I. 27: 213. On the episode, see Wood 2001: 33–4; Berschin 2005 [1986]. See also Wolfram and Maier, chapters 9 and 10 in this volume.

2. The best survey on the topic is Shaw 2002. See also Hultgård 2007.

of the dead. That Jonas had this character in mind when telling the story is far from certain, however. Philip Shaw has thoughtfully noted: "Woden is not a single phenomenon, but a complex of figures developing in various contexts for various reasons."[3] We know little about Jonas's Woden. This chapter is dedicated to this topic.

The *Vita Columbani* was written between 639 and 642.[4] Finding Woden in this context is peculiar. Early medieval authors, once faced with pagans, mostly used to describe their gods according to classical names and typologies.[5] For example, Gregory of Tours used Roman vocabulary and ancient deity names to narrate the pagan past of the Franks.[6] It seems that in early medieval Europe the gods of the Romans formed a trusted trope to describe the complex and elusive religiosity in the dark corners of the Christian world and beyond its frontiers. Therefore, a question would be how then would the readers of the *Vita* have understood the mention of Woden and his role in this beer ritual.[7] First, we can imagine that Jonas's audience would have agreed that the cold waters of the deep Lake Constance and mountains surrounded by chilly mist would have been seen as a credible stage for barbarian rituals and eldritch intervention. Ammianus Marcellinus had described the region as a metaphor for the barbarism within the empire.[8] Following the dissemination of the *Vita Columbani*, the place may have come to be seen as a nest of demons, appearing as early as the *Vita Galli vetustissima* in the early eighth century.[9]

Moreover, Jonas told his readers that Bregenz was a town at the edges of Germania. In this context, Jonas added that Woden, according to some, was Mercury.[10] This association was destined to enjoy an enduring success, but it is recorded for the first time here. Distant echoes could be found in Tacitus's remark that the Germani of his days worshipped Mercury above all the other gods.[11] The third day of the week, dedicated to Mercury in the Romance tongues, is named after Woden in many Germanic languages, allegedly since the fourth

3. Shaw 2002: ii. See also Meaney 1966.

4. On the date of composition, see Wood 1982: 63.

5. Palmer 2007: 411–7; Goetz 2013, 139–40.

6. *DLH* II.10, 29: 58–59, 74; Daly 1994.

7. On Jonas's audience, see O'Hara 2009.

8. Ammianus Marcellinus, *Rerum gestarum libri qui supersunt* XV.4.ii–vi: 126–8. Rollinger 2001; moreover, on the perception of Alpine landscape: Winckler 2014.

9. *Vita Galli vetustissima*. Berschin 2005 [1986]: 59. See further Fox and Dörler, chapters 12 and 13 in this volume, on the dating.

10. Donald Bullough proposed this to be a later interpolation: Bullough 1997: 19. On a votive altar to Mercury and figurines of Mercury from Bregenz, see O'Hara 2015, with further discussion in relation to Woden.

11. Tacitus, *De origine et situ Germanorum* 9: 142–4: *Deorum maxime Mercurium colunt, cui certis diebus humanis quoque hostiis litare fas habent.*

century AD. at the latest.[12] Still, it remains difficult to make sense of Jonas's early connection of Woden to Mercury. On the one hand, it seems probable that this association pre-existed Jonas, who simply reported what he had heard. On the other, it is possible that the author, against the backdrop of Tacitus's narrative, was among the first to compare Woden to Mercury, but this suggestion is difficult to prove because of *Germania's* elusive manuscript tradition.[13] Nevertheless, one element seems clear: Jonas wanted to help his readers identify a new character. In order to frame Woden, he told his audience that he was also Mercury, known from a plethora of narratives.

Indeed, in the days when Jonas was writing, mythology featuring an obscure and, as we will see, highly contradictory character called Woden was spreading in post-Roman Latin Christendom, engaging readers far and wide.[14] References to Woden are found in the Chronicle of Fredegar and the *Origo gentis Langobardorum*. Like Jonas's *Vita Columbani*, these two narratives were both written in the mid-seventh century. The stories are similar in character, although suggestive differences exist. They focus on the migration of the Lombards and the role of Woden in their identity and victories.

Although we cannot rule out that the idea that these narratives reported older traditions, the structure of the Chronicle of Fredegar argues in favor of Woden gaining great importance in the seventh century. As is well known, the third book of the chronicles follows the six-book version of the *Libri Historiarum* by Gregory of Tours. Writing at the end of the sixth century, Gregory narrated the episode of the Lombard invasion of Italy. In Gregory's narrative structure, the episode followed the rise of Emperor Justin II (565–578) and was contextualized in the historical developments of the late 560s.[15] Retelling this old story in the 660s, the author of the Chronicle of Fredegar introduced the Lombard invasion, narrating the distant past of the *gens*. He recalled their alleged Scandinavian origin, together with their confrontation with Woden on their long journey to Italy. In the story, the god granted the Lombards their name along with victory against their enemies.[16] In the middle of the seventh century, therefore, Woden found his place in a narrative which, in its sixth-century version, did not feature him.

This is not to say that Woden was purely an invention; I suspect the opposite to be the case. The name of the day Wednesday is among the strongest arguments

---

12. Green 2000: 236–53. See also Shaw 2007.
13. Haverfield 1916.
14. On the usage of the term mythology, see Kieckhefer 2006.
15. *DLH* IV.41: 174.
16. Fredegar III.65: 110.

for his antiquity, although not uncontroversial.[17] Some scholars sought evidence for an early Woden in place names or the iconography of some bracteates, metalwork allegedly portraying episodes of the Scandinavian sagas, even though these were not recorded in writing until centuries later.[18] An archaeological approach was also attempted by searching for clues of a pre-Christian religiosity involving Woden in much later English poetry.[19] If an older Woden existed, he nevertheless gained prominence among the elites of post-Roman Europe in the seventh century when three authors, although not entirely independently from one another, mentioned him for the first time in a very limited chronological frame, revealing a cluster of meaning.

Putting Jonas's story in its broader context, the direct association between Woden and paganism becomes problematic. On the one hand, the author clearly described Woden as a heathen deity, which in reality was one of the many manifestations of Satan, as was often the case. Many of his readers would have shared his thoughts. Two very famous inscribed brooches from Nordendorf, dated to the sixth or seventh century, banished Woden as a dark and lurking figure.[20] However, further insight stems from another mention of Woden, found in the eighth century *Abrenuntiatio Diaboli*. It is a short text surviving together with *Indiculus superstitionum et paganiarum*, a narrative compiled close to Saint Boniface's circle.[21] The *Abrenuntiatio* contains a formula in a Germanic language (which one is debated) spoken out to forsake the devil and his fellows, Woden, Thor, and Saxnot.[22] The formula was written for Latin-speaking clerics dealing with a vernacular flock. It is a brief text which may enrich the picture we have, suggesting that Woden, in the first half of the eighth century, may have lurked among the Christian communities of Germany. It becomes meaningful here to recall that according to Jonas, some Christians also attended the beer ritual. This apparent ambiguity finds confirmation in the Chronicle of Fredegar, in which Woden, ostensibly a heathen god, is also the granter of victory to a Christian people.

This suggestion seems to find further confirmation in the evidence stemming from Britain. Completing his *Historia ecclesiastica gentis Anglorum* around 731,

---

17. See the discussion in Shaw 2007.

18. On bracteates, see Behr 2000; following the numerous studies of Karl Hauck, who published *Zur ikonographie der Goldbrakteaten* in dozens of articles, which I cannot mention for reasons of space. On the methodological problem of these interpretations, see Starkey 1999 and Hines 1997: 392.

19. Ryan 1963; to be read with the response by Meaney 1966. See also North 1997.

20. Düwel 2008: 63–5.

21. Dierkens 1984. A different opinion is Shaw 2002: 85, who believes that this was composed around 800.

22. *Abrenuntiatio Diaboli: respondeat. ec forsacho allum dioboles uuercum and uuordum, Thunaer ende Uoden ende Saxnote ende allum them unholdum, the hira genotas sint.*

Bede remembered that the genealogies of the heptarchic kings of his own days originated from Woden's ancestry, who in the monk's mind seems to have been a ruler of the past. Bede narrated that Hengist and Horsa, the two heroes of the invasion of Britain, "were the sons of Wihtgils, son of Witta, son of Wecta, son of Woden, from whose stock the royal families of many kingdoms claim descent."[23] This famous passage gave rise to euhemeristic interpretations of Woden, who was thought to be a powerful king of a bygone time.[24] It now seems clear that searching for a human Woden at the roots of his mythology is questionable at best. Conversely, these daring interpretations make the point of noticing that a superhuman nature of Woden is not to be found in the *Historia ecclesiastica*. The distinction between Woden as a royal ancestor who lived in the past and Woden as a present demon turns out to be significant here. In the time following the circulation of Bede's narrative, Woden became the father of all the dynastic pedigrees of the great majority of English kings, mainly to be found in the Anglian collection.[25] These royal genealogies were the product of monks, who, like Bede, must have thought that ancestry from Woden was synonymous with Christian kingship.[26] As David Dumville summarized many years ago, a descent from Woden expressed royalty and the belief in an Anglian origin, rather than pagan faith.[27]

Making sense of these contradictory messages demands a better under-standing of the elusive Woden and his social functions in the seventh century. To achieve that, the best point of entry is the *Origo gentis Langobardorum*, which is the longest narrative dealing with the character. The text was perhaps redacted during the second reign of the Lombard king Perctarit (671–688), but some older textual layers point to the reign of King Rothari (636–654).[28] It is a rather anomalous text: a list of kings with a few extended narratives that show a keen taste for savage tales and barbarian things, becoming the clearest and boldest statement of non-Roman identity stemming from the early Middle Ages. Its production was the reflection of wider changes taking place inside the Lombard monarchy and in seventh-century Italian society. The narrative contains a longer version of the passage of the Chronicle of Fredegar mentioned above. The story is well known: coming from the harsh landscape of Scandinavia, in the narrative called Scadanan, the Lombards began a long march to Italy, fighting all the kings and peoples one by one who blocked their way. When

23. Bede, *HE* I.15: 50, trans. at 51.
24. See, e.g., Harrison 1976; John 1992.
25. Dumville 1976.
26. Sisam 1953.
27. Dumville 1977: 77–9.
28. *Origo gentis Langobardorum* 7: 6. Delogu 2010: 190

confronted by the Vandals, the Lombards invoked Woden. In one of the most famous episodes of early medieval literature, the superhuman creature granted the Lombards their name, along with victory against their enemies.[29] In this context, Woden is a peculiar character. He is married to a woman called Frea, and the two share a bed somehow overlooking the battlefield (in the sky? on a high mountain? an impressive tree?). In addition, although the whole episode has a strong Olympian flavor, the author of the *Origo gentis Langobardorum* was careful enough to never call Woden a god.

The gallery of barbarism and ancient ethnographic tropes embedded in the *Origo gentis Langobardorum* contrasted with the previous historical production at the Lombard court. During the long reign of Theodelinda and her husbands and son (589–626), Lombard history was recorded according to the master narrative of Christianity's triumph over heathenism. In the second decade of the seventh century, two authors, Secundus of Trent and an anonymous continuator of Prosper, followed the Roman tradition, compiling brief annals meant to be a continuation of the Christian works of historiography that Eusebius and Jerome had written in the fourth and fifth centuries.[30] The barbarian reading of the Lombard history that we find in the *Origo gentis Langobardorum* seems to have been a later development, a sort of "barbarian turn," which found resemblances in the historiography of neighboring post-Roman kingdoms.[31] Like the *Origo gentis Langobardorum*, many seventh-century narratives showed an interest in the origin and identity of the barbarian elites ruling post-Roman Europe. The values of descent and lineage were exalted, while elusive ancestors appeared in the distant past of the *gens*. I suggest that the Lombard allegiance to Woden made sense in this changed context, being an element of this self-barbarization of the Lombard aristocracies.

Two further points can be considered, both rather speculative. First, it seems that lineages originating with Woden spread on the borders of the Frankish lands.[32] In the middle of the seventh century, Woden was linked to Alamannia and the past of the Lombards, at the time ruling Italy. Since the middle and the end of the eighth century we have further attestations in Britain, Denmark, and Saxony. This leads to the second suggestion: Woden may have represented an effort to legitimize barbarian ancestry in the face of contenders, who could have claimed a more perfectly Christian or imperial heritage and in general a greater symbolic capital. We know that the Lombards may have discovered Woden in

---

29. *Origo gentis Langobardorum* 1: 2–3.
30. Pohl 2012; Gardiner 1983; Muhlberger 1984.
31. Borri 2014.
32. I owe this consideration to Katharina Winckler.

the years following the long truce with the Byzantine Empire, when the war against the Romans, who could claim an immense prestige, began again. The Woden ancestry among the Angles was counterbalanced by the Britons' claim of descent from a Roman emperor, the tyrant Magnus Maximus, who later became the great Macsen Wledig, as is shown by the oldest Welsh genealogies and in the famous inscription on the Pillar of Eliseg.[33] As we know that groups and identity cannot live in isolation, we can safely assume that Woden was meant to signify something, particularly on the borders.[34] Between the seventh and eighth centuries Woden seems to have given legitimacy and prestige to kings and aristocrats who were proud to boast of their barbarian heritage. He may have been part of a greater repertory of signs and signifiers for aristocrats who wanted to follow the larger-than-life barbarian conduct, perhaps characteristic of the age of migrations.[35]

In Jonas's narrative, Woden was related to alcohol consumption. It is well known that communal drinking was an important social act in numerous societies for many reasons, one being that alcoholic beverages are psychotropic agents, which offer relaxation and cement trust.[36] At the same time, the dangers of alcohol were notorious, and authorities constantly attempted regulation or prohibition. They were usually unsuccessful. In the early Middle Ages it was the clergy who generally tried to regulate the consumption of intoxicating beverages. Under criticism was not the drinking alone, but the lack of control that may have followed. The monastic rules prescribed, in fact, large amounts of alcohol consumption for monks as an essential part of their everyday diet, due to the nutritional value.[37] However, women and men did not consume alcohol for nourishment only, and losing control was an important part of drinking. This tendency seems to have been particularly strong among the aristocrats, who had the time and means to drink as much as they pleased. Through the ritualized consumption of intoxicating beverages, elites confirmed their social bonds and sometimes violently broke them.[38] Drinking was often an occasion for bragging, violence, sexual misconduct, and blasphemy. The literature of the Merovingian period is full of proud and lustful aristocrats drinking themselves into a stupor or drawing their swords to conclude a supper in tragedy.[39] A dramatic example

33. Dumville 1977: 75–6; on the pillar, see Higham 2002: 166–9.
34. Pohl 2013.
35. See the fascinating contribution by Wormald 2006 [1978]. On performative barbarism, see Halsall 2007: 477–8.
36. Dietler 2006; Douglas 1987.
37. See, however, Hocquet 1985.
38. Bullough 1990: 8; Hen 1995: 242–4; Althoff 1990: 203–11; Enright 1996: 69–96.
39. Hen 1995: 234–9.

of the discourse concerned with the escalating madness provoked by alcohol consumption may be read in the notorious episode of Sichar and Chramnesind, narrated by Gregory of Tours. From a series of drunken misunderstandings involving the two men (and many others), the region of Touraine was troubled for the best part of two years by vicious conflicts: buildings were burned, possessions and animals were stolen, and thirteen men lost their lives.[40] No wonder drinking to such extremes was perceived as something barbarian.[41] Forty years before Jonas wrote the *Vita Columbani*, the expression "to drink like Goths" may have circulated in Italy.[42] Earlier, Procopius had written that the Goths at the court of Amalasuntha (526–535), worried about the effeminate education imposed on young Athalaric, decided to raise him in the more masculine and tough Gothic way. The result was that Athalaric drank himself to death before he was eighteen.[43] It remains a matter of opinion whether beer played a specific role in this world of savage excess, different from that of other alcoholic drinks. An intoxicating drink with no religious functions, the beverage became the quintessential barbarian brew.[44] However, in the context of the *Vita Columbani* beer is also the monastic drink. Jonas narrated two miracles involving the multiplication and the preservation of beer.[45]

A few narratives, such as *Beowulf* or *Y Gododdin*, composed between the seventh and tenth centuries, charged the excessive aristocratic consumption of intoxicating beverages with heroic connotations.[46] The last warrior on his feet, elated and proud, staggering with a cup of mead in his hand and surrounded by collapsed fellow drinkers, must have had its appeal. Elsewhere, the drinking habits of the laity were watched with endless contempt.[47] Already in the Roman world, drunkenness, particularly if associated with a ruler, was a hideous practice and a formidable political accusation.[48] Closer to the days of Jonas, Caesarius of Arles was among the bitterest critics, dedicating three sermons to alcoholic debauchery.[49] Caesarius had great concern about overconsumption, accusing drunkards of committing the most lunatic and blasphemous things. In addition, he insinuated a connection between heavy drinking and paganism.[50]

40. *DLH* VII.47 and IX.19: 366–8, 432–34. The body count is from Halsall 1998: 2.
41. Shanzer 2002: 42.
42. Gregory the Great, *Dialogi* I.9. xiv: II:88.
43. Procopius of Caesarea, *Bella* V.3.xvi: III:27; Halsall 2002: 107–8.
44. Nelson 2008.
45. *VC* I.16–7: 179–83. See Maier, chapter 10 in this volume.
46. Edwards 1980; Bullough 1990.
47. Hen 1995: 234–49.
48. Humphrey 2002.
49. Caesarius of Arles, *Sermones* 46–47, 55: I, 205–15, 340–44; Bailey 2007.
50. Caesarius of Arles, *Sermones* 47, V: I, 214: *haec enim si pagani qui Deum ignorant faciant.* Hen 1995: 239.

Caesarius's followers received this portentous allegation: decades later, in a letter to Archbishop Cuthbert of Canterbury, Boniface wrote that drinking in excess was a wicked habit of the heathens (and the English).[51]

From this perspective, the passage in the *Vita Columbani* gains new insight. Jonas wrote that the Suebi had collected a *cupa* containing twenty *modia* of beer. That is about 170 liters of beer, almost 300 British pints. It was a ridiculous amount of alcohol, capable of driving a small army of barbarians crazy.[52] An episode narrated in the *Vita Vedastis*, written by Jonas in the same years as the *Vita Columbani*, could further enrich our understanding of this passage. Bishop Vedast, once on the estate of a certain Frankish noble called Hocinus, noticed that many barrels full of beer were stored in the lord's house for a local festivity or celebration attended also by King Chlothar I (511–558). Some of them were consecrated according to the pagan rite, the others according to the Christian one. The holy man made the sign of the cross over the barrels and the ones which had been hallowed according to the heathen custom suddenly burst.[53] The story is modeled on the very blueprint of the *Vita Columbani*. The great difference here is the absence of Woden. As Ian Wood has pointed out, we are probably dealing with social practices such as aristocratic feasting and communal drinking rather than with an active religiosity.[54] Moreover, I suspect that the author wanted to draw a line between drinking perceived as "Christian" or as "pagan." It is a discourse surviving in fragments, but the difference may have been in the manner and the amount of consumption; Jonas dismissed what he perceived as excessive and threatening drinking as heathen.[55]

The boundaries must have been vague, however. Many ecclesiastics found it intolerable that people used to drink to excess at festivities like Christmas or Easter, singing funny songs, dancing, and enjoying with the senses that which was meant to be a feast for the soul. It was a custom that mixed holy and worldly in a syncretic spiral of sin (and fun).[56] Other practices went further, gaining a darker aura. In Columbanus's *Paenitentiale*, a set of rules composed during the holy man's years in Burgundy, we read that Christian men had the bad habit of sharing food and drinks beside pagan sanctuaries (*iuxta fana*).[57] Columbanus

51. Boniface, *Epistulae* 78: 171: *Hoc enim malum speciale est paganorum et nostrae gentis.*
52. This consideration works only if the barbarians were fewer than fifty; otherwise the amount would have been fine.
53. Jonas of Bobbio, *Vita Vedastis* 7: 410.
54. Wood 2013: 4.
55. See also Maier, chapter 10 in this volume.
56. Brown 2000.
57. Columbanus, *Paenitentiale* B 24: 178: *Si quis autem laicus manducaverit aut biberit iuxta fana, si per ignorantiam fecerit, promittat deinceps quod numquam reiteret, et XL diebus in pane et aqua paeniteat.* On the rule, see Charles-Edwards 1997; for the dating, see Charles-Edwards 1997: 219. On the connection between Jonas's passage and Columbanus's penitential, see O'Hara 2015: 156.

was not the first man to fight these customs. It was a long-established and be-loved tradition of both pagans and Christians for centuries, which found its roots in the ancient life of the Mediterranean. It is clear, however, that the boundaries among heterodoxy, social drinking, and paganism became shadowy here.

Jonas is the only author linking excessive drinking to Woden. In this con-text, a revealing insight can be found in the Chronicle of Fredegar. The anony-mous author recorded that Woden was considered a god by the pagans (*gentes*), who called him by his name *fanatice*, "in a heathen way."[58] The translation I just proposed relies on Bruno Krusch's reading, which interpreted *fanatice* as an adverbial form of *fanatici*, which he read as a synonym for *gentiles*. It is of course correct and could be supported by the use of the word *fanatici* in further chronicles, that of Gregory of Tours in the first place.[59] However, the occurrence of *fanatice* is isolated in the chronicle, and Krusch's interpretation is mainly supported by the translation of *gentes* into pagans.[60] Conversely, this reading of *gens* seems questionable in the context of the chronicle.[61] If we read *gens* as people, as may be the case, other interpretations become feasible. The *gentes*, in fact, could have called Woden "fanatically," like madmen or in an exalted state, or they could have called him by his name like the people who met in the *fana* did.[62] In this context therefore, *fanatice* could denounce a broad semantic field, revealing excitement, alcohol consumption, or even meeting friends and fellows close to ancient shrines, as had been practiced for centuries. There the *gentes* may have raised a cup or two (or perhaps three) to Woden. Already Caesarius blamed drunkards for daring to toast to the angels.[63]

Pulling together the different accounts of Jonas and his contemporaries, we gain a glimpse of a twilight zone at the boundaries of orthodoxy, marked by pride in barbaric ancestry, heavy drinking, and a character called Woden.[64] Many would have considered these occasions of communality disgraceful, savage, and pagan. It is possible that the aim of Jonas's story was to warn the Columbanian *familia* of this new, dangerous mythology quickly spreading on the borders of the Frankish world. In order to underplay the significance of Woden, Jonas dismissed him as one of the devil's playthings, venerated only by

---

58. Fredegar III.65: 110: *Fertur desuper uterque falangiae vox dixisse: "Haec sunt Langobardi," quod ab his gentibus fertur eorum deo fuisse locutum, quem fanatice nominant Wodano.*

59. See *DLH* I.34: 24, II.10: 58, and II.27: 72.

60. MGH, *Scriptores rerum Merovingicarum* 2: 562.

61. On this see Fischer forthcoming.

62. On *fanatice*, see Ghosh 2016: 222–3. See also Blaise 1975: s.v. *fanaticus*. I am very grateful to Andreas Fischer and Cinzia Grifoni for their assistance with this.

63. Caesarius of Arles, *Sermones* 47, V: I, 214; Brown 2000: 2; Hen 1995: 239.

64. See Markus 1992: 157–8.

funny barbarians sitting in Germania, outside the civilized world. It was just an opinion, and a few decades later, powerful kings claimed that the blood of Woden was running through their veins, as a means of legitimacy, majesty, and authority.

If Jonas's voice was contested in the seventh century, it was only a matter of years before the Frankish expansion shed light on the shadowy corner occupied by Woden and his drinking friends. The Carolingians made the effort of representing the world before and around them as barbarous and pagan.[65] New rules of communality were enforced, and the aristocracies following the patterns of the Merovingian period were faced with new models of behavior, piety, and masculinity.[66] Drawing new boundaries and enforcing older ones, the authorities redefined what was Christian and what was pagan. In the process, many practices and beliefs were banished from the devout life; Woden may have been among them. Others were integrated into the Christian framework; Yitzhak Hen, following a suggestion from Heinrich Fichtenau, proposed that even a Carolingian way of drinking replaced the previous, wilder one of the seventh and eighth centuries.[67] Times had changed. By the turn of the eighth century, many would have agreed with Jonas that drinking with Woden was nothing more than drinking with the devil.

ACKNOWLEDGMENTS

The writing of this article was financed through the FWF Project 24823, The Transformation of Roman Dalmatia and the FWF F42, Visions of Community. I would like to thank Max Diesenberger, Andreas Fischer, Cinzia Grifoni, Rutger Kramer, Alexander O'Hara, Jelle Wassenaar, and Katharina Winckler.

BIBLIOGRAPHY

Abrenuntiatio Diaboli (1899). In E. Wadstein (ed.), *Kleinere altsächsisch Sprachdenkmäler: Mit Anmerkungen und Glossar*, Niederdeutsche Denkmäler 6. Norden and Leipzig, Soltau, 3.

Althoff, G. (1990) *Verwandte, Freunde und Getreue: Zum politischen Stellenwert der Gruppenbindungen im früheren Mittelalter*. Darmstadt, Wissenschaftliche Buchgesellschaft.

Ammianus Marcellinus (1935–1939) *Rerum gestarum libri qui supersunt*, ed. J. C. Rolfe. 3 vols. Loeb Classical Library 300, 315, 331. Cambridge, MA, and London, Harvard University Press.

65. Hen 2002.
66. Stone 2012; Noble 2007.
67. Hen 1995: 248–9; Fichtenau 1984: 86–7.

Bailey, L. (2007) "These Are Not Men: Sex and Drinks in the Sermons of Caesarius of Arles." *Journal of Early Christian Studies* 15: 23–43.

Behr, C. (2000) "The Origins of Kingship in Early Medieval Kent." *Early Medieval Europe* 9: 25–52.

Berschin, W. (2005 [1986]) "Columban und Gallus in Bregenz." In W. Berschin, *Mittellateinische Studien*. Heidelberg, Mattes, 57–63.

Blaise, A. (1975) *Lexicon latinitatis medii aeui praesertim ad res ecclesiasticas investigandas pertinens: Dictionnaire latin-français des auteurs du moyen-âge*. Medieval Latin Dictionaries 1. Turnhout, Brepols.

Boniface (1916) *Epistolae*. In M. Tangl (ed.), *Die Briefe des heiligen Bonifatius und Lullus*. MGH, *Epistolae Selectae* 1. Berlin, Weidmann.

Borri, F. (2014) "Romans Growing Beards: Identity and Historiography in Seventh-Century Italy." *Viator* 45: 39–71.

Brown, P. (2000) "Enjoying the Saints in Late Antiquity." *Early Medieval Europe* 9: 1–24.

Bullough, D. A. (1990) "Friends, Neighbours and Fellow-Drinkers: Aspects of Community and Conflict in the Early Medieval West." In *H. M. Chadwick Memorial Lectures* 1. Cambridge, Cambridge University Press.

Bullough, D. A. (1997) "The Career of Columbanus." In M. Lapidge (ed.), *Columbanus: Studies on the Latin Writings*. Studies in Celtic History 17. Woodbridge, The Boydell Press, 1–28.

Caesarius of Arles (1953) *Sermones*, ed. G. Morin. 2 vols. CC SL103-4. Turnhout, Brepols.

Charles-Edwards, T. M. (1997) "The Penitential of Columbanus." In M. Lapidge (ed.), *Columbanus: Studies on the Latin Writings*. Studies in Celtic History 17. Woodbridge, The Boydell Press, 217–39.

Columbanus (1970) *Paenitentiale*. In G. S. M. Walker (ed.), *Sancti Columbani Opera*. Scriptores Latini Hiberniae 2. Dublin, The Dublin Institute for Advanced Studies, 168–81.

Daly, W. M. (1994) "Clovis: How Barbaric, How Pagan?" *Speculum* 69: 619–64.

Delogu, P. (2010), *Le origini del medioevo: Studi sul settimo secolo*, Storia 57, Rome, Jouvence.

Dierkens, A. (1984) "Superstitions, christianisme et paganisme à la fin de l'époque mérovingienne: A propos de l'*Indiculus superstitionem et paganiarum*." In H. Hasquin (ed.), *Magie, sorcellerie, parapsychologie*. Brussels, Editions de l'Université de Bruxelles, 9–26.

Dietler, M. (2006) "Alcohol: Anthropological/Archaeological Perspectives." *Annual Review of Anthropology* 35: 229–49.

Douglas, M. (1987) "A Distinctive Anthropological Perspective." In M. Douglas (ed.), *Constructive Drinking: Perspectives on Drinking from Anthropology*. Cambridge, Cambridge University Press, 3–15.

Dumville, D. N. (1976) "The Anglian Collection of Royal Genealogies and Regnal Lists." *Anglo-Saxon England* 5: 23–50.

Dumville, D. N. (1977) "Kingship, Genealogies and Regnal Lists." In P. H. Sawyer and I. Wood (eds.), *Early Medieval Kingship*. Leeds, University Press, 72–104.

Düwel, K. (2008) *Runenkunde*. 4th edition. Stuttgart, Metzler.

Edwards, P. (1980) "Art and Alcoholism in Beowulf." *Durham University Journal* 72: 127–31.

Enright, M. (1996) *Lady with a Mead Cup: Ritual, Prophecy and Lordship in the European Warband from La Tène to the Viking Age*. Dublin, Four Courts Press.

Fichtenau, H. (1984) *Lebensordnungen des 10. Jahrhunderts: Studien über Denkart und Existenz im einstigen Karolingerreich*. Monographien zur Geschichte des Mittelalters 30. Stuttgart, Hiersemann.

Fischer, A. (forthcoming) *Die Fredegar-Chronik: Komposition und Kontextualisierung*. Habilitationsschrift Universität Berlin.

Gardiner, K. (1983) "Paul the Deacon and Secundus of Trento." In B. Croke and A. M. Emmett (eds.), *History and Historians in Late Antiquity*. Sydney, Pergamon Press, 147–53.

Ghosh, S. (2016) *Writing the Barbarian Past: Studies in Early Medieval Historical Narrative.* Brill's Series on the Early Middle Ages 24. Leiden and Boston, Brill.

Goetz, H.-W. (2013) *Die Wahrnehmung anderer Religionen und christlich-abendländisches Selbstverständnis im frühen und hohen Mittelalter (5.–12. Jahrhundert.*, 2 vols. Berlin, Akademie Verlag.

Gregory the Great (1978–1980) *Dialogi*, ed. Adalbert de Vogüé and Paul Antin. Sources Chrétiennes 251, 260, 265. Paris, Cerf.

Green, D. H. (2000) *Language and History in the Early Germanic World.* Cambridge, Cambridge University Press.

Halsall, G. (1998) "Violence and Society in the Early Medieval West: An Introductory Survey." In G. Halsall (ed.), *Violence and Society in the Early Medieval West.* Woodbridge, The Boydell Press, 1–45.

Halsall, G. (2002) "Funny Foreigners: Laughing with the Barbarians in Late Antiquity." In G. Halsall (ed.), *Humor, History and Politics in Late Antiquity and the Early Middle Ages*, Cambridge, Cambridge University Press, 89–113.

Halsall, G. (2007) *Barbarian Migrations and the Roman West, 376–568.* Cambridge, Cambridge University Press.

Harrison, K. (1976) "Woden." In G. Bonner (ed.), *Famulus Christi: Essays in Commemoration of the Thirteenth Centenary of the Birth of the Venerable.* London, S.P.C.K., 351–6.

Haverfield, F. (1916) "Tacitus during the Late Roman Period and the Middle Ages." *Journal of Roman Studies* 6: 196–201.

Hen, Y. (1995) *Culture and Religion in Merovingian Gaul A.D.: 481–751.* Culture Belief and Traditions 1. Leiden, Brill.

Hen, Y. (2002) "Paganism and Superstitions in the Time of Gregory of Tours: Une question mal posée!" In K. Mitchell and I. Wood (eds.), *The World of Gregory of Tours.* Leiden, Brill, 229–40.

Higham, N. J. (1992) *King Arthur: Myth-Making and History.* London and New York, Routledge.

Hines, J. (1997) "Religion: The Limits of Knowledge." In J. Hines (ed.), *The Anglo-Saxons from the Migration Period to the Eighth Century: An Ethnographic Perspective.* Woodbridge, The Boydell Press, 375–401.

Hocquet J.-C. (1985) "Le pain, le vin et la juste mesure à la table des moines carolingiens." *Annales ESC* 40: 661–86.

Hultgård, A. (2007) "Wotan-Odin." In *Reallexikon der Germanischen Altertumskunde* 35. Berlin, De Gruyter, 757–86.

Humphries, M. (2002) "The Lexicon of Abuse: Drunkenness and Political Illegitimacy in the Late Roman World." In G. Halsall (ed.), *Humor, History and Politics in Late Antiquity and the Early Middle Ages.* Cambridge, Cambridge University Press, 75–88.

John, E. (1992) "The Point of Woden." *Anglo-Saxon Studies in Archaeology and History* 5: 127–34.

Jonas of Bobbio (1896) *Vita Vedastis.* In B. Krusch (ed.), *Scriptores rerum Merovingicarum* 3. MGH. Hanover, Hahnsche Buchhandlung, 406–13.

Kieckhefer, R. (2006) "Mythologies of Witchcraft in the Fifteenth Century," *Magic, Ritual, and Witchcraft* 1: 79–107.

Markus, R. A. (1992) "From Caesarius to Boniface: Christianity and Paganism in Gaul." In *Le septième siècle, changements et continuités/The Seventh Century, Change and Continuity.* Studies of the Warburg Institute 42. London, Warburg Institute, 154–69.

Meaney, A. L. (1966) "Woden in England: A Reconsideration of the Evidence." *Folklore* 77: 105–15.

Muhlberger, S. (1984) "Heroic Kings and Unruly Generals: The 'Copenhagen' Continuation of Prosper Reconsidered." *Florilegium* 6: 50–70.

Nelson, M. (2008) *The Barbarian's Beverage: A History of Beer in Ancient Europe*. London and New York, Routledge.

Noble, T. F. X. (2007) "Secular Sanctity: Forging and Ethos for the Carolingian Nobility." In P. Wormald and J. Nelson (eds.), *Lay Intellectuals in the Carolingian World*. Cambridge, Cambridge University Press, 8–38.

North, R. (1997) *Heathen Gods in Old English Literature*. Cambridge, Cambridge University Press.

O'Hara, A. (2009) "The *Vita Columbani* in Merovingian Gaul." *Early Medieval Europe* 17: 126–53.

O'Hara, A. (2015) "Columbanus *ad locum*: The Establishment of the Monastic Foundations." *Peritia* 26: 143–70.

Origo gentis Langobardorum (1878). In G. Waitz (ed.), MGH, *Scriptores rerum Langobardicarum et Italicarum saec. VI–IX*. Hanover, Hahnsche Buchhandlung, 1–6.

Palmer, J. (2007) "Defining Paganism in the Carolingian World." *Early Medieval Europe* 15: 402–25.

Pohl, W. (2012) *Origo gentis Langobardorum*. In F. Lo Monaco and F. Mores (eds.), *I Longobardi e la storia: Un percorso attraverso le fonti*. Altomedioevo 7. Rome, Viella, 105–21.

Pohl, W. (2013) "Introduction: Strategies of Identification: A Methodological Profile." In W. Pohl and G. Heydemann (eds.), *Strategies of Identification. Ethnicity and Religion in Early Medieval Europe*. Cultural Encounters in Late Antiquity and the Middle Ages 13. Turnhout, Brepols, 1–64.

Procopius of Caesarea (1914–1928) *Bella*, ed. H. B. Dewig. Loeb Classical Library 48, 81, 107, 173, 217. Cambridge, MA, and London, Harvard University Press.

Rollinger, R. (2001) "Ammianus Marcellinus' Exkurs zu Alpenrhein und Bodensee." *Chiron* 31: 129–52.

Ryan, J. S. (1966) "Othin in England: Evidence from the Poetry for a Cult of Woden in Anglo-Saxon England." *Folklore* 74: 460–80.

Shanzer, D. (2002) "Laughter and Humour in the Early Medieval Latin West." In G. Halsall (ed.), *Humor, History and Politics in Late Antiquity and the Early Middle Ages*. Cambridge, Cambridge University Press, 25–47.

Shaw, P. (2002) "Uses of Wodan: The Development of His Cult and of Medieval Literary Responses to It." PhD thesis, University of Leeds.

Shaw, P. (2007) "The Origins of the Theophoric Week in the Germanic Languages." *Early Medieval Europe* 15: 386–401.

Sisam, K. (1953) "Anglo-Saxon Royal Genealogies." *Proceedings of the British Academy* 39: 287–348.

Starkey, K. (1999) "Imagining and Early Odin: Gold Bracteates as Visual Evidence?" *Scandinavian Studies* 71: 373–92.

Stone, R. (2012) *Morality and Masculinity in the Carolingian Empire*. Cambridge, Cambridge University Press.

Tacitus (1914) *De situ et origine Germanorum*. In W. Peterson and M. Hutton (eds.), *Germania, Agricola, Dialogue on Oratory*. Loeb Classical Library 35. Cambridge, MA, and London, Harvard University Press, 119–218.

Vita Galli vetustissima (1910). In B. Krusch (ed.), *Scriptores rerum Merovingicarum* 5. MGH. Hanover, Hahnsche Buchhandlung, 451–6.

Winckler, K. (2014) "Gemeine Plätze: Die Wahrnehmung der Alpen in (Spät)antike und (Früh)mittelalter." In U. Leitner (ed.), *Berg & Leute: Tirol als Landschaft und Identität.* Innsbruck, University Press, 302–24.

Wood, I. (1982) "The *Vita Columbani* and Merovingian Hagiography." *Peritia* 1: 63–80.

Wood, I. (2001) *The Missionary Life: Saints and the Evangelisation of Europe 400–1050.* Harlow, Pearson Education.

Wood, I. (2013) "The Pagans and the Other: Varying Presentations in the Early Middle Ages." *Networks and Neighbours* 1: 1–22

Wormald, P. (2006 [1978]) *Bede, Beowulf and the Conversion of the Anglo-Saxons.* In S. Baxter (ed.), *The Times of Bede: Studies in Early English Christian Society and its Historian.* Oxford, Blackwell, 30–105.

12

Between Metz and Überlingen

Columbanus and Gallus in Alamannia

YANIV FOX

Columbanus arrived in Francia in 591 and left for Italy in 612. In those twenty years, his efforts yielded three monasteries, as well as numerous relationships with Merovingian monarchs and potentates. In Italy, Columbanus founded Bobbio, the result of a close relationship with Queen Theodelinda and her husband, King Agilulf.[1] Among these accomplishments, the period in Bregenz stands out as an exceptional interlude, for a number of reasons. First, the region itself was probably not an integral part of Austrasia, unlike previous ventures, which were undertaken within Francia proper. The relationship between King Theudebert II, who ruled the eastern kingdom, and Duke Gunzo, head of the obscure Alamannian duchy to which Columbanus and his monks were dispatched, is difficult to ascertain. Second, it was different because no actual monastery resulted; Bregenz was a failure for everyone involved. Finally, the voyage to Alamannia contained an alleged "missionary dimension," something that was absent from earlier establishments.[2]

As I argue in this chapter, Bregenz was actually very similar to other ventures launched by the abbots of Luxeuil, and the reasons for its ultimate failure had very little to do with the hostility of the locals, which Walahfrid Strabo so vividly describes.[3] To understand the mission in Bregenz and its political overtones, a few words must first be said about Columbanus's modus operandi. The *Vita Columbani*, our best—and indeed at times our only—source for the early days in Burgundy, insists on portraying Columbanus as a rugged outdoorsman, a veritable man of the wild. His first destination in Burgundy was the *vasta heremus* of the Vosges, a place so unforgiving that it nearly drove the monastic population to the brink of starvation.[4] Next came Bregenz, another desolate

---

1. For a discussion of Columbanus's achievements, see Bullough 1997: 1–28.
2. See Wood 2001: 31–5; pace O'Hara 2015. For an analysis of lingering paganism and remnants of a pagan past in Gaul, see Hen 2002: 229–40. For the Carolingian stylization of mission in the ninth-century *Vitae Galli*, see Schwitter 2015.
3. Walahfrid, *Vita Galli*.
4. VC I.6: 163. For similar ideas in the work of Jonas of Bobbio, see Diem 2008: 29. For an in-depth discussion of Columbanus's and Gallus's interaction with their environment in the hagiography, see Rohr 2015. My sincere thanks to Franziska Schnoor for allowing me an early look at the manuscript.

ruin, and a second close encounter with fatal hunger.[5] Bobbio, Columbanus's final monastic foundation, was a secluded spot in the Apennine wilderness, where a dilapidated basilica dedicated to Saint Peter provided the only refuge from the elements. In order to make the site habitable, the monks had to carry heavy beams of fir wood through impenetrable brush and along steep and slippery footpaths, a task that was only achieved thanks to the miraculous powers of Columbanus.[6]

Jonas, who weaved this romantic ambience into his narrative, was himself an experienced adventurer. The time he had spent with Bishop Amandus working in the tenacious swamps of the Scheldt is colorfully described in the epistle that precedes the *Vita Columbani*.[7] However, when we put together what we know about how Columbanus operated with recent archaeological excavations carried out in Luxeuil and Annegray, Jonas's portrayals appear somewhat disingenuous.[8] Annegray, it seems, was not a desert at all, but rather a site of some regional importance, located along an important route connecting the Sanne and Moselle valleys. Recent excavations conducted at the site indicate that Annegray's immediate vicinity was probably inhabited at the time Columbanus and his monks settled there. As for Luxeuil, it too was not the secluded *eremus* of Jonas's prose, but a small hamlet, complete with a villa, a church with an adjoining graveyard, and a Roman bath.[9] Without a doubt, such a place was better suited to host Columbanus's monks, many of whom were sons of wealthy landowning families. More important, it presents Columbanus less as an uncompromising ascetic and more as a man attentive to the needs of his flock, which apparently had a proclivity for worldly comforts.

Should this surprise us? From what we are able to determine, Columbanus did not come from a humble background, although how high up the social ladder his family was located is difficult to say.[10] The *Vita Columbani* and the *Vita Agili* both place him in the company of very senior regional officials, not to mention his frequent visits with the king.[11] It is difficult to see how such an

---

5. *VC* I.27: 211.

6. *VC* I.30: 221–2. Cf. Ó Cróinín, chapter 2 in this volume.

7. *VC, Ep.*: 145: *Si enim me in hoc opere nequaquam indignum iudicassem, olim iam ad ea taxenda temeraria quamvis conatu adgressus fuissem, quaquam me et per triennium Oceani per ora vehit et Scarbea lintris abacta ascoque Scaldeus molles secando vias madefacit saepe et lenta palus Elnonis plantas ob venerabilis Amandi pontificis ferendum suffragium, qui his constitutis in locis veteris Sicambrorum errores evangelico mucrones coercet.* Wood 2001: 41–2.

8. For similar exaggerations, see Costambeys 2007: 7, n. 27.

9. Bully 2010: 39–43; Bully et al. 2015. Also, for a detailed discussion about the excavations at Annegray and Luxeuil, see Bully and Picard 2017.

10. Bullough 1997: 3. See, however, Ó Cróinín, chapter 2 in this volume.

11. *Vita Agili* I.3: 575.

audience would have come about without some formal letter of introduction or at least advance knowledge of his arrival.[12] To this we must add his highborn early recruits and the connections they brought with them, and suddenly it becomes much easier to imagine that Columbanus was not very different from the aristocratic founders that Luxeuil had spawned in great numbers a generation after his death.

The dynamics of the Irish practice of *peregrinatio* are poorly understood, not only in Columbanus's case but also for such figures as Fursey and Killian.[13] Yet the literary cargo these men had brought with them from Ireland and Britain,[14] and to an even greater extent the enthusiastic patrons who awaited them on the other side of the channel,[15] are a good indication that theirs were not blind missions undertaken by optimists. Rather, these would have been well-thought-out journeys, which in all likelihood entailed meticulous preparation on the part of both host and guest.[16]

Since Columbanus was greeted by patrons of considerable social standing on each and every one of his successful monastic enterprises, there is really no reason to assume that Bregenz was an exception, especially when it was Columbanus's Austrasian host, King Theudebert II, who suggested that the monks undertake a mission to Alamannia. A combination of several factors made the southern shores of Lake Constance an appealing spot to place an outpost. Theudebert was justifiably wary of the belligerent Alamanni to the east, who had recently raided the region, penetrating as far west as Avenches.[17] Furthermore, the outlying lands to the north, namely Alsace, were only annexed to Austrasia as part of an agreement between Theudebert and his younger brother, Theuderic II.[18] Theuderic was raised in the region and commanded significant local loyalty, something that worried Theudebert as tension between the brothers gradually mounted.[19]

For this plan to succeed, the participation of the local ruler was essential. Jonas does not name the duke in charge of the region, nor does he seem particularly inclined to elaborate on other aspects of Columbanus's Alamannian effort. Apart from a few miracle stories, very little about this period of Columbanus's

---

12. Perhaps facilitated through an existing network of Breton monks. See Wood, chapter 6 in this volume.

13. Hamann 2011: 1–41; Fox 2016: 53–67. See also Johnston, chapter 4 in this volume.

14. Ó Cróinín 1989: 49–55.

15. Fox 2014: 27–31, passim.

16. Compare, for example, the very different results of Amandus's planned and spontaneous missions. See *Vita Amandi I* 13–6: 436–44.

17. Fredegar IV.37: 29; Bachrach 1972: 81.

18. Fredegar IV.37: 29–30.

19. Fredegar IV.37: 29–30; Hummer 2005: 35–6

life is reported by Jonas. For more information, we must turn to the various hagiographical compositions commemorating Gallus, traditionally believed to have been a disciple of Columbanus who accompanied him from Ireland. It is here that we learn the duke's name (Gunzo) and of the woes that befell the monks after they incurred the hostility of the locals. Yet the various *Vitae Galli* were admittedly composed much later, and their portrayal of the events was written against a markedly different political backdrop.

THE SOURCES

Gallus's rich hagiographical tradition is remarkable. Not only have his deeds merited a supporting role in the *Vita Columbani*, but also, and more important, they have resulted in a lengthy process of hagiographical composition, versification, expansion, and revision in later centuries.[20] Yet a shadow of doubt hovers above even the most basic components of Gallus's story, such as whether or not he was even Irish.[21] If nothing else, Gallus is typical of other Irish saints on the Continent in the extremely complex relationship between his hagiographical portrayals and the actual nature of his historical activity. Over the years several historians have sought to disentangle the complications in Gallus's dossier, producing a varied set of proposed solutions.[22]

Given the voluminous literature on this question, I do not venture to speculate on the veracity of Gallus's Irish origins or on whether he was, in fact, a disciple of Columbanus. There are no decisive arguments either way, and uncovering Columbanus's relations with his disciple remains, as Donald Bullough has put it, the prerogative of the hagiographer; they are irrecoverable by the historian.[23]

It is also true, as Albrecht Diem has noted, that the regular regime portrayed in the later *vitae* should be regarded as a conscious attempt to bring the routines of Gallus's hermitage more closely in line with what Carolingian hagiographers perceived as the discipline practiced at Luxeuil.[24] Even if we could trust the hagiography entirely, we would not be correct in assuming that new Columbanian communities faithfully mimicked Luxeuil's monastic style; Columbanus felt free to incorporate continental influences,[25] and Gallus may have done the same, resulting in an idiosyncratic monastic regimen.

---

20. On this, see Schwitter 2015.
21. Wood 2015.
22. See, among many others, Prinz 1981: 80–1; Müller 1972: 209–49; Müller 1982: 330–41; Schär 2011: 19–50; Richter 2008: 33; Berschin 1975: 257–77.
23. Bullough 1997: 21. However, cf. Dörler's comments on Gallus in chapter 13 in this volume.
24. Diem 2015.
25. Stancliffe 2011: 17–28.

For understanding the political context in seventh-century Alamannia, which is the main purpose of this chapter, determining Gallus's Irish origins or the degree to which he was dependent on Luxovian regular traditions is less urgent. I cannot see any blatant factual impossibilities in the *vitae* of Gallus, and therefore I have opted to believe them, at least as they pertain to Gallus's Columbanian affiliation. It remains to be seen, then, how Gallus's hermitage in the Steinach mirrors Columbanian patterns.

The earliest composition chronicling the life of Gallus, a work termed the *Vita vetustissima* by the editors of the Monumenta Germaniae Historica, obviously has especial value for understanding the specifics of the Alamannian mission.[26] Yet the *vetustissima* is a composite fragment, whose narrative layers—each apparently composed at a different time—form an uneven whole. Various attempts have been made to date the *vetustissima*. Walter Berschin suggested that at its core, the piece contains a layer that should be dated to c. 680.[27] Using a series of stylistic and linguistic arguments, Raphael Schwitter has recently claimed that the earliest *Life* in its original form should, in fact, be dated to the 720s, a fact that has some bearing on its reliability as a historical source.[28]

For our purposes, the question of dating is acutely relevant because of the well-known tendency of hagiographical pieces to reflect contemporary concerns rather than confine themselves to historical reportage. Should we then interpret the problems encountered by Columbanus's monks or the various episcopal entanglements of Gallus—in other words, all of the material that deals with regional politics—as alluding to the pressures experienced by those persons or parties who commissioned the vita? Such a view is certainly less perilous, but by adhering to it, we voluntarily limit our ability to say much about Gallus's actual career.

There is nothing about the *vetustissima* that collides with what we know about the region in the early seventh century, although of course we are equally reliant on the works of Wetti and Walahfrid, both ninth-century compositions, to supplement our understanding. No doubt uncovering the historical context of Gallus's activities requires a delicate touch and ultimately, a measure of faith in our sources. Let us agree to proceed with due caution and see what may be said of the situation in the region in Columbanus's and Gallus's day.

---

26. *Vitae vetustissimae*: 251–6.
27. Berschin 1975: 274.
28. Schwitter 2011: 185–200.

DUKE GUNZO, HIS FAMILY, AND
THE ALAMANNIAN DUCHY

The identity of the duke who received Columbanus and his monks has been a cause for some speculation, especially since most of what we know about him is found in the ninth-century *Vitae Galli*.[29] His name, allegedly a hypocorism, has produced some fanciful attempts at reconstruction, ranging from the majestic-sounding Gundahar to the in my mind somewhat more plausible Cunzelen.[30] The latter option, suggested by Jäschke and Settipani, is reminiscent of the name borne by one of Gunzo's predecessors, Uncelen, who may also have been his father.[31] Gunzo's putative son Leuthar,[32] another *dux Alamannorum*, bears the name of an earlier duke, who led a Frankish-Alamannic expeditionary force across the Po as part of Theudebald's attempt to engage the Byzantines.[33]

If this hypothetical structure of the ducal family is to be believed, two conclusions may be drawn from it, which have some bearing on our interpretation of the role of Gunzo in the Columbanian effort. The first is that the family of this duke was intimately involved in the military campaigns of the Merovingians. Uncelen, Gunzo's purported father, was implicated in the lynching of the Burgundian mayor Protadius in 605, a move that temporarily prevented Austrasia and Burgundy from going to war.[34] Brunhild, the primary instigator of this conflict according to the Chronicle of Fredegar, avenged herself by having Uncelen deposed and mutilated.[35] Considering the predicament the ducal family was in, it is odd that Uncelen's son would be allowed to succeed him, adding an element of uncertainty to an already shaky identification. Still, this evokes the image of an Alamannian duchy that is well and truly integrated into the Frankish world, not the far-flung periphery Jonas made it out to be.

A second conclusion is that the dukes of this region were successful in carving out a hereditary niche for themselves, not unlike the Agilolfing duchy of Bavaria or the Etichonid duchy in Alsace. In fact, some scholars have chosen to regard both the Etichonids and the family of Gunzo as offshoots of the

---

29. Hen 1995: 194.

30. For Cunzelen see Settipani 1993: 87–8, n. 304–5; for Gundahar see Zöllner 1965: 127.

31. Jäschke 1974: 118ff.

32. Leuthar was also heavily involved in the power struggles between Austrasia's magnates. See Fredegar IV.88: 75. On Leuthar, see Ebling 1974: 182; for his familial relationship with Gunzo, see Settipani 2014: 276–7. For Leuthar's connection to Waldrada, the founder of Fridburga's nunnery at Metz, see Gauthier 1980: 295–6.

33. Agathias, *Histories*, I.6: 14; Gregory of Tours, *DLH* III.32: 128; Bachrach 1972: 27.

34. Fredegar IV.27: 18–9.

35. Ibid.

ancient and illustrious Agilolfing clan, the only identifiable group, apart from the Merovingians of course, that based its claim to power on its lineage.[36]

Using the available information, we may say very little about the nature of the duchy itself. Überlingen, where the duke was situated, may have been a permanent residence equipped with a governmental complex, or not; it is never actually stated.[37] The borders of the duchy itself are equally difficult to delineate; so much so, in fact, that several theories have suggested that we identify Gunzo with Duke Gundoin of Alsace, who donated the land for the Luxovian monastery of Grandval.[38] Without delving too much into the particulars of this theory, it does seem a rather unlikely notion. The children of both dukes had different names; they probably ruled over different territories; and Jonas, who was aware of both men, never sought to make this identification.[39]

Nevertheless, this confusion does allow us to make one important observation. As Max Schär has noted, the unit ruled from Überlingen was not *the* duchy of the Alamannians, if by this we wish to denote some politically or ethnically defined independent entity.[40] Gunzo, if he is indeed correctly identified, was not the native head of some confederation of trans-Rhenish *gentes*; he was a Frankish official sent to rule a region very similar to Alsace in terms of its relationship to the Frankish heartland: a periphery, ruled by proxy dukes, but gradually coming under closer Merovingian supervision.[41]

Talto, mentioned in the ninth-century *Casus sancti Galli*[42]—perhaps identical to the *tribunus Arbonensis* or *praefectus* mentioned in the *Vitae Galli*[43]—was possibly a subordinate of Gunzo. Talto also served as a *camerarius* of King Dagobert I and perhaps even served under Chlothar II, evidence that the leading men of the region were, first and foremost, Frankish officials who exercised their power through a recognized, structured hierarchy.[44] As head of this region, Gunzo was well placed to leverage both Theuderic and Theudebert, who courted him vigorously, and this in turn may shed some light on the context of Columbanus's and Gallus's activities in the region.

---

36. Fouracre 2000: 105–6. Interestingly, the internal dispute within the Huosi clan (one of the five named in the *Lex Baiuvariorum*) features the names Agilolf and Cunzo. See Wood 2006: 45–6.

37. Schär 2011: 222–3.

38. I use Luxovian here and not Columbanian because Grandval was a project initiated and directed by the leadership of Luxeuil. On this see Fox 2014: 87–9, 184–93. For Gundoin's establishments, see below.

39. For a summary of this theory, see Keller 1976: 27–30; Le Jan 1995: 401–2, n. 145.

40. Schär 2011: 224–5.

41. A very similar argument is made for Bavaria in Hammer 2011: 217–44.

42. Ratpert, *St. Galler Klostergeschichten*: 150: *Talto vir inlustris, Tagoberti scilicet regis camararius et postea comes eiusdem pagi.*

43. Wetti, *Vita Galli* 19, 21, 25: 266–7, 267–8, 270 (respectively); Walahfrid, *Vita Galli* I.19, I.21, I.25: 298–9, 299–300, 302–4 (respectively).

44. Schär 2015, 2011: 238–43.

While Theudebert's tactic was to invite the duke to cooperate on a lucrative monastic project, Theuderic took a more direct approach, offering to wed his son and heir, Sigibert II, to Gunzo's daughter Fridburga.[45] As with all the other protagonists in this drama, it must be iterated that the prince intended for Fridburga could possibly have been Sigibert III, Dagobert's firstborn, a point to which I return below. For now let us only say that the chronological constraints seem to favor the son of Theuderic, whose ephemeral reign lasted for several weeks before it was terminated by the advancing Neustrians.[46] If we recall that Brunhild was adamantly against pairing her progeny with high-profile brides—critical remarks voiced against this policy cost Columbanus his abbacy and Bishop Desiderius of Vienne his life[47]—we can recognize what a departure from custom it was. An experienced Brunhild astutely sensed that such a plan would expose the Burgundian royal house to pressure from prospective in-laws. Obviously, Gunzo was important enough to warrant an exception and justify the risk.

Now, we should assume that Columbanus's arrival was coordinated with Gunzo, who had ruled the region from the northern shores of Lake Constance. Bregenz was a project not dissimilar to the Bavarian mission undertaken some years later by Eustasius in Bavaria or to Waldebert's collaboration with Duke Gundoin of Alsace, mentioned briefly above.[48] The difference was that the political atmosphere in Alamannia changed quickly and violently, with the outbreak of war between Austrasia and Burgundy. After Theuderic's triumph, Columbanus's presence became a liability for Gunzo. Jonas admits as much, stating that the inauspicious change of ruler had convinced Columbanus to quit Bregenz for Italy.

Gallus's Alamannian Career

The tale of the monks' encounter with a party of heathens offering a sacrifice to Woden, which is described in the *Vita Columbani*, is expanded in Wetti's and Walahfrid's version of the *Vita Galli*.[49] The later accounts include an episode in which angry locals kill two of the monks and then complain to Gunzo, who has Columbanus and his disciples expelled from his territory.[50] Unlike Jonas's Columbanus, who sensed the unwelcome change in the political situation and departed, the monks of the *Vitae Galli* are reluctant to leave what they deem to

---

45. Wetti, *Vita Galli* 21: 267–8.

46. Fredegar IV.40: 32–3.

47. *Passio Desiderii*: 250–2.

48. For Bavaria see *VC* II.8: 243–4; *Vita Sadalbergae* 1: 51. For Grandval see *Vita Germani*: 25–40.

49. On this episode, see Shaw 2002: 118–27. See also the contributions of Borri and Maier, chapters 11 and 10 in this volume. Cf. O'Hara 2015.

50. Wetti, *Vita Galli* 6: 260–1; Walahfrid, *Vita Galli*, I.6: 289.

be a "lovely abode."[51] While Walahfrid is careful to conform to hagiographical conventions regarding Theuderic and Brunhild, he does not offer any explanation for the monks' departure, apart from the altercation with the locals. In this respect, the fragmentary *Vita vetustissima* contributes very little to our understanding of the events, so it would perhaps be preferable to accept Jonas's explanation, which pins the departure on the Burgundian military victory, as being closest to the truth.

So shortly after Theuderic's triumph, the group uprooted to Italy, leaving behind their friend Gallus, who was too ill to make the journey. Reading the *Vita Galli*, we get the distinct impression that unlike his vociferous master, Gallus was not perceived as a potential menace by the powers that be in Alamannia. The scope of his activity seems to have been more modest, and he was content to seclude himself in the Steinach valley, not far from where Columbanus's camp had been located. Yet Gallus succeeded in attracting a local following, and soon the news of his supernatural prowess reached Gunzo. The duke's daughter, Fridburga, was afflicted by a violent demonic possession. As a senior spiritual authority in the region, Gallus was called to intervene. A true recluse, Gallus refused to become involved, disobeying the duke's orders and evading his emissaries. Eventually, of course, Gallus consented and came to see Fridburga. Prayers and tears ensued, followed by a stern reprimand from Gallus, which convinced the demon to depart.[52]

Why Gallus felt it fitting to deny a suffering girl her cure is not adequately explained, but this episode, like much of what preceded it, betrays certain political overtones. Whether Fridburga's plight was real is inconsequential, yet what Gallus's reluctance teaches us is that he was probably wary of the duke's intentions, at least initially. His attempts to remain concealed from Gunzo's gaze could have had more to do with an air of suspicion that probably surrounded a disciple of Columbanus, a clear Theudebert partisan, operating at a time when the family of Theuderic seemed poised to take over Francia in its entirety. As the two bishops that Sigibert—or more likely his father—had sent to cure the girl clearly indicate, the well-being of Gunzo's family was never far from the king's mind.[53]

Reconciling the regnal chronology with the hagiographical portrayal of the Austrasian king in this episode poses some serious problems. Sigibert appears to be acting of his own volition when he dispatches bishops, issues orders, and eventually even cancels well-thought-out wedding plans, all very heavy and time-consuming demands on a boy-king whose rule lasted but a brief instant. While Jonas deliberately misrepresents the king who received Columbanus as Sigibert I (d. 575), this is highly unlikely to have been our Sigibert.[54] Apart from

---

51. Walahfrid, *Vita Galli*, I.8: 290.
52. Walahfrid, *Vita Galli* I.15–8: 295–8.
53. Walahfrid, *Vita Galli* I.16: 296–7.
54. Wood 1998: 110–1.

a few notable exceptions, most manuscripts of the *Vita Columbani* do have Sigibert I as the one welcoming Columbanus.[55] Still, this need not have confused the authors of the *Vitae Galli*, who would have read of Sigibert I's murder in a subsequent chapter,[56] located well before Columbanus set out on his mission to Bregenz, at the behest of Sigibert I's grandson.[57]

Conceivably, this hagiographical monarch could have been Sigibert III, who ruled for two decades from the early 630s. Of course that would either force us to accept him as the younger partner in a very awkward May-December romance or push the entire story forward in time, divorcing Gallus completely from the story of Columbanus, as indeed Hagen Keller has suggested.[58] Another option is to reject the historicity of this episode entirely. If we are unwilling to go that far, we may either conclude that the relationship between the Alamannic and the Austrasian courts was grossly exaggerated by Gallus's hagiographers, or, more likely, that the Austrasians were intent on marrying their young king to Fridburga, but that either Brunhild or some prominent noble was the one pulling the strings.

Gunzo sent his daughter to Sigibert, but the story did not conclude with a church wedding. Preparations for the ceremony were nearly complete when Fridburga had a change of heart. Overcome with religious zeal, she decided to spurn her royal fiancé in favor of the heavenly bridegroom. When he was told what had happened, the king took the news surprisingly well, appointing Fridburga as head of a convent in Metz.[59] This entire episode seems very suspect, not only because Sigibert was willing to toss aside a lucrative union to accommodate the whims of a girl he had only just met, but also because of the unexpected and anachronistic appearance of one Bishop Cyprian of Arles, who is inserted into the storyline as a rather transparent device to sway the king's opinion.[60]

On this point, Wetti's and Walahfrid's narratives are probably misinformed, and it is therefore tempting to speculate that Fridburga's dramatic wedding day

---

55. Including the oldest manuscript, St. Gallen, Stiftsbibliothek, 553. See O'Hara 2009: 150 n. 128.

56. Jonas blames this on Chilperic. See *VC* I.18: 186.

57. Unless, of course, we believe Brunhild on the question of Theudebert's origins. See *Fredegar* IV.27: 18.

58. Keller 1976: 23ff.

59. An episode reminiscent of the dynamic between Chlothar I and Radegund, herself a princess from a subjugated periphery. See Venantius Fortunatus, *Vita Radegundis* 5: 366–7.

60. Wetti, *Vita Galli* 22: 268: *inter quos Cyprianus Arlatensis [sic] praesul dixit*. The last bishop named Cyprian to have had any connection to Arles was actually a suffragan of the Arelate metropolitan from Toulon, who flourished in the early sixth century. See Duchesne 1907–1915: I.260, I.278. To continue the comparison with the previous note, Fridburga's Cyprian plays a similar role to Radegund's Médard of Noyon. See Venantius Fortunatus, *Vita Radegundis* 12: 368.

scene was a literary ploy designed to explain why the two never married and how she ended up as an abbess in Metz. Since the upheavals of 613 are nowhere mentioned in the *Vita Galli*, an alternative explanation was called for, but we could just as easily see how Chlothar's triumph over the Burgundians would have foiled such high-profile matrimonial designs.

GALLUS, THE CONSTANCE BISHOPRIC, AND THE ABBACY
OF LUXEUIL

What is also interesting about the story is that Gunzo, overcome with joy because of his daughter's miraculous recovery, decided to convoke a council with the intent of appointing Gallus bishop of Constance.[61] The duke was apparently secure enough in his position to circumvent canonical protocol and offer the bishopric to whomever healed his daughter. Again, Gallus's modesty prevented him from accepting the nomination, but it did not bar him from suggesting his own candidate, John (Iohannes), who accepted the appointment.[62]

Now, we could take Walahfrid at his word and explain this refusal as the result of Gallus's distaste for the worldly requirements of the office. This portrayal of events, in which Gallus easily convinces a surprisingly acquiescent duke of John's many qualities, seems to create more problems than it solves. To be sure, the role of John in the *Vita* is pivotal, although how useful it is for elucidating seventh-century realities is far from clear.[63]

This episode in particular is arguably much more instrumental for understanding how ninth-century hagiographers envisaged the correct relationship between the see of Constance and the monastic powerhouses operating within its jurisdiction: St Gallen and Reichenau. This becomes especially apparent when we examine the relationship between the two men. Before and after his ordination, John was still very much in a subordinate position to Gallus, who continued to instruct him on scripture and, one might presume, on other matters as well. It is perhaps no coincidence that the abbot-bishop who was most decisive in determining the legal standing of the various houses vis-à-vis the bishopric of Constance was another John (d. c. 782), whose tenure dictated the reality in which Wetti and Walahfrid operated and wrote.

---

61. See Halfond 2010: 35.

62. But not without first expectedly refusing the office. See Wetti, *Vita Galli* 24: 269–70; Walahfrid, *Vita Galli*, I.24: 302. For some famous examples of this topos, see Norton 2007: 191–6.

63. My thanks to Dagmar Ó Riain-Raedel for alerting me to the later context of this hagiographical passage.

Using power relations between a saint and his environment as a metonymy for later institutional hierarchies is of course a time-honored hagiographical technique, one that was probably employed here. Other aspects of the *Vita* were also subjected to thorough investigation. Raphael Schwitter has shown conclusively how language and imagery were employed to refashion the *Life's* protagonist; Gallus was thus transformed from recluse to missionary and finally to the apostle of Alamannia.

However, it is important not to overindulge in this interpretative technique, especially if it leads us to discard the hagiographical corpus as a source for studying the historical Gallus. The elements of the narrative that interest us here—the duchy, its relationship to the Merovingians, and its monastic policies—have not, after all, been made unrecognizable by the editorial process. Without compelling evidence to the contrary, departure from a literal understanding of the text may ultimately prove deleterious and counterproductive. The dismissive attitudes of Bruno Krusch and others toward Carolingian hagiographical réécriture have proven a serious obstacle to our understanding of the Merovingian landscape.[64] Since the *vetustissima* offers very few details, we are left to decide, again, whether to take the later *Vitae Galli* at their word. The next episode is perhaps slightly more helpful in this respect.

Gunzo was apparently not alone in recognizing Gallus's administrative qualities. After the death of Eustasius, a group of six monks came from Luxeuil to offer Gallus the abbacy.[65] Gallus refused yet again, but the fact that he was chosen implies that he was not a simple hermit but a man whose stature would allow him to hold his own in the company of kings and the highest Frankish aristocracy. His predecessor, Eustasius, was on friendly terms with King Chlothar II, while Waldebert, Luxeuil's third abbot, had political connections that spanned the breadth of Gaul. It is certainly possible that Gallus was apprehensive about taking on such a visible position, especially since he was already invested in an embryonic monastic community of his own, one that he may have felt would not survive his departure.[66]

Jonas does not mention that Gallus was considered for the abbacy of Luxeuil.[67] When he was conducting his research prior to composing the *Vita Columbani*, Jonas probably consulted Gallus, who was by then an old man.[68]

---

64. For discussion, see Kreiner 2014: 230–76.

65. Walahfrid, *Vita Galli* I.28: 305–7.

66. The *Life* describes a rudimentary community of twelve disciples and a church. See Walahfrid, *Vita Galli* I.26: 304: *Tempore subsequenti coepit virtutum cultor oratorium construere, mansiunculis per girum dispositis ad commanendum fratribus, quorum iam duodecim monastici sanctitate propositi roboratos doctrina et exemplis ad aeternorum desideria concitavit.*

67. A succinct version of the story appears in *Vita vetustissima* 3: 252–3.

68. See *VC, Ep.*: 145; Wood 1982: 75.

This is therefore an omission on Jonas's part, with direct bearing on the reliability of the *Vitae Galli*. Moreover, considering the prominent ties of both Eustasius and Waldebert to the regional elites around Luxeuil, to whom they were most likely also related,[69] it appears somewhat extraordinary that an outsider like Gallus should have been, almost by default, the man Luxeuil's community sought to succeed Eustasius. As in so many other aspects of the *Vitae Galli*, this too may have been a later addition based on no more than tradition. Alternatively, if we accept the theories put forward by Max Schär and Gerold Hilty, which viewed Gallus as a native of Alsace, his nomination could then be explained as having come with concrete regional advantages.[70] Finally, it is also not impossible to believe that Jonas omitted this episode so as not to portray Waldebert, the incumbent abbot of Luxeuil during the composition of the *Vita Columbani*, as the community's second choice.

Irrespective of Gallus's familial background, if true this episode makes clear that the lines of communication between Luxeuil and the hermitage in the Steinach remained open even after Columbanus's death, as Philipp Dörler also discusses in chapter 13 of this volume. The monks knew exactly where to find Gallus, and when in turn he needed to send his monk Magnoald to Bobbio, this was also done quite easily.[71] The eremitic community in the Steinach, however rudimentary it may have been, was probably perceived as part of the wider Columbanian *familia*. It did not have access to royal funds in the same way that Luxeuil or Bobbio had done, although the *Vita Galli* posits that Sigibert was willing to offer Gallus patronage, and in fact donated gifts of gold, silver, and possibly even land.[72] According to Wetti and Walahfrid, Gunzo and his deputies offered Gallus's hermitage material support and workers, and of course the duke's promise of the bishopric of Constance would have come with financial benefits.[73] Assuming these reports contain some kernel of historical truth, they appear to reflect a willingness to support monastic activity in the area.

Sigibert's rule was cut short, and so was any assistance Gallus may have been offered, at least until the situation stabilized. Gunzo's attitude with regard to the monastic community is very difficult to ascertain, but we may surmise that it did not develop into a large-scale and stable relationship of material and

---

69. Geary 1988: 172; Prinz 1965: 147, n. 135.

70. But with Irish (Schär) or Gallo-Roman (Hilty) ancestry. These theories are supported primarily by Gallus's ability to converse in the local dialect, or *barbarica locutio*. See Walahfrid, *Vita Galli* I.6: 289; Schär 2011: 51–76; Hilty 1985: 125–55.

71. For the close connections between St. Gallen and Bobbio, see also Zironi 2004: 90–103.

72. Walahfrid, *Vita Galli* I.21: 299–300: *Auri quoque libras duas et argenti pondo totidem cum epistula concessionis.*

73. Schär 2015.

spiritual exchange. Nevertheless, the Alamannic community probably operated under the same premise as the rest of the Columbanian houses—that is, a secular potentate supporting a monastic activist—although here, as in several other instances, construction and expansion of the original complex was kept relatively modest.[74] There is some archaeological evidence that points to local elite patronage, although the development of the site did not reach the scale of Columbanian projects in Neustria, for example, at least until the time of Otmar (abbot from 719–759).[75]

Conclusions

Understanding the nature of Gallus's activities in Alamannia is difficult in light of the many inconsistencies and textual lacunae found in the hagiographical corpus. Yet some, admittedly cautious, observations about its political context are not impossible to extract. Columbanus and his group of monks arrived in the region under the shadow of escalating tensions between Theudebert's Austrasia and Theuderic's Burgundy, whose hostility toward Columbanus was vividly explored in Jonas's composition. It is very likely, given Columbanus's previous attempts at monastic establishment, that he coordinated his efforts with the regional government, or that such provisions were made on his behalf by Theudebert's representatives. This is supported by the fact that ecclesiastical officeholders along the route knew of his voyage up the Rhine and offered their help.[76] Theudebert had a vested interest in the realization of an Alamannian outpost, but to an even greater extent in a successful collaboration with Duke Gunzo. Theuderic, too, wanted the duke based in Überlingen on his side and was willing to cement such an alliance with a marriage, a clear departure from the previous matrimonial policies of the Burgundian house.

For his part, Gunzo had to think hard where his allegiances lay. A wrong decision could have cost him his political career, if not worse, and he had the example of two predecessors—possibly ancestors?—to rely on. As long as the situation was relatively fluid, Gunzo could pursue both avenues, but once the armies of Theuderic prevailed in the ensuing conflict, the presence of Columbanus in the region became a disadvantage. The Irish abbot was curtly shown the door and had to pursue his journey into Italy. The story of Gallus's decision to remain in the area is perhaps true for no other reason than its unflattering depiction of both Gallus and Columbanus, set in an otherwise impeccable portrayal.[77]

74. See Fox 2014: 129–30 for comparable examples.
75. See Schindler 2015.
76. *VC* I.27: 212.
77. For a different interpretation, see Ó Riain-Raedel 2015.

It is when the hagiographical limelight turns to Gallus that things become murkier. His activities in the Steinach were probably not a secret, because Willimar, the ecclesiastical representative in the region, who was also known to the duke and the count, took Gallus in after Columbanus had left. Two of his clerics— Theodore and Magnoald—were charged with restoring Gallus's health, while a deacon, Hiltibod, found a spot for the hermitage. Gunzo soon became aware of Gallus's presence and summoned him to Überlingen, which initiated a chain of events that brought the humble ascetic to the attention of the king. We should not automatically assume that a partisan of Columbanus would incur the enmity of the Burgundian monarch, even if this were still Theuderic. Once Columbanus was gone, the king's attitude toward Luxeuil also changed for the better, following the entreaty of a monastic delegation that included Agilus—later the foremost figure in Eustasius's Bavarian mission—and Donatus, bishop of Besançon and founder of Jussa-moûtier.[78]

Columbanus's time in Bregenz, Gallus's activities in the Steinach, and indeed also the later projects in Alsace and Bavaria, should be construed as part of a greater program of Merovingian expansion and reorganization of the eastern Frankish frontier.[79] To this end royal funds were allocated, aristocratic patronage was enlisted, and the assistance of the secular clergy was secured, all with the aim of providing a supportive platform designed to facilitate the efforts of monastic figures. In this regard the *Vitae Galli*, with all of their obvious problems, paint a reasonably accurate picture of the region's integration into the Merovingian orbit.

Yet the benefits of monastic patronage extended beyond the scope of royal interest. The hagiographers Wetti and Walahfrid clearly worked very hard to accentuate Gallus's anchoritic tendencies. However, the fact that he was reluctantly and repeatedly dragged into the world of secular politics illustrates the effects a monastery—especially a royally funded one—would have on its surroundings. Like a finely crafted lens, a monastery had a way of harnessing energy from disparate sources into an effective beam of concentrated political and social power. As it matured, Columbanian monasticism exploited this medium to create vast and potent networks of *amicitia*. Influence and wealth flowed through much the same conduits that they had done in Bregenz and in the Steinach, giving rise to what Peter Brown has described as miniature "holy cities."[80]

Obviously, in Gallus's lifetime his little community did not succeed in doing this. One possible explanation for its stunted growth—and this, I admit, is sheer speculation—is the events of 613. To be sure, the rise to power of Chlothar

---

78. For Agilus see *VC* II.8: 245; for Donatus see *VC* I.14: 175–6.
79. See Wolfram, chapter 9 in this volume.
80. Brown 2013: 252–5.

generally benefited the interests of the Columbanian houses, but the fruits of this process only became apparent in the late 620s. Sigibert's overthrow denied Gallus's fledgling community critically needed financial support, and alternative sources were probably not forthcoming.[81] Other regional events, such as the Alethius affair and the internal crisis caused by Agrestius,[82] convinced Chlothar II to take a more distanced approach; he was clearly still undecided when he authorized the Council of Mâcon in 626.

When, two years later, Gallus was ostensibly offered the abbacy of Luxeuil, his community was not stable enough to be left to fend for itself. Ironically, the "underprivileged child" of the Columbanian familia later became its biggest success story, when on the site of Gallus's hermitage grew the great Carolingian house of St Gallen, although whether by that time there was actually anything "Columbanian" about it is open to debate.

BIBLIOGRAPHY

Agathias (1975) *The Histories*, ed. and trans. J. D. Frendo. Corpus fontium historiae Byzantinae, vol. 2a. Berlin and New York, W. De Gruyter.

Bachrach, B. S. (1972) *Merovingian Military Organization, 481–751*. Minneapolis, University of Minnesota Press.

Berschin, W. (1975) "Gallus abbas Vindicatus." *Historisches Jahrbuch der Görres-Gesellschaft* 95, 257–77.

Bobolenus (1910) *Vita Germani abbatis Grandivallensis*. In B. Krusch (ed.), *Scriptores rerum Merovingicarum* 5. MGH. Hanover, Hahnsche Buchhandlung, 25–40.

Brown, P. (2013) *The Rise of Western Christendom: Triumph and Diversity, A.D. 200–1000*. Oxford and Malden, MA, Blackwell.

Bullough, D. (1997) "The Career of Columbanus." In M. Lapidge (ed.), *Columbanus: Studies on the Latin Writings*. Woodbridge, Boydell Press, 1–28.

Bully, S. (2010) "L'église Saint-Martin de Luxeuil-les-Bains (Haute-Saône), deuxième campagne." *Bulletin du centre d'études médiévales d'Auxerre* 14: 39–43.

Bully, S. (2011) "Le site du monastère d'Annegray (Haute-Saône): Les prospections géophysiques." *Bulletin du centre d'études médiévales d'Auxerre* 15: 9–15.

Bully, S. and J.-M. Picard (2017) "*Mensa in deserto*: Reconciling Jonas's *Life of Columbanus* with Recent Archaeological Discoveries at Annegray and Luxeuil." In R. Flechner and M. N. Mhaonaigh (eds.), *Transforming Landscapes of Belief in the Early Medieval Insular World and Beyond: Converting the Isles*, vol. 2. Turnhout: Brepols.

Bully, S., et al. (2015) "Die Anfänge des Klosters von Luxeuil im Lichte jüngster archäologischer Untersuchungen (6.–9. Jahrhundert)." In F. Schnoor et al. (eds.), *Gallus in seiner Zeit: Leben, Wirken, Nachleben*. Sankt Gallen, Verlag am Klosterhof, 127–60.

81. The scope of the support provided in Talto's day is impossible to quantify, although Schär believes that Gallus received proprietary rights over his monastic compound in the 620s at the earliest. See Schär 2011: 244.

82. For Alethius, see Fredegar IV.44: 36–3; for Agrestius, *VC* II.9: 246–51.

Costambeys, M. (2007) *Power and Patronage in Early Medieval Italy: Local Society, Italian Politics and the Abbey of Farfa, c. 700–900*. Cambridge, Cambridge University Press.

Diem, A. (2008) "The Rule of an 'Iro-Egyptian' Monk in Gaul: Jonas' *Vita Iohannis* and the Construction of a Monastic Identity." *Revue Mabillon* 19: 5–50.

Diem, A. (2015) "Die *Regula Columbani* und die *Regula Sancti Galli*: Überlegungen zu den Gallusviten in ihrem karolingischen Kontext." In F. Schnoor et al. (eds.), *Gallus und Seine Zeit: Leben, Wirken, Nachleben*. Sankt Gallen, Verlag am Klosterhof, 65–98.

Duchesne, L. (1907–1915) *Fastes épiscopaux de l'ancienne Gaule*. 3 vols. Paris, Thorin & fils.

Ebling, H. (1974) *Prosopographie der Amtsträger des Merowingerreiches: Von Chlothar II. (613) bis Karl Martell (741)*. Beihefte der Francia, 2. Munich, Fink.

Fouracre, P. J. (2000) *The Age of Charles Martel*. Harlow, Longman.

Fox, Y. (2014) *Power and Religion in Merovingian Gaul: Columbanian Monasticism and the Frankish Elites*. Cambridge, Cambridge University Press.

Fox, Y. (2016) "The Political Context of Irish Monasticism in Francia: Another Look at the Sources." In R. Flechner and S. Meeder (eds.), *The Irish in Europe*. Basingstoke and New York, Palgrave Macmillan, 53–67.

Gauthier, N. (1980) *L'évangélisation des pays de la Moselle: La province romaine de Première Belgique entre Antiquité et Moyen-Age (IIIe–VIIIe siècles)*. Paris, E. de Boccard.

Geary, P. J. (1988) *Before France and Germany: The Creation and Transformation of the Merovingian World*. Oxford, Oxford University Press.

Halfond, G. I. (2010) *Archaeology of Frankish Church Councils, AD 511–768*. Leiden, Brill.

Hamann, S. (2011) "St. Fursa, the Genealogy of an Irish Saint: The Historical Person and His Cult." *Proceedings of the Royal Irish Academy* 112C: 1–41.

Hammer, C. I. (2011) "Early Merovingian Bavaria: A Late Antique Italian Perspective." *Journal of Late Antiquity* 4.2: 217–44.

Hen, Y. (1995) *Culture and Religion in Merovingian Gaul, A.D. 481–751*. Leiden, New York, and Köln, E. J. Brill.

Hen, Y. (2002) "Paganism and Superstitions in the Time of Gregory of Tours: Une question mal posée!" In K. Mitchell and I. N. Wood (eds.), *The World of Gregory of Tours*. Leiden, Brill, 229–40.

Hilty, G. (1985) "Gallus in Tuggen: Zur Frage der deutsch-romanischen Sprachgrenze im Linthgebiet vom 6. bis zum 9. Jahrhundert." *Vox Romanica* 44: 125–55.

Hummer, H. J. (2005) *Politics and Power in Early Medieval Europe: Alsace and the Frankish Realm, 600–1000*. Cambridge and New York, Cambridge University Press.

Jäschke, K.-U. (1974) "Kolumban von Luxeuil und sein Wirken im alamannischen Raum." In A. Borst (ed.), *Mönchtum, Episkopat und Adel zur Gründungszeit des Klosters Reichenau*. Vorträge und Forschungen, 20. Sigmaringen, J. Thorbecke, 77–130.

Keller, H. (1976) "Fränkisches Herrschaft und alemannisches Herzogtum im 6. und 7. Jahrhundert." *Zeitschrift für die Geschichte des Oberrheins* 124: 1–30.

Kreiner, J. (2014) *The Social Life of Hagiography in the Merovingian Kingdom*. Cambridge, Cambridge University Press.

Le Jan, R. (1995) *Famille et pouvoir dans le monde franc (VIIe–Xe siècle)*. Paris, Publications de la Sorbonne.

Müller, I. (1972) "Die älteste Gallus-Vita." *Zeitschrift für schweizerische Kirchengeschichte* 66: 209–49.

Müller, W. (1982) "Der Anteil der Iren an der Christianisierung der Alemannen." In H. Löwe (ed.), *Die Iren und Europa im früheren Mittelalter*, 2 vols. Stuttgart, Klett-Cotta, 1:330–41.

Norton, P. (2007) *Episcopal Elections, 250–600: Hierarchy and Popular Will in Late Antiquity*. Oxford, Oxford University Press.

Ó Cróinín, D. (1989) "Zur Frühzeit der irischen Mission in Europa." In J. Erichsen (ed.), *Killian: Mönch aus Irland, aller Franken Patron, 689–1989; Katalog der Sonder-Ausstellung zur 1300-Jahr-Feier des Kiliansmartyriums, 1. Juli 1989–1. Oktober 1989, Festung Marienburg Würzburg.* Würzburg and Munich, Mainfränkisches Museum, Haus der Bayerischen Geschichte: Bayerisches Landesamt für Denkmalpflege, 49–55.

O'Hara, A. (2009) "The *Vita Columbani* in Merovingian Gaul." *Early Medieval Europe* 17: 126–53.

O'Hara, A. (2015) "Columbanus *ad locum*: The Establishment of the Monastic Foundations." *Peritia* 26: 143–70.

Ó Riain-Raedel, D. (2015) "Bemerkungen zum hagiographischen Dossier des heiligen Gallus." In F. Schnoor et al. (eds.), *Gallus und Seine Zeit: Leben, Wirken und Nachleben.* Sankt Gallen, Verlag am Klosterhof, 223–42.

"*Passio sancti Desiderii episcopi Viennensis*" (1890) *Analecta Bollandiana* 9: 250–62.

Prinz, F. (1965) *Frühes Mönchtum im Frankenreich: Kutlur und Gesellschaft in Gallien, den Rheinlanden und Bayern am Beispiel der monastischen Entwicklung.* Vienna, Oldenbourg.

Prinz, F. (1981) "Columbanus, the Frankish Nobility and the Territories East of the Rhine." In H. B. Clarke and M. Brennan (eds.), *Columbanus and Merovingian Monasticism.* BAR International Series 113. Oxford, BAR, 73–87.

Ratpert (2002) *St. Galler Klostergeschichten (Casus sancti Galli).* In H. Steiner (ed.), *Scriptores rerum Germanicarum in usum scholarum saparatim editi,* 75. MGH. Hanover, Hahnsche Buchhandlung, 135–239.

Richter, M. (2008) *Bobbio in the Early Middle Ages: The Abiding Legacy of Columbanus.* Dublin, Four Courts Press.

Rohr, C. (2015) "Die Columbansvita und die Gallusviten als Quellen zur Mensch-Natur-Beziehung im Frühmittelalter." In F. Schnoor et al. (eds.), *Gallus und seine Zeit: Leben, Wirken, Nachleben.* Sankt Gallen, Verlag am Klosterhof, 19–38.

Schär, M. (2012) *Gallus: der Heilige in seiner Zeit.* Basel, Schwabe Verlag.

Schär, M. (2015) "Gallus' Eremitensiedlung im Steinachwald." In F. Schnoor et al. (eds.), *Gallus und seine Zeit: Leben, Wirken, Nachleben.* Sankt Gallen, Verlag am Klosterhof, 183–204.

Schindler, M. P. (2015) "Neue archäologische Erkenntnisse zu St. Gallen." In F. Schnoor et al. (eds.), *Gallus und seine Zeit: Leben, Wirken und Nachleben.* Sankt Gallen, Verlag am Klosterhof, 205–22.

Schwitter, R. (2011) "Zur Entstehungszeit der ältesten Teile der 'Vita s. Galli.'" *Mittellateinisches Jahrbuch* 46: 185–200.

Schwitter, R. (2015) "Vom Einsiedler zum Apostel Alemanniens: Karolingische 'réécriture hagiographique' am Beispiel der Vita sancti Galli." In F. Schnoor et al. (eds.), *Gallus in seiner Zeit: Leben, Wirken, Nachleben.* Sankt Gallen, Verlag am Klosterhof, 267–82.

Settipani, C. (1993) *La Préhistoire des Capétiens: 481–987.* Villeneuve d'Ascq, Patrick van Kerrebrouck.

Settipani, C. (2014) *Les ancêtres de Charlemagne.* 2nd edition. Paris, Prosopographia et Genealogica.

Shaw, P. A. (2002) "Uses of Wodan: The Development of his Cult and of Medieval Literary Responses to It." PhD thesis, University of Leeds.

Stancliffe, C. E. (2011) "Columbanus's Monasticism and the Sources of his Inspiration: From Basil to the Master?" In F. Edmonds and P. Russell (eds.), *Tome: Studies in Medieval Celtic History and Law in Honour of Thomas Charles-Edwards.* Studies in Celtic History, 31. Woodbridge, Boydell, 17–28.

Venantius Fortunatus (1888) *Vita Radegundis,* In B. Krusch (ed.), *Scriptores rerum Merovingicarum* 2. MGH. Hanover, Hahnsche Buchhandlung, 364–77.

Vita Agili abbatis Resbacensis (1743) In *Acta Sanctorum Aug.* VI. Antwerp, Bernard Albert van Plassche, 574–87.

Vita Amandi I (1910) In B. Krusch (ed.), *Scriptores rerum Merovingicarum* 5. MGH. Hanover, Hahnsche Buchhandlung, 428–49.

Vita Sadalbergae abbatissae Laudunensis (1910) In B. Krusch (ed.), *Scriptores rerum Merovingicarum* 5. MGH. Hannover, Hahnsche Buchhandlung, 40–66.

Vitae vetustissimae fragmentum (1902) In B. Krusch (ed.), *Scriptores rerum Merovingicarum* 4. MGH. Hanover, Hahnsche Buchhandlung, 251–56.

Walahfrid (1902) *Vita sancti Galli.* In B. Krusch (ed.), *Scriptores rerum Merovingicarum* 4. MGH. Hannover, Hahnsche Buchhandlung, 280–337.

Wood, I. N. (1982) "The *Vita Columbani* and Merovingian Hagiography." *Peritia* 1: 63–80.

Wood, I. N. (2001) *The Missionary Life: Saints and the Evangelisation of Europe, 400–1050.* Harlow, Longman.

Wood, I. N. (2015) "The Irish on the Continent in the Seventh Century." In F. Schnoor et al. (eds.), *Gallus und seine Zeit: Leben, Wirken, Nachleben.* Sankt Gallen, Verlag am Klosterhof, 39–54.

Wood, S. (2006) *The Proprietary Church in the Medieval West.* Oxford, Oxford University Press.

Zironi, A. (2004) *Il monastero longobardo di Bobbio: Crocevia di uomini, manoscritti e culture.* Spoleto, Centro italiano di studi sull'alto medioevo.

Zöllner, E. (1965) "Die Herkunft der Agilulfinger." In K. Bosl (ed.), *Zur Geschichte der Bayern.* Darmstadt, Wissenschaftliche Buchgesellschaft, 107–34.

13

Quicumque sunt rebelles, foras exeant!

Columbanus's Rebellious Disciple Gallus

PHILIPP DÖRLER

The Irish monk and missionary Columbanus is one of the most important figures in the Christianization of Europe in the early seventh century. His foundations and the many new monasteries established in the years following his death have been well studied. However, one of Columbanus's disciples is rarely discussed in this context: Gallus. He is, of course, no stranger, as he is well-known as the founder of the hermitage at the Steinach, where later the important monastery of St Gallen was founded. Yet Gallus is never considered an important part of the Columbanian monastic network, most likely because Gallus himself did not found a monastery.[1] It was almost another century later that Otmar established the monastery of St. Gallen, in 719. The monastery's foundation legend, however, links the monastery with Gallus and presents him as Columbanus's best-known rebellious disciple.[2]

This chapter focuses on the role Gallus played within the Columbanian movement and investigates the relationship between Gallus and the wider Columbanian *familia*. Why did the author of the first life of Gallus, the *Vita Vetustissima*, link his saint with Columbanus although their collaboration ended in conflict? And why did Gallus, unlike Columbanus, manage to settle in the Lake Constance region and to establish a long-lasting community at the river Steinach after a rift had developed between Columbanus and Gallus and after his teacher did not receive political support from the local rulers as well as from the Merovingian dynasty anymore? Which role did Gallus's foundation and its cooperation with the policymakers play in the implementation of Frankish or Alamannic power and influence in the Lake Constance region?

1. Without Columbanus's foundations "[h]is brief time as a missionary among Germanic pagans and heretics may well have had no enduring consequences." Bullough 1997: 28.

2. Locally the situation is quite different; in St. Gallen, Arbon, and Bregenz, Gallus is of great significance. This is confirmed by the local cult, veneration, and numerous publications for the broader public. See the publications on the occasion of the Gallus anniversaries celebrated in Arbon, St. Gallen and Bregenz: Schnoor 2015; *Ferment* 2 2012; Frei 2012; Katholische Kirchengemeinde Arbon 2012; Schmuki et al. 2011; Schär 2011; Schmid 2011; and Dörler et al. 2010 . See also Hilty 1997; Burmeister 1996; Duft 1966.

Unfortunately, we have hardly any sources for the early days of Gallus's foundation. The oldest text on Gallus is the *Vita Columbani*. Jonas, the author of the *Vita*, mentions Gallus only twice. We do not know for sure whether or not the monk mentioned in the *Vita Columbani* is the same Gallus who later founded the hermitage at the river Steinach.[3] Besides this, our most important source is the so-called *Vita Vetustissima*. This text was written by an anonymous author and is preserved in fragments. This makes dating difficult. Recent attempts have shown that the text was written in the early days of the monastery, between 720 and 725.[4]

Yet we can reconstruct the content of the *Vita Vetustissima* with sufficient certainty because we have two Carolingian revised versions of the same *Life*. Both texts rely heavily on the *Vetustissima*. The older text was written by the Reichenau monk Wetti, and just a few years later another reworked text was produced by Walahfrid Strabo that follows the *Vetustissima* even more closely. In the following discussion I use the fragments of the *Vita Vetustissima* as well as Walahfrid's revision for my line of argument.

What do we know about the composition of the *Vita Vetustissima*? There is not much known about the origin of the text. Concerning the author and the place of writing, we only have vague theories. Walter Berschin suggests St Gallen, whereas Michael Richter recently suggested Bobbio as the place of composition.[5] Taking the dating as well as the purpose of the work into account, it appears that the text was written at least in the sphere of influence of the St Gallen monastery.[6]

There is more to say about the *Vita Galli* by Walahfrid Strabo. Under Abbot Gozbert (816–837) St. Gallen became an imperial abbey and therefore independent from the bishopric of Constance (818). This new self-conception manifests itself in the *Life* written by Wetti sometime between 816 and 824. Yet the monastic community does not appear to have been satisfied with Wetti's version, and so Wetti's disciple Walahfrid was commissioned to write a more stylish version of the saint's life. It was not Walahfrid's intention to amend the

3. See the discussion on Gallus's historicity. Cf. Lieb 1952; Hebling and Hebling 1962; Lieb 1967: 81–83; and recently Richter 2009. Richter pleads for a monk from Luxeuil, as Jonas mainly bases his conclusions on information provided by Luxovian monks and he also mentions that Gallus often told him this story (Richter 2009: 138).

4. I do not follow Müller (1972) and Berschin (1986, 2007, 2012), who argue for an early dating, but Krusch (1902) and Schwitter (2011: 196). Schwitter argues for a dating to the early days of Abbot Otmar. With regard to content, he elaborates that there is no reason for the *Life*'s focus on the possessory relations of the young monastery in the 680s.

5. Berschin 1975; Richter 2009. St. Gallen as the *Life*'s place of origin is persuasive. Richter does not provide any evidence for his assumption.

6. Zironi 2004.

content. Both Wetti and Walahfrid Carolingianized the *Vetustissima* as they minimized the Alamannian element in the text.[7]

If we assume that Gallus presumably died sometime around 640 and we follow Raphael Schwitter's explanations about the dating of the text, then we have a gap of some eighty years between the saint's death and the writing of the text.[8] The *Vita Vetustissima* reports on the circumstances and necessities of the early eighth century. We have to bear this in mind when we want to say something about Gallus and the situation in his time.

The structure of the *Vita Vetustissima* is untypical for a saint's life in many respects. First, in all probability it begins with Gallus's teacher Columbanus and not with the saint himself. In the first few chapters the *Vita Vetustissima* is heavily dependent on Jonas's *Vita Columbani*, although it does not directly quote from it. The earliest surviving manuscript of the *Vita Columbani*, however, is a St. Gallen manuscript form the middle of the ninth century. It also includes the only copy of Wetti's *Vita Galli*.[9]

The independent narrative only starts with the joint missionary works in Tuggen and the onward journey from Lake Zurich to Arbon and Bregenz. Walahfrid reports:

And the blessed Gallus, a disciple of the holy man, equipped with faith, set the temples, where they sacrificed to the demons, on fire and threw all offerings he found into the lake. Out of anger and hate about that, they followed the saints and planned by mutual agreement to kill Gallus and to whip Columbanus and to banish him in disgrace from their region.[10]

Similarly, in Arbon it is not Columbanus but Gallus who speaks: "After they have had a rest, Gallus proclaimed the Word of God at the behest of Columbanus and revealed the truth of faith."[11] And again, on the initiative of Columbanus, it is Gallus who preaches when the monks reach Bregenz: "Columbanus assigned the blessed Gallus to lead back the people from the heretical belief of idolatry to the worship of God by salutary warning."[12] At this point Gallus emerges from

---

7. Berschin 1991: 286.

8. Schwitter 2011.

9. Stiftsbibliothek St. Gallen 2012, 553.

10. *Beatus quoque Gallus sancti viri discipulus, zelo pietatis armatus, fana, in quibus daemoniis sacrificabant, igni succendit, et quaecumque invenit oblata, dimersit in lacum. Qua causa permoti ira et invidia, sanctos insectabantur et communi consilio Gallum perimere voluerunt, Columbanum vero flagellis caesum et contumeliis affectum de suis finibus proturbare: Vita Galli I.4.*

11. *Postquam vero recubuerunt, iussione abbatis Gallus divina recitavit eloquia, profunda reserans veritas: Vita Galli I.5.*

12. *Columbanus itaque beato Gallo id iniunxit officii, ut populum ab errore idolatriae ad cultum Dei exhortation salutary revocaret, quia ipse hanc a Domino gratiam meruit: Vita Galli I.6.*

the shadows of his teacher for the first time. It is he who preaches on behalf of Columbanus. Interestingly, these fruitless mission attempts are not mentioned in the *Vita Columbani*. Why they appear in the *Lives of Gallus* has to be answered at a later point. In the *Vita Columbani*, however, the procurement of food for the monks is paramount in the Bregenz episode.

Second, the narration of Gallus's rift with his teacher and his subsequent excommunication is very unusual for a saint's life and adds to its veracity as a source. When Columbanus departs from Bregenz, Gallus stays, as he is ill with fever.[13] Columbanus commands him: "As long as I am alive, you shall not celebrate Mass."[14]

Even though Walahfrid does not explicitly mention excommunication in his version of the *Life*, it can safely be assumed that the *Vita Vetustissima* was referring to just such an excommunication when the monks of Bobbio delivered Columbanus's *baculum*, his abbatial staff, after his death to Gallus with the following comment: "During his lifetime, our master ordered that this crook should absolve Gallus of his excommunication."[15]

I completely agree with Walter Berschin that we can see this as definitive proof of Gallus's historicity.[16] The saint's excommunication is the decisive factor in Gallus's historicity. Yet there are also other cases of excommunicated saints, or saints against whom excommunication was threatened. The excommunication of Columba in his *Life* written by Adomnán is only one example, but in this case the excommunication was imposed on the saint by a synod and was later withdrawn.[17] Gallus is the only saint who was excommunicated by his own master because of disobedience. The saint abides by the rules and is therefore restricted in his religious observance. However, we have to take into consideration what *excommunicatio* meant in the early Middle Ages. In contrast to Carolingian times, there were two forms of excommunication in the early Middle Ages, according to Walter Berschin: a severe and a less severe one.[18] In the case of Gallus, its extent was somewhere in between. Columbanus, as his superior, simply banned Gallus as a priest from celebrating the Eucharist. The Carolingian revisers were not aware of the situation's severity anymore and therefore could easily delete the word *excommunicatio* and thereby tone down the situation.[19] For the author of the *Vita Vetustissima* this was obviously not

---

13. See Fox, chapter 12 in this volume, for the political context.

14. *Ne, me vivente in corpore, missam celebrare praesumas: Vita Galli* I.9.

15. *Dominus noster iussit nobis adhuc uiuens, ut per istum baculum Gallus fuisset absolutus ab excommunicatione: Vita Vetustissima* 1.

16. Berschin 1975: 273.

17. Adomnán, *Vita Columbae* III.4.

18. Berschin 1974: 132, 1986: 163.

19. Rohr 2001: 44.

possible. Probably the fact that Gallus had been excommunicated was still very present in the fledgling monastery. The *Vita Vetustissima* therefore had to justify Gallus's excommunication. Only later was Gallus stylized as the apostle of Alamannia; in the *Vita Vetustissima* Gallus's fever had the simple function of proving that Gallus was not simply disobedient, but that it was God's will that he stayed behind in the Lake Constance region. Despite the harshness of the reprimand, Gallus accepts the excommunication and remains in order to continue Columbanus's work in his own manner. With Columbanus's departure over the Alps for Italy, Gallus's missionary activity comes to an end.[20]

The conflict between the master and disciple enabled Gallus to plough his own furrow. Gallus is thus a successful representative of those other Columbanian disciples who broke with their master because of his severity.[21] Eventually, after Columbanus's death, the excommunication was lifted, and Gallus even received Columbanus's *baculum* as a sign of forgiveness and possibly designating him as Columbanus's successor instead of Athala, who became the second abbot of Bobbio.[22] The rift with his teacher also leads us to the core of the *Vita*. In the following chapters, the *Vita* reports on Gallus's hermitage by the river Steinach, on the healing of the Alamannic duke's daughter Fridburga through Gallus, and on the events concerning the elections of the bishop of Constance—in all of which the saint played a key role. The chronology and historicity of all the mentioned events have been heavily discussed.

Let us start with the historicity:

For this purpose they [the inhabitants of Bregenz] proceeded to the duke of the region, whose name was Gunzo, and accused the saints by saying that the public hunting was disturbed by the foreigners in that place. When he heard this, the duke enraged, sent messengers and ordered the servants of God to leave this place.[23]

---

20. Schwitter 2011: 193.

21. Gallus was not the only rebellious disciple. Richter convincingly argues that Abbot Athala was pushed out from Luxeuil and had to flee to Bobbio after a rebellion in the monastery took place. The severe Columbanian rule was loosened under Eustasius after Attala had left. Columbanus mentions the *rebelles* in a letter to the Frankish monks that reads like a response to a letter from Athala: *Quicumque sunt rebelles, foras exeant; quicumque sunt obedientes, ipsi fiant heredes.* ("Whoever are rebellious, let them depart away; whoever are obedient, let it be they who become my heirs." *Ep.* 4.3). Richter 2008: 53–5. Cf. Cugnier 2005. See also Diem, chapter 15 in this volume.

22. Schär 2011: 362.

23. *Qua etiam intentione locorum ipsorum ducem nomine Gunzonem adierunt et apud eum accusaverunt sanctos, dicentes, venationem publicam in eisdem locis propter illorum infestationem peregrinorum esse turbatam. Quo audito, dux furore succensus, missis nuntiis, famulos Dei de loco eodem discedere iussit: Vita Galli* I.8.

If we assume that Gallus is a historical character, then we can also assume that the hermitage at the river Steinach existed continuously from Gallus's lifetime until the foundation of the monastery in 719. The existence of hermitages at the site of subsequent monasteries can be shown at other places.[24] Yet the question concerning the relationship between Gallus and the Alamannic duke is more difficult to answer. This relationship is interesting in several respects. At first we have to answer the question of how it was possible for one of Columbanus's disciples to cooperate with the very same Duke Gunzo who had just expelled Columbanus from his region. It is likely that the foundation in Bregenz and the other monastic foundations of Columbanus were well-planned and supported by the local authorities. That Columbanus had to leave after a short time was probably not primarily related to his failed missionary attempts, but—as we know from the *Vita Columbani*[25]—to the death of his political patron Theudebert II and the coming to power of his brother, Theuderic II, from whom Columbanus had previously escaped from. Interestingly, the *Vita Galli* mentions another reason for the departure of the Columbanian community. The text continues:

> However, that does not satisfy the demons' companions, they also steal one of their cows and lead it into an inaccessible part of the woods. When two of the brothers follow their track, the thieves leap out, kill them, rob them and disappear.[26]

Given that the veneration of Gallus was regional, it does not come as a surprise that the motive for the banishment of the community was motivated by local politics. Yet the very same Gunzo who supported the hermitage later on was probably responsible for Columbanus's departure from the Lake Constance region. The two reasons are not contradictory, particularly as we can assume that the Alamannic duke was inaugurated by the king and the duke's rights were strongly restricted by the king. No definite statements can be made, as Gunzo is not mentioned in a document.[27] The influence of the Merovingian kings in early medieval Alamannia decreased from the 650s onward due to their loss of power, and the Alamannic dukes ruled more or less independently of the Frankish kings after 700.[28]

---

24. Cf. Borst 2010: 52.
25. *Vita Columbani* I.28.
26. *Sed neque hoc sufficit satellitibus daemonum, quin etiam vaccam eorum furto abstrahentes, in invia ducunt silvarum. Quos cum duo de fratribus e vestigio insecuntur, consurgentes latrunculi, interficiunt eos, et auferentes spolia eorum, discedunt:Vita Galli* I.8.
27. Borgolte 1986.
28. Niederstätter 1997: 216; Schär 2008: 351–2.

However, it seems that the account the life gives of Gunzo is historically wrong. It is likely that the Alamannic duke who expelled the Columbanian community was Gunzo's predecessor, Uncelen.[29] Or Gunzo was just politically powerful enough to protect Gallus. Following Hagen Keller, the first option becomes even more plausible; I think we also have to adjust the inner chronology of the *Vita*. As Hagen Keller has convincingly argued, the events in the *Life* were interchanged. The events of the episcopal elections as well as the story of the duke's daughter Fridburga did probably take place many years after Columbanus's death in the 640s. The fact that Ratpert mentions that Talto, King Dagobert's chamberlain, supported Gallus, provides further proof of this assumption.[30]

This means that there is practically no information about the early period of the hermitage. Between Columbanus's death in 615 and the events of the healing of Fridburga would be a gap of approximately two decades (with the exception of the information given by the *Vita* that monks from Luxeuil came to Gallus after Eustasius's death to offer him the abbacy of Luxeuil[31]).

The fact that we do not have any information about the early days is not surprising, given that Gallus as a disciple of Columbanus very possibly did not get any strong support from the Alamannic duke once Columbanus had left. Uncelen/Gunzo did no more than tolerate Gallus. Uncelen died in 613. The recent political change after the sudden death of King Theuderic II in the same year did improve the situation for Gallus. Brunhild did not succeed in establishing Theuderic's son Sigibert II as his successor, and King Chlothar II took over power in Austrasia. Already after the banishment from the Vosges, Chlothar had stood up for Columbanus's remaining in Gaul and had arranged to send him to Theudebert II. Thus, only one year after Columbanus's departure, a key patron of the Columbanian communities once again held sway in the Lake Constance region. From this point on, Gunzo could support Gallus's hermitage.

At that point, Columbanus had founded the monastery of Bobbio and was not willing to return to the Frankish kingdom. The attempt to get Columbanus to return through the agency of Eustasius of Luxeuil met with no success.[32] So we can reasonably assume that Chlothar II supported Gallus's hermitage.

After 613 Merovingian kings showed a more sustained interest in Alamannia. We do not know for sure if there was a *dux Alamannorum* between 610 and 630

---

29. Cf. Schär 2011: 225.
30. Talto is described as *Tagoberti scilicet regis camararius et postea comes eiusdem pagi* in the *Casus Sancti Galli* (Ratpert I.4). Cf. Keller 1976; Borgolte 1986: 242.
31. *Vita Galli* I.28.
32. *VC* I.30

for the whole of Alamannia.[33] By all means available, the kings themselves were intensively engaged in the political organization of Alamannia. The ecclesiastical reorganization under Chlothar's son Dagobert I played an important role in this process. Perhaps the bishopric of Vindonissa (Windisch) was transferred to Constance at that time.[34] With Dagobert we also arrive at the time when the bishop's election and the events of Gunzo and his daughter took place. The *Vita* tells us that the duke's daughter Fridburga asked the king: "I beg you, master, to support that man [Gallus] with your kind grace . . . (*Obsecro, domine, ut virum ipsum tuae gratiae foveas lenitate*)."[35]

The marriage of Fridburga and Sigibert III is proof of the strong relationship between the Alamannic dukes and the Merovingian kings and the important role Alamannia played at that time.[36] Sigibert is also known as a supporter of Columbanian communities.[37] In this respect, this marriage tie is definitely conceivable. However, that King Dagobert accepted without further ado that Gunzo's daughter canceled the marriage seems unlikely. Thus, we have to assume that the author invented the marriage in the 720s to establish a direct connection between his saint and the royal family. What is more, by doing so he could show that a connection to God and a saint was even more important than a connection to the royal family. At the same time, he could support the political independence of the Alamannic dukes. This marriage strengthened Gunzo's political power.[38]

The important role of Gallus in this story is interesting. Not only is Gallus directly connected with the families of the duke and the king, but these connections are obviously hierarchically organized: the duke is dependent on the saint, and the king accepts Fridburga's decision without question and consequently also the influence of the saint. The *Vita* therefore gives the impression that Gallus received absolute political aid from the Frankish as well as from the Alamannic rulers.

Besides the events of Fridburga's planned marriage, the *Vita* also reports on the episcopal elections of Constance at several points. This relation of gratitude and dependence is also shown when Gallus repeatedly rejects his appointment as bishop and pushes through his own protégé, John. In this regard, Gallus is acting very much like Columbanus's disciple. First, Gallus is asked to accept the bishopric after the bishop's death due to the duke's gratitude for his daughter's

---

33. Niederstätter 1997: 215–6.
34. Keller 1976: 13–14; cf. Prinz 1981.
35. *Vita Galli* I.21.
36. Fox, chapter 12 in this volume.
37. The support of Remaclus of Luxeuil is a good example; cf. Noël 1991.
38. Schär 2011: 224.

healing, but Gallus refuses to accept on the grounds that Columbanus is still alive.[39] Several years later at a ducal synod, he declines again and recommends his disciple, John.[40] Interestingly, there is no evidence of the king's influence on the election. Either Gunzo acted on behalf of the king or this would be another proof of the duke's strength in Alamannia.[41]

However, the events as reported in the *Vita* illustrate that not only the political rulers but also the bishopric of Constance are hierarchically dependent on Gallus, as the saint is on amicable terms with the bishop he puts forward. Taking into account that the bishopric of Constance was possibly not transferred from Vindonissa (Windisch) to Constance in 585–590 but under the reign of Dagobert, then it is dependent on St Gallen from the very beginning, according to the *Vita*.[42] Only after all these events does the *Vita* report on Columbanus's death: "until you get to the monastery of Bobbio and thoroughly obtain all details, that happened to my abbot, if he is still alive or if he died as it was revealed to me in a vision."[43]

Gallus hears of his teacher's death through a vision in his dream. That Gallus uses two different excuses for why he cannot be appointed as bishop could indicate that Columbanus died at an earlier date. When he was asked for the first time, Gallus replied that Columbanus was still alive; the second time, he stated that he was unsuitable because he was not born in the country. It can therefore be expected that Columbanus was already dead, at least when Gallus was asked the second time.

Why did the author modify the sequence of events? By doing so, he framed his two main stories—namely the story of the episcopal election and the healing of Fridburga—with events linked to Columbanus. Chapter I.26 reports on Columbanus's death in 615 and chapter I.28 on Eustasius's death in 629, and thereby the author links the monasteries of Bobbio as well as Luxeuil with the hermitage at the river Steinach just before reporting on the death of Gallus. This emphasizes that the hermitage was an essential part of the Columbanian monastic network.[44]

---

39. *Vita Galli* I.19.
40. *Vita Galli* I.24.
41. Schär 2011: 273.
42. Cf. Keller 1976: 18–22; Maurer 1993: 238–41. The episcopal list of 1143–1144 mentions a bishop Martianus before John, who would be the third bishop of Constance (*Series Episcoporum Constantiensium*, 325).
43. [U]sque dum veniens ad Bobium monasterium, et exquire Omnia diligenter, que acta sunt erga abbatem meum, si vivit an transivit, sicut mihi revelatum est per visionem: *Vita Vetustissima* 1.
44. Zironi 2004.

The juxtaposition of the three deaths could possibly also emphasize something else. Gallus came into conflict with his master and went his own way; so it also appears did Eustasius. It was Eustasius who was responsible for modifying Columbanus's monastic practices at Luxeuil. It was under his abbacy that he established the less severe *regula mixta* in Luxeuil, after his predecessor, Athala, had to flee to Bobbio following a rebellion among the Luxeuil monks. In the eyes of the author, both Gallus and Eustasius were competent successors to Columbanus.[45] Yet Gallus was offered not only the abbacy of Luxeuil but also Columbanus's abbatial staff.

What does this tell us about the aim of the *Vita Vetustissima* and Gallus's relationship to the wider Columbanian familia? Apart from the use of the *Vita Columbani* in the first chapters of the *Life*, we do not have additional evidence for a close relationship between the monasteries. Neither does the author tell us much about the monastic life in the Steinach hermitage. We do not know whether the *Regula Columbani* was in use there or not. The only thing we can say is that—in contrast to the *Vita Columbani*—obedience does not play an important role in the *Vita Vetustissima*. The period the *Vita* does tell us about is the period of the political reorganization of Alamannia.[46]

From another perspective, Gallus does not play an important role in Jonas's *Vita Columbani*. Jonas tells us about Gallus:

> At another time he was staying in the same wilderness, but not in the same place. Fifty days had already elapsed and only one of the brethren named Gallus was with him. Columbanus commanded Gallus to go to the Breuchin and catch fish. The latter went, took his boat and went to the Ognon river. After he had gotten there, and had thrown his net into the water he saw a great number of fish coming. But they were not caught in the net, and went off again as if they had struck a wall. After working there all day and not being able to catch a fish, he returned and told the father that his labour had been in vain. The latter scolded him for his disobedience in not going to the right place. Finally he said, "Go quickly to the place that you were ordered to try." Gallus went accordingly, placed his net in the water, and it was filled with so great a number of fish, that he could scarcely draw it. This did Gallus often tell us.[47]

---

45. VC II.10 and *Vita Galli* I.28 do not mention this event.
46. Cf. Keller 1976; Niederstätter 1997.
47. *Aliaque vice cum in eadem solitudine moraretur, non tamen eo in loco, iamque quinquaginta dies transierant, unusque tantum e fratribus cum eo erat Gallus nomine; cui ille imperat, ut ad Bruscam eat piscesque capiat. Ille abiit ratumque duxit, ut ad Lignonem amnem pergeret. Quo cum pervenisset, retem in alveum iactavisset, aspicit tantam multitudinem advenire nec prorsus retem tenere, sed, velut in parietem inpingerent, retro revertere. Laboravit itaque per totam diem neve unum capere quivit; reversus,*

Interestingly, this episode is immediately followed by a story about monks suffering from fever. Both episodes remind us of the importance of obedience to the abbot.[48] Gallus's disobedience is already evident in Jonas's account of Gallus. Irrespective of whether the Gallus in the *Vita Columbani* is the same person as the Gallus in the *Vita Vetustissima*,[49] we can take it for granted that the author of the *Vita Vetustissima* wants us to believe that he is referring to the same saint. The episode of the fishing saint is formative for the Gallus of the *Vita Vetustissima*, as it uses the motif of the fisher several times. The author describes the first time in Bregenz, when Gallus meets demons on Lake Constance: "And once, when he casted his nets into the lake, in the silence of the night he could hear a demon loudly calling another one by name from the top of the mountain close by, as if that one stayed in the lake."[50]

The second time the author mentions Gallus as a fisherman is in chapter I.28, when he wants to prepare a meal for the Luxeuil monks who visit him:

> [H]e himself took the net and one of his disciples, he went to the whirl-pool with the brothers, who had unexpectedly arrived, and said: "Let us see, if the compassionate Lord gives us some small fish to remedy our shortage."[51]

Yet if Gallus—as the *Vita Vetustissima* wants us to believe—enjoyed such a good reputation in the Columbanian monasteries that he was tipped as Columbanus's successor[52] and known personally to Jonas,[53] why is he not mentioned more prominently in the *Vita Columbani*? Is the answer simply because—as Rohr would argue[54]—his hermitage merely played a minor role within the Columbanian community? Or did Jonas say nothing about Gallus's excommunication precisely because he did not want to denigrate Gallus, whose activities

---

patri renuntiat de frustrato labore. Ille inoboedientem increpat, cur non ad denuntiatum locum properasset, aitque denuo: "Vade cito et ad denuntiatum perge locum." Pervenit itaque et undis rete opposuit, tantaque piscium copia est rete impletum, ut vix prae multitudine trahi potuisset. Haec nobis supra dictus Gallus sepe narravit: VC I.11.

48. *VC* I.12. Cf. Rohr 2001: 40.

49. Cf. footnote 3.

50. *Et dum quodam tempore retia sua mitteret in pelagus, in silentio noctis audivit daemonem magno vocis strepitu de vertice montis proximi vocantem quondam alterum nominatim, quasi in pelage commorantem: Vita Galli* I.7.

51. *[I]pse sumens rete et unum ex discipulis suis, cum fratribus qui supervenerant ivit ad gurgitem, dicens: "Videamus, utrum misericors Dominus aliquos nostris velit necessitatibus largiri pisciculos": Vita Galli* I.28.

52. Schär 2011: 362.

53. Cf. *VC* I.11: *Haec nobis supra dictus Gallus sepe narravit.* ("This did Gallus often tell us.")

54. Rohr 2001: 30.

in the Steinach do correspond to the Columbanian communities at the time of Jonas?

Most likely Gallus is not mentioned because the episode in Bregenz "reflected poorly on Columbanus and Gallus,"[55] as Richter noted. Jonas also did not mention the unsuccessful missionary attempts around Lake Zurich in Tuggen.[56] This failure might be an explanation for why Jonas did not mention these events. We know that Jonas also refrained from mentioning other controversial topics and was reticent in writing about people who were still alive (Abbess Burgundofara being a case in point). If we did not have Columbanus's own writings, we would know about neither the controversy over the dating of Easter[57] nor Columbanus's confrontation with the Gallic bishops.[58]

Why did the *Vita Vetustissima* add the events in Tuggen to the narrative? On first impression, Gallus does not seem to be very successful in his own *Vita*. What is the purpose of these episodes in the *Vita Vetustissima*? In my opinion, they fulfill two different functions. On the one hand, they provide the opportunity for Gallus to emerge from the shadows of his master. Gallus becomes the active player in his own drama. This is why the author emphasizes that Gallus spoke to the people in their own language.[59] The close relation to Columbanus—which is documented in the historical record—closely connects him to the Irish tradition. The episode is relevant for the author to show that Gallus asserted his independence from Columbanus and developed his own apostolate in the region.

On the other hand, the episode initiates the failure of Columbanian missionary work in the Lake Constance region and therefore supports the independent development of the disciple.[60] In the Vosges, Columbanus becomes visible not as a missionary, but as an abbot. This changes after the royal mission mandate that he gets from the Frankish king Theudebert II in 610. From now on he has to actively do missionary work.[61]

It would be going too far to say that the author of the *Vita Vetustissima* wants to criticize Columbanus by mentioning these episodes. Yet we can see

55. Richter 2002: 66.

56. *Vita Galli* I.4.

57. Columbanus, *Epp.* 1–3; Suso 1975: 171–5.

58. The *Vita Columbani* shows the conflicts only by subtle signals; cf. *VC* I.19.

59. To deduce that he is of Gallic origin from such evidence is as pointless as to prove the opposite by stating that only Irish kinsmen were allowed to follow Columbanus when he left Luxeuil, as we know that some monks joined him later. The question on Gallus's origin must remain open, but in my opinion it is not relevant. The important point is that the historical tradition remembers him as an Irishman.

60. As Columbanus felt free to depart from the teachings of his Irish masters, so Gallus may have thought likewise. Cf. Fox, chapter 12 in this volume.

61. Cf. O'Hara 2013, 2015 on Columbanus's monastic foundations.

that Columbanus as well as Gallus afterward did go back to the well-tried practices. Columbanus founded a monastery in Bobbio and Gallus a hermitage by the river Steinach. Both Columbanus and Gallus might have realized that their practice of missionary work could not succeed. This can explain that the hermitage founded by Gallus—at least according to the *Vita*—is reminiscent of an Irish monastery like Bangor. Gallus recognized the errors made in Tuggen and Bregenz and thus returned to former practices. Although only indirectly, we know that Gallus was not the only monk from the Columbanian communities who broke with Columbanus,[62] but by the foundation of his hermitage and its later fame as a monastic center he became Columbanus's best-known disciple.

The political circumstances soon allowed Gallus to gain a foothold in the region of Alamannia. Like Columbanus in the Vosges, Gallus could count on the support of the dynasty and the local potentates. Whereas in his early years his rift with Columbanus was important for his political survival, later on it became important once again to connect to his Columbanian past.

Gallus's relationship to Columbanus remained ambiguous, not least posthumously. According to the *Vita Vetustissima* Gallus had to fight hard for his independence, and he did distance himself from his master. At the same time, the author of his *Vita* skillfully tried to intertwine the lives of the two saints even after Columbanus had died. Gallus is presented to us as one of his disciples and his successor. Justification for Gallus's maverick disobedience and legitimization for Gallus as Columbanus's true successor were both equally important tasks of the *Vita*.

The unusual and unorthodox representation of Gallus in his *Vita* is the strongest argument for the important role Columbanus and his monasticism played in St. Gallen. The monastery remained an important center for preserving the memory of Columbanus and the Columbanian network; the later monastery's rich manuscript evidence is the best indication for this. When Otmar founded the monastery of St Gallen in 719, these kind of monasteries were highly attractive: both Luxeuil and Bobbio were exempted from episcopal supervision in 628, an exemption that would secure the monastery's independence from the bishopric of Constance. At the same time, the monastery of St. Gallen had to safeguard its preeminence in respect to the new neighboring Carolingian monasteries of Reichenau (724) and Pfäfers (735/740), and one way they did this was by looking back to the roots of their foundation in the seventh century and to Columbanus's rebellious disciple.

---

62. Richter 2009: 136.

ACKNOWLEDGMENTS

The research leading to these results has received funding from the European
Research Council under the European Union's Seventh Framework Programme
(FP7/2007-2013)/ERC grant agreement No. 269591.

BIBLIOGRAPHY

Adomnán (1991) *Vita Sancti Columbae*, ed. Alan Orr Anderson/Marjorie Ogilvie Anderson.
   Adomnán's Life of Columba. Oxford, Oxford University Press.
Berschin, W. (1974) "Die Anfänge der lateinischen Literatur unter den Alemannen." In W.
   Hübener (ed.), *Die Alemannen in der Frühzeit*. Bühl, Konkordia, 128–33.
Berschin, W. (1975) "Gallus Abbas Vindicatus." *Historisches Jahrbuch* 95: 257–77.
Berschin, W. (1986) "Columban und Gallus in Bregenz." *Montfort: Vierteljahresschrift
   für Geschichte und Gegenwart Vorarlbergs* 38.2: 160–4; repr. *Mittellateinische Studien*
   1(2002): 57–64.
Berschin, W. (1991) *Biographie und Epochenstil im lateinischen Mittelalter. 3. Karolingische
   Biographie: 750–920 n. Chr.* Stuttgart, Hiersemann.
Berschin, W. (2005) *Eremus und Insula: St. Gallen und die Reichenau im Mittelalter. Modell
   einer lateinischen Literaturlandschaft.* Wiesbaden, Reichert.
Berschin, W (2007) "Die karolingische Vita S. Galli Metrica (BHL NR. 3253), Werk eines Iren
   für St. Gallen?" *Revue Bénédictine* 117: 9–30.
Berschin, W (2012) "Zur Entstehungszeit der ältesten Teile der Vita s. Galli." *Mittellateinisches
   Jahrbuch* 47.1: 1–4.
Borgolte, M. (1986) *Die Grafen Alemanniens in merowingischer und karolingischer Zeit: Eine
   Prosopographie.* Sigmaringen, Thorbecke.
Borst, A. (2010) *Mönche am Bodensee: Spiritualität und Lebensformen vom frühen Mittelalter
   bis zur Reformationszeit.* Lengwil-Oberhofen, Libelle.
Bullough, D. (1997) "The Career of Columbanus." In M. Lapidge (ed.), *Columbanus: Studies
   on the Latin Writings.* Woodbridge, Boydell Press, 1–28.
Burmeister, K. H. (1996) "Ohne Bregenz kein Sankt Gallen: Der Weg des heiligen Gallus von
   Bregenz nach Sankt Gallen." *Schriften des Vereins für Geschichte des Bodensees und seiner
   Umgebung* 114: 5–16.
Cugnier, G. (2005) *Histoire du monastère de Luxeuil à travers ses abbés, 590–1790,* vol. 1, *Les
   trois premiers siècles, 590–888.* Langres, Dominique Guéniot.
Dörler, P., T. Klagian, and K. Dörler (2010) *Kolumban und Gallus: Mitgestalter eines kulturellen
   Umbruchs.* Schriften der Vorarlberger Landesbibliothek 22. Graz, Neugebauer.
Duft, J. (1966) "Die Bregenzer Sankt Gallus-Glocke in Sankt Gallen." *Montfort: Vierteljahresschrift
   für Geschichte und Gegenwart Vorarlbergs* 18: 425–35.
Ferment 2 (2012) *Aus der Wildnis wächst Neues.*
Frank, K. S. (1975) *Frühes Mönchtum im Abendland,* vol. 2, *Lebensgeschichten.* Zürich, Artemis.
Frei, R. (ed.) (2012) *Gallus-Wege: Zu Fuß von Bangor nach Sankt Gallen.* Herisau, Appenzeller
   Verlag.
Hebling, B., and H. Hebling (1962) "Der heilige Gallus in der Geschichte." *Schweizerische
   Zeitschrift für Geschichte* 12: 1–62.
Hilty, G. (1997) "Gallus in Bregenz." *Mondo Ladino* 21: 473–90.

Katholische Kirchengemeinde Arbon (2012) *Festgehalten Gallus am Bodensee*. Arbon, Katholische Kirchengemeinde Arbon.

Keller, H. (1976) "Fränkische Herrschaft und alemannisches Herzogtum im 6. und 7. Jahrhundert." *Zeitschrift für die Geschichte des Oberrheins* 124: 1–30.

Krusch, B. (1902) "Vita Galli Confessoris Triplex." In B. Krusch (ed.), *Scriptores rerum Merovingicarum* 4. MGH. Hanover, Hahnsche Buchhandlung, 229–51.

Lieb, H. (1952) "Tuggen und Bodman: Bemerkungen zu zwei römischen Itinerarstationen." *Schweizerische Zeitschrift für Geschichte* 2: 386–95.

Lieb, H., and R. Wüthrich (1967) *Lexicon topographicum der römischen und frühmittelalterlichen Schweiz 1: Römische Zeit, Süd- und Ostschweiz*. Bonn, Habelt.

Maurer, H. (1993) "Das Bistum Konstanz: Die Bischöfe." In B. Degler-Spengler, R. Reinhardt and F. X. Bischof, (eds.), *Helvetia Sacra*, vol. 1.2, *Das Bistum Konstanz, Das Erzbistum Mainz, Das Bistum St. Gallen*. Basel, Helbing & Lichtenhahn, 229–494.

Müller, I. (1972) "Die älteste Gallus-Vita." *Zeitschrift für schweizerische Kirchengeschichte* 66: 209–49.

Niederstätter, A. (1997) "Alemannen, Romanen, Ostgoten und Franken in der Bodenseeregion." *Montfort: Vierteljahresschrift für Geschichte und Gegenwart Vorarlbergs* 49.3: 207–24.

Noël, R. (1991) "Moines et nature sauvage dans l'Ardenne du haut Moyen Âge: Saint Remacle à Cugnon et à Stavelot-Malmédy." In J.-M. Duvosquel and A. Dierkens (eds.), *Villes et campagnes au Moyen Âge: Mélanges Georges Despy*. Liège, Éditions du Perron, 563–97.

O'Hara, A. (2013) "*Patria, Peregrinatio*, and *Paenitentia*: Identities of Alienation in the Seventh Century." In W. Pohl and G. Heydemann (eds.), *Post-Roman Transitions: Christian and Barbarian Identities in the Early Medieval West*. Turnhout, Brepols, 89–124.

O'Hara, A. (2015) "Columbanus *ad locum*: The Establishment of the Monastic Foundations." *Peritia* 26: 143–70.

Prinz, F. (1981) "Columbanus, the Frankish Nobility and the Territories East of the Rhine." In H. Clarke and M. Brennan (eds.), *Columbanus and Merovingian Monasticism*. Oxford, BAR, 73–87.

Ratpert (2002) *St. Galler Klostergeschichte (Casus sancti Galli)*, ed. Hannes Steiner. MGH, *Scriptores rerum Germanicarum in usum scholarum separatim editi* 75. Hanover, Hahnsche Buchhandlung.

Richter, M. (2002) "St. Gallen and the Irish in the Early Middle Ages." In M. Richter and J.-M. Picard (eds.), *Ogma: Essays in Celtic Studies in honour of Próinséas Ní Chatháin*. Dublin, Four Courts Press, 65–75.

Richter, M. (2008) *Bobbio in the Early Middle Ages: The Abiding Legacy of Columbanus*. Dublin, Four Courts Press.

Richter, M. (2009) "Der Aufenthalt des Hl: Columban im Bodenseeraum." In D. Walz (ed.), *Irische Mönche in Süddeutschland: Literarisches und kulturelles Wirken der Iren im Mittelalter*. Heidelberg, Mattes, 131–42.

Rohr, C. (2001) "Columban-Vita versus Gallus-Viten? Überlegungen zur Entstehung, Funktion und Historizität hagiographischer Literatur des Frühmittelalters." In G. Ammerer, C. Rohr, A. S. Weiß (eds.), *Tradition und Wandel. Beiträge zur Kirchen-, Gesellschafts- und Kulturgeschichte: Festschrift für Heinz Dopsch*. München, Oldenbourg, 27–45.

Schär, M. (2008) "St. Gallen zwischen Gallus und Otmar 640–720." *Schweizerische Zeitschrift für Religions- und Kulturgeschichte* 102: 317–59.

Schär, M. (2011) *Gallus: Der Heilige in seiner Zeit*. Basel, Schwabe.

Schmid, C. (2011) *Gallusland: Auf den Spuren des Heiligen Gallus*. Freiburg, Paulusverlag.

Schmuki, K., F. Schnoor, and E. Tremp (eds.) (2011) *Der Heilige Gallus 612–2012: Leben— Legende—Kult; Katalog zur Jahresausstellung in der Stiftsbibliothek St. Gallen.* St. Gallen, Verlag am Klosterhof.

Schnoor, F., K. Schmuki, E. Tremp, P. Erhart, and J. K. Hüeblin (eds.) (2015) *Gallus und seine Zeit: Leben, Wirken, Nachleben.* St. Gallen, Verlag am Klosterhof.

Schwitter, R. (2011) "Zur Entstehungszeit der ältesten Teile der Vita s. Galli." *Mittellateinisches Jahrbuch* 46.2: 185–200.

Series Episcoporum Constantiensium (1881) In G. Waitz (ed.), *Scriptores* 13. MGH. Hanover, Hahnsche Buchhandlung, 324–5.

Stiftsbibliothek St. Gallen (2012) *Vita Sancti Galli Vetustissima: Die älteste Lebensbeschreibung des heiligen Gallus.* St. Gallen, Verlag am Klosterhof.

Vita Galli = Walahfrid Strabo (1902) *Vita Galli.* In B. Krusch (ed.), *Scriptores rerum Merovingicarum* 4. MGH. Hanover, Hahnsche Buchhandlung, 280–337.

Vita Vetustissima = *Vita Galli Vetustissima* (1902) In B. Krusch (ed.), *Scriptores rerum Merovingicarum* 4. MGH. Hanover, Hahnsche Buchhandlung, 251–56.

Wetti (1902) *Vita Galli.* In B. Krusch (ed.), *Scriptores rerum Merovingicarum* 4. MGH. Hanover, Hahnsche Buchhandlung, 256–80.

Zironi, A. (2004) *Il Monastero Longobardo di Bobbio: Crocevia di uomini, manoscritti e culture.* Spoleto, Fondazione centro italiano di studi sull'alto medioevo.

PART V

Lombard Italy and Columbanus's Legacy

14

Columbanus, Bobbio, and the Lombards

STEFANO GASPARRI

The impacts of Columbanus and Irish monasticism on the Lombard and Frankish kingdoms differed sharply, to the extent that Bobbio remained the only Columbanian monastery in Italy. This fact is well known, although a definitive explanation has yet to be provided.[1] One of the chief difficulties in finding such an explanation derives from the sheer scarcity of the Italian sources in the period between the end of the sixth and the beginning of the seventh centuries. Paul the Deacon, who is our main point of reference for the entire history of Lombard Italy from the invasion until the end of the reign of King Liutprand (744), writes, for example, about Arioald (626–635) that "very little about the deeds of this king have reached our notice." Something similar could be said of practically the entire period, with a few exceptions that we discuss below. Immediately after that statement, Paul describes the foundation of Bobbio itself:

> It was about this time that the blessed Columbanus, born of the Irish people, came to Italy after he had built a monastery at a place known as Luxeuil in Gaul. He was received joyfully by the king of the Lombards and built the monastery known as Bobbio in the Cottian Alps, which lies 40 miles away from the city of Ticinum. Many possessions were lavished on this place by different princes and other Lombards and here there developed a great congregation of monks.[2]

Besides this passage, Bobbio only appears on one other occasion in the *Historia Langobardorum*, in Paul's description of the provinces of Italy. The monastery is named as one of the major centers of the fifth province, the Cottian Alps, alongside Acqui, Tortona, Genoa, and Savona. Bobbio is the only nonurban center

---

1. General studies on Bobbio are Richter 2008 and Polonio 1962.

2. Paul the Deacon, *Historia Langobardorum* IV.41: 134: *Circa haec tempora beatus Columbanus ex Scottorum gente oriundus, postquam in Gallia in loco qui Luxovium dicitur monasterium construxerat, in Italiam veniens, a Langobardorum rege gratanter exceptus est, coenobiumque quod Bobium appellatur in Alpibus Cottiis aedificavit, quod quadraginta milibus ab urbe dividitur Ticinensi. Quo in loco et multae possessiones a singulis principibus sive Langobardis largitae sunt, et magna ibi facta est congregatio monachorum.*

listed, in itself an indicator of its fame, which was firmly established by the end of the eighth century.[3]

Reading the text, Bobbio's connection with Pavia is immediately emphasized. This is more than simply a geographical connection; that Paul recorded the foundation of Bobbio immediately after his notice of Arioald's reign suggests that he understood there to be a special relationship between the monastery and the Lombard kings, one that went beyond donations of land. Nevertheless, Paul knew little about Bobbio, so little that he mistakenly associated its foundation with Arioald's reign. In reality Columbanus arrived in Italy in 612 or 613, toward the end of Agilulf's reign, and it was under this sovereign that the foundation of the monastery took place.[4] The diploma issued by Agilulf in favor of Columbanus has survived, albeit in a ninth-century copy whose authenticity, not least because of the great number of forgeries from Bobbio, has long been in question. Nevertheless, the overall content of the document certainly is authentic.[5] The diploma, while extensively interpolated, represents the earliest known example issued by a Lombard king. This too is further evidence of the importance of the monastery even at the beginning of its history.

The text of Agilulf's diploma describes the donation of the church of Saint Peter, in the place called Bobbio, "to the venerable man, the blessed Columbanus, and to his companions," so that the monks could settle there and own the land. The diploma establishes the boundaries of the church's possessions, which include half of a well (*puteus*), the ownership of which had already been conceded by the same king to Sundrarit. We know about Sundrarit from a narrative source, the "Continuator of Prosper," and he appears to have been an important figure at the royal court, so much so that in a subsequent diploma issued by Adaloald he is described as *vir magnificus*.[6] Furthermore (and this is of great significance), Agilulf's diploma ends with a prohibition on any royal official going against the judgments of the king expressed in the privilege; this is a powerful prohibition, although very different from the later formulas of immunity found in the Carolingian period.[7]

The contents of the diploma are confirmed by the account of the *Vita Columbani*, written by Jonas of Bobbio at the request of the abbot Bertulf. Jonas writes that Agilulf, after he had honorably received Columbanus, conceded to

---

3. Paul the Deacon, *Historia Langobardorum* II.16: 82.

4. For Polonio 1962: 10, the foundation date is 614.

5. *CDL* III.1: 3–7 (Milan, 24/07/613?).

6. For Sundrarit see *Prosperi Continuatio Hauniensis*: 640; for Adaloald's diploma see below, footnote 9.

7. *CDL* III.1: 7: *dantes quapropter omnibus ducibus, gastaldiis seu actionariis nostris omnimodis in mandatis ut nullus eorum contra hac precepti nostri pagina ire quandoque presumat.*

him the right to settle wherever he wanted to in Italy. Then, on the advice of a certain Iocundus, he identified the church of Saint Peter as the right place, situated "in the solitude of the countryside of the Apennines," where miraculous events had occurred.[8] The almost complete correspondence between Jonas's account and the content of the diploma, although seeming to confirm the substantial veracity of events, should nevertheless be viewed with caution. Indeed, while it is true that Jonas could have taken the diploma as a model, the opposite could equally have been the case: later copyists of the diploma could have interpolated the original text with references taken from the *Vita Columbani*.

Agilulf's privileges (possibly repeated later in a lost diploma granted to the second abbot Athala) were confirmed by his son Adaloald a few years later.[9] In the new diploma, it is written that the king, on Athala's request, issued the document during a visit to Bobbio to see Columbanus's tomb. Adaloald specifies that among the donations made by his father was "wood for cooking salt" (associated explicitly with Sundrarit's well), but the real novelty in this second diploma is to be found in the donation of mountain territory (the "small Alp called Pennice"), which had already been intended for the monastery by the king's mother, Theodelinda. The diploma says that the queen, "out of love for our father Columbanus" (who clearly had not died yet, so this must have been in 613) had climbed up the mountain "in order to see this place," an act that suggested her intention later to donate the land to the monastery.[10] Some years later, Adaloald again confirmed the donations made by him and his father to the third abbot, Bertulf. On this occasion, we also see recorded and confirmed possessions that were partially donated and partially sold to the monastery by a certain Zusso, probably on a date following the issue of the first diploma.[11] By now the original nucleus of the monastery's property was fully formed.

It is possible to define Bobbio as a royal monastery, as did older historiography, which was however strongly dependent on legal categories that are hardly appropriate for describing early medieval societies.[12] From what has been said so far it should be clear that there was in practice a very strong relationship between Bobbio and the Lombard royal family, represented by Agilulf, Theodelinda, and

8. *VC* I.30: 220–1.

9. *CDL* III.2: 7–12 (Pavia, 25/07/624?); III.3:14–5: *per hoc generale nostrum preceptum cedimus vobis ad limen Beati Petri ibidem in Dei nomine licentia habitandi et possidendi, undique fines decernimus, sicut a domno et genitore nostro [. . .] sancte memorie Columbano vel Atalane [abbates] concessum vel traditum fuit.*

10. *CDL* III.2:11: *ligna ad sales coquendas; alpecella que apellatur Pennice, ubi domna et genitrix nostra Theodelinda, gloriosissima regina, ob amore patris nostri Columbani ascendit ad locum istum previdendum.*

11. *CDL* III.3:12–5 (Pavia, 17/07/625/6): *quod vobis a Zussone [. . .] per donacione adque vindicione evenit.*

12. See Polonio 1962, with older bibliography.

Adaloald, a relationship established with the foundation of the monastery itself. This was the same family group that first attempted to make the royal office hereditary, and it is noteworthy that its members sought an element of continuity in their relationship with the monastery: all family members demonstrated a visible devotion to the house and its founder. It is important to underline, however, that the relationship with the royal court continued uninterrupted, even after the family's attempts to establish a dynasty were brought to an end with Adaloald's deposition in 626.

Indeed Arioald, the king who deposed Adaloald, played an important role in the monastery's history, even if he did not issue another diploma for Bobbio. He appears in the *Vita Columbani* with a double character. Initially he is presented with the typical negative traits of an Arian and a barbarian. Indeed, Jonas recounts that a monk of Bobbio, Blidulf, who had been sent to Pavia, was a victim of an ambush by one of Arioald's men, who at that time was still a duke. At Arioald's instigation, he had badly beaten the monk, but divine intervention restored him to good health and punished the assailant dreadfully, instilling in the duke at the same time a superstitious fear.[13] This is a typical narrative within its genre, in which Arioald is presented as a barbaric subverter of the Catholic faith. According to the account, even the gifts the duke sent to the monastery were refused by Abbot Athala, because they came from an Arian.

In the preceding chapter, however, Jonas had relayed a different story, which despite its position in the text in fact refers to a period after the aggression shown toward Blidulf, since Arioald is already shown to be king. The bishop of Tortona, Probus, who wanted to extend his control over the monastery, had sought the support of other northern Italian bishops, and together with them he requested the king's intervention. The king, however, who was the same Arioald who had earlier had the monk Blidulf beaten, replied that he was unable to intervene in a matter that could only be resolved by a synod, stating that in any case he could not favor "those who wished to provoke harm against a servant of God."[14]

In this case Arioald's behaviour is exemplary and very distant from that exhibited when he was duke. Taken together this shows that an association with a monastery like Bobbio was fundamental for the prestige of whoever held royal office, even if the sovereign was an Arian. Indeed, this was a relationship perhaps even more important than that with the bishops, which the Lombard kings also sought out, in a way comparable to their Frankish counterparts. Indeed

---

13. *VC* II.24: 286–9. On Jonas's *Vita Columbani* see Wood 1982: 63–80; O'Hara 2009: 126–53; O'Hara and Wood 2017.

14. *VC* II.23: 281–3.

Arioald, in his struggle to establish himself on the throne against Adaloald, had been supported by a number of northern Italian bishops, which aroused the severe protests of Pope Honorius I, who in 625 had written to the exarch of Italy, Isacius, requesting that he take severe measures against those bishops.[15] And yet the year after Honorius's letter, Arioald, as we have just seen, set himself against the very same bishops who had supported him, positioning himself in favour of Bobbio, even going so far as to assist, "with public support" (*supplimento publico*) Bertulf's mission to Pope Honorius in Rome (in which Jonas himself took part).[16]

The pope favored Bobbio and issued a bull in 628 that, placing the monastery under the jurisdiction of the Roman Church, proclaimed its exemption from any episcopal interference. The bull has survived—again as a copy—in a text that although far from correct is considered to be substantially authentic.[17] It can be read as the pope's response to the position of the northern bishops and, at the same time, an expression of his attempt to establish good relations with the Lombard court. Bobbio, therefore, emerges as a pawn in the wider, complex game of Italian politics.

We can trace the history of relations between the monastery and the Lombard court relatively well thanks to a series of royal diplomas, which have been preserved or recorded in other later diplomas. Privileges were issued by Kings Rothari, Rodoald (who confirmed the monastery's exemption from episcopal jurisdiction, in a text the authenticity of which is not assured), Grimoald, Cunipert, Liutprand, Ratchis, Aistulf, and Desiderius.[18] Out of all these sovereigns, the association with King Liutprand emerges as particularly important, as it was this king who commissioned the tombstone for Cumian, a monk of Irish origin who lived in Bobbio around the middle of the seventh century. The text of the epigraph inscribed on the tombstone requests that the saint intercede in favor of the king.[19] There also exists a stone fragment, preserved in the museum of Bobbio, that may even suggest the king stayed in the monastery.[20] He would have been the first to have done so after King Adaloald, approximately a century earlier, a testimony to a deep and uninterrupted link between court and cloister.

---

15. *Epistolae Langobardicae* 2: 694.

16. *VC* II.23: 282.

17. *CDSCB* 10: 100–3. Even Pope Theodore's bull of 643 (*CDSCB* 13:104–12) is considered today to be substantially authentic: Anton 1975: 55–9; Piazza 1997: 13–4.

18. *CDL* III.5:18–21 (Rodoald, Pavia, 4/11/625); 22:108–11 (Ratchis, Carbonara al Ticino, 5/08/747); other kings' diplomas are mentioned in *Ludovici II Diplomata* 31: 127–32.

19. *CDSCB* 20:122: *At pater egregie potens intercessor existe / pro gloriosissimo Liutprando rege qui tum/praetioso lapide tymbum decoravit devotus / sit ut manifestum almum ubi tegitur corpus.*

20. *CDSCB* 31:135: " +: D: LIUTPRAND REXV."

Liutprand himself, and Ratchis after him, had donated a number of revenues to the monastery deriving from a public *curtis* by Lake Garda, where even well into the ninth century the monastery had important possessions, including a church dedicated to Saint Columbanus.[21] Amid this uniform picture of donations we also find a notice of a different kind. We learn from a diploma issued by Ratchis in 747 that during Liutprand's reign a part of the property donated by a certain Hilpranda was taken from the monastery. Ratchis, after he had had three of his *silvani* verify its boundaries, completely restored the land to the monastery.[22] This was probably an instance of illegitimate occupation by local landowners, overturned by King Ratchis's intervention, and should certainly not be seen as evidence for any lack of support from Liutprand for the monastery. Such support, on the contrary, is amply demonstrated by the evidence presented above. Furthermore, the donor's name, Hilpranda, appears very rarely in the sources of the period and thus most likely belonged to a member of the same royal family as Liutprand and his nephew, Hildeprand, further strengthening their connection with Bobbio.[23]

All the donations made by the Lombard kings were later confirmed in a privilege issued by Louis II in 860, with the exception of those made by Rothari and Rodoald, the authenticity of which therefore remains in doubt.[24] This diploma (which was confirmed in 877 by Carloman), together with the first great *Adbreviato* of the monastery's property (composed only two years later), represents the endpoint, from the point of view of its property, of the monastery's history in the Lombard and Carolingian era.[25] Around thirty years previously, Wala had had an earlier register of the monastery's property drawn up, which indicated the essential outlines of its internal organization.[26]

It is not easy to go beyond these details, which with very few exceptions are almost entirely derived from Jonas's biography of Columbanus and the royal

---

21. Castagnetti 1979: 1: 137 (*Adbreviatio de rebus omnibus Ebobiensi monasterio pertinente*, 862), 2: 158 (*Adbreviatio de rebus omnibus Ebobiensi monasterio pertinente*, 863), 4: 180 (*Breviarium de terra sancti Columbani*, X–XI century). From the *curtis* were obtained cash and in-kind revenues, including the proceeds of a fishery. Noteworthy is also what is written in the *Adbreviatio* of 862 (1: 143): *In Caniano [near Pavia] xenodochium sancti Martini, quod datum fuit per iudicatum sancto Columbano, spetialiter in suo thesaurario perenniter inibi pertinens*; it is very likely that this *iudicatum* was of the Lombard period.

22. CDL III.22:110: *Manifestum est, eo quod ante hos annos temp[ore praecellentissimi] domni Liutprandi regis vobis subtractum est in aliquod fine nostra Turi[o et alpe nostra Carebalo, quod] per Hilpranda [. . .] in suprascriptum cenubium relaxatum est.*

23. See Jarnut 1973:145, which lists only the Hilpranda of Ratchis's diploma, and 147, where are listed some names (from Tuscany) in the masculine form Ilprandus-Ildiprandus.

24. *Ludovici II Diplomata* 31: 127–32 (Marengo, 7/10/860); Carloman's diploma (Cortenuova, 20/10/877): MGH, *Diplomata Regum Germaniae ex stirpe Karolinorum*, I.6: 292–4.

25. See footnote 21 for the two versions of the *Adbreviatio*.

26. *CDSCB* 36: 139–41.

diplomas. For this reason, while we can grasp a basic picture of Bobbio's relationship with the Lombard kings, its connection with the Lombard elite remains completely obscure. This could simply be the result of the destruction of private documents belonging to the monastery. However, since Bobbio did not undergo any particular disasters (such as fire or demolition) over the course of its history that would explain the loss of the oldest part of its archive, perhaps another explanation ought to be looked for. Comparison with other Italian monasteries shows that elsewhere private documents have partially survived, have been cited explicitly in later royal diplomas, or were copied into the great cartularies of the twelfth century (as was the case for Santa Maria at Farfa and San Vincenzo al Volturno). For Bobbio, by contrast, other than the two documents concerning Zusso and Hilpranda's property that we have mentioned, our only surviving private charter is found in a half-erased text (probably from the eighth century), over which Ratchis's 747 diploma was written.[27] The document must certainly have come from the monastery's archive. Furthermore, a guard-leaf from a Bobbio manuscript contains two notices that record the content of two documents, also attributable to the eighth century.[28] Nevertheless, for a monastery directly linked to the royal court, this is a very small quantity of documents.

Nor is it very useful, although it has been attempted, to reconstruct the monastery's Lombard-era possessions on the basis of working backward from the Carolingian diplomas. This is not only because it is difficult to distinguish the Carolingian donations from those of an earlier period, but also because in any case—even if we assume that the Lombard "stratum" could be identified—one would not be able to distinguish between private and public donations. Also, the fact that in Abbot Wala's *breve memorationis* (dated to 833–835), the basic text for this type of reconstruction, Bobbio's property is organized into *curtes*, further suggests that its possessions were mostly of a public origin. Such an origin is probably all the more probable for those more distant possessions, such as the *curtes* in Tuscia, or indeed the property by Lake Garda, not to mention the land in the capital, Pavia (in these last two cases we are dealing with *cellae* rather than *curtes*).[29]

It should be concluded, therefore, that private donations made a weak contribution to the formation of Bobbio's patrimony. In order to explain this (at least partially), it is relevant to consider the date of the house's foundation in the very first years of the seventh century. This was more than a century earlier than the foundation (or re-foundation) of all the other great monasteries of Italy,

27. *CDSCB* 28: 132.
28. *CDSCB* 30: 134–5.
29. See footnote 26.

including San Salvatore (later Santa Giulia) in Brescia, Novalesa, Nonantola, San Salvatore al monte Amiata, Farfa, San Vincenzo al Volturno, and Montecassino. This fact did not favor Bobbio, since during the seventh century the elites of the Lombard kingdom had not yet begun to make significant donations to monasteries, in contrast to what happened in the eighth century. Liutprand's legislation of 713, which legalized and encouraged donations *pro anima* and particularly benefited monasteries, certainly sanctioned an already existing situation, although not one that can have been much older.[30] We can state this with relative certainty because the preservation of Lombard private charters begins precisely at the beginning of the eighth century, increasing much more markedly only around the middle of that century. Clearly the conservation of these documents is owed to the fact that they contained donations to ecclesiastical institutions, which preserved them in their archives as a result.[31] By contrast seventh-century charters, which certainly must have existed, have been lost, as they were barely if at all connected to ecclesiastical institutions.

Thus the preservation of documents and the influx of donations to churches (and monasteries above all) were two contemporaneous processes. Such donations therefore were a phenomenon foreign to the long, seventh-century history of Bobbio. When donations did begin to increase, Bobbio found itself faced with many rivals, cutting it off first of all from a potential range of donations from beyond the region, which instead went to local monasteries, very many of them family foundations. At the local level, Bobbio cannot have benefited from the more modest wealth of the kingdom's northwest elites, who are barely represented in the surviving charters of the Lombard period (and not only those pertaining to Bobbio). As for Emilia, the region was a frontier zone and remained disputed until the 730s. Furthermore, Bobbio suffered in particular from the foundation of San Salvatore in Brescia, which became the royal monastery par excellence and attracted donations not only from the sovereigns, but also from the Lombard elites of the entire Po valley.[32] Bobbio's considerable patrimony, made visible by the polypytchs of the Carolingian era, was therefore fundamentally public in origin.

Bobbio's role within the history of the Lombard kingdom has traditionally been linked to three questions, which despite their interconnection, we consider separately here for greater clarity. The first problem concerns the Three Chapters heresy, its diffusion within the Lombard kingdom, and the schism associated with it after 606. It was then that the division took place between the

---

30. *Liutprandi leges*, 6: 140.
31. On the importance of this transformation, La Rocca 1997: 31–54 and 1998: 77–87.
32. Gasparri 1978: 429–42.

two seats of Aquileia and Grado.[33] The former was in Lombard territory and adhered to the Three Chapters, while the latter was Catholic and in Byzantine territory.

In Italian historiography, the Three Chapters heresy has always been considered to be of great significance for the interpretation of the history of the Lombard kingdom. This became all the more true after the studies of Giampiero Bognetti, who wrote in the first half of the twentieth century. According to Bognetti, whose influence on Italian early medieval historiography has been (and to some degree continues to be) enormous, the whole history of the kingdom was characterized by a long combat between Arians (who were almost pagans) and Catholics.[34] However, this is not an idea that current historiography accepts, because Arianism had no political role in Lombard Italy whatsoever; indeed, the traces it did leave are rather weak and disappeared rapidly.[35] For Bognetti, by contrast, the struggle continued well into the eighth century. As part of this history, the Three Chapters controversy was important because it supposedly represented an opportunity for the Lombard sovereigns (Agilulf and Theodelinda, and their son Adaloald) to construct a kind of "national church," which was Catholic but, through its adhesion to the Three Chapters, hostile to Byzantium. The religious unity of their subjects, it is argued, greatly increased the Lombard king's prestige and authority.[36]

Columbanus is located in this context, and he did indeed send one of his letters (the fifth) to Pope Boniface IV, urging him to assemble a council to re-solve the schism.[37] According to Bognetti's interpretation, and to very many others after him, it was necessary for the Lombard kings to isolate Rome from Byzantium, leading it to condemn the Fifth Council; in this way, the faith of the kingdom's Catholic subjects, who were faithful to Rome, would have been cemented, while at the same time definitively distancing them from Byzantium in religious matters.[38]

The number of anachronisms and unproven assumptions in Bognetti's writings are so great that it would take many pages to identify them all, a task I have already done elsewhere and thus do not repeat here.[39] I remain here with the facts as they appear in the sources.[40] Undoubtedly Agilulf and Theodelinda had

33. Paul the Deacon, *Historia Langobardorum* IV.33:127; Pohl 2007: 243–4.
34. Bognetti 1966 (first edition 1948).
35. Fanning 1981: 241–58; Pohl 2000: 47–58; Gasparri 2001: 219–53.
36. Referring to Agilulf, Columbanus wrote: *dolor eius est schisma populi* (*Ep.* 5.8: 44).
37. *Ep.* 5: 36–56; on Columbanus's *epistulae* see Wright 1997: 29–92; Leso 2013: 358–89 (with bibliography).
38. Bognetti 1966: 214–5 and 283.
39. Gasparri 2003: 3–28.
40. On the Three Chapters in general, see Chazelle and Cubitt 2007; for Italy see Azzara 2007: 209–22.

an acute interest in seeing the condemnation of the Fifth Council. Columbanus says so clearly: his letter to the pope is written on Agilulf's command (*iussio*); the king's intervention had provoked in him *stupor* and *sollicitudo*, and for this reason he could not evade the task. Columbanus, although he professes himself to be a humble *peregrinus*, was nevertheless strong in faith—immune to any heresy and faithful to the Roman Church—something he had always demonstrated together with all of his people, the Iberi, "inhabitants of the extreme ends of the world," and for that reason he was able to speak to the pope as a faithful disciple.[41] It remains an open question whether he knew in depth the content of the debates around the Three Chapters, but that is not particularly important, because in reality he is preoccupied with something else. This is above all a call for the unity of the church, necessary to combat its enemies: "Be vigilant, for the water is already entering the ship of the church, and the ship is in danger."[42]

It is interesting how Columbanus's letter reveals his proximity to the two sovereigns and their son, who twice in the letter are presented—very effectively—as profoundly involved in an attempt to overcome the division of the Christian people (the *scisma populi*) caused by the condemnation of the Three Chapters. And while Columbanus defines Agilulf as a *rex gentilis*, he simultaneously (with little logic) presents the same king, together with Theodelinda, as engaged in the struggle against the Arians: "And indeed the kings reinforced for a long time this Arian disgrace in this region, oppressing the Catholic faith; now they ask to strengthen our faith."[43]

It is possible that during his stay in Milan Columbanus came across Arian groups, against whom he directed his preaching, although there is nothing to prove that they were Lombards. Moreover, the character of the Lombard sovereigns appears contradictory in the eyes of the monk; ultimately he regards them as supporters of Catholicism, even if the king, Agilulf, had even recently come from an Arian background. However, no evidence allows us to deduce the existence of precisely defined religious "parties" in Lombard Italy, or indeed at court. Nor is it possible to identify Columbanus as a member of such a party. The simplest explanation is that the Irish abbot, strengthened by the purity of his faith, intervened at the urging of the king, who was willing to support his aspiration to build a monastery in Italy and strove to overcome the religious

---

41. *Epp.* 5.1: 37, 5.3: 38.

42. *Ep.* 5.3: 38: *Vigilate, quia aqua iam intravit in ecclesiae navem, et navis periclitatur.*

43. *Ep.* V.17: 54: *Reges namque Arrianam hanc labem in hac diu regione, calcando fidem caholicam, firmarunt; nunc nostram rogant roborari fidem.*

conflict that divided the population, the *scisma populi*. Attributing other roles to Columbanus, whether political or missionary, is not justified by the sources.[44]

The whole problem of Bobbio's relationship with the Three Chapters controversy demands one further reflection. Apart from Columbanus's letter, the affair is only mentioned in Bobbio's sources after the death of the house's founder in Book II of Jonas's *Vita Columbani*, in a long but rather obscure episode.[45] It concerns a monk named Agrestius, who had entered the monastery of Luxeuil during the time of Abbot Eustasius. Agrestius, driven by a desire to carry out missionary activity, had gone first to the Bavarians (with no success) and later to the diocese of Aquileia, where he joined the supporters of the Three Chapters schism. Jonas writes that at this point Agrestius had a notary, Aureus, send an *epistola venenosa* on behalf of King Adaloald to Abbot Athala at Bobbio, which evidently called on him to join the schismatics. Both here and later on, Jonas ridicules Agrestius's positions. Agrestius, however, did not give in. He returned to Luxeuil and there "with the thorns of schism he tempted" Abbot Eustasius, who nevertheless resisted. Thanks to the involvement of a number of Burgundian bishops, Agrestius managed to have the king, Chlothar, assemble a synod at Mâcon (in 626 or 627), although he was defeated there.[46]

Notably the Council of Mâcon did not actually discuss the schism. Instead, it discussed a number of practices associated with Columbanian monasticism, which according to Agrestius went against canon law and thus were to be considered heretical. Also surprising is that the problem of how to calculate Easter was not mentioned as one of these malpractices. Apart from that, Jonas completely discards discussion of the schism, despite what he wrote at the beginning about contacts between Agrestius and Eustasius, when he had tempted the abbot about the schism.

The whole series of events mostly appears as an internal development within Columbanian monasticism, which at the Council of Mâçon—according to Jonas's account—wished to demonstrate its complete alignment with Rome and its positions. This is confirmed by Jonas's description of the journey to Rome taken by Bertulf (whom we have mentioned already).[47] He underlines that Pope Honorius was above all concerned about the particular monastic practices of Bobbio's monks while, conversely, he was not at all concerned about their potential sympathy for the Three Chapters. According to Jonas, Honorius later

44. Leso 2010.
45. *VC* II 9: 246–51.
46. *VC* II 9: 248: *Eusthasium scismatis aculeis temptat.* See also Fischer and Wolfram, chapters 8 and 9 in this volume.
47. See text and n. 16.

urged Bertulf to pursue the struggle against the Arian heresy.[48] I maintain, however, that the pope's exhortation to continue fighting the "perfidy of the Arian pestilence" conforms to a topos of papal action rather than reflecting a real crisis on this front. Besides this, the only concrete measure taken by Honorious concerning heresy that we know about is the deposition of Fortunatus, the patriarch of Aquileia and a supporter of the Three Chapters, in favor of the Roman and Catholic Primigenius.[49] We know of no actions taken against the Arians.

In conclusion, the sources are contradictory. When reading Jonas in particular, it should be remembered that he wrote first and foremost to demonstrate the purity of faith of the monks of Bobbio and their fidelity to Rome. The Arians and supporters of the Three Chapters assume their roles within this narrative scheme, in which, however, the true contest concerned the particular customs of Irish monasticism. With his account, Jonas sought to affirm that all such customs that went against Roman tradition had already been abandoned. There is not, however, a single case in which we can deduce the existence of a surge in missionary activity (whether against Arians, supporters of the Three Chapters, or pagans), neither generally in the Lombard kingdom nor specifically in the territory where Bobbio was established. Bognetti's old hypothesis about the missions carried out by eastern monks has been definitively overturned, and there is no reason to substitute an equally implausible theory that attributes an equivalent role to the monks of Bobbio.[50]

As a consequence, it is incorrect to imagine that, by supporting Columbanus and granting him the land (and the church of Saint Peter) where he built his monastery, Agilulf intended to use Bobbio as a vehicle for conversion. Bognetti and his disciples presented the hypothesis that Agilulf wished to employ the monks of Bobbio in combating the "Arian nationalism" of the most conservative Lombard warriors.[51] These warriors supposedly lived in isolated military settlements (the famous—and equally fictional—*arimanniae*)[52] positioned along the Apennines on the Byzantine frontier with Liguria, territory that was effectively under the control of the Byzantine Empire until 643. According to Bognetti, had these warriors converted to Catholicism, they would have become more tightly bound to the activities of the monarchy (by now Catholic), strengthening its authority. Again, however, there is no evidence for such

---

48. *VC* II 23: 282–3.

49. *Epistolae Langobardicae* 3: 694–6 (November or December 625).

50. See Gasparri 2001: 225–32. The theory of the missionary role of Bobbio is still present in Italian historiography; see, e.g., Polonio 1962: 91–4; Zironi 2004: 9–21.

51. See above, footnote 37.

52. On the *arimanniae*, see Tabacco 1966; Jarnut 1971; Gasparri 1978; the first historian who interpreted the *arimanniae* as military settlements inside the kingdom was Bognetti 1938: 109–34.

missionary activity from Bobbio. The monastery's dependencies (the age of which we cannot determine) show no trace of missionary activity.

In conclusion, it is not justifiable to attribute to Bobbio a missionary role that is simply not attested by the sources. The theory derives from the belief that the primary task of the Irish monks was the conversion of pagans and Arians, but this has been disproved by the work of Ian Wood, which has demonstrated that the monks' basic goal was to promote their model of Christian life. Missionary work was simply a consequence of activity that had other ends.[53]

Alongside the Three Chapters controversy, the idea of a missionary vocation has been the second big problem to have concerned students of Bobbio. However, there remains one other theme, the third question that I referred to earlier: the notion of the monastery's "strategic"—indeed military—role. In this view, Bobbio was "a sentry in a recently conquered area, looking above all towards Liguria, still entirely in Byzantine hands."[54] This theory—which not only derives from Bognetti and Italian historians but has been put forward by, for example, Karl Schmid—has not solely been applied to Bobbio. Indeed, the idea almost always emerges when the foundation of a royal monastery is discussed. We find it for Farfa, on the borders of Rome's territory; for Nonantola, close to the Exarchate; and for San Salvatore al Monte Amiata in Tuscany, a region that was still not well-controlled by the kings in Pavia.[55] The sources say nothing at all about any of this. The Lombard monasteries never had a military function or a role in supervising frontiers or traffic intersections. Such an explanation for Bobbio fails to grasp the significance of its monastic settlement. Its relative proximity to roads, and its position between the Trebbia and Aveto valleys, enabled the monastery to intercept the flow of pilgrims on their way to Rome and thus to secure the provision and survival of the community. None of this was at all incompatible with the practice, typical of Irish monks, of choosing wild and remote locations for their foundations.

From the point of view of the king, the monastery, which developed under royal protection, undoubtedly projected a public presence in a particular territory. But in no way was it a strategic settlement in a military sense. This erroneous idea derives from an argument first put forward by Rudolf Schneider at the beginning of the twentieth century and later reprised and popularized—once again—by Bognetti. This view understood all Lombard settlement as linked to the military control of territory.[56] Monasteries too were situated within this

53. Wood 2001.
54. Quotation from Polonio 1962: 15. See also Destefanis 2002: 91–5.
55. Schmid 1972: 1–36.
56. Schneider 1924.

wider, general, strategic framework—which of course never existed. Such a conception of Lombard settlement, understood to have been rigidly separated from that of the Roman population, has largely been refuted, although some of its consequences—including that of viewing monasteries as strategic settlements—have yet to become outdated.[57]

Bobbio then had no strategic or military role, nor was it a major center of missionary activity. Moreover, the modest level of paganism in the region's countryside would not have justified such a role, nor would the hypothetical, Lombard *arimanniae*. Conversely, Bobbio represented the first, experimental example of a royal monastery in Lombard Italy, in a way that expressed the new politics of the kingdom under Agilulf and Theodelinda. With the most difficult phase of settlement and conquest over, the Lombard monarchy in this way developed new and more mature methods of government and power, following models from Byzantium as well as the neighboring Frankish kingdom. Among such methods, patronage of monasteries was one of the most typical examples, together with the foundation of churches (such as San Giovanni in Monza) or rituals of royal inauguration inspired by the Hippodrome in Constantinople.[58] Bobbio was thus the first example of a royal monastery, a model that was reprised with great success with San Salvatore of Brescia in the following century.[59] At the same time, it inaugurated a new phase of evolution for the Lombard kingdom and the politics of its kings. By now stably in control of their territory, they sought a deeper legitimacy for their power through an association with ecclesiastical institutions and thus prefigured models of practice that would become standard during the course of the eighth century.

BIBLIOGRAPHY

Anton, H. H. (1975) *Studien zu den Klösterprivilegien der Päpste im Frühen Mittelalter.* Beiträge zur Geschichte und Quellenkunde des Mittelalters 4. Berlin and New York.

Azzara, C. (2007) Il regno longobardo in Italia e i Tre Capitoli. In C. Chazelle and C. Cubitt (eds.), *The Crisis of the Oikoumene: The Three Chapters and the Failed Quest for Unity in the Sixth-Century Mediterranean.* Turnhout, Brepols, 209–22.

Bognetti, G. P. (1938) "Arimannie e guariganghe." In *Wirtschaft und Kultur: Festschrift zum 70. Geburtstag von A. Dopsch.* Leipzig, R. M. Rohrer Verlag, 109–34.

Bognetti, G. P (1966) *S. Maria foris portas e la storia religiosa dei Longobardi.* Milan, Giuffrè.

Castagnetti, A. (1979) "S. Colombano di Bobbio." In A. Castagnetti, M. Luzzati, G. Pasquali, and A. Vasina, *Inventari altomedievali di terre, coloni e redditi.* Roma, Istituto storico italiano per il medio evo, 119–92.

---

57. Gasparri 2003: 3–28.
58. Paul the Deacon, *Historia Langobardorum* III 35: 114 and IV 21: 123–4.
59. Gasparri 1978: 436–40.

Chazelle, C., and C. Cubitt (eds.) (2007) *The Crisis of the Oikoumene: The Three Chapters and the Failed Quest for Unity in the Sixth-Century Mediterranean.* Turnhout, Brepols.

Destefanis, E. (2002) *Il monastero di Bobbio in età altomedievale.* Firenze, All'insegna del giglio.

Diplomata Regum Germaniae ex stirpe Karolinorum (1934), ed. P. Kehr. MGH, Berlin, .

Epistole Langobardicae collectae (1892), ed. W. Gundlach. MGH, *Epistolae* III. Berlin.

Fanning, S. C. (1981) "Lombard Arianism Reconsidered." *Speculum* 56: 241–58.

Gasparri, S. (1978) "La questione degli arimanni." *Bullettino dell'Istituto storico italiano per il Medio Evo e Archivio Muratoriano* 87: 121–53.

Gasparri, S. (2001) "Roma e i Longobardi." In *Roma nell'alto medioevo*, I. Spoleto, Settimane di studio del Centro italiano di studi sull'alto medioevo, 48.

Gasparri, S. (2003) "I Germani immaginari e la realtà del regno: Cinquant'anni di studi sui Longobardi." In *I Longobardi dei ducati di Spoleto e Benevento*, I. Spoleto, Atti del XVI Congresso internazionale di studi sull'alto medioevo, 3–28.

Jarnut, J. (1971) "Beobachtungen zu den langobardischen Arimanni und Exercitales." *Zeitschrift für Rechtsgeschichte: Germanische Abteilung* 88: 1–28.

Jarnut, J. (1973) *Prosopographische und sozialgeschichtliche Studien zum Langobardenreich in Italien (568–774).* Bonn, L. Röhrscheid Verlag.

La Rocca, C. (1997) "Segni di distinzione: Dai corredi funerari alle donazioni 'post obitum' nel regno longobardo." In L. Paroli (ed.), *L'Italia centro-settentrionale in età longobarda.* Firenze, All'insegna del giglio, 31–54.

La Rocca, C. (1998) "Donare, distribuire, spezzare: Pratiche di conservazione della memoria e dello status in Italia tra VIII e IX secolo." In G. P. Brogiolo and G. Wataghin (eds.), *Sepolture tra IV e VIII secolo.* Padua, SAP, Società archeologica padana, 77–87.

Leso, T. (2010) "Iona hebraice, Peristera graece, Columba latine: Per un riesame critico delle fonti sull'esprienza colombaniana tra VI e VII secolo Francia e Italia." MPhil dissertation, Università degli Studi di Padova.

Leso, T. (2013) "Columbanus in Europe: The Evidence from the *Epistulae.*" *Early Medieval Europe* 21.4: 358–89.

Liuprandi Leges = Le leggi dei Longobardi: Storia, memorie e diritto di un popolo germanico (2005), ed. C. Azzara and S. Gasparri. Rome, Viella.

Ludovici II Diplomata (1994), ed. K. Wanner. Fonti per la storia dell'Italia medievale, Antiquitates 3. Rome, Istituto storico italiano per il medio evo.

O'Hara, A. (2009) "The Vita Columbani in Merovingian Gaul." *Early Medieval Europe* 17.2: 126–53.

O'Hara, A. and I. Wood (eds.) (2017) *Jonas of Bobbio: Life of Columbanus, Life of John of Réomé, and Life of Vedast.* Translated Texts for Historians 64. Liverpool, Liverpool University Press.

Paul the Deacon (1878) *Historia Langobardorum = Pauli Diaconi Historia Langobardorum.* In G. Waitz (ed.), *Scriptores rerum Langobardicarum et Italicarum saec.* VI–IX. MGH. Hanover, 12–178.

Piazza, A. (1997) *Monastero e vescovado di Bobbio (dalla fine del X agli inizi del XIII secolo).* Spoleto, Centro italiano di studi sull'alto medioevo.

Pohl, W. (2000) "Deliberate Ambiguity: The Lombards and Christianity." In G. Armstrong and I. N. Wood (eds.), *Christianizing Peoples and Converting Individuals.* Tourhout, Brepols, 47–58.

Pohl, W. (2007) "Heresy in Secundus and Paul the Deacon." In C. Chazelle and C. Cubitt (eds.), *The Crisis of the Oikoumene: The Three Chapters and the Failed Quest for Unity in the Sixth-Century Mediterranean.* Turnhout, Brepols, 243–64.

Polonio, V. (1962) *Il monastero di San Colombano di Bobbio dalla fondazione all'età carolingia.* Genoa, Palatio archiepiscopali Ianuensi.

Prosperi continuatio Hauniensis (1922), ed. R. Cessi. *Archivio Muratoriano* 22. 629–41.

Richter, M. (2008) *Bobbio in the Early Middle Ages: The Abiding Legacy of Columbanus.* Dublin, Four Courts Press.

Schmid, K. (1972) "Zur Ablösung der Langobardenherrschaft in Italien durch die Franken." *Quellen und Forschungen aus Italienischen Archiven und Bibliotheken* 52: 1–36.

Schneider, F. (1924) *Die Entstehung von Burg und Landgemeinde in Italien.* Berlin, W. Rothschild.

Tabacco, G. (1966) *I liberi del re nell'Italia carolingia e postcarolingia.* Spoleto Centro italiano di studi sull'alto medioevo.

Wood, I. N. (1982) "The Vita Columbani and Merovingian Hagiography." *Peritia* 1: 63–80.

Wood, I. N. (2001) *The Missionary Life: Saints and the Evangelisation of Europe.* Harlow, Routledge.

Wright, N. (1997) "Columbanus's *Epistulae.*" In M. Lapidge (ed.), *Columbanus: Studies on the Latin Writings.* Woodbridge, Boydell Press, 29–92.

Zironi, A. (2004). *Il monastero longobardo di Bobbio: Crocevia di uomini, manoscritti, culture.* Spoleto, Centro italiano di studi sull'alto medioevo.

15

Disputing Columbanus's Heritage: The Regula cuiusdam patris

(with a Translation of the Rule)

ALBRECHT DIEM

A good reader should take heed that he does not submit the scriptures to his understanding, but that he submits his understanding to the holy scriptures.[1]

This puzzling statement at the beginning of the *Regula cuiusdam patris* indicates trouble.[2] It implies that there is a "not so good" and insufficiently watchful reader who receives guidance from a heteronomous and utilitarian understanding of scripture.[3] Moreover, the author's appeal to a *bonus lector* implies a remarkable level of subjectivity because it envisions a monk as an autonomous, self-thinking reader in pursuit of his own understanding (*sensus*). As such, the first sentence of the *Regula cuiusdam patris* forms a very unusual variation of the invocation of the authority of the Bible and the *sancti patres* that we find in numerous other monastic normative texts.[4]

There is another reference to a self-thinking monastic reader, a *prudens lector vel auditor*, in Jonas of Bobbio's *Vita Columbani*. This reader is supposed to gain understanding of the nature and the extent of monastic discipline by reflecting

1. *Regula cuiusdam patris*, ch. 1.1, ed. Villegas 1973: 10: *Caveat lector bonus ne suo sensui obtemperet scripturas, sed scripturis sanctis obtemperet sensum suum.*
2. In secondary literature, the text usually appears under the title *Regula cuiusdam patris ad monachos*, which is not used in any of the manuscripts. The addition *ad monachos* was meant to distinguish the text from another seventh-century anonymous monastic rule, the *Regula cuiusdam ad virgines*. For a comparison of these two rules, see Diem and van der Meer 2016.
3. We have to ask whether *scripturae* and *scripturae sanctae* refer here only to the Bible or to a broader textual corpus. It is possible that the author deliberately makes a distinction between *scripturae* (of the Fathers) and the *scripturae sanctae* (of the Bible). Since the remainder of the Rule mainly engages with monastic authors (especially Cassian, Basil, and Columbanus) while using biblical passages often only in a supportive function, I assume that *scripturae* does indeed have a broader meaning than just Scripture.
4. For example *Regula Benedicti*, Prologue.1, ed. de Vogüé and Neufville 1972: 412; ch. 73, 672–4; *Regula magistri*, ch. 34.1–2, ed. de Vogüé 1964: 186–8; Caesarius of Arles, *Regula ad virgines*, ch. 1.2, ed. de Vogüé and Courreau 1988: 170; Columbanus, *Regula coenobialis*, ch. 1, ed. Walker 1957: 144, line 30; *Regula cuiusdam ad virgines*, ch. 6, ed. Migne 1862, col. 1059; ch. 22.1, col. 1068.

on the *regula* that Columbanus had established for his communities.[5] Jonas leaves open whether he is referring to the reader of a written *Regula Columbani* or directly addressing his own reader, which would imply that he claims that his work *is* in fact the *Regula Columbani*, presented in a narrative disguise.[6]

In this chapter I argue that the author of the *Regula cuiusdam patris* and Jonas of Bobbio had the same "Columbanian" *lector* in mind and competed for his or her compliance. Both make a vigorous claim for Columbanus's heritage and the true meaning of the *Regula Columbani* while propagating fundamentally different monastic ideals.

There is a curious intertextual relationship between the *lector bonus* of the *Regula cuiusdam patris* and Jonas of Bobbio's *prudens lector vel auditor*. The appeal to a mindful *lector bonus* that forms the beginning of the *Regula cuiusdam ad virgines* appears almost verbatim in the *Testimonia divinae scripturae*, a biblical and patristic florilegium that was compiled at the beginning of the seventh century. The *Testimonia* ascribes it to Augustine, though it is in fact a slightly rephrased quotation from Jerome's Commentary on the Gospel of Matthew. In its original, Jerome does refer to a *prudens lector*, using the expression that would later show up in Jonas's work.[7] This may be coincidental but could also indicate that Jonas was directly responding to the opening statement of the *Regula cuiusdam patris*. We will never know whether this was really the case, but I intend to show that the *Vita Columbani* and the *Regula cuiusdam patris* were both products of massive disruptions among the followers of Columbanus that occurred after the Irish abbot's death.

The *Regula cuiusdam patris* is a short treatise squeezed between the *Regula orientalis* and the monumental *Regula magistri* in Benedict of Aniane's famous collection of monastic rules.[8] Benedict of Aniane, presumably due to his own lack of information, does not provide us with a clue about its provenance and

---

5. Jonas, *VC* I.10, ed. Krusch 1905: 170, lines 10–15: *His ergo in locis monachorum plebes constitutas, ipse vicissim omnibus intereat regulamque, quam tenerent, Spiritu sancto repletus condedit, in quam, qualis et quantae disciplinae vir sanctus fuerit, prudens lector vel auditor agnoscit.* O'Hara and Wood 2017 published a complete new translation of the *VC*.

6. See Diem 2002, in which I argue that Jonas's references to the *Regula Columbani* do indeed not (or at least not exclusively) refer to the two written rules ascribed to Columbanus and that Jonas considered his *VC* the best textual representation of the *Regula Columbani*.

7. *Testimonia divinae scripturae*, prologue.10, ed. Lehner 1987: 56: *Caveat unusquisque lector, ne suo sensui obtemperat scripturas, sed scripturis sanctis obtemperat sensum suum.* On the date of the *Testimonia*, see ibid., 44. Jerome, *Commentariorum in Matheum libri IV*, I (Matt. 10:29–31), ed. Hulst/Adriaen 1969: 72, lines 1730–1032: *Prudens lector cave semper superstitiosam intellegentiam ut non tuo sensui adtemperes scripturas sed scripturis iungas sensum tuum et intellegas quid sequitur.* Defensor, *Liber Scintillarum* LXXXI, 10, ed. Rochais 1957: 231 quotes Jerome's words as well. Cfr de Vogüé 2006: 288. Cassian, *Institutiones* VII.16, ed. Guy 1965: 312 expresses a similar idea in different words.

8. Benedict of Aniane's collection survives in only one early medieval manuscript: Munich, Bayerische Staatsbibliothek, Clm 28118. We find the *Regula cuiusdam patris* on fol. 139–141v. On the *Codex Regularum*, see Hauke 1986: 7–13; Engelbert 2015, 2016. About a third of the *Regula cuiusdam*

authorship. The text has no prologue and no chapter list and is, unlike most other *regulae* in Benedict of Aniane's *Codex regularum*, not divided into chapters.[9] It is Benedict of Aniane who calls the text a *regula*; the epithets pamphlet or manifesto might be just as appropriate, as will be shown here.

The radical nature of this opening statement and the rather unusual addressee could have sparked at least some interest among monastic historians, yet scholarship so far has focused primarily on intertextuality rather than its historical context. In 1908 Louis Gougaud listed the *Regula cuiusdam patris* as among those monastic rules that showed Irish influence, without paying much attention to its content.[10] Fernando Villegas produced a critical edition in 1973, in which he identified most of its sources and concluded that the text is based on Columbanus's two monastic rules but does not show any direct connection to the *Regula Benedicti*.[11] Adalbert de Vogüé described the *Regula cuiusdam patris* and its sources in his monumental *Histoire littéraire du mouvement monastique* without attempting to place the work in a historical context.[12]

Since the *Regula cuiusdam patris* does not show any traces of the *Regula Benedicti* it was considered useless as a witness for the spread of the *Regula Benedicti* within the Columbanian monastic world. This may have contributed to the lack of interest in this text, which seemed to be noteworthy mainly because of its excessive habit of punishing a wide range of transgressions with either incarceration or expulsion. Indeed, in no other monastic rule does the *carcer* play such a prominent role, and no other author of a monastic rule is as eager to get rid of dysfunctional monks.[13] This approach to transgressions was rather anachronistic in the world of seventh-century Gaul, where monastic conversion was already considered irreversible.[14] Overall, the *Regula cuiusdam*

---

patris is also preserved in Benedict of Aniane, *Concordia Regularum*, ed. Bonnerue 1999. Some fragments appear in Smaragdus of St. Mihiel, *Expositio in Regulam S. Benedicti*, ed. Engelbert/Spannagl 1974. See also http://earlymedievalmonasticism.org/texts/Regula-cuiusdam-patris-ad-%20monachos.html.

9. The chapter division that we find in extant editions appears for the first time in the *editio princeps*: Holstenius 1661, pt. 2: 282–92. It is used here only for reasons of convenience, though it is at times misleading and should not determine our understanding of the text.

10. Gougaud 1908: 326–7.

11. Villegas 1973: esp. 135–40.

12. De Vogüé 2006: 287–305. The source references provided in my translation of the *Regula cuiusdam patris* are largely based on Villegas's and de Vogüé's findings.

13. De Vogüé 2006: 289 and 305. On incarceration, see Anaya Torres 2007: 11–23; on expulsion, see Ohm 1982: 150–1. It is symptomatic that the author uses no fewer than four different terms when referring to expulsion: *abscindere* (*Regula cuiusdam patris*, ch. 4.2: 14 and ch. 26.2: 30), *separare* (ch. 7.5: 15), *eicere* (ch. 8.7: 17; ch. 16.4: 14; ch. 18.1: 25), and *expellere* (ch. 17.4: 24). I briefly address the *Regula cuiusdam patris* in my study on monastic chastity because it is the only rule that explicitly mentions expulsion from the monastery as punishment for *fornicatio*. Cfr *Regula cuiusdam patris*, ch. 18.1–2: 25; Diem 2005: 266–72.

14. On the irreversibility of monastic vows, see Diem 2005: 196–9 with source references.

patris seems to conform to the cliché of a supposedly "Irish" strictness that had to be mitigated by the moderation and rationality of the *Regula Benedicti*.[15]

The *Regula cuiusdam patris* may not contain traces of the *Regula Benedicti*, but it uses, as Villegas and de Vogüé showed, a wide range of other sources, especially Columbanus's *Regula monachorum* and *Regula coenobialis*, the Latin translation of the *Regula Basilii*, and the works of John Cassian. It also contains one fragment of a sermon by Augustine, the already mentioned fragment of Jerome's Commentary on the Gospel of Matthew appearing in the *Testimonia divinae scripturae*, one allusion to Evagrius Ponticus's *Sententiae*, and a handful of vague similarities to Insular texts.[16]

The author of the *Regula cuiusdam patris* appears to have used an assemblage of memorized or paraphrased passages rather than quotations from his sources. Only the first two chapters of the Rule are a blend of literal (or almost literal) quotations from works of Jerome, Augustine, Cassian, and Columbanus. The rest of the text mainly consists of paraphrases, but there are also a considerable number of passages that cannot be traced to a source and should be considered the author's own contribution.[17] It is, however, important to note that the author of the *Regula cuiusdam patris* does not only paraphrase his sources but also "speaks" in their language, suggesting that he either had deeply absorbed the texts he cites or was quoting them from memory. He uses numerous terms and expressions that appear otherwise exclusively in Basil's, Cassian's, or Columbanus's works and applies them outside of their original contexts.[18]

The fact that the *Regula cuiusdam patris* uses both parts of Columbanus's Rule[19] but shows no traces of the *Regula Benedicti* suggests that it was written within a relatively short time frame between Columbanus's death and the moment when the *Regula Benedicti* got a foothold in the network of Columbanian foundations, which ultimately happened in the 630s.[20] Theoretically, the *Regula cuiusdam*

15. Cfr Ó Cróinín 2005: 19.

16. *Regula cuiusdam patris*, ch. 11.6: 19 paraphrases Evagrius Ponticus, *Sententiae*, ch. 39, ed. Leclercq 1951: 207. Similarities to Insular texts are listed in Villegas 1973: 144.

17. All sources are identified in the notes to the translation. Sources indicated with "cfr." are paraphrased or the basis of allusions; those without cfr. are quoted verbatim or almost verbatim.

18. For example, the expressions *corpus fraternitatis; corpus fraternus; corrigere; mandatum domini; notare; obtemperare; per nimiam humilitatem; propositum; unitas fratrum*, etc., are inspired by the Latin translation of the *Regula Basilii*. Cassian's work provides the expressions *compulsor; conventus; cum gaudio; discussio; excubiae; lapsus lugubris; puritas cordis; viam perfectionis aperire*; and *virtus oboedientiae*. In Columbanus's work we find the expressions *arbitrio uniuscuiusque senioris; paenitentia*; and *supellex*. Examples for recontextualizing allusions can be found in *Regula cuiusdam patris*, ch. 7.1: 15; ch. 9.3: 17; ch. 11.2: 18; ch. 13.1: 20; ch. 15.8: 22; ch. 16.3: 23; ch. 18.4: 25; ch. 20.6: 26; ch. 21.2: 27; ch. 24.3: 28; ch. 25.1: 29; ch. 28.6: 32; ch. 29.6: 33. Many of them are discussed in the footnotes of the English translation in the appendix.

19. Villegas 1973: 4 and 135–40. I assume that Columbanus's *Regula monachorum* and his *Regula coenobialis* originally formed one rule, as they appear in Benedict of Aniane, *Codex Regularum*, fol. 86v–98r. See Diem 2016a: 68–71.

20. The oldest texts mentioning the *Regula Benedicti* are the foundation charter for the monastery Solignac (632), ed. Krusch 1902: 747 and the Privilege for the monastery of Rebais (c. 637), ed. Pardessus 1849, vol. 2, no. 293: 61–63. On these documents, see Diem 2002: 77–89; and Ó Cróinín

patris could have written before Columbanus's death, expressing a dissenting voice in the conflicts unfolding in Luxeuil in 610 when its founder was sent into exile, but this is rather unlikely. We know from Columbanus's *Epistula* 4 that the community he left behind was in turmoil, although aside from briefly mentioning the question of the Easter date and disputes about the strictness of his Rule, he does not give much information about the matters in dispute.[21] Since the *Regula cuiusdam patris* does not contain allusions to the Easter question and generally imposes stricter punishments than Columbanus's Rule, it is unlikely that it expressed the dissenting views of the monks Columbanus had left behind in Luxeuil.

The Rule could, of course, also have been produced after the 630s. This would imply, however, that its author, who otherwise greedily drew on *auctoritates*, deliberately ignored the *Regula Benedicti*, which had already gained great authority and had formed a major source of inspiration for the two other preserved monastic rules produced in the Columbanian world, the *Regula Donati* and the *Regula cuiusdam ad virgines*.[22] Yet the spread of the *Regula Benedicti* forms, admittedly, a tentative *terminus ante quem*.

If we cautiously date the text between 615 and 635, it would be, aside from Jonas of Bobbio's *Vita Columbani*, one of the very few sources on the beginning of what historians describe as the "Columbanian" monastic movement.[23] It is the purpose of this chapter to show that the *Regula cuiusdam patris* can indeed be related to the events that took place in the first two decades after

---

2005: 15–17. Another early witness would be the privilege of Pope Theodore for Bobbio, dated to 643, ed. Cipolla 1918: 109, though its authenticity is rather doubtful, as discussed in Anton 1975: 58–59. and also cfr also Gasparri, chapter 14 in this volume. On the *Regula Benedicti* in Columbanian monasteries, see Dunn 2000: 173–7. The question of whether Columbanus himself knew the *Regula Benedicti* is a matter of dispute. Charles-Edwards 2000: 383–8 discusses the state of research and follows de Vogüé's argument that Columbanus was already familiar with the *Regula Benedicti*, which is based on rather loose word parallels. See de Vogüé 1972: 163–6. Stancliffe 2011: 23–5 points out, in my opionon correctly, that the verbal parallels between Columbanus's *Regula monachorum* and the *Regula Benedicti* are not strong enough to make a case, especially since they apply to the *Regula Magistri* as well.

21. Columbanus, *Ep.* 4, ed. Walker 1957: 26–37, esp. ch. 3: 28 on the Easter controversy, and ch. 4: 28–30 on the strictness of the Rule. See also Bullough 1997: 16–18.

22. See Diem 2007b and 2016a on the *Regula cuiusdam ad virgines* and Diem 2012 on the *Regula Donati*. The *Regula Benedicti* is mentioned (along with the *Regula Columbani*) in every preserved episcopal privilege issued for a Columbanian monastery, which implies that the Rule was known throughout the network of "Columbanian" monasteries. On episcopal privileges, see Diem 2002: 77–84.

23. As will appear from this study, "Columbanian," "Hiberno-Frankish," and "Iro-Fränkisch" are highly problematic categories that unjustifiably imply a high level of uniformity among the monasteries that place themselves in the tradition of Columbanus. These terms should be used, if at all, with caution and necessary qualifications. See also Wood 1998; Fox 2014: 13–8.

Columbanus's death. It provides crucial new insights into the early history of Columbanian monasticism.

Jonas of Bobbio's *Vita Columbani* makes a strong claim for how Columbanus should be remembered and how his legacy ought to continue in Luxeuil, Bobbio, and the numerous male and female monastic communities that were founded under the *Regula Columbani* soon after his death.[24] Moreover, the text invokes Columbanus's and his successors' sanctity, their miracles, and instances of divine intervention to show how Columbanus's ascetic zeal and strictness could transform into a livable monastic regime without corrupting his ideals. Jonas explains to his readers why Columbanus's communities of hard-working radical ascetics, who were always on the verge of starvation, could become powerful monastic institutions under a much more moderate regime. He shows how they became part of the political landscape of the Frankish and Lombard kingdoms and how Columbanus's successors, particularly the abbots Eustasius of Luxeuil and Athala and Bertulf of Bobbio, carefully guarded, implemented, and defended his *regula, doctrina*, and *instituta*.[25]

It is now widely accepted that Jonas was no objective chronicler but rather a vigorous spokesperson of one of the parties involved in giving Columbanian monasticism its shape. His *Vita Columbani* was commissioned by Abbot Bertulf of Bobbio and dedicated to Abbot Waldebert of Luxeuil as well as the Bobbio community and may have been written as an attempt to create unanimity between Columbanus's main foundations and, as it were, to peacefully divide his heritage between them.[26] Part of this endeavor was to reshape Columbanus as a founding saint who conformed to the monastic ideals that were deployed by his successors. Consequently, Jonas's Columbanus was considerably different from the person we encounter in Columbanus's preserved works.[27]

---

24. *VC* I.26: 209–10 and II.10: 255–6. On Jonas's strategies to claim Columbanus's memory, see Dunn 2008; Diem 2007a.

25. A theoretical framework for the transition from charismatic communities to monastic institutions is provided by Max Weber's studies on charisma: Weber 1968: esp. 18–61; 253–67; see also Diem 2007a. On the junction of *vita* and *regula* in medieval monasticism, see Agamben 2013. Brown 2015: 181–200 provides the best synthesis of Columbanian monastic ideals, placing them in the broader context of late antique and early medieval Christian practice and doctrinal developments. On Athala and Eustasius as guardians of the *regula*, see Jonas, *VC* II.1: 231: *Ergo cum egregie post beatum Columbanum supradictum coenobium regeret et in omni disciplina regularis tenoris erudiret.* On Eustasius, see II.9: 246: *Cumque iam haberetur ab omnibus gratus, ut nullus se beatum Columbanum perdidisse gemeret, qui eius doctrinis inbutus fuisset, presertim cum cernerent in discipulum magistri instituta manare . . . ;* 248–9: *. . . non ambigens de beati Eusthasii auctoritate et doctrina, quod omnes adversantes sanctae regulae prudentia et faciditate, administrante sibi Spiritu sancto superaret.*

26. Jonas, *VC*, prologue: 144–8; Diem 2007a: 551–2.

27. On the differences between the "historical" Columbanus and the hagiographic creation, see Wood 1998; Charles-Edwards 2000: 345–7; Stancliffe 2001; and Dunn 2008.

Jonas does not conceal the fact that Bobbio and Luxeuil and its affiliations were shaken by conflicts on the question of who could claim Columbanus's legacy and who embodied his ideals. A certain monk named Roccolenus led a group who attacked Abbot Athala of Bobbio and then left the monastery in anger, to settle elsewhere.[28] On another occasion, Eustasius was attacked by the monk Agrestius, who attempted to find support in Bobbio and to take control of several affiliations of Luxeuil. Eustasius had to defend himself and the *Regula Columbani* (as he claimed) against Agrestius's attacks at an episcopal council that was held in Mâcon in 626 or 627.[29] Jonas notes that the perpetrators of both insurgencies eventually fell prey to divine punishment after refusing to do penance and to reconcile with their communities. For Jonas, God had clearly proven them wrong.[30]

I propose that the *Regula cuiusdam patris* gives voice to at least one, and perhaps even both, of the parties that rose up against Columbanus's successors and made a claim on his heritage. The *quidam pater* who wrote the Rule may have been none other than Agrestius himself[31] or someone of his circle, such as Amatus or Romaric, the founders of Remiremont who had, according to Jonas, supported Agrestius's case until they switched sides and made peace with Eustasius.[32]

Aside from shedding new light on the early history of Columbanian monasticism, my analysis of the *Regula cuiusdam patris* may provide us with some guidance in reading early medieval monastic rules in general.[33] As great as Benedict of Aniane's merits for the preservation of the early medieval tradition of monastic rules may have been, he misleads us at one central point. The eminent Carolingian monastic reformer wanted to convey the idea that the *Regula Benedicti* was in fact the perfect synthesis of the entire tradition of Latin monastic Rules. His *Codex Regularum* presents all monastic rules for monks as *one* comprehensive *Regula patrum*, with a prologue that happens to be the prologue of the *Regula Benedicti*.[34] His *Concordia regularum* makes a similar point,

28. *VC* II.1: 231–2. On the monastic revolt against Athala, see Stancliffe 2001: 205 and Dunn 2008: 8–18. Dunn links the uprising directly to the overly strict provisions in Columbanus's *Regula coenobialis* and to the fact that Athala represents the shift from a charismatic leader to a monastic administrator.

29. *VC* II.9–10: 246–57.

30. *VC* II.1: 232, II.10: 253–4. See also II.19: 273–4; Kreiner 2014b: 127.

31. Despite the little information we have about Agrestius (all coming from Jonas's *VC*), modern scholars have transformed him into quite a prolific author. Felice Lifshitz suggests that due to his Aquileian contacts and his position on the Three Chapter Controversy, he may have been involved in the compilation of the *Martyrologium Hieroniminanum*. Helmut Reimitz discusses the possibility that Agrestius was the author of parts of the Fredegar Chronicle. See Lifshitz 2006: 16–20; and Reimitz 2015: 191–5, elaborating on the hypothesis of Schürer 1900: 85–8.

32. On Agrestius's activities in Remiremont, see Folz 1980: 19–20. The *Vita Amati* 3, ed. Krusch 1902: 216 describes Amatus as *cum monasticis normis semper incumbens*.

33. On the genre of monastic rules, see Diem and Rousseau 2017.

34. Benedict of Aniane's collection begins with *Incipit prologus sanctorum regulae patrum*

emphasizing that monks should study all the rules he had collected because they represent one monastic ideal.[35]

The *Regula cuiusdam patris* shows that there was in fact no *Concordia* (see Damian Bracken's contriution in this volume, chapter 2), but that monastic rules expressed radically different viewpoints on monastic practices, ideals, and their theological grounding. These dissenting viewpoints were often expressed through a critical dialogue with previously written rules. Many *regulae* emerged in a moment of crisis that made it impossible to fall back on the repertoire of norms and guidelines that were available at that moment.[36] The *Regula cuiusdam patris* provides a particularly detailed case study of such a moment of crisis.

At first glance, the text is just a blend of paraphrases of fragments from the works of Basil, Cassian, and Columbanus. A closer look, however, shows that after its programmatic opening statement, the remainder of the Rule takes selected themes and phrases from Columbanus's Rule, particularly his *Regula monachorum*, as a point of departure and supplements them with ideas from his other sources. It is, in fact, a critical commentary on the *Regula Columbani* and not just a mixed rule. The text gives—very much in line with what he stated in the beginning—Columbanus's Rule a new *sensus*, one that the author of the *Regula cuiusdam patris* considered to conform with the *scripturae*, in this case mainly the works of Basil and Cassian. In doing so, the author followed in the footsteps of Columbanus himself, whose Rule was indebted to Basil's and Cassian's works as well.[37]

The result of this endeavor is not particularly edifying. It is a work that does not conceal the author's fury at a disrupted community, in which anger, slander, and disobedience prevail. The text seems to propose not much more than disposing of disobedient or disgruntled monks and those who violate the monastic precepts or the *mandata domini* ("commands of the Lord"). The language

---

monachorum, followed by the prologue of the *Regula Benedicti*, though Benedict is never mentioned by name. The *Regula magistri*, the last rule for monks in the collection, ends with *Explicit regula sanctorum patrum*. See Munich, Bayerische Staatsbibliothek Clm 28118, fol. 1r and 184v. The fact that Benedict of Aniane presented all his rules for monks as one rule has been overlooked in previous studies on his collection.

35. Benedict of Aniane, *Concordia regularum*, prologus 9–10, ed. Bonnerue 1999: 3.

36. Diem 2005: 131–46. For another case study, Aurelianus's revision of Caesarius of Arles's *Regula ad virgines*, see Diem 2014.

37. See also Villegas 1973: 135–40. On the reception of Cassian, see Stevenson 1997: 208–9; Lake 2011; and Stancliffe 2011. It is noteworthy that Basil and Cassian provided textual material for several rules, especially the *Regula Eugipii*, ed. Villegas and de Vogüé 1974, a rule-florilegium that may have been produced at roughly the same time, though independently from the *Regula cuiusdam patris*. Eugippius used, aside from the works of Basil and Cassian, Augustine's Rule and the *Regula magistri*. See also Dunn 2008: 19.

of the *Regula cuiusdam patris* is drastic, one might almost say fiery. For example, the text explains the expulsion of monks for disobedience with words from Matthew 5:29: "For it is better for you that one of your members perishes that that the entire body enters the fire of hell."[38] Someone who shows anger and does not repent will also expect to burn in hell. His putrefied wounds have to be burned out by the healing punishment of fire and be cut open by an incision of the spiritual knife.[39] The Rule calls an incompetent abbot a "murderer of souls"[40] and quotes in the context of negligent seniors the biblical word: "Go, cursed into eternal fire, which is prepared for you by the devil and his angels."[41] Every monk needs to rise at the first word of a request "as if the coal of the burning fire has descended upon him."[42]

First I describe a possible historical context for the the *Regula cuiusdam patris* and show how it could be related to to the uprisings in Bobbio and Luxeuil. After that I show that the author's concern was not merely limited to recommending the expulsion of monks and abbots from the monastery and threatening them with the punishment of hell. Instead, he tried to do justice to a disrupted community at a programmatic level and to provide an elaborate theological reflection on the purpose of monastic life, while offering an alternative to the prevailing Columbanian monastic theology.

The Historical Context

In his *Vita Columbani*, Jonas of Bobbio describes two major uprisings after Columbanus's death; one took place in Bobbio, the other in Luxeuil and its affiliated communities. Athala, who succeeded Columbanus as abbot of Bobbio, had to defend his position against a dissenting group of monks who refused to submit to his authority, allegedly "because they could not bear the power of excessive ardor and carry the weight of strict discipline." Athala eventually let them leave the monastery. They did not, however, return into the lay world but established new monastic communities, which indicates that the dissenters

---

38. *Regula cuiusdam patris*, ch. 4.2–3: 13–4: *Si autem post examinationem carceris reprobus invenitur semel et bis, iterum atque iterum, abscindendus est ab omni fraternitatis corpore, secundum mandatum domini dicentis: expedit enim tibi ut pereat unum de membris tuis, quam totum corpus tuum eat in gehennam ignis, et: quia modicum fermentum totam massam corrumpit.*

39. *Regula cuiusdam patris*, ch. 9.1–3: 17: *Si quis iracundus inventus fuerit ex fratribus, reus erit in concilio gehennae ignis nisi paeniteat. Et vulenera putrefacta castigatio ignis medicamento exurenda sunt et tumidum vulnus spiritalis ferri sectione utatur.*

40. *Regula cuiusdam patris*, ch. 20.3: 26: . . . *hic non solum principatu fratrum indignuns est, verum etiam homicida animarum iudicandus est.*

41. *Regula cuiusdam patris*, ch. 24.8: 29, quoting Matt. 25:41–2.

42. *Regula cuiusdam patris*, ch. 29.3: 33, quoting Rom. 12:20.

were sincere monks rather than just rebels who had renounced their monastic profession.[43]

Jonas relates that after having left Bobbio, the group of rebels went to different places: "Some were received among the ocean's bays, others tried to gain freedom in the desert."[44] A number of details of the *Regula cuiusdam patris* strikingly resonate with the needs of the monks who left Bobbio. The *Regula cuiusdam patris* addresses, differently from all other monastic rules, a dispersed community of monks living close to the seaside,[45] in the mountains, and in barren regions.[46] Its members earned their living in a variety of ways that were determined by regional circumstances.[47] The Rule refers numerous times to several *seniores* holding leadership functions, which implies that each group of monks had its own leader and that an abbot, maybe with an *equonomus* as his deputy, ruled the entire decentralized community.[48] The *Regula cuiusdam patris* prohibits healthy monks from traveling on horseback or in a cart, while allowing the frail ones to do so, which implies that monks, even old, lame, and sick ones, often traveled back and forth between different monastic settlements.[49]

Although Jonas does not mention this explicitly, it is likely that there was a connection between the uprising in Bobbio and the conflict that was instigated by Agrestius only a couple of years later. As already discussed by others in this volume, Agrestius was a Burgundian courtier who became a monk at Luxeuil because he was *cordis conpunctione tactus* ("touched by contrition of heart") and left all his worldly possessions behind. Even Jonas, who otherwise calls him

43. *VC* II.1: 231: . . . *qui se aiebant nimiae fervoris auctoritatem ferre non posse et arduae disciplinae pondera portare non valere; . . . Cum nihil iam proficere cerneret nec alibi trahentes animos suae societatis abenis inretiri posse vidisset, pertinaces ire sinit; qui postquam segregati ab eo, alii eorum marinis sunt sinibus recoepti, alii locum heremi ob libertatem habendam petire.*

44. See previous footnote.

45. This is implied by *Regula cuiusdam patris*, ch. 15.5: 22: . . . *sive in caelo, sive in terra, sive in mari, seu in omnibus creaturis dei.* See also Gougaud 1908: 327.

46. *Regula cuiusdam patris*, ch. 22.1: 27: *Fratribus quibus habitatio in stereli terra, id est absque pane, et sunt in montanis, et infructuosis, modicum lactis permittimus cum aqua mixtum.*

47. *Regula cuiusdam patris*, ch. 13.1–2: 20–1: *Arbitrio uniuscuiusque senioris relinquendum est, unde annuum panem monasterio suo provideat: si ex sarculo aut bubus, ut aliquibus most est, sicut nobis; aut artificiis, sive negotiis, sive ex conductione mercedis, sive ex quolibet opere Quomodo res et ratio et situs loci unicuique permiserit, semper laborandum est, et lex dei, quae sive visibilia sive invisibilia continent, observanda est.*

48. See especially *Regula cuiusdam patris*, ch. 13.1: 20 (see previous footnote). It seems that one of these *seniores* also performed the function of abbot. See ch. 20.1: 26: *Si quis ex senioribus sive is qui abbas nuncupatur, voluptuosus exsistat et ebriosus et dives* ... This abbot was not necessarily always present; see ch. 5.1: 14: *Non omnibus praesente abbate vel equonomo obtemperandum* ...

49. *Regula cuiusdam patris*, ch. 21: 27: *Monachos in curribus et in equis discurrere, praeter infirmos, et debiles, et clodos, non permittimus.* Dunn 2008: 18–19 argues that Bobbio itself was a community consisting of various cells and small affiliations. Her assumption is primarily based on the most likely forged Privilege of Pope Theodore for Bobbio from 643, ed. Cipolla 1918: 108–12 .

a new Cain, acknowledges his initial good intentions.[50] Agrestius undertook, against Eustasius's wish, a missionary journey, which failed miserably. He went to Aquileia and joined the heretical party in the Three Chapter Controversy (as Columbanus himself may have done before him) and tried to gain support for his doctrinal viewpoints from Eustasius and Athala.[51] As a result, Eustasius had him evicted from Luxeuil.[52] At least that is what Jonas tells us, but this is probably not the whole story.

After his expulsion, Agrestius used his old political connections from his past as *notarius* at the court of King Theuderic II to attack the *Regula Columbani* as *canonicae institutionis aliena* ("contrary to canonical practice") and to utter, "grunting like a pig," allegations of heresy against Columbanus and Eustasius, who, as Jonas emphasizes several times, embodied the *regula, doctrina*, and *instituta* of his master.[53] Eustasius had to defend himself and the *sancta regula* (as Jonas calls it) at an episcopal council gathered in 626 or 627 in Mâcon—and it is noteworthy that there is no precedent of using the allegation of heresy in the context of monastic practice or the content of a monastic rule.

Assuming that the Council of Mâcon may have been a turning point in the history of Columbanian monasticism, historians have developed various scenarios of what was really at stake when Eustasius and the *Regula Columbani* stood trial in Mâcon. Their arguments mostly evolve around what Jonas did *not* say or what he addressed only in allusions. In the most extensive study of the Agrestius conflict currently available, Bruno Dumézil points out the striking parallels between Columbanus's own biography, ideals, and rhetoric and what we have come to know about Agrestius. Dumézil argues that Agrestius may have considered himself the true successor of Columbanus and a defender of his master's ascetic zeal, particularly the practice of *peregrinatio*, and his doctrinal views on the Three Chapters. Agrestius never made headway against Eustasius, who submitted Luxeuil and its affiliates to the political agenda of Clothar II,

---

50. *VC* II.9: 246: . . . *et quadam cordis conpunctione tactus, omnia quae possederat relinquens, ad Luxovium veniens, se et sua omnia supradicto patri tradiderat.*

51. Columbanus addresses the Three Chapter Controversy in *Ep.* 5, ed. Walker 1957: 36–57, urging Pope Boniface IV to reconcile with his theological opponents. The question of which standpoint Columbanus himself held remains unclear, though he was certainly critical of Pope Vigilius and (supportively) critical of Boniface. See Gray and Herren 1994; Bullough 1997: 23–25; Wood 1998: 100–2; Wood 2007: 328–39; Kreiner 2014a: 125–6.

52. *VC* II.9: 248: *Sed postquam salutaribus monitis mentem peste corruptam et salubre antidoto curare nequisset, a suo ac suorum collegio segregavit.*

53. *VC* II.9: 248: . . . *sed cum nihil eius inperitia facere quivissset, beati Columbani religio offendit, adversus regulam eius lanuino dente garriens ac velut caenosa sues gruniens . . . ; 248–9: Cumque nihil profecisset, statuit, ut sinodali examinatione probaretur, non ambigens de beati Eusthasii auctoritate et doctrina, quod omnes adversantes sanctae regulae prudentia et facidatate, administrante sibi Spiritu sancto superaret; 250: Audito Eustasius hereseo nomine se vel suos cum magistro vocatos, ait . . .*

whom Jonas depicts as a staunch supporter of Columbanus's foundations.[54] The rebellious monk got, as Dumézil argues, a forum and support due to still-lingering conflicts between the Burgundian aristocracy, particularly the Burgundian mayor of the palace Warnachar, and the Neustrian political elite. In Dumézil's eyes the Agrestius conflict was thus a combination of a personal drama, a dispute about monastic values and practices, and political tensions that had their roots in the showdown of 614 when Clothar II had taken control over all the Merovingian kingdoms.[55] Ian Wood, Clare Stancliffe, Thomas Charles-Edwards, and Yaniv Fox assume, with different emphases, that the Council of Mâcon was motivated by the conflicts about the calculation of Easter,[56] the Three Chapter Controversy,[57] or the still-lingering clash between Irish and continental monastic practice exemplified by the Irish tonsure.[58] Mark Stransbury argues that, aside from the Irish tonsure, even the use of the Insular script was a matter of dispute.[59] Clare Stancliffe and Thomas Charles-Edwards suggest, moreover, that there was a link between the Council of Mâcon and the transition from a pure observance of the *Regula Columbani* to the use of a combined *Regula Benedicti et Columbani*—a process that eventually led to the disappearance of the *Regula Columbani*.[60]

All speculations about the true—and allegedly concealed—agenda of the Council of Mâcon are based on strong arguments. It is indeed likely that Jonas suppressed topics at stake at the Council of Mâcon that did not fit his agenda and might throw an unfavorable light on Columbanus or cause trouble for his successors. Jonas is discreet about the Easter controversy, Columbanus's position on the Aquileian schism, the difficult relationship between the Irish holy man and the local Gallic bishops, and the spread of the *Regula Benedicti* among Columbanian monasteries. The dramatic depiction of the confrontation between Columbanus and Theuderic II that Jonas provides in the first book of his *Vita Columbani* certainly simplified the relationship between Merovingian rulers and Columbanus's monastic foundations.[61]

---

54. *VC* I.24: 206–8, I.30: 222–3, II.9: 246–8.

55. Dumézil 2007.

56. Dunn 2008: 3; Charles-Edwards 2000: 364–7, who places the Council of Mâcon in the wider context of the relationship between the papacy and the Irish Church.

57. Wood 1998: 101–2; Charles-Edwards 2000: 365–7; Stancliffe 2001: 206; Lifshitz 2006: 16–20; Kreiner 2014a: 125–8.

58. On the Irish tonsure, see Fox 2014: 228–30.

59. Stransbury 2011, based on *VC* I.9: 251: . . . *calumniatur capitis comam aliter tondi, alium caracterem exprimi et ab omnium mores disciscere.* He understands *caracter* as a reference to written letters.

60. Charles-Edwards 2000: 383–90; Stancliffe 2001: 211–3. On the replacement of the *Regula Columbani*, see also Prinz 1965: 263–92.

61. On the relationship between Columbanus and the Merovingian rulers, especially Brunhild, see Wood 1998.

Nevertheless, I want to draw attention to the topics of contention that Jonas *did* mention in his depiction of the showdown of Mâcon. After all, Jonas wrote the *Vita Columbani* for an audience that could have witnessed the Council of Mâcon.[62] Jonas may have determined where to place his emphasis and what to suppress, but he was certainly not in a position to work with alternative facts. We can assume that he chose topics suitable to discredit Agrestius by reducing his attacks to trivialities that Eustasius could easily refute. But there is probably still more behind these attacks, and there are striking links to the content of the *Regula cuiusdam patris*.

According to Jonas, Agrestius attacked three aspects of Columbanus's Rule. First was the practice of making the sign of the cross over a spoon whenever it is used, and second was the requirement of asking for a blessing while entering or leaving a building of the monastery.[63] Finally he accused Columbanus of having added extra elements to the Mass through an overabundance of prayers and collects.[64] The first two accusations refer to practices mentioned in Columbanus's *Regula coenobialis*.[65] The third one resonates with the liturgical program of Columbanus's *Regula monachorum*, which indeed requires, depending on the season and the day of the week, at least twenty-four psalms to be sung at the hour of the morning office:

> But towards morning twice ten and twice two are determined, as has been said, during the seasons of short nights, while more, as I have already said, are always ordained for the night of the Lord's Day and Sabbath vigil, on which seventy-five are sung individually in the course of one office.[66]

In an afterthought, after having been refuted by Eustasius on these grievances, Agrestius attacked the manner of tonsure (and maybe the Irish script, if Mark Stransbury is right) as deviating from the *mores omnium* ("the customs of everyone").[67]

---

62. Dumézil 2007: 136. On the constraints of writing hagiography for a contemporary audience, see Fouracre 1990: 11–2.

63. *VC* II.9: 249–50: *Cumque illi urguerent, tandem criminis causam depromit, se suae regulae habere, cocleam, quam lamberent, crebro crucis signo signari et ingressum cuiuslibet domus intra coenubium tam introiens quam egrediens benedictionem postulare.*

64. *VC* II.9: 250: *At ille prorumpit, se scire Columbanum a ceterorum mores disciscere et ipsa missarum sollemnia multiplicatione orationum vel collectarum celebrare et multa alia superflua, quae cum auctori acsi heresea tradita execrari debere.*

65. Columbanus, *Regula coenobialis*, ch. 1: 146: *Et qui non signaverit coclear quo lambit sex percussionibus*; ch. 3: 146–48: *Qui egrediens domum ad orationem poscendam non se humiliaverit et post acceptam benedictionem non se signaverit, crucem non adierit, XII percussionibus emendare statuitur.*

66. Columbanus, *Regula monachorum*, ch. 7: 130–33: *Ad matutinum vero bis deni bisque bini per tempora brevium, ut dictum est, noctium dispositi, pluribus, iam ut dixi, semper nocti dominicae ac sabbati vigiliae deputatis, in quibus sub uno cursu LXXV singillatim cantantur.*

67. *VC* II.9: 251: *His et horum similibus responsis confusus Agrestius, addit garrulitatis noxam, calumniatur capitis comam aliter tondi, alium caracterem exprimi et ab omnium mores disciscere.*

The three main accusations against the *sancta regula*—and Eustasius's responses to each of them—could, as trivial as they sound, stand for more than petty disagreements on details of monastic practice. All of them relate in a broad sense to ritual practices that Agrestius calls superfluous and Eustasius calls powerful.[68] The first one addresses a ritual sanctifying and protecting mundane material objects—and this applies, as Eustasius emphasizes in his response, not only to spoons but also, for example, to vessels and cups. Using the sign of the cross is, as Eustasius explains, an effective means of self-defense against the devil.[69] The second one criticizes a ritual that defines the monastery as a space whose boundaries should be crossed with caution and in connection with an act of prayer. In his response Eustasius emphasizes again the protective character of prayer. He compares the blessing and the sign of the cross when entering or leaving a building with the salutary effect of entering the Church through baptism—which implies that the act of blessing at entry and exit is by no means a trivial matter.[70] Agrestius's third accusation not only addresses the Mass, as we can conclude from Eustasius's reply, but also questions the beneficial impact of intercessory prayer in general and the assumption that pressing God through prayers has a salutary effect. All three accusations relate in different ways to the main challenge of Columbanian monasticism as Jonas describes it in his *Vita Columbani*: the question of what constitutes sanctity and how far the spiritual power of the monks could reach. Jonas explains that every object that belongs to the monastery partakes in its sanctity, using a beautiful fable in the first book of his *Vita Columbani*. He tells about a raven who stole a glove from the monastery and later, remorsefully, returned it.[71] The notion of the monastery as a sacred space with highly precarious boundaries is one of the recurring themes of Jonas's first book and the main reason given for the fatal showdown between King Theuderic II and Columbanus.[72] The monks' power of intercession, the

---

68. Cfr Kreiner 2014a: 218–9.

69. *VC* II.9: 250: "*Nequaquam,*" inquit, "*reor contrarium esse religioni, si coclea, qua christianus lambit, vel quodcumque vas aut poculum crucis signo muniri, cum per adventum signi dominici pellatur pestis adversantis inimici.*"

70. *VC* II.9: 250: "*Introeunte vel monacho cellulam vel exeunte benedictionem Domini armari ratum duco iuxta psalmistae vocem: Dominus custodit te ab omni malo: custodiat animam tuam Dominus. Dominus custodiat introitum tuum et exitum tuum ex hoc nunc et usque in saeculum. Licet hoc ad unumquemque christianum refertur, ut gratia baptismi per fidem in ecclesia introeunte servetur et usque ad finiem perseverantiae vigore firmetur, tamen cotidianum motum, sive in ingressu vel egressu seu progressu, unumquemque nostrum signo crucis armari vel benedictione sodalium roborari fas duco.*"

71. *VC* I.15: 178–9. For an analysis of this episode and references to other Columbanian sources on the sacredness of mundane objects, see Diem 2016b.

72. *VC* I.19: 190. I discuss this event and its implication for Columbanian concepts of space and boundaries in Diem 2007a. See also Charles-Edwards 2000: 357–8 and 382–3.

raison d'être for Columbanian monasteries, depended heavily on the impenetrability of its spatial boundaries and the correctness of its rituals.

In her reading of the Agrestius conflict and the Council of Mâcon, Jamie Kreiner suggests that the entire conflict—in extension of the Aquileian schism—may be "rooted in different ideas about what kinds of actions were necessary for the soul's salvation."[73] In 1997 Donald Bullough had already formulated the idea that Agrestius's critique may have been targeted at confession, penance, and the notion of absolution.[74] Both suggestions are compelling and deserve a fuller examination, particularly in the context of the *Regula cuiusdam patris*.

Its author vigorously refutes all attachment to material objects and requires the strictest austerity.[75] Moreover, the *Regula cuiusdam patris* is strikingly devoid of references or even allusions to any ritual other than the regular *conventus* and the Mass.[76] The author condemns negligence in handling monastic tools, but he certainly does not see them as objects requiring prayer.[77] The text does not contain the faintest reference to monastic space and boundaries; on the contrary, it seems to have been written for a community held together by ideas and practices rather than within a shared sacred space. There is no prayer for the sinful, no prayer on someone else's behalf, and no prayer or any other ritual to receive forgiveness for one's sin or to attain salvation.

Another potential link between the opposition against Columbanus's successors and the content of the *Regula cuiusdam patris* can be found in their attitude toward penance. Jonas of Bobbio ascribes to the rebels of Bobbio and Luxeuil a position that is, at first sight, egregious: a denial of the power of penance. Athala's opponents in Bobbio and Agrestius faced death and damnation because they scorned the monastery as a *locus paenitentiae*, and it is striking that Jonas uses this term in both cases.[78] The monastery envisioned by the *Regula cuiusdam patris* is indeed no *locus paenitentiae*.

Fernando Villegas has shown in his edition of the *Regula cuiusdam patris* that the chapters on monastic transgressions were largely based on regulations of the *Regula coenobialis*, the second part of Columbanus's Rule. A comparison

---

73. Kreiner 2014b: 127.
74. Bullough 1997: 13.
75. *Regula cuiusdam patris*, ch. 12–15: 20–22.
76. *Regula cuiusdam patris*, ch. 30–31: 34–35.
77. *Regula cuiusdam patris*, ch. 28: 31–2.
78. *VC* II.1: 232: *At vero alii, qui verecundia praeveniente vel temeritate hac arrogantiae vitio maculati redire noluerunt et datum locum paenitentiae contempserunt, diversis mortibus sunt direpti;* ch. 10: 254: *Nullum etenim Dominus perire desiderat, sed semper quamvis gravibus delictis obrutum per paenitentiae fomenta redire expectat. Cumque sibi sepius paenitentiae locum datum non cognovisset, ut Eusthasii sententia ad iudicium invocantis praevaleret, ante triginta dierum circulo quam vertentis anni meta compleretur, a servo suo quem ipse redemerat secure percussus interiit.*

of both texts reveals, however, that the *Regula cuiusdam patris* by no means reproduces Columbanus's verdicts but imposes entirely different and apparently stricter sanctions on the same transgressions. Where Columbanus requires bodily punishment and fasting according to a fixed penitential tariff (following the model of penitential handbooks),[79] the author of the *Regula cuiusdam patris* imposes imprisonment and expulsion and emphasizes that the punishment has to be determined according to the circumstances and the motivations of the perpetrator through the discernment of the superior.

The fact that the author used the *Regula coenobialis* but then deliberately chose a different set of sanctions indicates that he considered what he found in Columbanus's Rule to be inadequate. The following chart contains some examples of the author's revisions, and it is noteworthy that most of them come from chapter 10 of the *Regula coenobialis*, which may already have belonged to the sections of the Rule that were added after Columbanus's death.[80] So we do not know whether the author of the *Regula cuiusdam patris* did indeed rewrite Columbanus's own work or that of his successors.

Columbanus, *Regula coenobialis*	*Regula cuiusdam patris*
ch. 10: **Si quis frater inoboediens** *fuerit, duos dies una paxmate et aqua.*	ch. 4: **Si quis frater** *inventus* **fuerit inoboediens** *abbati sive equonomo sive alicui ex fratribus, mittendus est in carcerem et paeniteat quantum iudicaverit senior. Si autem post examinationem carceris reprobus invenitur semel et bis, iterum atque iterum, abscindendus est ab omni fraternitatis corpore . . .*
ch. 10: **Si quis** *veniam non petit aut dicit* **excusationem**, *duos dies uno paxmatio et aqua.*	ch. 7: **Si quis** *tardior ad veniam inventus fuerit, sive aliqua verba religioni contraria, sive pro* **excusatione** *delicti sui protulerit, mittendus est in carcerem et paeniteat secundum quod iudicaverit senior usquequo corrigatur.*
ch. 10: **Si quis murmura**t, *duos dies uno paxmatio et aqua.*	ch. 6: **Si quis** *frater* **murmura**ns *inventus fuerit, hic ipse mittendus est in carcerem et opus eius abiciatur. Penitentiam agat secundum examen senioris, si permittatur ei satisfaciet.*
ch. 10: *Si alius contendit* **mendacium** *. . . duos dies uno paxmatio et aqua.*	ch. 8: **Mendacium** *et iuramentum sive verbum otiosum per omne corpus fraternitatis damnandum est. Si quis ex fratribus cum quo aliquid horum inventum fuerit mittendus est in carcerem et paeniteat usquequo a vitio corrigatur.*
ch. 10: **Si quis detra**ctaverit abbati **suo**, *VII dies uno paxmatio et aqua.*	ch. 26: **Si quis** *seniori* **suo detra**xerit, *non seniori detrahit, sed domino, cuius opus facit senior. Si vero hoc frequenter faciat abscidatur a fraternitate ac sollicitudine fraterni corporis.*

79. Meens 2014: 40–69; Charles-Edwards 1997.
80. Bullough 1997: 11.

These deliberate alterations of Columbanus's Rule may indicate that the author of the *Regula cuiusdam patris* regarded the tariffed penitential system and the comparatively lenient sanctions as unsuitable for restoring order in a deeply disrupted community. I suggest, however, that they also reflect a more fundamental theological disagreement on the effects of *paenitentia*. Columbanus's *Regula coenobialis* begins with a theologically bold premise:

> It has been ordained, my dearest brethren, by the holy fathers that we make confession before meal or before entering our beds or whenever it is opportune of all failings, not only mortal ones, but also of minor omissions since confession and penance free from death.[81]

This statement resonates with Jonas's repeated emphasis on the salutary effects of *medicamenta paenitentiae* in his *Vita Columbani*,[82] but also with ideas on the salutary effect of confession and penance as laid out in the *Regula Donati* and the *Regula cuiusdam ad virgines*, the two other preserved "Columbanian" monastic rules.[83] Confession and the *medicamenta paenitentiae* lead to salvation (or at least avoid damnation). Evading them may be fatal, as Jonas emphasizes not only in the context of those rebels who remain renegades, but also in an episode in the section of the *Vita Columbani* dealing with the miracles at the monastery of Faremoutiers. Jonas tells here about two nuns who incurred eternal damnation because of their refusal to confess and to take the *medicamenta penitentiae*.[84]

Despite all the references to transgressions, punishment, and *paenitentia* in the *Regula cuiusdam patris*, the idea that penance may have a salutary effect is just as absent as any reference to intercessory prayer as the community's contribution to the project of salvation. As far as the text addresses *paenitentia*, its objective is to correct behavior and to gain the community's forgiveness rather than to reach

---

81. Columbanus, *Regula coenobialis*, ch. 1: 144–5: *Statutum est, fratres carissimi, a sanctis patribus, ut demus confessionem ante mensam sive ante lectorum introitum aut quandocumque fuerit facile de omnibus non solum capitalibus criminibus sed etiam de minoribus neglegentiis quia confessio et paenitentia de morte liberant.* See also Meens 2014: 54–7.

82. Jonas claims in *VC* I.5: 161, that the *medicamenta paenitentiae* had been abandoned through the negligence of the bishops. Moreover, he claims that people from everywhere flocked to the monastery to receive the *medicamenta paenitentiae* (I.10: 170). Some of the rebels against Athala returned to the monastery and saved their souls by seeking the *medicamenta paenitentiae* (II.1: 232). Eustasius provides the *medicamenta paenitentiae* to the monks of Rebais and to their neighbors, which implies that this was also available to laypeople (II.8: 245). A nun receives salvation through the *medicamenta paenitentiae*, as does a group of monks in Bobbio (II.15: 265, II.25: 290). On the notion of *medicamenta paenitentiae* in Jonas's work and other Frankish sources, see also Meens 2014: 70–81.

83. Donatus, *Regula ad virgines*, ed. Zimmerl-Panagl 2015, ch. 19.3–5: 157; ch. 23: 159–60; *Regula cuiusdam ad virgines*, ch. 5–7, col. 1058–60. See also Diem 2011: 93–7, 2012: 32–6.

84. *VC* II.19: 271–5, esp. 273. See also Kreiner 2014a: 116–28, identifying the notion of repentance as means of salvation as a Columbanian contribution.

God's pardon.[85] There is no mention of *medicamenta paenitentiae*, which might have been a direct affront against those in Luxeuil and Bobbio who considered the *medicamenta paenitentiae* an essential part of Columbanus's legacy.

The author of the *Regula cuiusdam patris* does, however, present an alternative. The entire Rule is, as it were, enclosed by two statements on the remedies against one's sinful state. For the *Regula cuiusdam patris* the Eucharist holds the position that is in other Columbanian rules held by *paenitentia*. In the first chapter of the *Regula cuiusdam patris*, the author states in words inspired by Augustine: "The chalice of suffering (or of the Passion) is bitter but it entirely heals all diseases. The chalice of suffering is bitter, but when the physician drinks it first, the sick man shall not hesitate to drink."[86] The Rule ends with this precept: "On Sundays, one always has to receive the Eucharist as a remedy (*remedium*) for sins. But we have to approach the body and blood of our Lord Jesus Christ with all holiness of the heart and the body."[87]

The author of the *Regula cuisudam patris* operates within the same framework of medical metaphors, but his *medicamenta* are indeed entirely different from the *medicamenta paenitentiae* that are, as Jonas of Bobbio claims, essential to Columbanus's monastic ideal. It was certainly no trivial theological matter whether the remedies of penance, confession, and mutual prayer might ensure salvation or if the Eucharist alone was enough. The question may have been serious enough to prompt mutual accusations of heresy, and at least in Jonas's eyes, Athala's critics and Agrestius signed their fate by disregarding the power of penance.[88]

Agrestius's third attack on the *Regula Columbani* and Eustasius's response can be linked to the question of what constitutes a proper *medicamentum*. Jonas reports that Agrestius accused the monks of Luxeuil of adding to the Mass through an overabundance of superfluous prayers.[89] Eustasius responded that these prayers are not superfluous at all, but indeed highly effective. Chapter 7 of Columbanus's *Regula monachorum* explicitly refers to the practice of

---

85. See *Regula cuiusdam patris*, ch. 7.4, ch. 8.2, ch. 10.4, ch. 20.6, ch. 27.2.

86. *Regula cuiusdam patris*, ch. 1.2–3: 10: *Calix passionis amarus est, sed omnes morbos penitus curat; calix passionis amarus est, sed cum prior biberit medicus ne bibere dubitet aegrotus.*

87. *Regula cuiusdam patris*, ch. 32: 35: *In diebus vero dominicis eucaristia semper accipienda est ad remedium peccatorum. Sed cum puro corde et omni sanctiate cordis et corporis oportet nos accedere at corpus et sanguinem domini nostri iesu christi. Amen.*

88. Charles-Edwards 1997: 236–47 states that, contrary to what one might have expected, Columbanian penitential practice did not find any resistance among the Gallic clergy. The *Regula cuiusdam patris* might provide what he had expected to find.

89. *VC* II.9: 250: *At ille prorumpit, se scire Columbanum a ceterorum mores disciscere et ipsa missarum sollemnia multiplicatione orationum vel collectarum celebrare et multa alia superflua, quae cum auctori acsi heresea tradita execrari debere.*

intercession through prayer,[90] and we find a similar intercessory formula in the Bobbio Missal.[91] Moreover, Columbanus's *Regula monachorum* does, as already mentioned, frame the Mass with an enormous number of psalms.[92] The *Regula cuiusdam patris*, rather differently, declares the Mass to be the only way of receiving forgiveness for one's sins. The liturgical program of the *Regula cuiusdam patris* limits the number of psalms the monks have to sing at the office hours and omits the intercessory *versicula* that Columbanus's *Regula monachorum* requires after each daily hour. Moreover, the *Regula cuiusdam patris* replaced Columbanus's terms for monastic liturgy, *cursus, synaxis*, and *hora*,[93] with the rather neutral term *conventus* ("gathering").

Aside from not mentioning any intercessory activities, the main liturgical difference between Columbanus's *Regula monachorum* and the *Regula cuiusdam patris* is that the *Regula cuiusdam patris* does not assign any psalms during morning Mass, which is entirely in line with Agrestius's critique on Columbanian practice:

One has to come together in the church for three gatherings (*conventus*) during the day and three times during the night. At each daytime gathering three psalms are to be sung. But at the nighttime gatherings twelve psalms will be sung, except at the Mass that is celebrated at dawn. At

90. Columbanus, *Regula monachorum*, ch. 7: 130: *Igitur iuxta vires consideranda vigilia est, maxime cum ab auctore salutis nostrae iubemur vigilare et orare omni tempore, et Paulus praecipit: sine intermissione orate. Sed quia orationum canonicarum noscendus est modus, in quo omnes simul orantes horis convenient statutis, quibus absolutis unusquisque in cubiculo suo orare debet, per diurnas terni psalmi horas pro operum interpositione statuti sunt a senioribus nostris cum versiculorum augmento intervenientium pro peccatis primum nostris, deinde pro omni populo christiano, deinde pro sacerdotibus et reliquis deo consecrates sacrae plebis gradibus, postremo pro elemosinas facientibus, postea pro pace regum, novissime pro inimicis, ne illis deus statuat in peccatum quod persecuntur et detrahunt nobis, quia nesciunt quid faciunt.*

91. *Missale Bobbiense*, no. 438, ed. Lowe 1920: 130: *Maiestatem tuam clementissime pater exoramus pro fratribus et sororibus nostris seo omnibus benefactoribus nostris vel qui se in nostris oracionibus conmendaverunt tam pro vivos quam et solutis debitum mortuis quorum elimosinas erogandas suscepemus vel quorum animas ad memorando conscripsemus vel quorum nomina super sanctum alterio scripta adest Evidenter concede propicius ut haec sacra oblacio mortuis prosit ad veniam et vivis proficiat ad salutem et fidelibus tuis pro quibus oblacionem offerimus indulgenciam tuae pietatis succurrat.*

92. Columbanus, *Regula monachorum*, ch. 7: 128–32, esp. 130–2: *Ad matutinum vero bis deni bisque bini per tempora brevium, ut dictum est, noctium dispositi, pluribus, iam ut dixi, semper nocti dominicae ac sabbati vigiliae deputatis, in quibus sub uno cursu LXXV singillatim cantantur.* [. . .] *Noctibus vero reverentissimis dominicis scilicet vel sabbatis ad matutinum ter idem volvitur numerus, id est ter denis et VI psalmis.* Stancliffe 2011: 20 observes that Columbanus's liturgical order is in general following that of Cassian, with the exception of this extreme number of psalms at the morning office. On the excessiveness of Columbanus's liturgical program, see also Stevenson 1997: 209–13, who also provides evidence that celebrating Mass at dawn was a common practice.

93. The expression *conventus* rarely appears in monastic rules, though John Cassian uses it.

each nighttime gathering, prayers and two readings, one from the Old Testament and one from the New Testament are to be recited. At the gatherings on Saturday and Sunday Mass has to be celebrated until cockcrow. And as far as the strength of each one can endure, vigils should be held.[94]

Both the last statement—*quomodo vires uniuscuiusdque suffere poterint*—and the subsequent chapter on arriving on time for the office give the impression that liturgy was not of central importance for the author of the *Regula cuiusdam patris*. The author states that those who arrive after the first psalm may not join the *conventus*. They have to ask for pardon afterward. Whoever does this more often receives a reprimand. For the night prayers, lenience is granted until the second psalm.[95] This mild reproach toward a lack of liturgical discipline is remarkable if we compare it to the draconic punishments the author of the *Regula cuiusdam patris* imposes for other transgressions. Most other monastic rules are much more preoccupied with liturgical discipline than the *Regula cuiusdam patris* is.[96] For the author of the *Regula cuiusdam patris*, work, austerity, and obedience to the *mandata dei* seem to be much more important than penance and liturgical rigor.

In the next section of my analysis I focus on a number of other particularities of the *Regula cuisudam patris* that can be understood as consequences of its theological program and make the text unique among all textual witnesses of Columbanian monasticism: its concept of monastic renunciation, its work ethic, its notion of authority, and eventually, its concept of *oboedientia*.

Renuntiatio: *The Monastic Ideal of the* Regula cuiusdam patris

As already stated, the *Regula cuiusdam patris* begins with a reference to the *calix passionis* that needs to be taken as a remedy. It is the responsibility of any *senior*

---

94. *Regula cuiusdam patris*, ch. 30.1–5: 34: *Tribus conventibus diei, totidemque noctis tempore in ecclesia conveniendum; tres psalmi in unoquoque conventu diei canendi sunt; duodecim vero nocturnis conventibus cantabuntur, praeter illam missam quae celebratur ortu solis. Orationes vero et duae lectiones, una de veteri testamenti et alia de novo, in singulis noctis conventibus dicendae sunt. In his vero conventibus, id est sabbati et dominicae, usque ad gallorum cantus missa celebranda est. Et quomodo vires uniuscuiusque sufferre poterint excubiae pre agendae sunt.*

95. *Regula cuiusdam patris*, ch. 31: 34–5: *Is vero qui ad primum psalmum in die non occurrit, in conventum fratrum non recipietur. Sed postea in public veniam petat. Si vero frequenter hoc faciat, confutabitur usque dum corrigatur.*

96. See, for example, *Regula coenobialis*, ch. 2: 140; ch. 4: 148; ch. 12: 160, lines 19–25; ch. 14: 162; ch. 15: 166, lines 9–19; *Regula cuiusdam ad virgines*, ch. 2.18–19, col. 1055; ch. 8, col. 1061.

to act as a model, both by drinking from the *calix passionis* and by attaining the necessary *sanctitas cordis et corporis*.[97] The Rule ends with the requirement to approach the Eucharist with a pure heart and in all holiness of heart and body (*cum puro corde et omni sanctitate cordis et corporis*) in order to receive healing.[98] In the middle section of the Rule (chapters 14–15 in the modern chapter division) the author requires three renunciations that define the way of life every monk has professed.[99] Here we find an outline of how this *puritas cordis et corporis* can be achieved and what drinking the *calix passionis* actually entails:

> God's law, which comprises the visible and the invisible, is always to be followed. None of the commands of God, be it a large one or the smallest one, may be passed by because *whoever transgresses against one rule is made guilty of all of them.* The monastic way of life that we have promised, needs to be practiced and carried out with our whole heart and with all love. It consists of three renunciations.
>
> First we must cast off all of our power (*facultas*) and all the riches of the world must be recognized by us as alien.
>
> In the second place we have to leave all vices of the flesh and the soul behind and we have to free ourselves from them and *all anger, bitterness, shouting and blasphemy should be taken from you, along with all malice.*
>
> The third renunciation is that of all things that are seen in the sky, on earth, in the sea or in all of his creatures we do not only put nothing on equal footing with God, but we should also regard all these things as inferior to ourselves, since we strive beyond all these things for the heavenly kingdom and the knowledge of God. And therefore we do not direct our attention very much to these things that serve vanity and that will pass soon, according to what the Apostle says: *Everything that is visible is temporal, but what is invisible is eternal.*[100]

97. *Regula cuiusdam patris*, ch. 1.3–4: 10 and ch. 24.4: 28.

98. *Regula cuiusdam patris*, ch. 32: 35. *Puritas cordis* is a key concept in the monastic theology of John Cassian. See Von Nagel 1978; Diem 2005: 95–112.

99. Cfr. also de Vogüé 2006: 293–7.

100. *Regula cuiusdam patris*, ch. 14.2 and ch. 15: 21–22: *Et lex dei, quae sive visibilia sive invisibilia continent, observanda est. Et nihil ex mandatis dei, sive magnum sive minimum, praetereundum est: quia qui transgreditur unum factus est omnis reus. Propositum monachi quod promisimus, ex toto corde nostro et ex tota dilectione exercendum est et faciendum, quod in tribus abrenuntiationibus consistit. Primo omnium omnes facultates nostras respuere debemus et omnes divitiae mundi alienae esse a nobis noscuntur. Deinde*

This chapter, arguably the programmatic core of the *Regula cuiusdam patris*, shows how the author composed his text as a critical response to Columbanus's Rule. The *Regula monachorum* contains a similar triad, but on *perfectio*, and this triad is somewhat hidden away in a chapter on greed: "Thus them nakedness and disdain of riches are the first perfection of monks, but the second is the purging of vices, the third the most perfect and perpetual love of God and unceasing affection for things divine, which follows from the forgetfulness of earthly things."[101] Columbanus's short triad on *perfectio* is inspired by a section from the third book of Cassians's *Collationes* on the topic of monastic renunciation.[102] The author of the *Regula cuiusdam patris* was probably inspired by Columbanus's *Regula monachorum*, but he did not just rephrase what he found there. Instead, he went back to its source, Cassian, and proposed a different and much more radical *sensus* of Cassian's words—an interpretation that very much reads like a statement *against* monks who failed to live up to this *propositum* by not renouncing their *facultas*, by quarreling, and by seeing monastic life as an endeavor that is entangled in the world.

It makes sense to read the three renunciations in particular as a polemic against the direction Columbanian monasticism had taken after Columbanus's death and as a contribution to the debates instigated by Agrestius. Aristocrats who entered Columbanian monasteries may have renounced their property, but they certainly kept their *facultas* by remaining part of powerful family structures, as Yaniv Fox and Jamie Kreiner have shown.[103] There was a lot of "anger, bitterness, shouting and blasphemy" in Bobbio and Luxeuil and, of course, it is always the other party that is to be blamed for it. Moreover, it may have been easy to accuse places like Luxeuil, which gained significant political and economic power, of having the wrong priorities and focusing on the visible and temporal.

---

in secundo loco, omnia vitia carnis et animae relinquenda sunt et carenda: et omnis ira et indignation, et clamor, et blasphemia auferatur a vobis cum omni militia. Tertia igitur abrenuntiatio est, haec omnia quaecumque videntur, sive in caelo, sive in terra, sive in mari, seu in omnibus creaturis dei, non solum nihil ex his adsimilari domino debemus sed omnia etiam illa inferior a nostri arbitrari a nobis oportet: qui utpote nos ultra illa ad caelorum regna et ad ipsius domini notitiam extendimus. Et ideo his vanitati servientibus et mox transeuntibus non magnopere intendimus; secundum quod apostolus dicit: omnia quae videntur temporalia sunt, quae autem non videntur aeterna sunt. The chapter division in Villegas's edition, which starts chapter 15 with *Propositum monachi*, makes no sense here.

101. Columbanus, *Regula monachorum*, ch. 4: 126–7, lines 20–23: *Ideo ergo nuditas et facultatum contemptus prima perfectio est monachorum, secunda vero purgatio vitiorum, tertia perfectissima dei continuata dilectio ac divinorum iugis amor, qui terrenorum succedit oblivioni.*

102. Cassian, *Collationes* III.6, ed. Pichery 1955: 145. See also de Vogüé 2007: 257–62 and Stancliffe 2011: 19–20, who discusses Cassian's impact on Columbanus's monastic theology in general.

103. Fox 2014: 27–135 and Kreiner 2014a: 201–29 show to what extent the rhetoric of renunciation in Columbanian monasticism clashed with the reality of aristocratic patronage and political integration.

Austerity and Manual Labor

The definition of the *propositum monachi* in chapter 15 of the *Regula cuiusdam patris* is flanked by two sets of regulations that may be related to the discontent that inspired the three renunciacions. In chapters 12–14 the author requires strict austerity and independence from external support. Monks have to perform manual labor to sustain the community on a very basic level. All surplus needs to be spent on supporting the poor.[104] The specifics of the community's location determine the source of income: potentially agriculture, livestock, trade, handicrafts, and maybe even day labor.

The *Regula cuiusdam patris* was clearly not written for a community that enjoyed lavish support from kings and aristocrats and could concentrate on prayer instead of doing manual labor. Its economic ideal could not have been more different from that expressed in the already mentioned privilege for Rebais from 637, the oldest preserved privilege for an affiliation of Luxeuil. Protecting their property seems to have been a major concern of the founders of Rebais:

> As to anything that is given to the monks of the said monastery who live there under evangelical order of life whether by themselves, by their parents, or by royal gift or by other Christians, that is fields, slaves, service, holy books or other things, that are meant to belong to the divine service, or other objects, and things which are given to the altar—both the things they have already got and those they will receive: whatever they have received by inspiration of God, must neither during my own life nor under my successors, be alienated or diminished by any of the clergy or bishops, or by the lofty power of a king, for their own use.[105]

One of the narrative lines in Jonas's *Vita Columbani* describes and legitimates the transition that the communities underwent in the course of Columbanus's lifetime and under the regime of his successors. Numerous miracles and signs of God's favor sanctioned, as it were, the transition from a community of poor

104. *Regula cuiusdam patris*, ch. 12: 20: *Nihil quaerere debemus ex his quae ad saeculum pertinent, praeter cotidianum panem nostrum, et breve vestimentum quo induamur. Haec ipsa sine sollicitudine a nobis requirantur; ne inueniamur aliquando de regno dei non cogitare, et dicatur de nobis: haec omnia gentes requirunt. Verumtamen monachos semper oportet laborare, et sine sollicitudine vitam suam transigere. Omnia quaecumque laboraverint, excepto ut supra diximus pane exiguo et vestimento, pauperibus distribuant. Cura pauperum semper facienda est, et omnia nostra cum caritate fiant; et sine caritate infructuosa sunt apud deum opera nostra.*

105. Episcopal privilege for the monastery of Rebais (c. 637), ed. Pardessus 1849: 60: . . . *ut quidquid praedicti monasterii, vel monachis ibidem sub evangelica religione viventibus, ab ipsis eorumque parentibus, vel regio munere seu a quibuslibet Christianis, in agris, mancipiis, ministerio, sacris voluminibus, vel quibuscumque speciebus quae ad ornatum divini cultus pertinere noscitur, aut caeteris rebus, collata, aut deinceps collatura sunt, seu quod ad altare fuerit oblatum, ut ad quemcumque. Deo inspirante, transmissum, praesentis vitae nostrae successorumque nostrorum, nullus sibi exinde aliquid clericorum aut pontificum, vel regalis sublimitas suis usibus usurpare aut minuere praesumant.*

and hard-working monks under a leader who lived a strictly ascetic life into a well-endowed and politically connected network of monastic foundations led by capable administrators and receiving privileges such as that for Rebais.[106]

Incapable Superiors

The *Regula cuiusdam patris* discusses (more extensively than any other monstic rule) what characterizes a worthy or unworthy superior and how the monks should deal with an incapable abbot. The Rule condemns abbots and *seniores* who neglect their own monasteries, do not care for their monks' spiritual or physical needs, engage in worldly politics, travel around, do not live according to the standards they impose on others, and act out of anger or favoritism.[107] Moreover, the text warns that monks (and implicitly abbots) should not establish close relations with female communities.[108]

Much of what the *Regula cuiusdam patris* criticizes about the behavior of abbots and other superiors could be directly applied to Eustasius. Jonas and other hagiographers praise him as a tirelessly traveling negotiator on behalf of a flourishing monastic network. He founded new monasteries; served as a missionary; and maintained close ties to the royal court and to Frankish aristocrats, whose houses

---

106. See, for example, *VC* I.30: 223 on Luxeuil receiving protection and lavish material support from King Clothar II.

107. *Regula cuiusdam patris*, ch. 1.3–4: 10: *Calix passionis amarus est, sed cum prior biberit medicus ne bibere dubitet aegrotus. Oportet namque illum qui alterius vulnera mederi cupit ab omi languoris morbo alienum sanumque subsistere*; ch. 19: 25–6: *Non quisquam congregationi fratrum praeesse permittendus, nisi qui oboediendo didicerit ea quae aliis praecipi debeant sed si forte in scripturis sanctis satis sufficienter instructus est, tamen si factorurn gestis adhibeat fidem, id est ea quae docet, opere conpleverit, humilitatem et caritatem, patientiam et mansuaetudinem ostendendo, et voluntatem senioris implendo, et omnia mandata domini agendo*; ch. 20: 26: *Si quis ex senioribus sive is qui abbas nuncupatur, voluptuosus exsistat et ebriosus et dives, et qui huic saeculo conformatur, id est in curribus et in equis, de loco ad locum discurrat, hic non solum principatu fratrum indignus est, verum etiam homicida animarum iudicandus est, et alius monasterio eius praeesse constituatur. Sin vero non poterint monachi ab illo exeant, et ille exeommunicetur. Si vero paeniteat, subdat se sub manibus senioris et servituti se subiciat, donec probaverit is qui praeest*; ch. 24: 28–9: *Quomodo seniorem oportet fieri ad fratres? Tamquam si nutrix foveat parvulos suos, diligens et confortans singulos; et viam perfectionis eis aperiat; et ipse praecedat in omni perfectione et sanctitate cordis et corporis; et sine ulla acceptione personarum omnis pariter et sincera dilectione, tamquam notos proprios ex toto corde diligat. Si vero viderit aliquem illorum mandatum domini praeterire, non ira erga eum moveatur sed cum miseratione et conpassione; secundum illum qui dixit: quis infirmatur et ego non infirmor; quis scandalizatur et ego non uror? Si vero neglegens in his quae ad usus corporis et animae pertinent, sine dubio subicietur illi sententiae quae dicit: ite maledicti in ignem aeternum qui preparatus est diabolo et angelis eius. Esurivi enim et non dedistis mihi manducare; sitivi et non dedistis mihi bibere, et ea quae secuntur. Et maledictus homo qui facit operae dei neglegenter*; ch. 25: 29: *Si quis a senioribus et abbatibus iracundus inventus fuerit, notetur usquequo corrigatur. Si vero ab hoc vitio insanabilis fuerit, ab imperio fratrum destruendus. Quoniam sive iuste sive iniuste irasci non oportet.*

108. *Regula cuiusdam patris*, ch. 18.2: 25: *Sorores igitur raro videndae sunt et frequenter loqui ad eas velle prohibemus, ne occasionem inveniamur dare infirmis.*

he frequently visited. In sum, Jonas praised him as a highly skilled monk-politician who obviously had not cut his aristocratic roots; instead he extensively used them to the material and economic benefit of his communities.[109] Eustasius was not only present at the foundation of numerous monasteries but also interacted closely with aristocratic ladies and future abbesses, such as Burgundofara and Sadalberga.[110] Luxeuil itself was not much more than a base camp for him, and it is telling that Jonas repeatedly calls him *abbas*, but never *abbas Luxoviensis*.[111]

Even if the author of the *Regula cuiusdam patris* did not have Eustasius in mind when he talked about the "pleasure-seeking, sottish, and opulent" abbot, who "is shaped by this world," who "travels back and forth in a cart or on horseback," and who "is not only unworthy of ruling over the brothers, but should be condemned as a murderer of souls," it is clear that his ideal of a capable abbot was hardly compatible with the life Eustasius led, even according to his own hagiographer.

Obedience

One of the central themes of the *Regula cuiusdam patris* is *oboedientia*—and we should not assume that this term, as the author uses it, covers exactly the same range of meanings as the modern expression "obedience."[112] Almost half of the text discusses different aspects and implications of *oboedientia* and manifestations of disobedience. The author's point of departure is the first chapter of Columbanus's *Regula monachorum*, which demands unconditional obedience *usque ad mortem*[113] and makes each monk who shows resistance responsible for the acts of any other monk who might be prone to disobedience:

> At the first word of a senior, all on hearing should rise to obey, since their obedience is shown to God, as our Lord Jesus Christ says: *He who*

109. E.g., *VC* II.7–10: 240–57; *Vita Agili*, ch. 12–16, ed. Stiltingus 1886: col. 580A–E; *Vita Amati*, ch. 5, ed. Krusch 1902: 217; *Vita Sadalbergae*, ch. 1–4, ch. 7–8, ed. Krusch 1910: 50–4; Fredegar IV.44, ed. Krusch 1888: 142–143. Especially *VC* II.7: 241: *Evenit, ut pro communi necessitate ad regem Chlotharium pergeret, qui eo tempore in ultimis Galliae finibus Oceani maris vicina inhabitabat. Fuit ergo arrepti itineris via per saltum pagumque Briegium perventumque ad quaedam villam Changerici quo dudum magister quantisper moraverat.* See also Diem 2007a; Kreiner 2014a: 190–1.

110. *VC* II.7: 243: *Monasteriumque Christi virginum super paternernum solum inter fluvios Mugram et Albam aedificat fratresque, qui aedificandi curam habeant, deputat; germanum puellae Chagnoaldum et Waldebertum, qui ei postea successit, ut regulam doceant, decernit.*

111. Diem 2007a: 552.

112. See also de Vogüé 2006: 290–3, commenting on the sources of the chapters of the *Regula cuiusdam patris* on obedience.

113. De Vogüé 2007: 253–5. See also *VC* I.12: 172–3, which exemplifies Columbanus's demand for unconditional obedience: Columbanus sends a group of sick monks out to work. Only those who follow his orders without hesitation are miraculously healed.

hears you hears Me. Therefore if anyone hearing the word does not rise at once, he is to be judged disobedient. But he who answers back incurs the charge of insubordination, and thus is not only guilty of disobedience, but also, by opening the way of answering back for others, is to be regarded as a destroyer of many. Yet if any murmurs, he too, as though not obeying heartily, must be considered disobedient. Therefore let his work be rejected, until his goodwill be made known. But up to what measure is obedience laid down? Up to death it is assuredly enjoined, since Christ obeyed the Father up to death for us. [...] Thus nothing must be refused in their obedience by Christ's true disciples, however hard and difficult it be, but it must be seized with zeal, with gladness, since if obedience is not of this nature, it will not be pleasing to the Lord Who says: *And he who does not take his cross and follow Me, is not worthy of Me.* And thus He says of the worthy disciple, how that *Where I am, there is My servant also with Me.*[114]

Columbanus's concept of obedience does not differ fundamentally from that expressed in the *Regula Benedicti*, which equally places unconditional obedience at the center of monastic life and requires that monks have to perform even impossible and morally questionable tasks if the abbot requires them to do so.[115] Columbanus and the author of the *Regula Benedicti* share in particular the notion that an obedient monk delegates the responsibility for his deeds to the superior whose orders he follows.[116]

---

114. Columbanus, *Regula monachorum* ch. 1, ed./transl. Walker 1957: 122–5: *Ad primum verbum senioris omnes ad oboediendum audientes surgere oportet, quia oboedientia deo exhibetur, dicente domino nostro Iesu Christo: Qui vos audit me audit. Si quis igitur verbum audiens non statim surrexerit inoboediens iudicandus est. Qui autem contradixerit contumaciae crimen incurrit, et ideo non solum inoboedientiae reus est, sed etiam contradictionis aditum aliis aperiens multorum destructor aestimandus est. Si quis vero murmuraverit, et ipse tamquam non ex voto oboediens inoboediens putandus est. Idcirco opus eius abiiciatur, donec illius bona voluntas cognoscatur. Oboedientia autem usque ad quem modum definitur? Usque ad mortem certe praecepta est, quia Christus usque ad mortem oboedivit patri pro nobis. [...] Nihil itaque recusandum est oboedientibus veris Christi discipulis, quamvis durum et arduum sit, sed cum fervore, cum laetitia arripiendum est, quia si talis non fuerit oboedientia, non erit acceptabilis domino qui ait: Et qui non accipit crucem suam et sequitur me, non est me dignus. Et ideo dicit de digno discipulo: ut Ubi ego sum, ibi et minister meus mecum.*

115. See *Regula Benedicti*, prologue, 2–3: 412; ch. 3.6: 452–4; ch. 4.61: 460–2; ch. 5: 464–8; ch. 7.34–43: 480–2; ch. 23: 542; ch. 58.7–8: 626–8; ch. 58.17: 630; ch. 68: 664; ch. 71: 668; esp. ch. 4.61: 460: *praeceptis abbatis in omnibus oboedire, etiam si ipse aliter—quod absit!—agat, memores illud dominicum praeceptum: Quae dicunt facite, quae autem faciunt facere nolite.* On similarities between Benedict's and Columbanus's notions of obedience, see De Bhaldraithe 1983: 69–71. It is remarkable that modern commentators on the *Regula Benedicti* usually try to mitigate the mandate of unconditional obedience and to sideline the notion of delegated responsibility of the abbot. As such, they propose an understanding of the *Regula Benedicti* that comes close to what the *Regula cuiusdam patris* proposes. See Leclercq 1965; de Vogüé 1979: 197–200, 224–41; Kardong 1983; Böckmann 1994; Puzicha 2009.

116. As in the *Regula Benedicti*, Columbanus even develops the idea that obedience delegates the responsibility for one's salvation to the abbot. Compare *Regula Benedicti*, ch. 2.6–10: 442, and Columbanus,

At first glance the *Regula cuiusdam patris* seems to elaborate Columbanus's strict notion of obedience by expanding it with assertions from Basil and Cassian. The author emphasizes even more than Columbanus the performative side of obedience: monks have to rise at the first word when they hear an order or a request and throw themselves to the ground whenever criticism is afoot.[117] Obedience has to be performed *usque ad mortem*, promptly and without hesitation.[118] Following one's own *iudicium* instead of the advice (*consilia*) of the *seniores* leads directly into the open arms of the devil.[119] Moreover, the Rule addresses numerous manifestations of disobedience, such as murmuring, defending one's own acts, lying and swearing, anger, slander, and contempt.[120] These transgressions in particular are to be punished by imprisonment and, if necessary, expulsion. Even stronger than Columbanus, the *Regula cuiusdam patris* emphasizes that obedience needs to be performed with joy. Whatever a monk performs against his will is to be considered worthless.[121]

Yet despite all these similarities, the *Regula cuiusdam patris* develops, entirely in line with its opening statement, a notion of *oboedientia* that is fundamentally different from that of Columbanus (and, in fact, the *Regula Benedicti*). First, *oboedientia* is a *virtus*, a virtue to be attained—a notion that is inspired by John Cassian's work.[122] It is much more than simply fulfilling orders in a chain of

Regula monachorum, ch. 9: 138–40. See Kreiner 2014b: 142 for the notion of delegated responsibility in Columbanian hagiographic texts.

117. *Regula cuiusdam patris*, ch. 3.2–3: 11: *Et ad primum verbum senioris omnes qui audierint ex fratribus adsurgere oportet. Et qui non surrexerit veniam petat et paeniteat quantum iudicaverit senior;* ch. 7.1–2: 15: *Ad primum verbum discussionis senioris sive equonomi, sive alicuius fratris, venia petenda est et tamdiu in terra prostratus donec senior discussionem consummaverit. Si autem senior discussionem iteraverit, et ipse veniam iterare debet;* ch. 29.1–3: 32–3: *Si quis ad vocem conpulsoris sive invitantis ad aliud quodcumque non statim surrexerit, hic inobediens reus est. Petat veniam ad deum et iterare non praesumant. Quoniam oportet unumquemque ad primum vocem invitantis adsurgere; velut carbo ignis ardentis descendisset super eum.*

118. *Regula cuiusdam patris*, ch. 3.5: 12: *Oboedientia usque ad mortem facienda est secundum exemplum domini oboediens patris usque ad mortem;* ch. 23: 28: *Quomodo nos oboedire ei oportet, qui nos ad opus mandati cohortatur? Sicut infans obtemperat nutrici suae quad ad ubera sua eum invitat; immo si quid promptius et celeries, pro eo quod multum pretiosior vita futura quam praesens, oboedientiam usque ad mortem oportet.* This section is inspired by *Regula Basilii*, ch. 15: 64–65, ch. 46: 90, ch. 112: 138–9.

119. *Regula cuiusdam patris*, ch. 1.5: 10: *Nullo alio vitio diabolus monachum perdit ac trahit ad mortem, quam cum eum neglectis seniorum consiliis suo iudicio defensionique conspexerit confidere.* This section is inspired by Cassian, *Collationes* II.1: 123.

120. *Regula cuiusdam patris*, ch. 4: 13–14; ch. 6: 14; ch. 7.3–5: 15; ch. 8–10: 16–18; ch. 26–27: 30–31.

121. *Regula cuiusdam patris*, ch. 29.6–8: 33: *Cum gaudio semper operandum est et nihil cum tristita faciendum; et semper dicendum est: gaudete in domino iusti et semper decet conlaudatio; et iterum apostolus dicit: gaudete in domino semper, iterum dico gaudete. Si autem triste aliquid oblatum fuerit a nobis in donis dei, non erit acceptabile apud deum.*

122. *Regula cuiusdam patris*, ch. 3.1: 11: *Deinde virtus oboedientiae expetenda est et secundum vires uniuscuiusque exercenda est.* See, for example, Cassian, *Institutiones* IV.12: 136.

command. *Oboedientia* has a horizontal aspect and needs to be a guideline for how monks interact with each other and how they should obey those who are directly senior to them. This horizontal obedience stands on an equal footing with obedience to the abbot.[123] Superiors have to show obedience toward their inferiors as well through their love,[124] through their care for spiritual but also bodily needs,[125] and by not showing anger or favoritism.[126] Most importantly, *oboedientia* has to be performed unconditionally, *usque ad mortem*, not toward the superior but toward the *mandata domini*—a term that is absent in Columbanus's Rule but ubiquitous in the *Regula cuiusdam patris*[127] and inspired by Basil's Rule, where it appears numerous times.[128] As long as a superior acts and gives orders in accordance with the *mandata domini*, a monk has to obey him unconditionally.[129] If a superior acts contrary to the *mandata domini*, a monk has the right and the duty to renounce deference, to excommunicate his superior, to depose him, or, if this is impossible, to leave the monastery.[130] The different notions of obedience in Columbanus's Rule and in the *Regula cuiusdam patris* may simply have been motivated by the transition from a charismatic leader

---

123. *Regula cuiusdam patris*, ch. 3.6: 13: *Et unusquisque oportet fratri suo servire sicut abbatis proprio vel patri sicut apostolus dicit: servite invicem in timore christi, et iterum: omnia vestra cum caritate fiant*; ch. 5: 14: *Non omnibus presente abbate vel equonomo obtemperandum quia unus non occurit admones, sed tamen unusquisque fatri senior oboedire contendat sicut domino. Quicquid facit proximo suo, domino facere non ambigat.*

124. *Regula cuiusdam patris*, ch. 24.1/6: 28.

125. *Regula cuiusdam patris*, ch. 24.8: 29: *Si vero neglegens in his quae ad usus corporis et animae pertinent, sine dubio subicietur illi Sententiae quae dicit: ite maledicti in ignem aeternum qui preparatus est diabolo et angelis eius. Esuriui enim et non dedistis mihi manducare; sitivi et non dedistis mihi bibere.*

126. *Regula cuiusdam patris*, ch. 25: 29: *Si quis a senioribus et abbatibus iracundus inventus fuerit, notetur usquequo corrigatur. Si vero ab hoc vitio insanabilis fuerit, ab imperio fratrum destruendus est. Quoniam sive iuste sive iniuste irasci non oportet.*

127. *Regula cuiusdam patris*, ch. 2.2: 11: *et proximum magnopere diligendum esse secundum mandatum domini*; ch. 14.3: 21: *Et nihil ex mandatis dei, sive magnum sive minimum praetereundum est: quia qui transgreditur unum factus est omnium reus.* See also ch. 19.3: 25–26, ch. 23.1: 28.

128. Basil develops throughout his Rule a notion of obedience, which is primarily oriented toward the *mandata dei*, very much in line with what the *Regula cuiusdam patris* proposes. See *Regula Basilii*, ch. 1–3: 8–32, ch. 12–13: 58–63, ch. 46: 90, ch. 83–84: 117–9, ch. 106: 134, ch. 126: 155–6, ch. 150: 175–6, esp. ch. 13.8–9: 62: *Si autem contrarium aliquid mandatis dei vel quod ea corrumpere videatur aut contaminare facere iubemur ab aliquo, tempus est nos dicere Obtemperare oportet deo magis quam hominibus, et rursum meminisse domini dicentis Alieni autem vocem non sequuntur, sed fugiunt ab eo quoniam nesciunt alienorum vocem.*

129. *Regula cuiusdam patris*, ch. 19: 25–26: *Non quisquam congregationi fratrum praeesse permittendus, nisi qui oboediendo didicerit ea quae aliis praecipi debeant sed si forte in scripturis sanctis satis sufficienter instructus est, tamen si factorum gestis adhibeat fidem, id est ea quae docet, opere conpleverit, humilitatem et caritatem, patientiam et mansuaetudinem ostendendo, et voluntatem senioris implendo, et omnia mandata domini agendo*; ch. 23.3: 28: *Immo si quid promptius et celerius, pro eo quod multum pretiosior vita future quam praesens, oboedientiam usque ad mortem oportet*; ch. 27.3: 31: *Et omnia quaecumque senior praeceperit secundum mandatum domini explenda sunt.*

130. *Regula cuiusdam patris*, ch. 20.4–5: 26: *et alius monasterio eius praeesse constituatur. Sin vero non poterint monachi ab illo exeant, et ille excommunicetur.*

who could claim to embody the *mandata dei* to a monastic administrator whose orders could certainly diverge from it. Nevertheless, these notions have theological implications profound enough to stir up mutual accusations of heresy, since they reach the core of a monastic discipline and self-understanding.

My observations on the clash between *oboedientia* as self-denying submission to a superior and *oboedientia* as a *sensus*-directed unconditional submission to the *mandata domini* are strikingly congruent with Eoin de Bhaldraithe's more general observations on Continental and Insular notions of obedience.[131] He contrasts the unconditional obedience and nonresistance that he finds in the *Regula Magistri*, the *Regula Benedicti*, and Columbanus's Rule (which he considers a product of Continental monastic traditions rather than a specifically Irish Rule)[132] with the *Regula Basilii* on the one hand (which places the *mandata domini* and the gospel at the center of unconditional *oboedientia*)[133] and the Irish monastic rules on the other hand, which do not operate on the assumption that unconditional obedience to the superior is an ascetic achievement or a tool for salvation.[134] In Irish rules, obedience means, if it is mentioned at all, following the rule of the gospel, observing the monastic rule, and carrying out one's duties.[135] In this regard, the *Regula cuiusdam patris* might indeed be more "Irish" than the *Regula Columbani* as we know it and as evoked by Jonas of Bobbio.

CONCLUSION

It is likely that the *Regula cuiusdam patris* gave voice to a group of dissenters against the abbots of Luxeuil and Bobbio and their claim to implement Columbanus's Rule and to be his legitimate successors. Even Jonas's undoubtedly distorted depiction of the conflicts in Bobbio and Luxeuil allows us to identify connections between the topics at stake and the content of the *Regula cuiusdam patris*. Some of the disputed topics in which the *Regula cuiusdam*

131. De Bhaldraithe 1983.
132. Stancliffe 2011: 18–24 makes a similar point, analyzing to what extent Columbanus's works were inspired by sources he encountered on the Continent, particularly the works of Basil and Cassian.
133. De Bhaldraithe 1983: 66–7.
134. See also Dunn 2000: 171, 2008: 6–7; Stancliffe 2011: 25–8.
135. See, e.g., *Rule of Ailbe*, ch. 27b, trans. Ó Maidin 1996: 23: "When, through obedience, they go to carry out their duties, let their spirit be 'This is a heavy task brother, let me do it'"; *Rule of Carthage for monks*, ch. 8: 68: "Show humility and joy towards friend and stranger alike, and homage, obedience, and fealty towards every person"; ch. 16: 69: "Let us reverence the seniors and be submissive to them, let us instruct the juniors with profit and diligence"; and *Rule of Carthage of the Céli Dé*, ch. 9: 70: "The juniors are to practice obedience as is their due, since the one who is idle is submissive to the Devil." De Bhaldraithe 1983: 72–4 provides more examples.

patris diverts from Columbanian monasticism (at least as it is described by Jonas) reach into the core of monastic self-understanding and its theological basis: prayer, penance, austerity, manual labor, monastic economy, interactions with the outside world, obedience, and the notion of monastic space. Are these connections sufficient to resolve the riddle of the *quidam pater* and to rename the Rule as *Regula Agrestii*? Probably not. Yet what we see in the *Regula cuiusdam patris* is an angry voice that shows that Columbanian monasticism was by no means the undisputed result of an organic development that gave monastic ideals, practice, and theological grounding a place in a post-Roman society.

Peter Brown ends his magnificent study on wealth, charity, and redemption in the late antique and early medieval world with a sketch of Columbanus's monastic ideal and the monastic movement that emerged in his name. For Brown, Columbanian monasticism completes a circle that leads us back to the roots of the notion of human agency and the belief in the power of charity as a means to attain salvation that is indeed within reach. Columbanus's monks had become the "new" and much more convenient poor.[136]

If we look at what Brown rightfully identified as the characteristics of Columbanus and Columbanian monasticism, we find elements that the author of the *Regula cuiusdam patris* would have emphatically embraced: the aim for austerity, the ascetic exercises, the personal renunciation of property, silence, and the imperative of mutual love. But we find much more that he would have vigorously refuted. The monasteries our author envisioned were not places of political and economic power built on fiscal land and surrounded by ditches, hedges, and palisades to create a holy space.[137] The *Regula cuiusdam patris* addresses communities in places so barren that the monks have to supplement their diet with a glass of diluted milk; the text addresses monks willing to rent out their labor to strangers to gain their daily bread and their simple garb. Its author did not offer a "monasticism for everyone," which would allow one to choose between putting on a monastic habit or crafting a secular variation on the ascetic theme. His monks would not have allowed outsiders to participate in the monastic endeavor and to share any of their *lucrum* and *merces* by trading charity with intercessory prayer.[138] For him, unconditional and unquestioning submission, elaborate rituals of confession and carefully

136. Brown 2015: 196.
137. Brown 2015: 185.
138. Brown 2015: 195–7. On *merces* and *lucrum*, see Diem and van der Meer 2016: 81–6.

calibrated penance, and strict liturgical discipline were suitable neither for getting closer to salvation nor for producing a tradable surplus of sanctity.[139] His monks had to defend their independence through the work of their hands, and the surplus they produced was meant to support the "old" poor. Where Columbanus pushed for an attainable *perfectio*, the *Regula cuiusdam patris* talked about *renuntiatio*.

All this does not by any means imply that Peter Brown is wrong. The monastic ideal envisioned and described by Jonas of Bobbio prevailed and to a large extent shaped what monasticism would become in later centuries. Yet the *Regula cuiusdam patris* may have been part of an undercurrent of dissent or at least unease with the transformation of asceticism that leads us from Anthony's cave to Kornelienmünster.

It is time to return again to the opening statement of the *Regula cuiusdam patris*, the appeal to the cautious *lector bonus*. Peter Brown shows how deeply Columbanus was indebted to the Continental monastic traditions and its textual manifestations, and it is clear that Jonas also considered himself a *prudentissimus lector*. Brown shows how much of the optimism, the sense of agency, and the notion of a salvation within reach formed a return to texts and ideas that had already been around for a long time and needed to be transformed and adjusted to fit into a distinctly post-Roman world.

The author of the *Regula cuiusdam patris* shared some of this optimism. Salvation and forgiveness of sins were also in reach for him, but he strongly disagreed with the means, the instruments, and the practices that Columbanus and Jonas claimed to have found in the works of the *scripturae* of the *sancti patres*. "You read the right books," he cried out, "but you got it all wrong."

139. Brown 2015: 188–91.

The Regula cuiusdam patris: *Translation and Commentary*

Note on the translation: I have tried to provide a translation that is as literal as possible, keeping the sentence structure intact, even if the result is not beautiful in style. The footnotes provide cross references, alternative translations of ambiguous passages, and references to sources the author may have used. I also indicate which parts of the Rule have been used in Benedict of Aniane's *Concordia regularum* and in Smaragdus's *Expositio Regulae*. Where I use "cfr," the author paraphrased his source text instead of quoting it verbatim.

In the name of the Father, the Son, and the Holy Spirit[140]

Here begins the *Rule* of a certain father[141]

1 1 A good reader should take heed that he does not submit the scriptures to his understanding, but that he submits his understanding to the holy scriptures.[142] 2 The chalice of suffering is bitter, but it entirely heals all diseases.[143] 3 The chalice of suffering is bitter, but when the physician drinks it first, the sick man shall not hesitate to drink.[144] 4 For someone who desires to heal the wounds of others ought to remain free from the disease of weariness and stay healthy.[145] 5 By no other vice does the devil destroy a monk and draws him to death as when he observes that a monk trusts in his own judgement and justification while ignoring the counsel of the elder.[146]

2 1 In the first place one has to fear and love God with all one's heart, all one's soul and all one's strength 2 and, above all, one's neighbor is to be loved according to the precept of the Lord.[147]

---

140. The *Regula cuiusdam patris* is the only monastic rule that begins with an invocation of the Trinity.

141. Please note that the chapter division is not based on the text as it appears in the extant manuscripts. It should be used with caution because it might predermine how we read the text.

142. *Testimonia Divinae Scripturae*, prologue.10, ed. Lehner 1987: 56; similar to Jerome, *Commentariorum in Matheum libri IV*, I (Matt. 10:29–31), ed. Hurst/Adriaen 1969: 72, l. 1730–1032, also in Defensor, *Liber Scintillarum* LXXXI.10, ed. Rochais 1957: 231. A similar statement, though phrased differently and addressing a very specific example, appears in Cassian, *Institutiones* VII.16: 312–4.

143. Chalice of the Passion: *calix passionis*.

144. *Calix passionis amarus est, sed omnes morbos penitus curat; calix passionis amarus est, sed cum prior biberit medicus ne bibere dubitet aegrotus.* Cfr Augustine, *Sermo* 329 *in natali martyrum*, ch. 2, PL 38, col. 1455: *Calix passionis amarus et salubris: calix quem nisi prius biberet medicus, tangere timeret aegrotus.*

145. Cassian, *Institutiones* VIII.5: 344.

146. Cassian, *Collationes* II.11.7: 123. Chapter 1.5 of the *Regula cuiusdam patris* appears in Benedict of Aniane, *Concordia regularum*, ch. 6.11: 92.

147. Cfr Columbanus, *Regula monachorum*, prologue: 122; Matt. 22:37; Mark 12:30–3; Luke 10:27. The author adds two aspects to Columbanus's text. First he replaces *deum diligere* with *deum timendum et diligendum est*, then he inserts a reference to the *mandatum Domini*. The notion of loving *and* fearing God at the same time can be found in a number of Irish monastic rules, for example, *Rule of Comghall*,

3 1 Then one has to strive for the virtue of obedience.[148] It should be exercised by each one according to his strength.[149] 2 And it behooves all brothers who hear it to rise at the first word of a senior. 3 Let someone who does not rise, ask for pardon and do as much penance as the senior determines.[150] 4 He should carry out what he is ordered to do, even if it seems to be harsh.[151] 5 Obedience needs to be rendered until death, according to the example of the Lord, *who obeyed the father until death*.[152] 6 And it behooves everyone to serve his brother as if he were his own abbot or father, as the Apostle said: *Serve each other in the fear of the Lord*,[153] 7 and, once more: *All your affairs should be done with love*.[154]

4 1 If a brother is found[155] to be disobedient towards his abbot, the prior (*equonomus*)[156] or any brother, he is to be sent to prison.[157] Let him do as much penance as the senior determines.[158] 2 But if he, after having been tested by the prison,[159] is found condemnable once or twice or time and again, he needs to be torn off from the entire body of the community,[160]

---

ch. 8, trans. Ó Maidin 1996: 32: "Through fear comes the love of the King who heals every ill; for love of him we carry out his will and cherish his commandments"; *Rule of Cormac Mac Ciolionán*, ch. 7: 56: "It is no error, and certainly no heresy, to say that the love of God demands fear of him." See also *Rule of Carthage*, ch. 38: 78; *The Alphabet of Devotion*, ch. 4: 162. The *mandatum Domini* appear at several instances in the *Regula cuiusdam patris* and numerous times in the *Regula Basilii*.

148. The notion of *virtus oboedientiae* appears especially in the work of John Cassian. See, for example, *Institutiones* IV.12: 136.

149. This statement cannot be traced back to any source.

150. Cfr Columbanus, *Regula monachorum*, ch. 1: 122. The author adds *veniam petat et paeniteat quantum iudicaverit senior*—a sanction that can be found at several instances in the *Regula cuiusdam patris*.

151. Chapter 3.1–4 of the *Regula cuiusdam patris* appears in Smaragdus, *Expositio*, ch. 71.2: 322.

152. Phil. 2:8. Cfr Columbanus, *Regula monachorum*, ch. 1: 122–4.

153. Eph. 5:21: *subiecti invicem in timore Christi*; here: *servite invicem in timore Christi*. This variant seems to be unique. Maybe the author conflated Eph. 5:21 with Gal. 5:13: *Per caritatem servite invicem*. Chapter 3.4–6 of the *Regula cuiusdam patris* appears in Smaragdus, *Expositio*, ch. 71.5: 332.

154. We find the requirement of acting solely out of love, for example, in *Regula cuiusdam ad virgines*, ch. 5, col. 1058–9 and ch. 22, col. 1068–70, and in *Regula Benedicti*, ch. 71: 668. *Omnia vestra cum caritate fiant*, cfr 1 Cor. 16:14: *omnia vestra in caritate fiant*. The variant *onia vestra cum caritate fiant* is found otherwise only in Augustine, *De gratia et libero arbitrio*, ch. 17, *PL* 44, col. 902, and *De correptione et gratia*, ch. 3, *PL* 44, col. 918. Chapter 3 of the *Regula cuiusdam patris* appears in Benedict of Aniane, *Concordia regularum*, ch. 76.14: 663–4.

155. *Inventus fuerit* appears eight times in this rule. It is used both in John Cassian's work and in the *Regula Basilii*.

156. The text uses the term *equonomus* (instead of *praepositus*). It is also found (as *oeconomus*) in Columbanus, *Regula coenobialis*, ch. 8: 152 and ch. 12: 160. See also de Vogüé 2006: 292.

157. *Carcer*. The term *ergastulum* is more widely used.

158. Columbanus, *Regula coenobialis*, ch. 10: 158 punishes disobedience with two days of fasting on water and bread.

159. The expression *examinatio carceris* (also in *Regula cuiusdam patris*, ch. 8.7) appears in the so-called Second Synod of Patrick, ch. 22, ed. Bieler 1963: 192, though with a completely different meaning, referring to the "prison of the flesh."

160. *Corpus fraternitatis* appears at several places in the *Regula Basilii*.

3 according to the precept of the Lord, who says: *For it is better for you if one of your members perishes that if the entire body enters the Hell of fire.*[161] 4 And: *Because only a little yeast ruins the entire dough.*[162]

5 1 In the presence of the abbot or prior one does not have to obey everyone, because a single [monk] cannot serve everyone [at the same time]. 2 But every brother should strive to obey his senior as he would obey the Lord. 3 He should not doubt that whatever he does for his neighbor he does for the Lord.[163]

6 1 If a brother is found to be grumbling, he is to be sent to prison and his work should be thrown away.[164] 2 Let him do penance according to the consideration of his senior. 3 If it is permitted to him, he may do satisfaction.[165] 4 But if he does this more often, he is to be thrown out of the monastery.

7 1 At the first word of a reproach[166] by a senior, a prior or any brother one needs to ask for pardon and remain prostrated on the ground until the senior completes his reproach.[167] 2 But if a senior repeats his reproach, [a monk] also needs to ask for pardon again. 3 If someone is found to be slower in asking for pardon or if he utters words that contradict piety or are meant to defend his offence, 4 he is to be sent to prison and he should do penance according to the judgment of the abbot, until he improves himself.[168] 5 But if he is found to be stubborn, he needs to be removed from the brothers.[169]

8 1 Lying, swearing or idle talk are to be condemned by the entire body of the community.[170] 2 If there is a brother with whom any of these (behaviors)

---

161. Matt. 5:29, also used in *Regula Basilii*, ch. 26.5: 74, ch. 76.3: 110, ch. 175.4: 199.

162. 1 Cor. 5:6 is also used in *Regula Basilii*, ch. 175: 198–9, which probably served as a model for this and all the other chapters on expulsion.

163. Cfr Matt. 25:40. This chapter cannot be traced to a specific source and might relate to a concrete conflict in the monastery.

164. Cfr *Regula Basilii*, ch. 71.1: 107; Columbanus, *Regula monachorum*, ch. 1: 122–4; Columbanus, *Regula coenobialis*, ch. 10: 158, punishes grumbling with two days' fasting on bread and water.

165. This section might be inspired by *Regula Basilii*, ch. 70: 106 on contradicting a senior.

166. *Discussio*. The expression probably comes from Cassian's work.

167. Cassian, *Institutiones* IV.16.1: 140 and Columbanus, *Regula coenobialis*, ch. 15: 166 use similar wording (*tamdiu prostratus in terram veniam postulabit, donec orationum consumetur sollempnitas*) in the context of negligently breaking or losing things.

168. Columbanus, *Regula coenobialis*, ch. 5: 150 imposes in this case a penance of fifty blows with a stick and in ch. 10 two days of fasting on bread and water.

169. Chapter 7 of the *Regula cuiusdam patris* appears in Benedict of Aniane, *Concordia regularum*, ch. 76.13: 663 and in Smaragdus, *Expositio*, ch. 71.9: 333.

170. *Per omne corpus fraternitatis* is ambiguous. It means that lying, swearing, and idle talk are to be condemned either *by* the entire community or *within* the entire community. Columbanus, *Regula*

are discovered, he is to be sent to prison. Let him do penance until he is corrected from this vice, 3 *for a mouth that lies, kills the soul*,[171] 4 and in the Gospel the Lord has prohibited swearing, with these words: *For I tell you that you should not swear at all.*[172] 5 Moreover he says: *Men will give account at the Day of Judgment for every idle word that they will have spoken.*[173] 6 And the Apostle says: *Let no evil speech come out of our mouth, unless it is a speech valuable for the edification of faith so that it gives joy to those who hear.*[174] 7 But if a brother, after being tested by the prison,[175] is unable to avoid this vice, he is to be thrown out from the brothers and condemned.

9 1 If one of the brothers is found to be irascible, he will be guilty of the fire of Hell at the court,[176] unless he does penance. 2 The putrefied wounds are to be burned out with the remedy of fire as punishment,[177] 3 and the swollen wound should receive the incision of the spiritual knife.[178] 4 Thus, capital and lethal offences, which lead to death, behoove to be healed and treated harshly according to the judgment of the abbot or prior, until he (the brother) improves and is healed.[179]

10 1 If a brother says a word about another brother who does not hear it or is absent 2 and it does not pertain to his praise and love, he is to be condemned[180] as if he is a blasphemer. 3 Let him immediately ask God for pardon[181] and confess to the brother what he said about him. 4 If he is found to do this more often, he is to be sent to prison and he should do

coenobialis, ch. 9: 154 imposes for idle talk two hours of silence or twelve lashes; ch. 10: 158 imposes for lying a penance of two days' fasting on bread and water.

171. Wisd. 1:11.
172. Matt. 5:34.
173. Matt. 12:36.
174. Eph. 4:29. Cfr *Regula Basilii*, ch. 40.4: 85–6.
175. Also *Regula cuiusdam patris*, ch. 4.2: 13.
176. Cfr Matt. 5:22.
177. In manuscript Munich, Clm 28118, fol. 139v the original text *castigatio ignis medicamento* was emended by a hand from the fifteenth century to *castigatione, id est, ignis medicamento* ("punishment, that is, remedy of fire"). The original may have been simply *castigationis medicamento*.
178. Cfr *Regula Basilii*, ch. 76: 110. The phrasing might be influenced by Cassian, *Institutiones* X, ch. 7.7: 398 (though the context is different).
179. Despite some vague allusions to Basil and Cassian, this section has no clearly identifiable source. Its drastic phrasing indicates the urgency of the matter.
180. *Iudicandus est* (also *Regula cuiusdam patris*, ch. 20.3: 26, ch. 28.2/4: 31). The expression appears in Columbanus, *Regula monachorum*, ch. 1: 122, and three times in the *Regula Basilii*.
181. The requirement to ask God for pardon (*venia*), instead of from the community or the brother in question (also in *Regula cuiusdam patris*, ch. 17.3: 24), is also found in penitential literature, for example in *Paenitentiale Vinniani*, ch. 29, ed. Bieler 1963: 84; *Paenitentiale Bigotianum* II.10: 222; *Paenitentiale Ps.-Theodori* 12, ch. 11, ed. Körntgen/van Rhijn/Meens 2009: 22, 29.3, and 33.2.

harsh penance until he learns what the Apostle said: *Your speech should be seasoned with salt.*[182] 5 His offence shall not be forgiven until he has asked for pardon from all brothers. After having asked for pardon, it shall be forgiven.[183]

11 1 With regard to abstinence from food,[184] *one* rule is to be followed by all the brothers, except for those who are old, sick or children. 2 *One* measure applies to all circumstances.[185] That is to say: from the ninth hour until the following, one has to abstain from food.[186] 3 Neither before nor after the meal, which is served to all brothers together at mealtime, may the mouth indulge in anything, unless sickness or difference in age or bodily condition compels this.[187] 4 But one may never eat until satiety.[188] 5 Monks, for whom the world is crucified for Christ's sake and who are crucified to the world,[189] have to refrain from meat and wine or any drink that can lead to drunkenness,[190] and may not receive it. 6 For monks there should be no feasts in this world, except that food is a little more exquisite for the arrival of guests, who should be received like Christ for the sake of love.[191]

---

182. Cfr Col. 4:6: *Sermo vester semper sit in gratia, sale conditus.* The variant used here (*sermo eorum conditus sit sale*) is most likely based on *Regula Basilii*, ch. 136.5: 165–6 (*sermo eorum sale conditus sit*).

183. The prohibition against bad-mouthing a brother does not appear in any other rule and is phrased entirely independently. This points, again, to the urgency of the matter in the specific context in which the rule was written.

184. Note that the author uses *abstinentia*, not *ieiunium* (fasting). The notion of fasting as ascetic practice is not present in the *Regula cuiusdam patris*. The Rule does not mention any periods of fasting.

185. *Una mensura sit in omnibus* appears in an entirely different context (general applicability of the *mandata dei*) in *Regula Basilii*, ch. 114.1: 140. *In omnibus* could refer to persons but also to things. Since other monastic rules determine mealtimes according to the seasons, I assume that the author had circumstances rather than persons in mind. A similar emphasis on uniformity appears in *Regula cuiusdam patris*, ch. 30: 34. The author seems to dislike the practice of adjusting regulations to seasons and specific circumstances.

186. This regulation makes sense only in response to a practice that is common elsewhere. According to *Regula Benedicti*, ch. 39.1: 576, and *Regula cuiusdam ad virgines*, ch. 11.3, col. 1063, the meal usually takes place at the ninth hour. Columbanus, *Regula monachorum*, ch. 3: 124–6 stipulates that meals should take place at Vespers. Several rules determine mealtimes according to the seasons. We find the recommendation not to eat at the ninth hour also in Ps-Columbanus, *De octo vitiis principalibus*, ed. Walker 1957: 210. Cfr de Vogüé 2006: 294.

187. Cfr Cassian, *Institutiones* IV.18: 144.

188. Cfr *Regula Basilii*, ch. 9.7: 47. *Regula cuiusdam patris*, ch. 11 appears in Benedict of Aniane, *Concordia regularum*, ch. 52.31: 459–60.

189. Cfr Gal. 6:14, which is used in numerous monastic rules.

190. Columbanus, *Regula monachorum*, ch. 3: 124–6 requires moderation in drinking but does not entirely prohibit the drinking of wine. Several penances imposed in his *Paenitentiale* include abstinence from wine. See also *Vita Sadalbergae*, ch. 20, ed. Krusch 1910: 61 on serving wine and beer on the occasion of a visit from Abbot Waldebert.

191. *Et ferias monacho non esse super terram.* Cfr Evagrius Ponticus, *Sententiae*, ch. 39, ed. Leclercq 1951: 207: *quia non est festivitas apud monachos super terram.* This is the only allusion to Evagrius's

7 Yet abstinence is to be concealed lest we fall prey to the vice of ostentation, which is above all vices the most serious one.[192]

12 1 We may not desire any of the things that pertain to the world except for our daily bread and the short vestment that we wear. 2 Even for these things we should ask without anxiety (*sollicitudo*), lest at some point it is found out about us that we did not ponder about the Kingdom of God and it is said about us: *The gentiles have asked for all this.*[193] 3 Yet it is appropriate for monks to work at all times and to spend their lives without anxiety. 4 Everything they gain through their work, except the abovesaid—a little bread and clothing—should be divided among the poor. 5 Care for the poor is to be performed at all times and *everything we do should be done with love.*[194] Without love our work is barren in the eyes of God.[195]

13 1 It is to be left to the discretion of the respective senior,[196] from where he provides the yearly bread for his monastery,[197] 2 be it from agriculture, livestock—as it is common for some others and for us—from handicraft, commerce, day labor,[198] or any other work.

14 1 One should not care so much about what everyone works at, but how everyone lives. 2 One should always work as the condition and the circumstances and the setting of a place permit.[199] God's law, which comprises the visible and the invisible, is always to be followed. 3 None of the commands of God, be it a large one or the smallest one, may be passed over because *whoever transgresses against one rule is made guilty of all of them.*[200]

Sententiae in the *Regula cuiusdam patris*. Other monastic rules also imply that the arrival of guests was a reason to break the fast. See, for example, *Regula cuiusdam ad virgines*, ch. 11, col. 1063. Chapter 11.5–6 of the *Regula cuiusdam patris* appears in Smaragdus, *Expositio*, ch. 40.6: 258.

192. The very last aspect (concealing abstinence) has no precedent in other rules. Chapter 11.5–7 of the *Regula cuiusdam patris* appears in Benedict of Aniane, *Concordia regularum*, ch. 48.17: 425.

193. Matt. 6:32.

194. 1 Cor. 16:14.

195. This chapter is inspired by *Regula Basilii*, ch. 127: 158–8, which argues that not having *sollicitudo* is entirely compatible with the requirement to work in order to care for one's neighbor.

196. The phrase *arbitrio uniuscuiusque senioris* comes from Columbanus, *Regula coenobialis*, ch. 9: 154, although it is used there in an entirely different context: the senior's decision when penitents are allowed to wash their hair.

197. One would expect daily bread, but this might refer to a practice of baking bread once a year and drying it, as it is described, for example, in the *Rules of Shenute*, ch. 178 and ch. 381, ed. Layton 2014: 160, 251.

198. *Conductio mercedis*, literally "hiring of wages." I assume that this refers to something we would call day labor.

199. Certainly at this point, the chapter division is misleading.

200. Cfr James 2:10. This entire section cannot be traced back to the texts the author used and might be a genuine contribution: a strongly moralistic commentary on monastic labor, self-sufficiency, and economy that implies that especially in this regard the *mandata dei* are often disobeyed.

15 1 The monastic way of life that we have promised, needs to be practiced and carried out with our whole heart and with all love. It consists of three renunciations. 2 First we must cast off all of our power (*facultas*)[201] 3 and all the riches of the world are recognized by us as alien. 4 In the second place we have to leave all vices of the flesh and the soul behind and we have to free us from them, and *all anger, bitterness, shouting and blasphemy should be taken from you, along with all malice*.[202] 5 The third renunciation is that of all things that are seen in the sky, on earth, in the sea or in all of his creatures, we do not only put nothing on equal footing with God, but we should also regard all these things as inferior to ourselves, since we strive beyond all these things for the Heavenly Kingdom and the knowledge of God. 8 And therefore we do not direct our attention very much to these things that serve vanity and that will soon fade, according to what the Apostle says: *Everything that is visible is temporal, but what is invisible is eternal*.[203]

16 1 We have to follow silence in everything and the discipline of being silent has to be kept under all circumstances, but especially at Mass[204] and at table. 2 But on all occasions nothing should be spoken except for what necessity requires. 3 If someone, disregarding this discipline, responds with shouting or harsh words, he should be reproached until he is corrected.[205] 4 But if he cannot be healed from this vice, he should be thrown out of the community of the brothers.[206]

17 1 One may not have and hold anything as if it belongs to oneself, but especially among monks *all things should be held in common*.[207] 2 Someone

---

201. The expression *facultas* appears in a similar context in Cassian's and Columbanus's work. I consider the common translation as "richness" or "wealth" to be imprecise. *Facultas* is rather the power that comes with wealth. The target group of Columbanian monasteries were aristocrats who held positions of power in the world. The Rule aims at preventing them from retaining their secular power positions while living in the monastery. On the entanglement of wealth and power in the context of Columbanian monasticism, see Kreiner 2014a: 201–13.

202. Eph. 4:31.

203. 2 Cor. 4:18. This section paraphrases Cassian, *Collationes* III.6.1–3: 145 on the three renunciations. Columbanus, *Regula monachorum*, ch. 4: 126 alludes briefly and rather peripherally to the same passage of Cassian in the context of greed. The author of the *Regula cuiusdam patris* went back to the original text and placed the three renunciations in the center of both the monastic *propositum* and the Rule itself.

204. The emphasis on silence *iuxta missam* (at Mass) is unique and may be seen in the light of *Regula cuiusdam patris*, ch. 32 and possibly in the context of Agrestius's critique on the overabundance of prayers performed at Mass, as mentioned in *VC* II.9: 250.

205. Cfr *Regula Basilii*, ch. 45: 89. The phrase *notetur usquequo corrigatur* (also in *Regula cuiusdam patris*, ch. 25.1) appears in *Regula Basilii*, ch. 112.2: 138 in the context of favoritism.

206. Chapter 16 of the *Regula cuiusdam patris* appears in Benedict of Aniane, *Concordia regularum*, ch. 9.7: 125.

207. Acts 4:32.

who says that this or that belongs to him has committed a sin in the eyes of God 3 unless it was just a slip of the tongue.[208] But even for this he should ask God for pardon[209] and he should henceforth be careful and not dare to repeat it. 4 If someone appears to be incurable from this vice, he is to be expelled from all the brothers, 5 for the vice of avarice is the most serious among all vices and *the root of all evil is avarice.*[210]

18 1 If a brother falls through a misdeed that is even sadder[211]—that of fornication—he is to be thrown out of the community of the brothers and he should do penance in another region until his death.[212] 2 Therefore sisters should be visited rarely, and we prohibit anyone from wanting to speak with them frequently, lest we are found giving opportunity to the weak.[213] 3 We prescribe, however, striving to excel wholeheartedly in kindness and generosity to them, because they are members of Christ and mothers of the Lord and Christ has redeemed us through a virgin. 4 But gifts should be sent to them through the most trustworthy and reliable persons, so that the occasion of slander is avoided because of the most evil people.[214]

19 1 No one should be allowed to be the head of a community of brothers unless he has learned through obedience those things that need to be enjoined to others. [He is suitable] if he happens to be sufficiently trained in the sacred scriptures, and under the condition that he trusts the deeds of those who perform them, 3 that is to say that he makes the things he teaches complete though his work by showing humility and love, patience and mildness and by fulfilling the will of a senior himself and carrying out all commands of the Lord.[215]

---

208. Columbanus, *Regula coenobialis*, ch. 2: 146 punishes this with six blows with a stick. The practice of policing the use of the possessive pronoun comes from Cassian, *Institutiones* IV.13: 136–8.

209. See note on *Regula cuiusdam patris*, ch. 10.3.

210. 1 Tim. 6:10, probably quoted from Cassian, *Institutiones* VII.6: 298. Chapter 17 of the *Regula cuiusdam patris* appears in Benedict of Aniane, *Concordia regularum*, ch. 42.20: 357.

211. *Lugubriori lapsu*, probably inspired by Cassian, *Collationes* XVIII.16, ed. Pichery 1959: 33.

212. Cfr Columbanus, *Poenitentiale* B, ch. 2, ed. Walker 1957: 172. No other monastic rule addresses *fornicatio* as explicitly and imposes this sanction.

213. Cfr *Regula Basilii*, ch. 198.t/2: 216.

214. *Regula Basilii*, ch. 7.4: 39 uses the same phrase in an entirely different context: the oblation of children, which has to take place in front of witnesses and with the consent of the parents.

215. Cfr Cassian, *Institutiones* II.3.3: 62. It is possible that chapter 19 of the *Regula cuiusdam patris* is corrupt. The first and the third parts of the sentence fit together well, but it is hardly possible to fit in the two conditional clauses in between these parts. An alternative translation for *tamen si factorum gestis adhibeat fidem* ("that he trusts the deeds of those who perform them") would be "that he shows trustworthiness in the performance of his deeds."

20 1 If any of the seniors, or the one who is called abbot, appears to be pleasure-seeking, sottish, and opulent, 2 or to be someone who is shaped by this world and, for example, travels back and forth in a cart or on horse-back,[216] 3 he is not only unworthy of ruling over the brothers, but to be condemned as a murderer of souls,[217] 4 and another should be appointed to be at the head of the monastery. 5 If the monks are not able to do this, they should leave him (the abbot) and he should be excommunicated. 6 But if he does penance, let him give himself over to the hands of a senior and submit himself to serfdom as long as the one who is the superior considers it appropriate.[218]

21 1 We do not permit that monks travel back and forth in carts and on horse-back, except for the sick, the weak, and the lame. 2 Those who do this are not part of the community of the brothers.[219]

22 1 Brothers who have their dwelling on barren land, that is that they have no bread, and those who stay in the mountains or wastelands, are allowed to have a little milk, mixed with water. 2 But we do not permit a monk to live together with women, that is, with mothers and sisters.[220]

23 1 How do they have to obey the one who exhorts us to the assigned work? 2 Like an infant follows his nurse who invites him to her breast. 3 Yet how much more does one have to obey until death for the sake of the future life, which is much more precious than the present life.[221]

24 1 How should a senior behave towards the brothers? 2 *Just as a nurse who cherishes her little ones,*[222] loving and comforting each of them. 3

---

216. Cfr Ps. 19/20.8. Villegas sees here and in the next two chapters parallels with the First Synod of Patrick, ch. 9, ed. Bieler 1963: 54, which prohibits monks from traveling in a cart together with a virgin. I do not see this connection. See, however, Bede, *HE* III.5: 226 on Aidan always traveling on foot.

217. Cfr *Regula Basilii*, ch. 119.5: 146. Basil uses the same expression, *homicida animarum*, for superiors who are negligent in teaching.

218. *Donec probaverit is qui praeest.* This phrase appears in a different context (anger) in *Regula Basilii*, ch. 96.1: 128. Even though the author uses fragments from the *Regula Basilii*, this section is unique in describing what disqualifies a superior, imposing sanctions on him, and allowing monks to abandon him. Chapter 20 of the *Regula cuiusdam patris* appears in Benedict of Aniane, *Concordia regularum*, ch. 5.19: 82.

219. *Alieni sint ab unitate fratrum.* This phrase appears in a different context (grumbling) in *Regula Basilii*, ch. 71.1: 107. The fact that the sick, old, and lame are allowed to travel in this way indicates that it was by no means uncommon to travel back and forth between different locations. One just had to go by foot. Chapter 21 of the *Regula cuiusdam patris* appears in Benedict of Aniane, *Concordia regularum*, ch. 5.19: 82.

220. Columbanus, *Regula coenobialis*, ch. 13: 162, punishes sleeping (*dormire*) in the same house with women with one or two days of fasting on bread and water. The author of the *Regula cuiusdam patris* uses *habitare*, which implies that monks could possibly stay for a longer period outside the monastery.

221. Cfr *Regula Basilii*, ch. 84.1–2: 118. It does not make much sense to separate chapter 23 of the *Regula cuiusdam patris* from chapter 24.

222. Cfr *Regula Basilii*, ch. 15.3: 64–5; 1 Thess. 2:7.

And he should open up to them the path of perfection[223] 4 and walk ahead of them in all perfection and sanctity of heart and body,[224] 5 and he must without any regard for the individual person love everyone in equal and honest love with all his heart as if they were his sons.[225] 6 But if he sees one of them disregarding the orders of the Lord, he should not be moved by anger towards him, but by remorse and compassion, 7 according to him who has said: *Who is weak and I don't get weak? Who is scandalized and I do not burn?*[226] 8 But if he is negligent in matters that concern the benefit of body and soul, he will without doubt submit himself to the sentence of the one who says: *Go, accursed, into the eternal fire, which is prepared by the devil and his messengers. For I was hungry and you have not given me to eat; I was thirsty and you have not given me to drink,* and so forth. [227] And: *Accursed is the man who does the work of God negligently.*[228]

25 1 If someone among the seniors and the abbots is found to be irascible, he should be reproached until he improves himself.[229] 2 But if he is incurable of this vice, he is to be stripped of the rule over the brothers, because—justly or unjustly—one may not get angry.[230]

26 1 If someone slanders his senior, he does not slander his senior but the Lord, whose work the senior does.[231] 2 But if he does this more often, he should be torn from the brotherhood and from the care of the brotherly body. 3 If he does penance, his sins are to be forgiven him. 4 The Prophet says: *I have punished the one who secretly slanders his neighbor.* [232]

---

223. *Viam perfectionis eis aperiat.* Cassian, *Institutiones* X.10: 404 uses the same expression in the context of manual work.

224. Cfr *Regula cuiusdam patris*, ch. 32.2: 35. *Sanctitas cordis et corporis* cannot be traced in any other source.

225. The manuscript gives *notos* ("acquaintances") without any corrections. I assume, however, that we would have found *natos* ("sons") in the original text, which makes much more sense.

226. 2 Cor. 11:29. Cfr *Regula Basilii*, ch. 46.4–5: 90. Basil uses only the first half of the biblical quotation. The author of the *Regula cuiusdam patris* completed it.

227. Matt. 25:41–42.

228. Jer. 48:10; cfr *Regula Basilii*, ch. 113: 139.

229. *Notetur usquequo corrigatur* (also in *Regula cuiusdam patris*, ch. 16.3: 23) appears in a different context (unjust favoritism) in *Regula Basilii*, ch. 112.2: 138. The expression *notare* ("to reproach") appears several times in the *Regula Basilii*.

230. Cfr also Cassian, *Institutiones* VIII.22: 364–6. Chapter 25 of the *Regula cuiusdam patris* appears in Benedict of Aniane, *Concordia regularum*, ch. 37.12: 321.

231. Cfr Columbanus, *Regula coenobialis*, ch. 10: 160, imposing a penance of seven days on bread and water; Columbanus, *Paenitentiale* A, ch. 10: 170 imposes seven days of penance.

232. Psalm 100/101.5. Cfr *Regula Basilii*, ch. 43: 88. Chapter 25 of the *Regula cuiusdam patris* appears in Benedict of Aniane, *Concordia regularum*, ch. 31.21: 276–7. There is no reason to separate chapter 27 from chapter 28.

27 1 If someone is found to despise his senior for whatever reason, he does not despise the man but God, etc.[233] 2 If someone does this, he should do penance and reconcile with his senior. 3 And whatever the senior commands, is to be fulfilled in accordance with the order of the Lord.[234]

28 1 If a brother is found to be negligent in dealing with the utensils of the monastery, 2 he is to be judged to be guilty of sacred property. 3 If someone sees a problem and he fails to take care of it and resolve it the same day, 4 he is as well to be judged as someone who neglects and destroys holy property.[235] 5 For it behooves everyone to work and to act more considerate to the property of the monastery, as if one were the lord over everything and rules over everything.[236] 6 Conversely, a monk should consider himself in greatest humility[237] like a stranger, 7 so that he does not ask for anything of the monastic property except for his daily bread.

29 1 If someone does not rise immediately when he hears a word of someone who orders or requires or does anything of that sort, he is guilty of disobedience. 2 He should ask God for pardon and should not dare to repeat it, 3 because everyone has to rise at the first word of someone who makes a request, as if *the coal of burning fire descended upon him.*[238] 4 Obedience that is not of such sort we have described, is dead and is not acceptable in the eyes of God. 5 *For everything that does not come out of piety is a sin.*[239] 6 Monks always have to work with joy, and nothing should be done in sadness. 7 At all time they should pray: *You, the just, rejoice in the Lord who always is to be praised.*[240] 8 Furthermore, the Apostle says: *Always rejoice in the Lord, and again I say to you: rejoice!*[241] 9 But if we bring anything forward in sadness, it will not be acceptable in the eyes of God.[242]

233. 1 Thess. 4:8.

234. The author uses here *secundum*, not *tamquam*, which implies that only those commands are to be obeyed that are in accordance with the *mandata dei*. Cfr also Columbanus, *Paenitentiale* A, ch. 11: 170. Chapter 27 of the *Regula cuisdam patris* appears in Benedict of Aniane, *Concordia regularum*, ch. 31.21: 277.

235. Cfr Cassian, *Institutiones* IV.20: 148–50.

236. Cfr Cassian, *Institutiones* IV.14: 138 . . . *et omnibus dominetur. Dominari* is a deponent. If the author misunderstood it as passive construction, it would be "and is ruled by everything," which admittedly would make more sense.

237. *Per nimiam humilitatem* appears in the context of clothing in *Regula Basilii*, ch. 11.5: 52.

238. Rom. 12:20.

239. Rom. 14:23.

240. Ps. 32/33.1 (*Psalterium Romanum*). Chapter 29.5–6 of the *Regula cuiusdam patris* is not inspired by any of the sources the author used, though *cum gaudio* appears in Cassian's *Collationes* in different contexts.

241. Phil. 4:4.

242. Cfr (on the entire chapter) Columbanus, *Regula monachorum*, ch. 1: 122–4. Chapter 29 of the *Regula cuiusdam patris* appears in Benedict of Aniane, *Concordia regularum*, ch. 8.6: 113.

30 1 One has to come together in the church for three gatherings[243] during the day and three times during the night. 2 At each daytime gathering three psalms are to be sung.[244] 3 But at the nighttime gatherings twelve psalms will be sung, except at the Mass that is celebrated at dawn.[245] 4 At each nightime gathering, prayers and two readings, one from the Old Testament and one from the New Testament, are to be recited.[246] 5 At the gatherings on Saturday and Sunday, Mass has to be celebrated until cockcrow.[247] 6 And as far as the strength of each one can endure, vigils[248] should be held.[249]

31 1 Someone who at daytime does not arrive at the first psalm, may not be admitted to the community of the brothers, 2 but afterwards he has to ask for pardon in public. 3 If he does this more often, he will be restrained until he may be corrected. 4 At night, a respite is given until the second psalm.[250]

32 1 On Sundays one has always to receive the Eucharist as a remedy for sins.[251] 2 But we have to approach the body and blood of our Lord Jesus Christ with all holiness of heart and body.[252] Amen.

ACKNOWLEDGMENTS

The research for this chapter contributes to the Spezialforschungsbereich F 4202 Visions of Community, funded by the Austrian Science Fund (FWF), the Faculty of History and Cultural Sciences of the University of Vienna, and the Austrian Academy of Sciences. It was completed during a research leave at the Institute for Advanced Study in Princeton when I was a fellow of

243. *Conventus.* The expression rarely appears in monastic rules, though John Cassian uses it. Columbanus uses the terms *synaxis, cursus,* and *hora.* It is possible that the author's word choice expresses a different understanding of the role of monastic hours than that of Columbanus.

244. Cfr Columbanus, *Regula monachorum,* ch. 7: 130, which requires the same number of psalms at daytime but adds a number of intercessory prayers for the remedy of the sins of the monks themselves and different groups of clerics and laypeople. Cfr also Cassian, *Institutiones* II.4–6: 64–70.

245. Columbanus, *Regula monachorum,* ch. 7: 130–2 requires, depending on the season, at least twelve psalms for the Vigil office and between twenty-four and thirty-six psalms at morning Mass.

246. Cfr Cassian, *Institutiones* II.4: 64, II.6: 68–70.

247. Cfr Cassian, *Institutiones* III.5.2: 106.

248. The author uses *excubiae* instead of *vigilia.* He took this expression from Cassian's work.

249. Diverting from Cassian, *Institutiones* II.13: 82.

250. Cfr Cassian, *Institutiones* III.7.2: 108–10.

251. Cfr Cassian, *Institutiones* III.2: 92–4.

252. *Sanctitas cordis et corporis* (also in ch. 24.4) appears in no other text. On the entire chapter, cfr Columbanus, *Paenitentiale* B, ch. 30: 180.

the American Council of Learned Societies. I would like to thank Courtney Booker, Joshua Campbell, Giles Constable, Patrick Geary, Alexander O'Hara, Julian Hendrix, Matthieu van der Meer, and Ian Wood for their comments and feedback on different versions of the text.

BIBLIOGRAPHY

Agamben, G. (2013) *The Highest Poverty: Monastic Rules and Form-of-Life*. Stanford, CA, Stanford University Press.

Anaya Torres, J. M. (2007) *La expulsión de los religiosos: Un recorrido histórico que muestra interés pastoral de la Iglesia*. Rome, Pontificia Università Gregoriana.

Anton, H. H. (1975) *Studien zu den Klosterprivilegien der Päpste im frühen Mittelalter*. Berlin and New York, De Gruyter.

Augustine (1865) *De correptione et gratia*. PL 44, col. 915–44.

Augustine (1865) *De gratia et libero arbitrio*. PL 44, col. 882–909.

Augustine (1845) *Sermo 329 in natali martyrum*. PL 38, col. 1455–6.

Aurelianus of Arles (1975) *Regula ad monachos*, ed. A. Schmidt, "Zur Komposition der Mönchsregel des Heiligen Aurelian von Arles I." *Studia Monastica* 17: 237–56.

Basil (1986) *Regula a Rufino latine versa*, ed. K. Zelzer. CSEL 86. Vienna, Hoelder-Pichler-Temsky.

Benedict of Aniane (1999) *Concordia Regularum*, ed. P. Bonnerue. CCCM 168A. Turnhout, Brepols.

Bieler, L. (ed.) (1963) *The Irish Penitentials*. Dublin, Dublin Institute for Advanced Studies.

Böckmann, A. (1994) "RB5: Benedict's Chapter on Obedience." *American Benedictine Review* 45: 109–30.

Brown, P. (2015). *The Ransom of the Soul. Afterlife and Wealth in Early Western Christianity*. Cambridge, MA, Harvard University Press.

Bullough, D. (1997) "The Career of Columbanus." In M. Lapidge (ed.), *Columbanus: Studies on the Latin Writings*. Woodbridge, Boydell, 1–28.

Caesarius of Arles (1988) "Regula ad virgines." In A. de Vogüé and J. Courreau (eds.), *OEuvres Monastiques*. vol. 1. SC 345. Paris, Cerf, 170–272.

Caesarius of Arles (1994) "Regula ad monachos." In A. de Vogüé and J. Courreau (eds.), *OEuvres Monastiques*, vol. 2. SC 398. Paris, Cerf, 204–26.

Cassian (1955/1958/1959) *Collationes*, ed. E. Pichery. SC 42/54/64. Paris, Cerf.

Cassian (1965) *Institutiones*, ed. Jean-Claude Guy. SC 105. Paris, Cerf.

Charles-Edwards, T. M. (1997) "The Penitential of Columbanus." In M. Lapidge (ed.), *Columbanus: Studies on the Latin Writings*. Woodbridge, Boydell, 217–39.

Charles-Edwards, T. M. (2000) *Early Christian Ireland*. Cambridge, Cambridge University Press.

Charta Eligii (1902) In B. Krusch (ed.), *Scriptores rerum Merovingicarum* 4. MGH. Hanover and Leipzig, 746–9.

Cipolla, C. (ed.) (1918) *Codice Diplomatico del Monastero di San Columbano di Bobbio fino all'anno MCCVIII*, vol. 1. Rome, Tipografia del Senato.

Columbanus (1957a) *Poenitentiale*. In G. S. M. Walker (ed. and trans.), *Sancti Columbani Opera*. Dublin, Dublin Institute for Advanced Studies, 168–81.

Columbanus (1957b) *Regula coenobialis*. In G. S. M. Walker (ed. and trans.), *Sancti Columbani Opera*. Dublin: Dublin Institute for Advanced Studies, 142–69.

Columbanus (1957c) *Regula monachorum*. In G. S. M. Walker (ed. and trans.), *Sancti Columbani Opera*. Dublin: Dublin Institute for Advanced Studies, 122–43.

Columbanus (1957d) Epistula 5. In G. S. M. Walker (ed. and trans.), *Sancti Columbani Opera*. Dublin: Dublin Institute for Advanced Studies, 36–57.

De Bhaldraithe, E. (1983) "Obedience: The Doctrine of Irish Monastic Rules." *Monastic Studies* 14: 63–84.

De Vogüé, A. (1979) *Community and Abbot in the Rule of St. Benedict*, trans. C. Philippi. Kamamazoo, Cistercian Publications.

De Vogüé, A. (2006) *Histoire littéraire du mouvement monastique dans l'antiquité*, vol. 10. Paris, Cerf.

De Vogüé, A. (2007) "L'idéal monastique de Saint Colomban." *Médiévales* 52: 253–68.

Defensor (1957) *Liber Scintillarum*, ed. Henricus M. Rochais. *CCSL* 117. Turnhout, Brepols.

Diem, A. (2002) "Was bedeutet Regula Columbani?" In M. Diesenberger and W. Pohl (eds.), *Integration und Herrschaft: Ethnische Identitäten und soziale Organisation im Frühmittelalter*. Vienna, Verlag der Österreichischen Akademie der Wissenschaften, 63–89.

Diem, A. (2005) *Das monastische Experiment: Die Rolle der Keuschheit bei der Entstehung des westlichen Klosterwesens*. Münster, LIT-Verlag.

Diem, A. (2007a) "Monks, Kings and the Transformation of Sanctity: Jonas of Bobbio and the End of the Holy Man." *Speculum* 82: 521–9.

Diem, A. (2007b) "Rewriting Benedict: The *regula cuiusdam ad virgines* and Intertextuality as Tool to Construct a Monastic Identity." *Journal of Medieval Latin* 17: 313–28.

Diem, A. (2011) "Das Ende des monastischen Experiments: Liebe, Beichte und Schweigen in der regula cuiusdam ad virgines (mit einer Übersetzung im Anhang)." In G. Melville and A. Müller (eds.), *Female vita religiosa between Late Antiquity and the High Middle Ages: Structures, Developments and Spatial Contexts*. Münster and Berlin, LIT-Verlag, 81–136.

Diem, A. (2012) "New Ideas Expressed in Old Words: The Regula Donati on Female Monastic Life and Monastic Spirituality." *Viator* 43: 1–38.

Diem, A. (2013) "Who Is Allowed to Pray for the King? Saint-Maurice d'Agaune and the Creation of a Burgundian Identity." In G. Heydemann and W. Pohl (eds.), *Post-RomanTransitions: Christian and Barbarian Identities in the Early Medieval West*. Turnhout, Brepols, 47–88.

Diem, A. (2014) ". . . *ut si professus fuerit se omnia impleturum, tunc excipiatur*: Observations on the Rules for Monks and Nuns of Caesarius and Aurelianus of Arles." In V. Zimmerl-Panagl, L. J. Dorfbauer, and C. Weidmann (eds.), *Edition und Erforschung lateinischer patristischer Texte, 150 Jahre CSEL: Festschrift für Kurt Smolak zum 70. Geburtstag*. Berlin and Boston, De Gruyter, 191–224.

Diem, A. (2016a) "Columbanian Monastic Rules: Dissent and Experiment." In R. Flechner and S. Meeder (eds.), *The Irish in Europe in the Early Middle Ages: Identity, Culture and Religion*. London and New York, Palgrave Macmillan, 68–85 and 248–9.

Diem, A. (2016b) "The Stolen Glove: On the Hierarchy and Power of Objects in Columbanian Monasteries." In K. Pansters and A. Plunkett-Latimer (eds.), *Shaping Stability. Normative Sources and the Regulation of Religious Life, 800–1500*. Turnhout, Brepols, 51–67.

Diem, A., and M. van der Meer (2016) *Die Columbanischen Klosterregeln: Regula cuiusdam patris; Regula cuiusdam ad virgines; Regelfragment De accedendo*. St. Ottilien, EOS-Editions.

Diem, A., and P. Rousseau (2017) "Monastic Rules." In I. Cochelin and A. Beach (eds.), *The Cambridge History of Western Medieval Monasticism*, vol. 1. Cambridge, Cambridge University Press.

Donatus (2015) *Regula ad virgines*, ed. V. Zimmerl-Panagl. *CSEL* 98, Monastica 1. Berlin, De Gruyter.

Dumézil, B. (2007) "L'affaire Agrestius de Luxeuil: hérésie et régionalisme dans la Burgondie du VIIe siècle." *Médiévales* 52: 135–52.

Dunn, M. (2000) *The Emergence of Monasticism: From the Desert Fathers to the Early Middle Ages*. Oxford, Blackwell.

Dunn, M. (2008) "Columbanus, Charisma and the Revolt of the Monks of Bobbio." *Peritia* 20: 1–27.

Engelbert, P. (2015) "Benedikt von Aniane und der Codex regularum Clm 28118 der bayerischen Staatsbibliothek München." *Studia Monastica* 57: 69–90.

Engelbert, P. (ed.) (2016) *Der Codex Regularum des Benedikt von Aniane: Faksimile der Handschrift Clm 28118 der Bayerischen Staatsbibliothek München*. St. Ottilien, EOS-Editions.

Evagrius Ponticus (1951). *Sententiae*, ed. J. Leclercq, "L'ancienne version latine des sentences d'Evagre pour les moines," *Scriptorium* 5: 195–213.

Folz, R. (1980) "Remiremont dans le mouvement colombanien." In M. Parisse (ed.), *Remiremont, l'abbaye et la ville: Actes des journées d'études vosgiennes Remiremont 17–20 avril 1980*. Nancy, Université de Nancy II, 15–27.

Foundation Charter for the Monastery Solignac (632) (1902) In B. Krusch (ed.), *Scriptores rerum Merovingicarum* 4. MGH. Hanover and Leipzig, Hahnsche Buchhandlung, 746–8.

Fouracre, P. (1990) "Merovingian History and Merovingian Hagiography." *Past and Present* 127: 3–38.

Fox, Y. (2014) *Power and Religion in Merovingian Gaul: Columbanian Monasticism and the Frankish Elites*. Cambridge, Cambridge University Press.

Fredegar (1888) Chronicarum libri IV, ed. B. Krusch. In Scriptores rerum Merovingicarum 2. MGH. Hanover, Hahnsche Buchhandlung.

Gougaud, L. (1908) "Inventaire des règles monastiques irlandaises." *Revue Bénédictine* 25: 167–84 and 321–33.

Gray, P. T. R., and M. W. Herren (1994) "Columbanus and the Three Chapters Controversy—A New Approach." *Journal of Theological Studies* 45: 160–70.

Hauke, H. (1986) *Katalog der lateinischen Handschriften der Bayerischen Staatsbibliothek München: Clm 28111–28254*. Wiesbaden, Harrasowitz.

Holstenius, L. (1661) *Codex Regularum quas sancti patres monachis et virginibus sanctimonialibus servandas praescripsere*. Rome, V. Mascordus.

Jerome (1969) *Commentariorum in Matheum libri IV*, ed. M. Adriaen and D. Hurst. *CCSL* 77. Turnhout, Brepols.

Kardong, T. (1983) "Hard Obedience: Benedict's Chapter on Obedience." *Regulae Benedicti Studia* 12: 193–202.

Kreiner, J. (2014a) *The Social Life of Hagiography in the Merovingian Kingdom*. Cambridge, Cambridge University Press.

Kreiner, J. (2014b) "Autopsies and Philosophies of a Merovingian Life: Death, Responsibility, Salvation." *Journal of Early Christian Studies* 22: 113–52.

Lake, S. (2011) "Usage of the Writing of John Cassian in Some Early British and Irish Writings." *Journal of the Australian Early Medieval Association* 7: 95–121.

Layton, B. (ed. and trans.) (2014) *The Canons of Our Fathers: Monastic Rules of Shenoute*. Oxford, Oxford University Press.

Leclercq, J. (1965) "Religious Obedience According to the 'Rule of St. Benedict.'" *American Benedictine Review* 16: 183–93.

Lifshitz, F. (2006) *The Name of the Saint: The Martyrology of Jerome and Access to the Sacred in Francia, 627–827*. Notre Dame, IN, University of Notre Dame Press.

Meens, R. (2014) *Penance in Medieval Europe*. Cambridge, Cambridge University Press.

Missale Bobbiense (1920), ed. E. A. Lowe. London, Henry Bradshaw Society.

Ó Cróinín, D. (2005). "A Tale of Two Rules: Benedict and Columbanus." In M. Browne and C. Ó Clabaigh (eds.), *The Irish Benedictines: A History*. Dublin, Columba Press, 11–24.

O'Hara, A., and I. N. Wood (2017) *Jonas of Bobbio. Life of Columbanus, Life of John of Réomé, and Life of Vedast*. Translated with introduction and commentary. Liverpool, Liverpool University Press.

Ó Maidin, U. (trans.) (1996) *The Celtic Monk: Rules and Writings of Early Irish Monks*. Kalamazoo, Cistercian Publications.

Ohm, J. (1982). "Der Begriff *carcer* in Klosterregeln des Frankenreichs." In J. F. Angerer and J. Lenzenweger (eds.), *Consuetudines Monasticae: Eine Festgabe für Kassius Hallinger aus Anlass seines 70. Geburtstages*. Rome, Pontificio Ateneo S. Anselmo, 145–55.

Paenitentiale Ps.-Theodori (2009), ed. L. Körntgen, C. van Rhijn, and R. Meens. CCSL 156B. Turnhout, Brepols.

Pardessus, J.-M. (ed.) (1849) *Diplomata: Chartae, Epistolae, Leges aliaque instrumenta ad res Gallo-Francicas spectantia*, vol. 2. Paris, Ex. Typ. Regio.

Prinz, F. (1965) *Frühes Mönchtum im Frankenreich. Kultur und Gesellschaft in Gallien, den Rheinlanden und Bayern am Beispiel der monastischen Entwicklung (4. bis 8. Jahrhundert*. Munich, Oldenbourg.

Ps.-Columbanus, *De Octo Vitiis Principalibus*. In G. S. M. Walker (ed. and trans.), *Sancti Columbani Opera*. Dublin: Dublin Institute for Advanced Studies, 210–213.

Puzicha, M. (2009) "Propria Voluntas: Self-Will and One's Own Will: Self-Realization and Self-Determination in the Rule of Benedict." *American Benedictine Review* 60: 244–52.

Regula Benedicti (1972), ed. A. de Vogüé and J. Neufville. SC 181–2. Paris, Cerf.

Regula cuiusdam ad virgines (1862), ed. J.-P. Migne. PL 88. Paris, col. 1053–70. (I am preparing a new critical edition.)

Regula cuiusdam patris, ed. F. Villegas (1973). "La 'Regula cuiusdam Patris ad monachos': Ses sources littéraires et ses rapports avec la 'Regula monachorum' de Colomban." *Revue d'Histoire de la Spiritualité* 49: 3–36 and 135–44.

Regula Eugipii (1974), ed. F. Villegas and A. de Vogüé. CSEL 87. Vienna, Hoelder-Pichler-Temsky.

Regula magistri (1964), ed. A. de Vogüé. SC 105–6. Paris, Cerf.

Reimitz, H. (2015) *History, Frankish Identity and the Framing of Western Ethnicity, 550–850*. Cambridge, Cambridge University Press.

Schürer, G. (1900) *Der Verfasser der sogenannten Fredegar-Chronik*. Freiburg, Commissionsverlag der Universitätsbuchhandlung.

Smaragdus of St. Mihiel (1974) *Expositio in Regulam S. Benedicti*, ed. Alfred Spannagel and Pius Engelbert. *Corpus Consuetudinum Monasticarum*, vol. 8. Siegburg, Schmitt.

Stancliffe, C. (2001) "Jonas's Life of Columbanus and His Disciples." In J. Carey, M. Herbert, and P. Ó Riain (eds.), *Studies in Irish Hagiography: Saints and Scholars*. Dublin, Four Courts Press, 189–220.

Stancliffe, C. (2011) "Columbanus's Monasticism and the Sources of His Inspiration: From Basil to the Master?" In F. Edmonds and P. Russell (eds.), *Tome: Studies in Medieval Celtic History and Law in Honour of Thomas Charles-Edwards*. Cambridge, Cambridge University Press, 17–28.

Stevenson, J. B. (1997). "The Monastic Rules of Columbanus." In M. Lapidge (ed.), *Columbanus: Studies on the Latin Writings*. Woodbridge, Boydell Press, 203–16.

Stransbury, M. (2011) "Agrestius et l'écriture de Luxeuil." In M. Picard (ed.), *Autour du Scriptorium de Luxeuil*. Luxeuil-les-Bains: Association des Amis de saint Colomban, 68–71.

Testimonia Divinae Scripturae (1987), ed. Abert Lehner. *CCSL* 108D. Turnhout, Brepols.

Villegas, F. (1973) "La 'Regula cuiusdam Patris ad monachos': Ses sources littéraires et ses rapports avec la 'Regula monachorum' de Colomban." *Revue d'Histoire de la Spiritualité* 49: 3–36 and 135–44.

Vita Agili (1868) In J. Stiltingus (ed.), *Acta Sanctorum*. August VI. Paris and Rome, Victor Palmé, 574–84.

Vita Amati (1902) In B. Krusch (ed.), *Scriptores rerum Merovingicarum* 4 MGH. Hanover and Leipzig, 215–21.

Vita Sadalbergae abbatissae Laudunensis (1910) In B. Krusch (ed.), *Scriptores rerum Merovingicarum* 5. MGH. Hanover and Leipzig, 49–66.

Von Nagel, D. (1978) "Puritas cordis—Reinheit des Herzens: Sinn und Ziel einer Mönchsübung nach den Schriften des Johannes Kassian." In G. Stachel (ed.), *Munen muso: Ungegenständliche Meditation; Festschrift für Hugo M. Enomiya-Lasalle zum 80. Geburtstag*. Mainz, Matthias-Grünewald-Verlag, 127–55.

Weber, M. (1968) *On Charisma and Institution Building*, trans. Shmuel Noah Eisenstadt. Chicago, University of Chicago Press.

Wood, I. N. (1998) "Jonas, the Merovingians, and Pope Honorius: *Diplomata* and the *Vita Columbani*." In A. C. Murray (ed.), *After Rome's Fall: Narrators and Sources of Early Medieval History; Essays Presented to Walter Goffart*. Toronto, University of Toronto Press, 99–120.

Wood, I. N. (2007) "The Franks and Papal Theology, 550–660." In C. Chazelle and C. Cubitt (eds.), *The Crisis of the Oikomene: The Three Chapters and the Failed Quest for Unity in the Sixth-Century Medierranean*. Turnhout, Brepols, 223–41.

Index

Abbelenus, bishop of Geneva, 144, 148–150, 152
Abnoba, Celtic goddess, 184
Abrenuntiatio Diaboli, 192
absolution, 273
acculturation, 72
Achpoet's *Confession*, 177
Acts of the Apostles, 33, 184
Adaloald, Lombard king, 82, 147, 244–247, 251, 253
Adalram, archbishop of Salzburg, 171
Adomnán of Iona, *Vita Columbae*
  Aidus Niger in, 59
  convention of Druim Cett in, 64
  Comgall of Bangor in, 94
  portrayal of Columba in 97, 228
  Uinnianus in, 93
Afra, Saint, 166
Agathias of Myrina, 180, 181
Agaune, 150
Agilolfing, dukes, 165, 167, 210
Agilulf, Lombard king
  Arian beliefs of, 31
  patron of Columbanus, 12, 81, 244, 252
  Theodelinda and, 82, 84, 205, 251, 256
Agilus, abbot of Rebais, 146
Agrestius, renegade monk of Luxeuil
  attitude to penance, 276
  in Bavaria, 147
  conflict with Eustasius at Synod of Mâcon, 148–155, 157, 169, 220, 253, 268–273
  depiction in *Vita Columbani*, 158
  link with Burgundian factions, 144
  Regula cuiusdam patris, 265, 280

Aguntum/Lienz, 167
Aistulf, Lombard king, 247
Alamanni, 168, 170, 179, 180–181, 207, 209
Alamannia
  burial rites in, 181
  Christianization of, 12, 232
  Columbanus in, 7, 11, 168, 207
  depictions of, 182
  duchy of, 205
  duke of, 230
  Gallus in, 171, 216, 229, 237
  king of, 179
  in seventh century, 209, 212–213, 218, 230–234
  paganism in, 179
  ritual in, 184
  sword sheath found in, 182
  Woden linked to, 194
Alethius affair, 220
Allemannische Gedichte, 179
Alsace, 207, 210, 219
Alveto valley, 255
Amalasuntha, Gothic king, 196
Amandus, missionary bishop, 155, 160, 167, 169, 171, 206
Amatus, abbot of Remiremont, 146, 147, 149, 150, 156, 265
Ambrose of Milan, bishop, 34, 38, 39, 41, 85
amicitia, 135, 219
Ammianus Marcellinus, 181, 190
Amra Choluimb Chille, 97
Aneirin, Welsh poet, 63
Angers, 105, 106
Angles/Anglo-Saxon, 60–63, 129, 169, 170, 193, 195

Anglo-Saxon Chronicle, 60
Anicetus, pope, 20, 44
Anjou, 105
Annals of Tighernach, 62
Annals of Ulster, 60, 63, 64
Annegray, monastery of, 11, 76, 109,
    120, 206
Anonymous continuator of Prosper, 194
Anthony of Egypt, 70, 183, 289
Antiphonary of Bangor, 97
Apennines, mountain range, 12, 245, 254
Aquilean schism, 147, 251, 269, 270, 273. *See
    also* Three Chapters Controversy
Arbon, 227
archives, ecclesiastical, 250
Arduinna, Celtic goddess, 184
Arian heresy
    Bobbio and, 254–255
    Columbanus's work against, 81, 143, 252
    Lombards and, 82, 251, 254–255
    in *Vita Columbani*, 246
arimanniae, Lombard military settlements,
    254, 256
Arioald, Lombard king, 83, 243, 246, 247
Aristides, 35
aristocracies, barbarian, 194, 195, 199
Artemis, 184
ascetic exile (*peregrinatio*), 8, 10
asceticism, 25, 177, 185, 289
Athala, second abbot of Bobbio
    Gallus and, 229
    letter of Agrestius and, 147, 152, 253
    rebel monks and, 234, 264–267, 269
    royal patronage of Bobbio and, 245
Athalaric, 196
Auf der Läschitz, 172
Augsburg, 180
Augustine of Canterbury, 116, 118, 119
Augustine of Hippo
    choir metaphor and, 36
    concord and, 27, 33, 38
    identification and, 9
    influence of, 262, 276
    monogamous ideals of, 73
    nature of the state and, 43–44
    Paulus Orosius and, 39
    ship metaphor and, 28
Augustus, Roman emperor, 22
Auraicept na nÉces, 182
Aurelia, church in Bregenz dedicated to
    Saint, 169

Aureus, notary of King Adaloald, 253
Austrasia, 12, 76, 78, 205, 210, 218, 231
Austria, 168, 169
Authari, Lombard king, 82, 166
Authari, king, 166
authority, 25, 26, 27, 43, 278
Autiernus, Columbanian monk, 107
Autun, 155
avarice, 121, 297
Avars, xi, 167
Avenches, 207

B-ware pottery, 93
Baden-Württemberg, 179
Báetán, 93
Balts, 171
Bamburgh, 63, 64
Bangor, monastery of, 5, 10, 53, 55–56, 73,
    91–92, 94, 96–97, 108, 237
baptism, 137, 183, 272
barbarian
    ancestry, 198
    barbarism, 194
    depiction of, 181, 199, 246
    drinking to extremes and, 196
    identity, 12
    kingdoms, 14
    language, 171
    rituals of, 178, 189–190
Barrach, Dáire, 54, 56
Basil, monastic rule of, 97, 266, 285, 286
battle of Tolbiac, 179
Bavaria, 11, 146, 153, 165–166, 168–169, 219
Bavarian Romans, 172
Bavarians, 144, 146, 147, 168, 169
Bayeux, 105
Bécc Bairrche, 56
Bede, 60, 61, 116, 170, 193
beer, 177, 178, 179, 182, 183, 185, 189, 192, 196
beheading of animals, 181
Belfast Lough, 92
Benedict of Aniane, *Concordia regularum*,
    260, 261, 265, 290
Benedict XVI, pope, 4
Beowulf, 196
Beppolen, Frankish general, 105, 108, 110
Bernicia, kingdom of, 60, 61, 63
Berschin, Walter, 209, 226, 228
Bertulf, abbot of Bobbio, 245, 253, 254, 264
Bishop of Milan, 117
Bishop of Rome, 29, 31, 32, 41

bishops, 6, 29, 113, 136, 150, 153, 158, 169
Blidulf, monk of Bobbio, 246
Bobbio
  abbey church of Saint Peter, 244, 245, 254
  Adbrevatio, 248
  Agrestius and, 265, 276, 280
  Bobbio Missal, 277
  Bobbio Sacramentary, 137n97
  community of, 254, 264
  connection with other Columbanian
    foundations, 77, 217, 233, 237
  establishment of, 12, 81, 205–206, 231,
    243–245
  Gallus and abbacy of Bobbio, 228, 229
  Jonas's entry into, 70
  monastic rebellion in, 13, 234, 253,
    267–268, 273
  monastic archive, 249
  papal bull for, 159, 247
  patrimony of, 82, 249–250
  as royal monastery, 254–256
  Vita Vetustissima and, 226
Bodic, Breton *comes*, 104
body metaphor, 37, 40, 42, 44
Bognetti, Giampiero, 251, 254, 255
Boniface, Anglo-Saxon bishop, 169, 192, 197
Boniface IV, pope, 27–38, 40, 44–45, 83,
  154–158, 252
Bonosus/ Bonosians, 146, 155
Book of Armagh, 56
Bóruma, Brian, Irish king, 60
Boyne, river, 92
bracteates, 192
Bregenz
  activity of Gallus in, 227–229, 235–237
  Columbanus and, 108, 168
  Columbanus's mission in, 205, 214, 219
  Columbanus's monastery in, 207, 212, 230
  locals of, 170, 171
  location of, 189
Brescia, San Salvatore, later Santa Giulia,
  250, 256
Brigit, *Vita prima* of, 75, 137
Britain, 93, 95, 125, 135, 192, 207
British
  Church, 125, 126, 128
  ethnic group, 43, 60
  kingdoms, 61–64
  monks/monasticism, 11, 95, 96, 107,
    110, 132
  penitential genre, 71n14

  term, 104
  territory, 105–106
Britons, xi, 60, 95, 104, 108, 110, 116, 117, 195
Brittany, 10, 76, 103, 104, 107
Britto, 104
Broërec, 106
Brown, Peter, 9, 219, 288, 289
Brunhild, Queen, 7, 76
  conflict with Columbanus, 131
  involvement in marriage of Theuderic,
    133–135
  politics, 210, 214, 231
  portrayal of, 74–75, 77– 78, 85, 132
Bullough , Donald, 58, 72, 208, 273
Burgundofara, abbess of Faremoutiers, 75,
  145, 149, 236, 283
Burgundy, kingdom of, 6, 11, 69, 76, 210, 218
  bishops of, 121
  Columbanus expelled from, 78
  Columbanus in, 106, 197, 205
  Columbanus's move to, 107, 108, 109,
    110, 131
  Eustasius's mission in, 153, 155, 166
  factions in, 144, 152
  Frankish court of, 134
burials, multiple and horse, 181
Byzantium/ Byzantine Empire, 155, 195,
  251, 254

Caesarius of Arles, bishop, 196, 198
Cairell mac Muiredaig, 93
Candidus, representative of Pope Gregory
  the Great, 115, 116, 122, 130
Capraria, island of, 118
Carantanians, 11, 167, 172
Carantoc, British abbot of Salicis, 110
carcer, 261
Carinthia, 171
Carloman, 248
Carolingians, 199
Cashel, Co. Tipperary, 59
Cassian, John, 97, 262, 266, 280, 285
Casus sancti Galli, 211
catechumenate, 183
Cathechesis Cracoviensis, 30
Catholicism, 251, 252, 254
Celts/Celtic, 125, 184, 185
ceramic, 165
Chagneric, father of Burgundofara, 145
Chalcedon, Council of, 156, 157
Chalon-sur-Saône, 78, 115, 155, 156

Chanao, Breton *comes*, 104, 106
Charente, river, 93
charms and amulets, 181
charters, private, 249, 250
Chiemsee, Lake, 165
Childebert II, king of Burgundy and
    Austrasia, 76, 77, 109, 121, 131, 156
Chilperic, Frankish king, 105, 129, 130
Chlothar I, king of Neustria, 197
Chlothar II, king of Neustria
    court of, 9, 211
    depiction in *Vita Columbani*, 81, 132,
        145, 148
    ecclesiastical organization in Alamannia
        under, 232
    enemy of Brunhild, 76–77
    and Gallus's hermitage, 231
    son of Fredegund, 105
    support for Eustasius, 167, 216
    and Synod of Mâcon, 152–153, 220, 253
choir, image of, 35–38
Chozil, prince, 171
Chramnesind, 196
Christianization, 12, 73, 74, 146, 160, 167, 181,
    189, 225
chronicle, earliest Irish, 71
Chronicle of Fredegar. *See* Fredegar
Chundo, 108, 109, 110
Cicero, 38, 39, 40, 43
Ciesburc, 180
Civil war, 34, 44
Clement of Rome, pope, 26
Clichy, Council of, 154
Clovis, Frankish king, 104
Collectio Canonum Hibernensis, 80
Colmán, name, 98
Colmán, son of Cormac Camshrón, 54
Columba, abbot of Iona, xiii, 3, 4, 10, 64, 65,
    91, 95, 97, 98, 228
Columbanian monastic network
    conflicts in, 145, 150, 152, 169, 229, 280
    Gallus's connection with, 209, 217, 218,
        220, 225, 233, 234, 237
    missionary work, 236
    monasteries, xiv, 243
    monastic rules, 263, 275
    new foundations, 208
    orthodoxy, 156, 158, 198
    patronage of, 77, 219, 232
    practice, 267, 272, 273, 277, 288

Regula Benedicti, 261, 270
relationship to bishops, 78
relationship to Rome and papacy, 159, 253
Synod of Mâcon, 269
Vita Columbani as source for, 264–265
Columbanus
    and Agrestius, 157
    in Alamannia, 205–208, 213, 218–219
    Arian heresy, 81
    attitude to authority, 25, 36, 156
    attitude to Gallic bishops, 20, 126
    author of *Precamur patrem*, 97
    baculum, 228, 229
    birth in Leinster, 3, 53–54, 55, 91
    and Bishop Uinnianus, 94, 98
    and British Church, 95
    British monks of, 110
    Brittany, 103, 104, 107–109
    as catalyst, 8
    church dedicated to, 248
    conflict and, 7
    correspondence with Gregory the Great,
        23, 115–116, 118–123, 125, 127
    cultural identity, 69
    family background of, 72–74, 76
    fosterage, 58
    and Gallus, 227–228, 233, 234, 236
    ideal of ascetic exile, 5, 9, 75
    idea of Europe and, 6
    Ireland, political context in, 64, 65
    Irish customs, 79–80
    Jonas's representation of, 71, 78, 154, 178,
        270, 272
    legacy of, 13, 30, 177, 260, 264–265, 276
    and Lombards, 251–254
    Merovingians, 130–136, 145
    as a missionary, 167–168, 171, 225, 237
    monastic founder, 11, 113, 243, 244
    monastic ideal, 276, 289
    paganism and, 12, 143, 170, 183, 185
    penitential, 95, 96
    Robert Schuman and, 4
    Rule of, 147, 259, 262, 263, 266, 271, 274,
        275, 285–288
    Three Chapters, 269
    ties to Uí Bairrche, 56, 60, 62
    tomb of, 245
    in Ulster, 92
    view of Church, 28, 29, 31, 32, 35, 37,
        40–42, 43, 44

view of Roman Empire, 34
women, relationship to, 70, 83, 85, 86
writings of, 19, 84, 114
Columbus, 116
Comgall, abbot of Bangor, 53, 58, 74, 91, 94
Comininus, British monk of
    Columbanus, 107
Conailli Muirtheimne, 59
Concord/*concordia*, 10, 20–22, 24, 28–29,
    31–36, 39, 40, 43, 44
Concordia regularum, Benedict of Aniane,
    265, 266, 290
confession, 136, 273, 275
Congal Cloén, 65
Connaid Cerr, king of Dál Riata, 62
Conomor, Breton *comes*, 104
Conon, abbot of Lérins, 116
Constance, 207, 217, 225, 232
    bishopric of, 215, 226, 229, 233, 237
    Lake of, 11, 168, 178, 189, 190, 212, 229, 230,
        235–236 (*see also* Lacus Venetus)
Constantinople, 158, 168, 171
Constantinople, Council of, 158
Continuator of Prosper, 244
conversion, 167, 169
Coroticus, British chieftain, 40, 129
Corpus Genealogiarum Sanctorum
    Hiberniae, 95
Cottonian Alps, 243
Council of Mâcon (*see* Mâcon, synod of)
Cruithin, 59, 62, 64, 65, 92
Cruithnechán, 94
cultic practice, 185
cultural consolidation, 71
cultural hybridity, 7, 8
Cumian, tombstone in Bobbio, 247
Cumméne Find, abbot of Iona, 65
Cunipert, Lombard king, 247
Cunzelen, duke, 210
Cuthbert, archbishop of Canterbury, 197
Cyprian of Carthage, bishop, 27, 28, 44
Cyrian, bishop of Arles, 214
Cyuuari, 180

Dagán, bishop, 116, 129
Dagobert I, Frankish king, 169, 211, 231, 232
Dál Cormaic, 54
Dál Fiatach, 56, 57, 58, 59, 60
Dál nAraidi, 59
Dál Riata, 59, 60, 61, 62, 64, 65

Dannheimer, Hermann, 165, 166
Danube, river, xi, 169, 179
Davidson, Hilda Ellis, 182
De duodecim abusiuis saeculi, 41, 44, 45
De Excidio Britonum, 107, 125, 127. *See
    also* Gildas
Degsastan, battle of, 60, 62, 64
Deira, 61
Déisi of Munster, 57
demons, 183, 184, 190, 227, 230, 235
Dennán, 93
Deorad Dé, 75
Derry, Co., 64
Desiderius, Lombard king, 247
Desiderius, bishop of Vienne, 79, 121, 133, 212
devil, 170, 182, 184, 189, 272, 285, 290, 299
Diana, cult of at Ephesus, 184
diploma, royal, 247, 248, 249
Dísert Diarmada (Castledermot), Co.
    Kildare, 56
disobedience, 228, 234, 235, 237, 266, 267,
    283, 284, 285, 300
divorce, 73
doctrina, 264, 269
Domangart, 61
donations to churches, 250
Dopsch, Heinz, 165, 166
Down, Co., 59, 98
Downpatrick, Co. Down, 93
drinking, 177, 186, 196, 198, 199, 294
druid, 137
Druim Cett, 64, 65
Dub-dá-chrich, Irish bishop, 166
Dublittir, 172
Duft, Johannes, 171
Duibthrian, 97
Dumbarton, Scotland, 61

E-ware pottery, 92, 93
Eanfrith, brother of Æthelfrith, 61
Easter
    conflict over, 6, 25, 113, 134, 138, 270
    dating of, 20, 21, 78, 114, 119–120, 123, 132, 263
    Gallic bishops, 45, 115, 124, 154
    Jonas and, 70, 144, 236, 253
    unity and, 31, 43
Ebrachar, Frankish general, 105, 106, 108, 110
Edwin, English king, 64
Elbe, river, 179, 180
elites, 71, 73, 75, 192, 195, 217, 218, 250

Elmet, 61, 63
Elnone, 160
Emilia, 250
Émíne, Saint, 56
Emly, Co. Tipperary, 59
Époisses, 131, 135, 137
Ermenberga, 133, 135
Ermenrich of Ellwangen, 30
Esau, brother of Jacob, 33, 34, 35
Etherius of Lyon, bishop, 121
ethnic, xii, 43, 71, 171, 104
ethnographers, 181
ethnographic tropes, 194
Etichonid, ducal dynasty of Alsace, 210
Eucharist, 128, 184, 228, 276, 279, 301
Eunius, bishop of Vannes, 105
Eunocus, Columbanian monk, 107
Europe, xi, 4–6, 10, 13–14, 143, 161, 171, 189
Eusebius, church historian, 185, 194
Eustasius, second abbot of Luxeuil
   Agrestius affair and, 143–152, 157, 253, 269,
      271–272
   Evangelization and, 11, 155
   Gallus as potential successor, 216–217
   mission in Bavaria, 165–169, 212
   successor to Columbanus, 231, 234,
      264–265, 282–283
Eutyches, 156, 157
Evagrius Ponticus's *Sententiae*, 262
evangelization, 143, 144, 145, 166, 189
Exarchate, 255
excommunication, 128, 135, 137, 228, 298
exile, 8, 58, 69, 78, 113, 133
exorcism of demons, 183
expulsion from monastery, 261, 267, 285
Ezekiel, 97, 115, 125, 129

Fanatice, 198
Faremoutiers, convent of, 75, 275
Farfa, monastery of, 249, 250
Faustus of Riez, bishop, 97
feasting, 135, 197
female communities, 282
Fiachna, 64
Fiachra of Slébte (Sletty), Saint, 56
Fid Eoin, battle of, 62
Fifth Ecumenical Council, 251, 252
Finnian, 124, 126, 127
Finnian's *Penitential*, 124
Florian, Saint, 166

Fontaine, monastery of, 76, 117, 178
food placed in graves, 181
fornication, 128, 297
Forth, Firth of, 61
Fortunatus, patriarch of Aquileia, 254
fosterage, 58, 74, 76
Foyle, Lough, 92
Fragmenta Gildae, 94. *See also* Gildas,
   Fragment 7
Francia, 103, 205, 213
Franks, 104, 171, 180
Frankish
   army, 108
   authority, 106, 211
   Columbanus and, 69
   elites, 5, 7, 8, 194
   king, 10, 179
   kingdoms, 143, 198, 243, 264
   mission to Bavaria, 168
   nobles, 197, 182
   pagan past, 190
Frea, Germanic goddess, 194
Fredegar, 106, 133, 135, 191–193, 198, 210
Fredegund, Frankish queen of
   Chlothar I, 105
Fridburga, daughter of duke of Alamannia,
   212–214, 229, 231– 233
Friuli, 167
frontier, xi, 6, 8, 14, 24, 61, 190, 219, 250,
   254–255
Fursey, Irish monastic founder, 207

Gallic bishops
   Columbanus's celebration of Easter and,
      119–120, 134, 144, 270
   Columbanus's conflict with, 8, 11, 19–20,
      45, 78, 114
   Columbanus's letter to, 36–37, 107
   simony and Columbanus's criticism of,
      122–124, 126
Gallic Church, 118, 120
Gallic clergy, 27, 31, 37, 79
Gallus, Columbanian monk and hermit
   and abbacy of Luxeuil, 216–217
   and Alamannia, 213, 216, 218, 219–220,
      230–237
   and Columbanian network, 225, 226
   ethnicity of, 53n5, 171, 208, 217
   hagiographic depiction of, 30, 209, 216,
      226–227, 229

historicity of, 228
influence and achievements of, 12
Garda, Lake, 248, 249
Garibald I, duke, 166
Garibald II, duke, 166
Gaul, Merovingian
   Columbanus's arrival in, 21, 91, 113, 127
   communication with, 118–119
   feasting in, 135
   ritual economy of, 6
   sexual practices in, 79
   state of religion in, 137, 143, 155
   women in, 73
Gemmán, teacher of Columba of Iona, 94
gender, 71, 72, 81, 84
gens/gentes, 6, 71, 143, 145, 147, 168, 189, 194,
   198, 211
Germania, 168, 170, 189, 191, 199
Germani, 181, 185, 190
gift/-s, 6, 23, 117, 131, 136, 217, 246,
   281, 297
Gildas, 11, 79, 94–96, 106–107, 110, 114, 120,
   124–128, 138
   De Excidio Britonum, 97, 98
   Fragment 7, 127, 128
Godinus, 152
gods of the Romans, 190
Gorgonia, 118
Gospel of Nicodemus, 97
Goths, to drink like, 196
Gougaud, Louis, 261
Gozbert, abbot of St Gallen, 226
Grado, 251
Grandval, monastery of, 211
Gregory of Nazianus, *Orationes*, 97
Gregory of Tours, bishop
   account of Guntram's campaign in
      Brittany, 108–110
   Alamanni and, 170
   depiction of Gallic clergy, 125
   depiction of pagan past, 190, 198
   fellow bishops and, 129–130
   and feud of Sichar and Chramnesind, 196
   and Lombard invasion of Italy, 191
   portrayal of Brunhild, 77
Gregory the Great, pope
   as authority for Columbanus, 11, 44,
      113–117, 121, 127
   Columbanus informant for, 122–123
   correspondence of, 82, 116, 154

and cult of Saint Pancras, 117
as diplomat, 138
ideas on peace and unity, 14, 23–25, 32
Grimald of St Gallen, abbot, 30
Grimoald, Lombard king, 247
Gundahar, duke of Alamannia, 210
Gundeberga, 83
Gundlach, Wilhelm, 42
Gundoin, duke of Alsace, 211, 212
Guntram I, king of Burgundy, 11, 105,
   107–110
Gunzo, duke of Alamannia, 205, 208,
   210–212, 229–231, 233
Gurgan, British monk of Columbanus,
   53, 107
Gutenstein, 182
Gwallawg, king, 63
Gwynnog ap Gildas of *Bonedd y Sant*, 95

hagiography, 183, 208, 218
Hailfingen, bronze disk, 182
harmony. *See Homonia*
heathen/-s, 168, 192, 194, 197, 212. *See*
   also pagan
Hemmaberg, Carinthia, 172
Hengist, brother of Horsa, 170, 193
heresy, 81, 143–145, 148, 153–155, 159–160,
   166, 252, 269, 287
heretics, 85, 146, 155
Hermenigild, son of Visigothic king
   Leovigild, 133
Herrenchiemsee, Bavaria, 11, 168, 166, 168
Hiberno-Frankish mission, 169
Hiberno-Latin writings, 80
Hilpranda, benefactor of Bobbio, 248, 249
Hiltibod, deacon of Gallus, 219
Hilty, Gerold, 217
Historia ecclesiastica gentis Anglorum, Bede,
   192. *See also* Bede
Historia Langobardorum, Paul the Deacon,
   243. *See also* Paul the Deacon
Histories, Gregory of Tours, 104, 106, 191.
   See also Gregory of Tours
historiography, xiii, 34, 194, 251
Hocinus, Frankish noble, 197
holy space, 136, 288
Homonoia, ("harmony"), 33, 36, 38
Honorius I, pope, 159, 247, 253, 254
Horsa, brother of Hengist, 170, 193
hostages, 59

Iberi, xii, 252
identities, xiii, 8, 9, 72
Ignatius, Saint, *Letter to the Ephesians*, 35
Illyrians, 185
Imblech Ibair, 59
imprisonment, 261, 285. *See also* carcer
Indiculus superstitionum et paganiarum, 192
instituta, 264, 269
Insular, 7, 11, 12, 29, 113, 128, 130, 133, 135
    script, 270
    texts, 262
intercessory prayer. *See* prayer
Interpretatio Christiani, 184
Iocundus, agent of King Agilulf, 245
Iona/Í, island of, 94, 97, 98
Ireland
    beer and, 185
    Columbanus and, 3, 6, 69, 72, 75, 96–97,
        107, 127, 135, 137, 138
    depiction of, 30, 85
    kings of, 60
    political context of, 10, 64, 76
    trade and, 93, 106
    women in, 77, 79
Irish
    annals, 92
    Church, 43, 95, 116, 119, 127
    of Dál Riata, 61
    elites, 73
    ethnicity, 43, 71, 137, 208
    exegete, 28
    influence, 207, 261
    and Isle of Man, 59
    manner of life, 41, 117
    monasticism, 80, 96, 254, 255, 270
    monastic rules, 287
    monks of Columbanus, 132, 168
    scholars, 21, 26, 72, 79, 114
Isacius, exarch of Italy, 247
Isidore of Seville, *History of the Goths*, xiii
Isidore of Seville, xii, 33, 35
Islandmagee, Co. Antrim, 59
Isle of Man, 59, 64
Italian bishops, 246–247
Italy, 21, 83, 108, 193, 196, 205, 212, 218, 243,
    245, 252

Jacob, brother of Esau, 33, 34, 35
Jerome, 97, 185, 194, 262
    Commentary on Isaiah, 126

Commentary on the Gospel of Matthew,
    260, 262
Jews, xi, 31, 114, 123
Jezebel, 75, 77, 131
John XXIII, pope, 3
John/Iohannes, bishop of Constance,
    215, 233
Jonas of Bobbio, xiii, 11, 12
    Agrestius affair, 157
    Bavaria, 169
    and Bishop Amandus, 206
    Bobbio monks, 254
    and *damnatio memoriae* of Brunhild, 81
    drunkenness, 196, 198
    and Eustasius, 145–147, 149–151
    and Gallus, 216, 226, 234–236
    Germania, 171
    hagiographer of Columbanus, 53–54, 58,
        72–74, 91, 103, 107–109, 132–134, 137, 213
    monastic rebellions, 267–268, 270,
        275, 289
    and *Regula cuiusdam patris*, 260, 276
    representation of Columbanus, 71, 78,
        85–86, 154, 168
    silences of, 113, 144
    Slavs, 11
    Woden and, 12, 170, 190–191
Jupiter, Roman god, 183
Justin II, emperor, 191
Justus, 116

Keller, Hagan, 214, 231
Kelly, Joseph, 124
Kilian, Irish monk and missionary, 185, 207
Konstantinos/Cyril, apostle to Slavs, 171
Korneliemünster, 289
Kreiner, Jamie, 273, 280
Kršna Vas, 172
Krusch, Bruno, 135, 145, 216, 198

Lacus Venetus, 171. *See also* Constance,
    Lake of
Lateran Council, 159
Laurence, Roman missionary to England,
    116, 119, 129
law, 71, 73, 79, 85
Leinster, region of Ireland, 3, 10, 53, 54, 56,
    57–58, 91
Leo the Great, pope, 156
Leo XIII, pope, 3

Leovigild, 133
Lérins, monastery of, 118
Lethet (Knocklayd, Co. Antrim?), 59
Leuthar, 210
Lex Bavariorum, 167
Libanius, 22, 23
Liber in Gloria Martyrum, 104
Libri Historiarum, Gregory of Tours. See
    Histories
Life of Abbán, 54
Life of Brigit, 137
Life of Cainnech, 54
Life of Fintan/Munnu of Tech Munnu, 54
Life of Gallus. See *Vitae Galli*
Life of Gildas, 106
Life of Severinus, 172
Liguria, 254, 255
liturgy, 183, 277, 289
Liutprand, Lombard king, 243, 247, 248
Loire, river, 93, 106
Lombard
    aristocracies, 194
    court, 247
    elites, 5, 249
    Italy, 7, 12, 251, 256
    kingdom, 243, 244, 249, 250, 254, 264
    law, 82
    monarchy, 193, 256
    monasteries, 255
    settlement, 256
    warriors, 254
Lombards
    Arian and pagan, 82, 143, 252
    disruptions in northern Italy, 118
    Woden and, 191, 194
Louis II, king, 248
Louth, Co., 59
Luke's Gospel, 177
Luni, 118, 119
Luxeuil
    14th centenary conference in 1950, 3–5
    Agrestius and renegade monks of, 11, 13,
        144, 147, 253, 267–269, 273
    archaeological excavations of, 206
    cellarer of, 177
    church dedication to Saint Peter, 118
    Columbanus's banishment from, 168, 263
    Columbanus's legacy in, 264–265
    foundations of, 123, 207, 281
    Gallus and, 216, 217, 231

    Merovingians and, 78, 79, 103, 132
    missionaries from, 165, 166
    monastic community of, 76, 120, 169
    monastic life in, 208, 234, 276, 280
    mission and, 145, 146, 153
    Paul the Deacon reference to, 243
    Privilege for, 159
    Remiremont and, 147, 150
    septa secretiora of, 80
    Suebian bandits near, 171

mac Báetáin, Fiachna, 63
mac Báetán, Máel Umai, 60
mac Cairill, Báetán , 59, 60, 61, 64, 65
mac Cáirthinn, Móenach, 54
mac Conaing, Rigullán, 62
mac Cuill, Saint, 56
mac Diarmata, Cormac, 54, 55, 60, 65
mac Echach, Dícuil, king, 62
mac Echach, Fáilbe, 62
mac Eochada, Niall, 56
mac Gabráin, Áedán, 59, 61, 62, 64, 65
mac Maíl na mBó, 56
mac Óengusa, Rotha, 57
mac Scandail, Máel Cáich, king of
    Cruithin, 62
mac Suibni, Áed Dub, 59
mac Táil, Saint, 56
Macliaw, Breton *comes*, 104, 106
Mâcon, synod of
    Chlothar II and, 220
    Easter controversy and, 134, 270
    Jonas's depiction of, 149, 150, 154, 158–159,
        253, 265, 271
    political factions and, 152
    as turning point, 269, 273
Macsen Wledig, 195
Maelruain, founder of monastery of
    Tallaght, 185, 186
Mag Roth, battle of, 65
Maglocunus, British monk, 98
Magnoald, companion of Gallus, 217, 219
Magnus Maximus, Roman emperor, 129, 195
Marcellus, Saint, 109
Marienberg, Würzburg, 184
Maritain, Jacques, 3, 4
marital customs, 72, 76, 122
Martin I, pope, 155, 156, 159, 160
Martin, Saint, 107, 129, 183
Mass, 271, 273, 276, 277, 278, 296, 301

medicamenta paenitentiae, 146, 153, 161, 275, 276
Meic Ainmirech, Domnall mac Áedo, 65
Mellitus, 116
Mercury, Roman god, 170, 182, 183, 189, 190, 191
Merovingian Gaul. *See* Gaul, Merovingian
Merovingian kingdoms, 143, 157, 270
Merovingian/s
  and Alamannia, 210
  and Bretons, 105
  Columbanus and, 62, 76, 81, 86, 113, 138
  concubinage, 78
  Jonas and, 132
  queens, 77, 134
  rivalries of, 60
Methodios, apostle to Slavs, 171
Metz, 12, 214, 215
Michael III, Byzantine emperor, 168
microloga, 158
Milan, 83, 85, 143, 252
Minerva, Roman goddess, 183
miracles, 179, 185, 245, 281
miracle stories, 177, 178, 207
mission, 169, 209, 237
  activity, 229, 254, 255, 256
  unsuccessful attempts, 236
missionary, 160, 169, 179, 205, 269, 282
Mo Sinnu moccu Min, 91, 94
Mo-Sníthech, Muiredach, 54
monarchia, 146
monasteries
  economy, 288
  ideals, 260
  monastic discipline, 259, 287
  network, 282
  patronage of, 256
  rule, 132, 137, 195, 260, 265, 266, 268, 275, 278
  space, 136, 288
  as strategic settlements, 255, 256
Monothelitism, 155, 159
Montecassino, monastery of, 250
Monza, monastery of San Giovanni, 256
Morbihan, Golfe de, 11, 103–108, 110
Morcant, British king, 63
Moselle, river, 206
Moville, Co. Down, 91–97
Münchhöf-Homberg, 181
Munster, region in Ireland, 59

Naiton, son of Gildas, 95
Nantes, 103, 104, 105, 106, 107
Nazarius, Saint, 104
Nelson, Max, 185
Nendrum, monastery of, 92, 94, 97
Nestorius, 156, 157
Neustria, kingdom of, 218
Neustrian/s, 105, 212, 270
Nicea, Council of, 156
Nitra, 171
Noah, 126, 127
Nonantola, monastery of, 250, 255
Nonnosus, Saint, 172
Nordendorf fibulae, 170, 192
Noricum, region of, 167
Northumbria/-ns, 61, 62, 64
Novalesa, monastery of, 250

obedience, 234–235, 284–285, 288, 291
Oberflacht, 181
Óðinn, Norse god, 182, 189
Ogam, 182
Old Slovene, 172
Origo gentis Langobardorum, xiii, 191, 193–194
Orléans, 155
Osraige, 55
Osric, son of Alfred, 62
Otmar, abbot of St Gallen, 218, 225, 237
Ovid, Roman poet, 14, 177

Pace et Concordia, 26, 27. *See also* concord
Paenitentiale, 197
pagan
  Anglo-Saxons, 129
  Alammanian, 180
  cultic practices, 185
  custom, 183
  gods, 170
  Ireland, 74
  Lombards, 82
  religion, 181
  ritual, 179, 197
  sanctuary, 184
paganism, 143, 166, 192, 196, 256
pagans, 146, 168, 169, 183, 184, 190, 254, 255
Pancras, Saint, Roman martyr, 117
papacy, 12, 20–21, 83, 134, 154–156, 159–161
papal bull for Bobbio, 247
Passio Kiliani, 184. *See also* Killian
Patrick, Saint, 40, 56, 129

Paul the Deacon, 243, 244
Paul the hermit, 70
Paul, Saint, 25, 31, 36, 37, 39, 40, 41, 42, 43,
    117, 126, 129
Paulinus of Nola, 40
Paulus Orosius, 39
Pavia, 244, 246, 249, 255
Pax Augusta, 22
Pax Romana, 22, 34
penance, 273, 288, 291–294, 299–300
penitentiae medicamenta, 143
penitential system, 275
penitentials, 71, 96, 128
Pennice, mountain, 245
Perctarit, Lombard king, 193
peregrinatio, 74, 75, 85, 168, 189, 269, 207,
    252. *See also* ascetic exile
Peter and Paul, harmony and
    concord, 32, 35
Peter, Saint, 29, 31, 35, 84, 117, 118, 206
Pfäfers, 237
Photinus/Photinians, 146, 155
Pictland, 61
Picts, 60
pilgrims, 121, 255
place names, 192
plebs, 146
Pliezhausen, 182
Po valley, 250
Poitiers, nuns of, 109
Poitou, 105
Polycarp, bishop, 20, 44
polypytchs, 250
Pomerius, *De uita contemplative*, 29, 31
Praefatio Gildae de Poenitentia, 96
Praetextatus, bishop, 129
prayer, 136, 148, 213, 271, 272, 273, 281,
    288, 300
Precamur patrem, 97
Primigenius, 254
prior (*eqonomus*), 292
Priscillian, 129
prison, 291, 292, 293. *See also* imprisonment
    and *carcer*
privileges, 159, 282
pro anima donations, 250
Probus, bishop of Tortona, 246
Procopius, 196
Protadius, 135, 210
provincia Sequanorum, 145

Prudentius, 32
Pseudo-Clement, letter to James, 29

Raetia, 170
Rance, 103
Ratchis, Lombard king, 247, 248, 249
Ratislav, prince, 168
Ratpert, Lombard king, 231
Rebais, privilege for, 281, 282
Rebecca, 33, 34, 84
reciprocal relations (reciprocity), 6, 7
Regalis, bishop, 105
regula, 259, 261, 264, 269
Regula ad virgines, Caesarius of
    Arles, 136
Regula Basilii, 128, 262, 287
Regula Benedicti
    excommunication in, 128
    influence of, 261–263
    obedience and, 284–285, 287
    precedence of, 265
    use in Columbanian monasteries, 270
Regula coenobialis, Columbanus, 262, 271,
    273–275
Regula Columbani
    attacks on, 269–270, 276
    criticism of, 149
    Gallus's hermitage and, 234
    monastic communities and, 264–265
    Vita Columbani and, 260, 287
Regula cuiusdam ad virgines, Jonas of
    Bobbio, 260, 263, 275
Regula cuiusdam patris
    Bible and, 259–260
    factional disputes and, 13, 263, 265–268, 271
    features of, 273–278, 281–283, 285–289
    Irish influence and, 261
    sources for, 262, 280
Regula Donati, 263
Regula magistri, 128, 260, 287
regula mixta, 234
Regula monachorum, Columbanus, 179,
    262, 266, 271, 276–277, 280, 283
Regula orientalis, 260
Regula pastoralis, Gregory the Great,
    115–116, 118–120
Reichenau, monastery of, 215, 237
relics, 117, 156
religio, 137, 138
religious deviance, 153

Remiremont, monastery of, 147, 149–150, 157, 161, 265
Rennes, 105
rex gentilis, Agilulf as, 252
Rheged, kingdom of, 61, 63
Rhine, river, 179, 218
Rhone valley, 118
Rhydderch, king, 63
Richter, Michael, 226, 236
ritual blowing, 183
rituals of royal inauguration, 256
Roccolanus, rebellious monk, 265
Rodoald, Lombard king, 247
Roman
    Church, 153, 247, 252 (*see also* papacy)
    Empire, 9, 10, 14, 21, 34, 166, 168
    law, 82
    martyr, 117
    tradition, 254
Romans, 34, 168, 181
Romaric, founder of Remiremont, 146–147, 149, 157, 265
Rome
    dating of Easter and, 114
    focus for Christian unity, 31
    Jonas of Bobbio and, 159, 253–254
    letters from, 119
    martyrdom of Peter and
        Paul in, 34
    territory of, 255
    travel to, 155–156
Rothari, Lombard king, 83, 193, 247
royal court, 246, 282
    genealogies, 193
    monasteries, 255, 256
    space, 136
Rufinus, 97
runes, 189

Saale, river, 179–180
sacrificium profanum, 189
Sadalberga, abbess, 146, 283
Sagittarius, bishop, 109
Saint-Coloumb, Brittany, 103, 110
Salicis, monastery of, 11, 110
Salonius, bishop, 109
Saltair na Rann, 181
Salzburg, 166, 171, 172
Samo, king, 167, 169
San Salvatore al monte Amiata, monastery of, 250, 255

San Vincenzo al Volturno, monastery of, 249, 250
sancta regula, 272
Sanne, river, 206
Satan, 45, 115, 192. *See also* devil
Saxnot, 192
Saxon/s, 104, 105
Scandinavia, 181, 192, 193
Schäferdiek, Knut, 184, 185
Schär, Max, 211, 217
Scheldt, river, 160, 206
Schmid, Karl, 255
Schneider, Rudolf, 255
Schuman, Robert, 3, 13, 14
Schwitter, Raphael, 209, 216, 227
Scotland, 59, 63
Scottus anonymus, 30
Scrabo Hill, Co. Down, 92, 93
scriptures, 259, 290, 297
Scythians, 185
Secundus of Trent, bishop, 194
Semnones tribe, 180
Seneca, 41
septa secretiora, 80
Sextus Iulius Africanus, 185
sexual regulation, 73
Shaw, Philip, 190
ship image and metaphor, 27–31
shunning, 97, 113, 128, 129
Sichar, 196
Sigibert I, Frankish king, 77, 91, 109, 131, 213, 214
Sigibert II, Frankish king, 212
Sigibert III, Frankish king, 212–214, 232
simony, 121, 122, 125, 130
Sinilis, teacher of Columbanus (abbot of Bangor?), 58, 91, 94
Sinell, bishop of Moville, 91
sinus Brittanicus, 103–104, 106–110
Slavonic, 167
Slavs, xi, 11, 167–171
Slovakia, 171
Sluagad Fiachna meic Báitáin co Dún nGuaire i Saxanaib, 63
Smaragdus, *Expositio Regulae*, 290
Song of Songs, 115
St Gallen, monastery of, 12, 215, 220, 225–226, 233, 237
St-Gildas-de-Rhuys, Brittany, 106
status, 10, 72, 76, 78, 80, 84, 125
Steinach, Gallus's hermitage at the, 213, 219, 225, 226

connection with Columbanian
    communities, 209, 217, 233
continuity of, 230
monastic life in, 234, 237
Stoic, 22, 24, 41
Strangford Lough, 92–93
Strathclyde, 61, 63
Suebi/Alamanni, 170, 171, 180, 189, 197. *See
    also* Alamanni
Sulpicius Severus, hagiographer of Saint
    Martin, 97, 183
Sundrarit, Lombard warlord, 244
Susa, birthplace of Jonas of Bobbio, 53
Switzerland, 6, 12, 168
Syagrius of Autun, bishop, 121

Tacitus, Roman historian, 180, 190
Taliesin, Welsh poet, 63
Tallaght, monastery of, 185
Talto, 211, 231
Tara, 54
Tertullian, 183
Testimonia divinae scripturae, 260, 262
Teurnia, *metropolis Norici*, 172
Theodelinda, queen of the Lombards
    Bavarian origins of, 166
    Bobbio and, 245, 256
    Columbanus and, 12, 81, 82, 205
    Lombard history and, 194
    as queen, 83–85
    Rome and, 31
    Three Chapters and, 251–252
Theodore, companion of Gallus, 219
Theudebald, king of Austrasia, 210
Theudebert II, king of Austrasia
    Alamannia and, 168, 207
    Duke Gunzo and, 205, 211–213
    son of Childebert II, 131
    support for Columbanus, 12, 230, 236
Theuderic II, king of Burgundy
    Agrestius and, 144
    Alsace, 207
    Brunhild's influence on, 77–78, 81
    Columbanus and, 6, 79, 80, 132, 230, 270, 272
    and Duke Gunzo, 211, 212
    exile of Columbanus, 103, 134–136
    family of, 213, 231
    illegitimate sons of, 78
    planned marriage of, 133
    son of Childebert II, 131
    visit to Luxeuil, 137

Theudila, sister of Theuderic II, 133
Thor, Germanic god, 170, 192
Three Chapters Controversy
    Agrestius and, 147, 157–158, 169, 269–270
    authority of Rome and, 31, 156
    Bobbio and, 253, 255
    Columbanus and, 12, 70, 252
    Italian historiography and, 251
    Pope Honorius I and, 254
    Pope Vigilius and, 35
    schism and, 83, 250–251
    Vita Columbani and, 154
Tighernach of Clones, Irish saint, 56
Tomus, of Pope Leo the Great, 115, 156–157
tonsure, 149, 270–271
Torslunda, Sweden, 182
Tours/Touraine, 105, 106, 196
Treticus of Lyon, bishop, 148
trial by battle, 109
troscad, 79, 137
Tuggen, 227, 236
Týr, Germanic god, 180

Ua Áedo Róin, Diarmait, Irish king, 56
Überlingen, 211, 218, 219
Uí Bairche, 10, 54–58
Uí Cennselaig, 54, 55, 57
Uí Dúnlainge, 57
Uí Néill, 60, 61, 64–65
Uinnianus, bishop, 10, 93–96, 98
Uinnianus, *Penitentialis Uinniani*, 96
Ulaid, 59–60, 64–65, 92–93
Ulster, 10, 56, 58–64, 91–93
Uncelen, duke of Alamannia, 210, 231
United European federation, 4
Uppsala, Sweden, 182
uprisings in Bobbio and Luxeuil, 13, 144,
    150, 234, 267
Urbgen (Urien), British king, 63

Valsgärde graves, 182
Vandals, 194
Vannes/Vannetais, 104–108
Vedast, bishop of Arras, 170, 182–183, 197
Venantius Fortunatus, xiii, 97
Venantius, bishop of Luni, 24, 116
Veneti/ Venetia, 170, 171
Venus, goddess, 183
Vergilius, bishop of Arles, 121
Victorian Easter cycle, 21. *See also* Easter
Victorius of Aquitaine, 114, 118, 119, 123

Vidimaclis, 105
Vigilius, pope, 158
vigils, 96, 278, 301
Vilaine, valley of the, 105, 106
Villegas, Fernando, 261, 262, 273
Vindonissa (Windisch), bishopric of, 232, 233
Virgil of Salzburg, bishop, 11, 166, 167
Virgil, Roman poet, 97
Vistula, river, 171
Vita Agili, 206
Vita Amati, 157
Vita Columbani, Jonas of Bobbio
    Agrestius in, 158
    audience of, 77, 131, 271
    beer miracles in, 177, 185, 197
    Bobbio diploma, 244–245, 246, 248, 253
    Columbanus in, 70, 91, 205–206
    Columbanus's failed missionary attempts
        in, 230
    confrontation between Theuderic and
        Columbanus in, 270
    Eustasius in, 147, 151
    Gallus in, 208, 226, 228, 234–235
    heresy and, 154, 155, 159
    influence on *Vita Sadalbergae*, 161
    Irish elements in, 80
    legacy of Columbanus and, 264
    manuscripts of, 13
    medicamenta penitentiae, 275
    models for, 183
    orthodoxy and, 143, 145
    prudens lector in, 259–260
    Sigibert I in, 214
    as source for Columbanian monasticism,
        165, 263, 272, 281
    Vita Vetustissima and, 227, 234
    Woden story in, 170, 190
    women in, 71, 74–75, 78, 81, 85
    writing of, 160, 196, 216
Vita Galli, 210, 212, 215, 226, 230
Vita Martini, 183
Vita Sadalbergae, 161
Vita Tripartita (on Patrick), 57

Vita Vedastis, 182, 183, 197
Vita Vetustissima (on Gallus), 190, 209, 213,
    225–229, 234–237
Vitae Galli, 208, 211, 217, 219
Vosges, 11, 107–110, 171, 205, 236, 237

Wala, abbot of Bobbio, 248
Walahfrid Strabo, monk of Reichenau and
    hagiographer of Gallus, 205, 209, 213,
    214–215, 217, 219, 226–228
Waldebert, third abbot of Luxeuil, 151, 212,
    216–217, 264
Walker, G. S. M., xi, 42, 115
Wandregisel, abbot of Fontenelle, 155, 156
Warasqui/Warasci, 144, 145, 155, 166
Warnachar, Burgundian mayor of the
    palace, 144, 148–150, 152, 270
Waroch, Breton *comes*, 104, 105, 106,
    107, 110
weapon sacrifice, 181
Welsh genealogies, 195
Wends/Winds/Windisch, 171
Wetti, monk of Reichenau and hagiographer
    of Gallus, 209, 214–215, 217, 219,
    226–227
Wiliachar, 106, 108
Willimar, benefactor of Gallus, 219
Witteric, Visgothic king, 134
Woden, Germanic god, 170, 182–183, 185,
    189–195, 198–199, 212
Woluntioi, tribe, 92
women, 10, 70–77, 80–81, 85, 122, 195, 298
Wood, Ian, 11, 80, 168, 197, 255
Woods, David, 107
Würzburg, 184, 185

Y Gododdin, 196

Ziu, Germanic god, 180
Ziuvari, 170
Zurich, Lake, 168, 227, 236
Zusso, benefactor of Bobbio monastery,
    245, 249